AF605925

The Civil War as Global Conflict

THE CAROLINA LOWCOUNTRY AND THE ATLANTIC WORLD

Sponsored by the Program in the Carolina Lowcountry and the Atlantic World of the College of Charleston

Money, Trade, and Power
Edited by Jack P. Greene, Rosemary Brana-Shute, and Randy J. Sparks

The Impact of the Haitian Revolution in the Atlantic World
Edited by David P. Geggus

London Booksellers and American Customers
James Raven

Memory and Identity
Edited by Bertrand Van Ruymbeke and Randy J. Sparks

This Remote Part of the World
Bradford J. Wood

The Final Victims
James A. McMillin

The Atlantic Economy during the Seventeenth and Eighteenth Centuries
Edited by Peter A. Coclanis

From New Babylon to Eden
Bertrand Van Ruymbeke

Saints and Their Cults in the Atlantic World
Edited by Margaret Cormack

Who Shall Rule at Home?
Jonathan Mercantini

To Make This Land Our Own
Arlin C. Migliazzo

Votaries of Apollo
Nicholas Michael Butler

Fighting for Honor
T. J. Desch Obi

Paths to Freedom
Edited by Rosemary Brana-Shute and Randy J. Sparks

Material Culture in Anglo-America
Edited by David S. Shields

The Fruits of Exile
Edited by Richard Bodek and Simon Lewis

The Irish in the Atlantic World
Edited by David T. Gleeson

Ambiguous Anniversary
Edited by David T. Gleeson and Simon Lewis

Creating and Contesting Carolina
Edited by Michelle LeMaster and Bradford J. Wood

The CIVIL WAR as GLOBAL CONFLICT

Transnational Meanings of the American Civil War

Edited by David T. Gleeson and Simon Lewis

THE UNIVERSITY OF SOUTH CAROLINA PRESS

Published by the University of South Carolina Press
Columbia, South Carolina 29208

www.sc.edu/uscpress

Manufactured in the United States of America

23 22 21 20 19 18 17 16 15 14
10 9 8 7 6 5 4 3 2 1

Library of Congress Cataloging-in-Publication Data

The Civil War as global conflict : transnational meanings of the American Civil War / edited by David T. Gleeson and Simon Lewis.

pages cm. — (The Carolina Lowcountry and the Atlantic world)

Includes bibliographical references and index.

ISBN 978-1-61117-325-3 (hardbound : alk. paper) — ISBN 978-1-61117-326-0 (ebook) 1. United States—History—Civil War, 1861–1865—Causes. 2. United States—History—Civil War, 1861–1865—Political aspects. 3. United States—History—Civil War, 1861–1865—Social aspects. 4. United States—History—Civil War, 1861–1865—Influence. I. Gleeson, David T., editor of compilation. II. Lewis, Simon, 1960–, editor of compilation.

E459.C59 2014
973.7—dc23
2013036702

This book was printed on a recycled paper with
30 percent postconsumer waste content.

CONTENTS

Acknowledgments vii

Introduction 1
David T. Gleeson and Simon Lewis

Why Civil War? The Politics of Slavery in Comparative Perspective: The United States, Cuba, and Brazil 14
Edward B. Rugemer

King Cotton, Emperor Slavery: Antebellum Slaveholders and the World Economy 36
Matthew Karp

"If it is still impossible . . . to advocate slavery. . . it has . . . become a habit persistently to write down freedom": Britain, the Civil War, and Race 56
Hugh Dubrulle

"Two irreconcilable peoples"? Ethnic Nationalism in the Confederacy 85
James M. McPherson

Proving Their Loyalty to the Republic: English Immigrants and the American Civil War 98
David T. Gleeson

"A new expression of that *entente cordiale?*" Russian-American Relations and the "Fleet Episode" of 1863 116
Alexander Noonan

The Rhine River: The Impact of the German States on Transatlantic Diplomacy 146
Niels Eichhorn

Lex Talionis in the U.S. Civil War: Retaliation and the Limits of Atrocity 172
Aaron Sheehan-Dean

Fulfilling "The president's duty to communicate": The Civil War and the Creation of the *Foreign Relations of the United States* Series 190
Aaron W. Marrs

"They had heard of emancipation and the enfranchisement of their race": The African American Colonists of Samaná, Reconstruction, and the State of Santo Domingo 211
Christopher Wilkins

Nurse as Icon: Florence Nightingale's Impact on Women in the American Civil War 235
Jane E. Schultz

Race, Romance, and "The spectacle of unknowing" in *Gone with the Wind*: A South African Response 253
Lesley Marx

Coda: Roundtable on Memory 275
O. Vernon Burton, Edmund L. Drago, W. Eric Emerson, Joseph McGill, Theodore Rosengarten, Amanda Foreman

Contributors 297
Index 301

ACKNOWLEDGMENTS

As directors of the Program in the Carolina Lowcountry and Atlantic World (CLAW) at the College of Charleston planning our activities in the early 2000s, we both recognized that 2011 was going to be an important year for the city, state, region and nation in which we were based. Thus the conference that spawned this volume had long been in the "hopper," and as a result we have had a lot of support, which we would like to recognize here. Our colleagues in the CLAW program, Lisa Randle and John White, were instrumental in helping pull off what became a large and important conference attracting scholars from all over the world and from all sections of the community. Heather Gilbert provided vital Web support. Our executive director, Dr. OrvilleVernon Burton, now of Clemson University, provided valuable advice and was instrumental in securing us prestigious plenary speakers. In the history department at the College of Charleston, Drs. Lee Drago and Bernard Powers helped both intellectually and physically with the conference. Dr. Scott Peeples, in the English department, gave us some good insights and sources. Administrative and graduate assistants Tara Miller, Maggie Lally, and Dana Woodcock did some excellent last-minute formatting for us. Also at the College, Deans David Cohen and Cynthia Lowenthal were always supportive of our efforts. We thank them for that. The 2011 conference received important financial support from the Humanities Council of South Carolina and the School of Arts and Social Sciences at Northumbria University in the UK. Professor McPherson's conference keynote lecture, revised and reprinted in this volume, was sponsored by the Wells Fargo [formerly Wachovia] Distinguished Public Lecture Series.

For the volume we acknowledge the continued guidance and advice from the staff at the University of South Carolina Press. We want to specifically recognize the hard work of Alex Moore, Linda Fogle, Karen Beidel, and Elizabeth Jones. All of our contributors have been excellent to work with and have helped us to put together this collection in a timely and efficient manner. We appreciate too the valuable suggestions for improvement made by the two anonymous reviewers for this project.

David Gleeson also particularly wants to recognize the support of his colleagues at Northumbria University in the British and Irish Worlds and U.S. history research groups, especially Professor Donald M. MacRaild, Dr. Sylvia Ellis, and Dr. Tanja Bueltmann. Department head Professor David Walker and Dean of Arts and Social Sciences Professor Lynn Dodd were also very supportive of this project. Gleeson's essay in this volume is a result of his involvement in the Locating the Hidden Diaspora: The English in North America in Transatlantic Perspective Project at Northumbria, which is funded in part by the UK Arts and Humanities Research Council.

Finally, we would both like to thank our families, Amy, Emma, and Aidan Gleeson, Janet Watts, and Megan, Zoë, and Oliver Lewis, who have put up with the late-night edits, Skype calls, and so on inherent in a transatlantic collaboration. We truly do appreciate their continued patience and support.

DAVID T. GLEESON AND SIMON LEWIS

Introduction

The American Civil War is one of the most written-about events in history, and in many ways it is one that is the most thoroughly "known" already. If you go almost anywhere in the United States where there was a battle, you are almost certain to encounter someone who knows the terrain of that battlefield to within the last inch and who can tell you the precise development of the fighting to within a minute. Professional historians of the Civil War will all tell you stories of encountering phenomenally knowledgeable (and equally opinionated) audience members at public lectures they have given. In addition to having exhaustive knowledge of battles, campaigns, and strategies, we also know a very great deal about the individuals involved, particularly the political and military leaders. Prior to 2009, it was already claimed that Abraham Lincoln was the subject of more biographies than any other person in world history, and yet the bicentenary of his birth produced even more scholarly and popular analysis, notably Eric Foner's *The Fiery Trial: Abraham Lincoln and American Slavery* (which won the Pulitzer Prize, the Lincoln Prize, and the Bancroft Prize) and O. Vernon Burton's *The Age of Lincoln* (which won the Heartland Prize). There is a similarly unquenchable interest in the foot soldiers, too, resulting, among other things, in extensive reenactment organizations. All too often in public consciousness, though, the laudable focus on soldiering leads to comparisons between the moral character and military skill of Billy Yank and Johnny Reb that can still in some circles feed into cycles of justification and recrimination. Periodic flare-ups of controversy over such perennially potent symbols as the Confederate flag illustrate just how deep sectional feeling can still run. Current antigovernment attitudes in the United States have given new life to anti-Union rhetoric all over the country as seen, for instance, in an op-ed by the veteran environmentalist and secession advocate Kirkpatrick Sale in the Charleston *Post and Courier* arguing that the war "was not a civil war, second that it was the Union that started it, and third that it was not started over slavery."[1]

Despite the apparently comprehensive coverage and interminable, seemingly intractable disagreement, it seems as if the public desire not just to revisit familiar territory but to discover new details or to explore new avenues of thought on the Civil War is unquenchable. Recent years have seen growth, for instance, in the number of more socially oriented histories, notably represented by women writers on mourning (Drew Gilpin Faust's *Republic of Suffering*), women and gender (Joan Cashin's *First Lady of the Confederacy: Varina Davis's Civil War;* Catherine Clinton and Nina Silber's *Battle Scars: Gender and Sexuality in the American Civil War*), and the home front (Lee Drago's *Confederate Phoenix*).[2] This volume sets out to shed light on a further avenue of thought that has been surprisingly neglected: thinking of the war not just as a local conflict but as a global one, whose causes, conditions, and consequences were all affected by transnational concerns and whose outcome in turn has had profound effects on world history. There have of course been works examining the diplomatic efforts of both the federal and the Confederate governments as well as the impact of the war on specific countries such as Ireland and Great Britain, but here we hope to provide a more global approach that moves beyond diplomacy, important though it is, to examine issues such as ethnicity, national identity, gender, and memory in the transnational context of the Civil War.[3] Breaking out of the intense localism of much of the historiography also allows us better to break out of the tendency—in public consciousness as in history courses—to isolate the war in time, too, as if it were not only an exclusively American event but one that lasted specifically from 1861 to 1865.

Looking at the war in a transnational perspective and as part of a broader sweep of global history draws attention to the way in which the pre-1861 world differs massively from the post-1865 world, the shape of which we now take pretty much for granted. Although, obviously, the events of 1861–65 are not solely responsible for the current shape of the world, it is very difficult for us not to have its current shape in mind as we look back, to think in terms of American global power, for instance, or in terms of the dominance of the discourse of democracy and universal suffrage long before those were anything like securely established. Specifically, we need to remember that the 1860 United States, while adding territory by expanding westward, was still limited to thirty-three states; the Canadian provinces of British North America were not yet confederated; Alaska was still Russian; Great Britain was the dominant global naval power; and, while European empires still exerted imperial control over most of the globe, they all faced actual or potential colonial rebellion abroad (in India, Mexico, and Cuba, for instance) and the rise of nationalism at home that was transforming the continent's political shape (via the establishment of the new nations of Italy and Germany, for example). The essays in this volume underscore the fact that the civil war in America was by no means the only conflict that the British and

French Empires, for example, needed to think about (see the chapter by Niels Eichhorn). Furthermore, it was neither the closest to home nor, despite being the bloodiest in U.S. history, the deadliest of contemporary conflicts; its death toll was dwarfed by what was going on in China, and its per capita death rate was exceeded many times over by that of Paraguay's bloodletting (see the chapter by Aaron Sheehan-Dean).[4]

At the same time as attitudes to nation and empire were in flux (see the chapter by James McPherson), attitudes to citizenship and democracy were also far from fixed or stable, and attitudes to race and slavery were the subject of fierce debate (see the chapter by Hugh Dubrulle). The United States was worryingly radical (to some) in promoting the principles and practices of democracy and well in advance of the United Kingdom, for instance, in establishing universal (male) suffrage—something that even the hotly contested British Reform Bill of 1867 did not achieve; Russia, meanwhile, whose fleet visits to New York and San Francisco were taken as symbolizing that vast country's diplomatic support of the United States, moved to free the serfs from 1861 on (see the chapter by Alexander Noonan). Attempting to understand the Civil War in global context means refusing to see the conflict in isolation from these factors.

Most profoundly, perhaps, such an attempt insists that we cannot understand the impact of the war and the "new birth of freedom" without thinking globally (see the chapter by James McPherson). Our present-day assumptions about universal human rights, for instance, which seem so secure and unquestionable (in principle, at least—the practice, as we know all too well, is a very different matter), might eventually have been reached had the Confederate States of America come into being as an independent nation, but the process whereby they might have done so is difficult to conceive (and would almost certainly have been extraordinarily bloody). Without a Union victory the consolidation of "Western" faith in democracy and individual freedom made manifest in eighteenth-century revolutions in British colonial America, in France, and in Haiti might well have stalled, halting the seemingly inevitable onward march from the eighteenth- and nineteenth-century discourse of natural rights toward the post–World War II world's shared beliefs in human rights.

One of the consequences of considering the war in temporal isolation has been to separate it not just from its long-standing *causes* (e.g., in the failure of the Constitutional Convention to deal with the question of slavery at a national level) but also from its aftermath and from the uneven implementation of the principles it theoretically enshrined. In particular, the worldwide memory of the war erases the retreat from democracy in the South and the resubjugation in a different form of the African American population in favor of a glamorized popular version encapsulated in, for example, *Gone with the Wind*. That film's iconic stature (and hence its influence on popular memory) is perhaps indicated by the fact that, however rampant its shortcomings as "history" may be, it was featured at the Oscars ceremony of 2011, the 150th anniversary of the Civil War, because it had won the Academy Award for best movie of the year in 1939, the first year the awards ceremony was televised. So, although Lincoln's words from the Gettysburg Address and his second inaugural oration may be widely remembered and staples of American classrooms, they certainly have not been able to control or contain the "meaning" of the war nationally or internationally. Lesley Marx's chapter on the resonance of *Gone with the Wind* in apartheid South Africa draws particularly intriguing conclusions as to the role of American popular culture in globalizing ideas of race via the (mis)remembering of national history and nationalist historiography.

However broad our perspective may be, all history is written from a particular vantage point. This volume is the latest in the Carolina Lowcountry and Atlantic World (CLAW) series to emerge from a conference convened by the CLAW program at the College of Charleston; one of the program's goals is precisely to promote public understanding of local historical experience in a broader international context. In line with that goal, our commemoration of the war aims to break out of some of the narrow binarisms that dog the public discourse about it.[5] The conference coincided with the dates of Lincoln's inaugurations both in 1861 and in 1865—when he famously declared in the latter "with malice toward none" and "charity toward all"—and we set out on this conference and on the broader commemoration with just such a reconciliatory spirit—duly critical but not divisive. Our focus on transnational aspects of the war highlights the fact that national fragmentation, nationalism, and the assertion of state rights were not unique to these shores in the mid-nineteenth century; likewise, slavery and racism were neither exclusively southern issues nor exclusively American ones. The central conundrum confronting the young American nation was one that European nations also confronted as the Age of Enlightenment morphed into the era of Imperialism. Britain, France, Spain, and Portugal might all have abolished slavery by the end of the nineteenth century, but many of their non-European colonial subjects were still emulating the first American patriots by taking up arms against colonial rule until late into the twentieth century. And many of the leaders of African independence movements were inspired not only by the ideals of the American Revolution but also by the subsequent generations of African American leaders who still had to fight for their freedom long after 1776 and well beyond 1865.[6]

Drawing attention to these global issues to frame the war in transnational ways might, however, have been the easy part of our task. Living and working in Charleston, South Carolina, where South Carolina's Ordinance of Secession was signed and where the bombardment of Fort Sumter signaled the outbreak of hostilities, we were (and remain) acutely conscious that nothing the CLAW program has done up to now—not even our commemoration of the bicentenary of the banning of the international slave trade—has quite as much potential for opening old sores as the Civil War sesquicentennial. Attitudes to the Civil War are as divided and divisive as election attack ads, and those divisions remain conspicuously attractive to contemporary journalists. In December, another organization's commemorative event drew local, national, and even international attention. The Secession Gala, hosted by the Sons of Confederate Veterans to celebrate South Carolina's "second declaration of independence," attracted widespread media coverage in the United States and further afield and prompted a demonstration by the NAACP, which vigorously denounced the commemoration of an event it considered tantamount to a treasonous attack on the United States. This kind of polarization made good copy and was picked up on by one of the British journalists in attendance in a particularly arch manner. David Usborne of London's *Independent* newspaper likened the event to a pantomime, writing: "The pantomime season lasted only a day in Charleston SC this year, but no one can say the amateur dramatics—and the audience participation—did not have a special intensity about them. The American Civil War wasn't about slavery, honestly. Oh, yes, it was! Oh, no it wasn't! Oh, yes, it was!"[7] Conscious of some of the shortcomings and plain bad outcomes of the centennial commemorations, we feel that it is absolutely incumbent on us to attempt to move the public away from those pantomime-like North-South, black-white, blue-gray binaries.[8] The attempt to reframe the Civil War as a conflict with significant transnational roots and consequences is driven therefore not just by a desire to get the history right but also by a hope that we can find a way to talk about that history in the light of twenty-first-century realities.

Coverage of the various commemorations of the first shots of the war suggest that the sesquicentennial is already on track to move beyond the binary. April 12, 2011, drew even more journalists to Charleston than the Secession Ball had done. Coverage in outlets as diverse as Al Jazeera and *The Guardian*, however, noted the civility of the main commemorations, which included a very dramatic splitting of a searchlight beam above Fort Sumter at precisely the hour of the first shot. Al Jazeera described the commemoration as "a more historically accurate and inclusive event" than the Centennial, and Amanda Foreman, writing in *The Guardian*, opened her article "The American Civil War Battles Go On" by directly contrasting the South's celebratory commemorations of 1961 with the more "somber approach" in 2011.[9]

In invitations to our keynote speakers for the March 2011 conference, we referred to another seemingly intractable political situation that appears finally to have moved toward healing: that of Ulster. In "Whatever You Way, Say Nothing," one of his very moving poems about the "troubles" in Northern Ireland, Seamus Heaney talks about the way in which people on either side of the sectarian/

political divides that rendered his home province a battle zone for the best part of three decades seemed almost possessive of their "competence with pain," all too ready to "hug our little destiny again." Heaney was suggesting that people needed to get a wider perspective on their situation, to see themselves from the outside, not from their narrow bunkers—"besieged within the siege," as he put it in the same poem—in order to break out from the political impasse in which they found themselves and to see their common humanity. We would like to think that understanding the Civil War in global contexts might have just such an effect in our community; sad to admit, such an effect is still needed. If you read the online comments to local newspaper coverage of the sesquicentennial so far, it is immediately apparent that many people's minds here are open in the same way they're open in Heaney's poem—open only, that is, "as a trap."[10]

In short, we would like to suggest that this volume goes beyond the norms of academic collections—it goes beyond the academic and bears the additional burden of social responsibility. One indication of that is our inclusion of a series of brief "think pieces" on the subject of memory by a distinguished and varied group of historians, preservationists, and reenactors. During the panel discussion in which these pieces originated, David Gleeson posed the frequently asked question whether we might not be better off just forgetting the war. As Joe McGill promptly replied, the genie is out of the bottle on this particular issue—it's not just the thousands of books, it's not just the national parks at battle sites, it's the monuments, the reenactments, the curio stalls, it's the vigorous trade in memorabilia. Memory of the war is alive and thriving—though it may not necessarily always be healthy or conducive to good health. Michael Allen, another of the panelists, in fact used the metaphor of the "virus" that is endemic in public consciousness. So the question then becomes: how do those of us who practice history in an academic and public way help people remember the war in ways that respect people's personal connections to it but that do not deny or soft-pedal the real and important causes and consequences of the conflict at the time and since? By extending the purely parochial debates ridiculed by some as "pantomime," we hope to shed new light while simultaneously reducing the heat on a very hot subject through reasoned debate, informed by scholarship as well as opinion. Perhaps in a small way our work in public and in print can promote a South where public memory can be less contested and society thus less conflictual. Ultimately, we believe that this volume, in opening out new trajectories of thinking about the Civil War and its immediate and long-term consequences, does just that.

The volume is arranged in three sections. In the first, Edward B. Rugemer, Matthew Karp, Hugh Dubrulle, and James M. McPherson all present truly global overviews on the war's relation to global economic forces, to global attitudes to race, slavery, and ethnicity, and to nationalism and citizenship. The second section, comprising essays by David T. Gleeson, Alexander Noonan, and Niels

Eichhorn, looks at particular manifestations of some of those issues and the local complications of national affiliation and international relations, specifically in relation to English Americans, the importance of German politics to British policy, and the meaning of the Russian fleet visits to the United States in 1863. The final section of the volume brings together essays that assess the war's significance internationally in a variety of fields: military principles (Sheehan-Dean), international relations (Marrs), the expansion of antiracist ideology (Wilkins), nursing (Schultz), and popular culture (Marx).

The volume opens with a comprehensive essay confronting the key question of why, uniquely among New World slave societies, it took a civil war to end slavery in the United States. In his first book, *The Problem of Emancipation: The Caribbean Roots of the American Civil War* (Louisiana State University Press, 2008), Edward B. Rugemer argued that the abolition of slavery in the British West Indies in 1834—especially the slave rebellions that preceded abolition—had a significant impact on the political contest over slavery in the United States and shaped the coming of the Civil War. Here, Rugemer extends his challenge to the practice of examining the antebellum struggle over slavery in the United States in isolation by comparing and contrasting the situations in Brazil and Cuba with that in the United States. Like his award-winning book, Rugemer's essay highlights the usefulness of this approach to American history.

Matthew Karp takes a similarly broad approach to his reconsideration of the origins of the war, arguing that the South's confidence was based not solely on the belief that cotton was king but also on an even more deep-seated assumption that slavery was both essential and unassailable. Hugh Dubrulle's essay, which very neatly takes the attitudes and beliefs of Fanny Kemble and her daughter as indicators of how attitudes toward race and slavery changed transnationally—Kemble herself having lived in both Britain and the United States—from the first three decades of the nineteenth century to the next three confirms Karp's insights that by 1860 the plantocracy had become thoroughly self-assured in the belief that slavery was right and proper. James M. McPherson puts a different tweak on the idea of race and ethnicity by examining the ways in which leading southerners (or, following Walter Scott, "Southroners") attempted to divide themselves from (white) Northerners not just on cultural or ideological grounds but also on grounds of race, thus inventing a nationality akin to that of new European "nations."[11] McPherson shows how widespread—and how specious—were the claims that southerners were "cavaliers" descended from noble Normans, while northerners were a lesser race of Anglo-Saxon "churls." He also acknowledges, however, that the South did make a serious attempt to create an ethnic nationalism distinct from the civic one that had driven American identity since the Revolution and became reinforced in the Northern states as they fought to preserve their Union and stand up for its Constitution.

David Gleeson's essay indicates that, however essentialist the spurious notions of ethnic nationalism may have been, for English-descended Americans in the North, questions of ethnic and national affiliation posed practical problems to the English for historical and political reasons. What made English Americans' positions politically sensitive had nothing to do with whether or not they were supposedly Saxons or Normans; it depended simply on the fact that memory of war between the United Kingdom and the United States was still so fresh and contemporary diplomatic relations were so frequently very tense, almost leading to war in late 1861 over the so-called *Trent* Affair. It was a revitalizing of American civic nationalism around the issue of emancipation that provided an opportunity for English immigrants, who swore loyalty to a monarch, to reconnect to an American identity.

While the relationship between the United States and the United Kingdom has been widely studied and while twentieth-century history has cast the two nations as fast allies, the relationship between the United States and Russia has veered between that of wartime allies in both world wars to vehemently opposed ideological adversaries during the Cold War. Alexander Noonan's essay on the visit of two naval squadrons to New York and to San Francisco in 1863 shows how these rather enigmatic visits provoked different interpretations at the time and how similarly diverse interpretations flourished in the twentieth century. The visits may not have had any bearing on the prosecution or outcome of the war militarily, but they were important diplomatically, and they show how the need to be diplomatic, to keep one's diplomatic cards close to one's chest, allows the interpretation of such events to be colored by contemporary ideology. Noonan's essay, therefore, like much of this volume, performs a double function of explicating the history of the visit while also proffering a historiographical critique, inviting us to acknowledge how past and present interact to create history.

Niels Eichhorn's essay gives us a more straightforward but no less fascinating insight into the complexity of European politics in the 1860s, arguing that intra-European relations played a significant role in keeping Britain and France out of the Civil War. Tensions within Europe—notably, as Eichhorn shows, on the Rhine—meant that Britain and France simply could not afford to intervene in the war. In fact, devastating though the war may have been in American history, as far as Britain was concerned, the sectional war across the Atlantic was, relatively speaking, a sideshow; stretched thin in Europe and hyperconscious of the possibility of war on the Rhine, Britain responded to the Civil War in a manner governed less by the principles at stake in the war than by the pragmatic need to avoid intervention.

Beginning the next section, Aaron Sheehan-Dean's essay on the conduct of the war brings a valuable international and legal dimension to the military history of the war, focusing on the international "law of war" and its execution by various commanders in the field. The issue of international law in American wars is still very much a live one in current conflicts, and Sheehan-Dean highlights the Civil War origins of this debate. Aaron Marrs takes a different tack, going beyond the immediate impact of various diplomatic efforts covered well elsewhere and analyzing instead the war's longer-term impact on American foreign policy, in this case the Foreign Relations of the United States [Documents] Series from the U.S. State Department. Although the Civil War was a "domestic" war, its impact on the practice of foreign relations in the United States was profound. Secretary of State William Henry Seward knew the importance of influencing foreign opinion but also of rallying the American people behind the Lincoln administration's diplomatic efforts. Although primarily aimed at providing documents for Congressional and public perusal, the series has been and remains a boon to diplomatic historians studying American foreign conflicts ever since. Christopher Wilkins's essay examines a specific foreign policy area influenced by the Civil War, Santo Domingo, and American attempts to annex it after the Civil War. While historians of Reconstruction and American foreign relations have explored this episode, Wilkins focuses on the Caribbean side of the story, particularly on a group of African American colonists who began to take a second look at the United States in the heady early days of Radical Reconstruction when political racial equality seemed a real possibility in their and/or their parents' former home.

Jane E. Schultz's essay indicates the impact the war had on the nursing profession internationally. In the 1850s Florence Nightingale, the British pioneer of women's nursing, had begun to transform the profession through her work in the Crimean War. Her iconic status gave her enormous influence both in the Union and in the Confederacy. As Schultz indicates, Southern nurses found Nightingale an especially appropriate inspiration whose representation as a chivalric and romantic figure fitted their own attitudes to war. But Nightingale—or her transatlantic reputation—did even more than inspire women on both sides of the conflict to become nurses or to professionalize nursing internationally. Schultz argues that women saw the opening that Nightingale had made as allowing them to claim a place in the polity long before suffragists were able to get them a more direct link.

The final essay of the volume deals with one of the most enduring popular representations of the Civil War, David O. Selznick's "classic" movie drawn from Margaret Mitchell's *Gone with the Wind.* Framed by a personal narrative within a particular South African set of circumstances and taking a richly interdisciplinary, cultural studies approach, Lesley Marx draws intriguing comparisons between South Africa and the United States. Without losing sight of geographical and historical specificity, Marx points to fascinating similarities not only between the actual history of the processes of race and nation formation in both countries but also in the way that film narratives have fostered specifically racialized memories of those processes. Drawing on the work of Patricia Yaeger, Marx describes how readily *Gone with the Wind*'s "spectacle of unknowing" has fed into white South Africans' (mis)understanding of their own racialized historiography. Marx's references to the recent revisionist histories on the Anglo-Boer War in South Africa that pay due attention to the impact of that war and its aftermath on black South Africans suggest that there is scope for more comparative work on the two situations.

The apparently tangential subject matter of these last two essays hints at the extraordinary range of ways in which the American Civil War affected everyday life well beyond the battlefield, the development of military technology, and so on. A truly comprehensive volume covering the transnational significance of the war would include essays on the development of photography and its importance in journalism and journalism's ability to sway public opinion. It would also look at the ways in which the nature of the warfare affected the ways in which poets and other writers responded to war. As Paul Fussell has famously written about World War I and modern memory, the emotional—specifically elegiac—response of poets reminds us that "objective" history can reduce human beings to ciphers. But, while Fussell focused on the unprecedented death toll of the Great War, he omitted any mention of the way the American Civil War had already given the world an example of the mechanization of war and its consequent capacity for mass slaughter.[12] Even in the few years between 1855 and 1865, the poetic forms used by Alfred, Lord Tennyson had already been rendered obsolete (or at least outdated) by Whitman and Melville. Wilfred Owen may have seemed revolutionary to some readers when he asked what funeral rites there might be for men who "die like cattle" and for defending the bluntness of his poetry with the famous claim that "the Poetry is in the pity," but Melville and Whitman had preceded him by some fifty years.[13] Melville, for instance, writing in response to the military novelty of naval warfare involving ironclads, had written "plain mechanic power / Plied cogently in War now placed— / Where War belongs— / Among the trades and artisans." With "warriors . . . now but operatives," war poetry needed to be "Plain" and "ponderous" rather than "nimble," and victories needed to be hailed "without the gaud / Of glory."[14]

While we expect the current volume to be among the first of many that attempt to broaden the scholarship on the Civil War, it behooves us to remember that for each of the fallen and for each family that suffered directly, the memory of the war can never be less than local, intensely personal in fact. The attempt to globalize should not allow us to abstract the conflict or to forget that if such conflicts are to be avoided we have to remember them at the individual, human level. As the Caribbean poet Derek Walcott, channeling John Donne, writes in response to the ruins of a "great house" in another former slave society, "all in compassion ends."[15] In that spirit, we have added as a sort of coda a selection of more subjective responses to the question of memory: in this particular place, so defined by the events and the memory of the Civil War, what do and should we remember, and how and why should we remember it? O. Vernon Burton, Lee Drago, W. Eric Emerson, Amanda Foreman, Joe McGill, and Ted Rosengarten are all in their own way public historians or cultural workers deeply invested in the lived experience of the Civil War, its causes and consequences. Referring to their varied personal experience—as white and black southerners, as a Vietnam War veteran, as an Anglo-American, as the son of Jewish immigrants—these writers offer responses that graphically reveal the imbrication of the global and the local, their individual backgrounds embodying both the history of national, racial, sectarian, and religious conflict worldwide and the possibility of postconflict reconciliation. In direct, personal language, they round this volume out with eloquent assertions of the need for tolerance alongside a fierce commitment to the application of principles of liberty and justice established by the Thirteenth, Fourteenth, and Fifteenth Amendments. Those gains must be remembered alongside the dreadful loss of life and property as a bulwark to ensure the perpetuation and the perfection of those principles.

NOTES

1. Eric Foner, *The Fiery Trial: Abraham Lincoln and American Slavery* (New York: Norton, 2011); Orville Vernon Burton, *The Age of Lincoln* (New York: Hill and Wang, 2008); Kirkpatrick Sale, "Understanding the Sesquicentennial—and the War's Real Causes," Charleston *Post and Courier,* April 5, 2011. http://www.postandcourier.com/news/2011/apr/05/understanding-the-sesquicentennial-and-the-wars/ (accessed December 6, 2011).

2. Drew Gilpin Faust, *This Republic of Suffering: Death and the American Civil War* (New York: Random House, 2009); Joan Cashin, *First Lady of the Confederacy: Varina Davis's Civil War* (Cambridge, Mass.: Belknap, 2006); Catherine Clinton and Nina Silber, *Battle Scars: Gender and Sexuality in the American Civil War* (New York: Oxford University Press, 2006); Edmund L. Drago, *Confederate Phoenix: Rebel Children and Their Families in South Carolina* (New York: Fordham University Press, 2008).

3. See, for example, Howard Jones, *Blue and Gray Diplomacy: A History of Union and Confederate Foreign Relations* (Chapel Hill: University of North Carolina Press, 2009); Joseph M. Hernon Jr., *Celts, Catholics and Copperheads: Ireland Views the American Civil War* (Columbus: Ohio State University Press, 1968); R. J. M. Blackett, *Divided Hearts: Britain and the American Civil War* (Baton Rouge: Louisiana State University Press, 2000); Amanda M. Foreman, *A World on Fire: Britain's Crucial Role in the American Civil War* (New York: Random House, 2011). For an attempt to examine Abraham Lincoln's global significance, see Richard Carwardine and Jay Sexton, eds., *The Global Lincoln* (New York: Oxford University Press, 2011).

4. James M. McPherson, *Battle Cry of Freedom: The Civil War Era* (repr., New York: Oxford University Press, 2003), 854. Even with new analysis that may increase the

death toll from the war, the total scale of the conflict pales in comparison to that of the contemporary wars in China and Paraguay. J. David Hacker, "A Census-Based Count of the Civil War Dead," *Civil War History* 57 (December 2011): 307–48; Thomas H. Reilly, *The Taiping Heavenly Kingdom: Rebellion and the Blasphemy of Empire* (Seattle: University of Washington Press, 2010), 3–4, 148–49, 157–69; Christopher Leuchars, *To the Bitter End: Paraguay and the War of the Triple Alliance* (Westport, Conn.: Greenwood Press, 2002).

5. For a skeptical initial examination of the significance of the American Civil War see Jeffrey R. K. Ritchie, "Was U.S. Emancipation Exceptional in the Atlantic, or Other Worlds?" in *The American South and the Atlantic World*, ed. Brian Ward, Martyn Bone, and William A. Link (Gainesville: University Press of Florida, 2013), 149-69.

6. American influence on African liberation struggles includes both the influence of the grand national narrative from Washington and Jefferson through Lincoln, and the specifically African American narrative that applies American ideals of liberty to notions of pan-Africanism. Exemplary in this regard is Nelson Mandela's account of his first visit to New York on release from jail in South Africa in 1990. Mandela recalls: "I spoke to a great crowd at Yankee Stadium, telling them that an unbreakable umbilical cord connected black South Africans and black Americans, for we were together children of Africa. There was a kinship between the two, I said, that had been inspired by such great Americans as WEB Du Bois, Marcus Garvey, and Martin Luther King Jr . . . . I said that as freedom fighters we could not have known of such men as George Washington, Abraham Lincoln and Thomas Jefferson 'and not been moved to act as they were moved to act'" (*Long Walk to Freedom.* Abacus: London, 1995. 698.) For a nineteenth-century example of the influence of the Civil War on the South African struggle for political equality see George M. Frederickson, *Black Liberation: A Comparative History of Black Ideologies in the United States and South Africa* (New York: Oxford University Press, 1995), 37-38.

7. David Usborne, "The Debate That Still Divides a Nation—150 Years On," *Independent,* December 7, 2010. http://www.independent.co.uk/news/world/americas/the-debate-that-still-divides-a-nation-ndash-150-years-on-2166348.html (accessed December 6, 2011).

8. See Robert J. Cook, *Troubled Commemoration: The American Civil War Centennial, 1961–1965* (Baton Rouge: Louisiana State University Press, 2007). The Centennial Commission got off to a very bad start in 1961 when one of New Jersey's commissioners, an African American, was denied accommodation at Charleston's Francis Marion Hotel. President Kennedy intervened by shifting the Commission's meeting to federally owned property on the Charleston naval base. That same year, the South Carolina legislature ran the Confederate battle flag up the flagpole on top of the state capitol in Columbia; it stayed there for nearly forty years, creating considerable controversy and rancor before being moved to a site on the statehouse grounds in 2000.

9. Al Jazeera, "US Marks Civil War Anniversary," http://cc.bingj.com/cache.aspx?q=al+jazeera+english+American+Civil+war&d=4559417406915848&mkt=en-US&setlang=en-US&w=73f960b1,a50039c8 (accessed December 6, 2011); Amanda Foreman, "The American Civil War Battles Go On," *The Guardian,* April 11, 2011. http://www

.guardian.co.uk/commentisfree/cifamerica/2011/apr/11/american-civil-war-150-years (accessed December 6, 2011).

10. Seamus Heaney, *Opened Ground: Selected Poems 1966–1996* (New York: Farrar, Straus and Giroux, 1998), 123–25.

11. A new book by Paul Quigley reinforces this view of southern nationalism taking its inspiration from American models. See *Shifting Grounds: Nationalism and the American South* (New York: Oxford University Press, 2011).

12. Paul Fussell, *The Great War and Modern Memory* (New York: Oxford University Press [Twenty-Fifth Anniversary Edition], 2000), 338.

13. Wilfred Owen, "Anthem for Doomed Youth," "Preface," *The Collected Poems of Wilfred Owen*, ed. C. Day-Lewis (New York: New Directions, 1965), 44, 31.

14. Herman Melville, "A Utilitarian View of the *Monitor*'s Fight," *Battle-Pieces and Aspects of the War* (Amherst: University of Massachusetts Press, 1972), 61–62. We are grateful to Dr. Scott Peeples for this reference.

15. Derek Walcott, "Ruins of a Great House," *Collected Poems 1948–1984* (New York: Farrar, Straus and Giroux, 1986), 19–21.

EDWARD B. RUGEMER

Why Civil War?

The Politics of Slavery in Comparative Perspective

The United States, Cuba, and Brazil

In January 1861 James DeBow of New Orleans published an article in his widely read *Review* addressed to the "non-slaveholders of the South." DeBow explained why secession was not simply an elite movement and why poor whites would benefit from their support of a Confederacy founded on slavery. White men, even those who did not own slaves, would suffer if slavery were abolished, which DeBow considered practically inevitable now with the election of Abraham Lincoln. DeBow strengthened his argument by referring to the recent history of slavery elsewhere in the Americas. "Brazil," he argued, "is the only South American state which has prospered. Cuba, by her slave labor, showers wealth upon old Spain, while the British West India colonies . . . have been reduced to beggary. St. Domingo shared the same fate, and the poor whites massacred equally with the rich."[1]

With these three sentences DeBow illustrated some of the transatlantic dimensions of secessionist thought in the aftermath of Lincoln's election. From the Revolution until 1860, the political struggles over the future of slavery had visited every empire and nation throughout the Atlantic world. DeBow's reference to "St. Domingo," its poverty, and the massacre of whites was shorthand for all white southerners needed to know about the Haitian Revolution. In 1790 French Saint-Domingue was the world's greatest producer of sugar and coffee. The Haitian Revolution—the only successful slave insurrection in human history—crushed slavery in that island, but it also destroyed the island's economy. DeBow placed St. Domingo in the same category as the British West Indies; in 1834 Great Britain had abolished slavery in its Caribbean empire, and, indeed, the sugar industry of those islands had severely declined. In contrast to these colonies where slavery had been abolished, DeBow noted Cuba and Brazil, which, like the United States, had not abolished slavery and had flourished.[2]

DeBow's article presented two of the arguments that secessionists made that drew on the recent history of slavery and abolition in the Atlantic World. First, secessionists argued that with the election of Lincoln slave insurrections were a more dangerous threat. This belief came from the dominant interpretation of the Haitian Revolution, which held that it had been caused by abolitionist agitation. For secessionists, the ascendance of an abolitionist like Lincoln to the seat of federal authority meant that abolitionism would follow the lines of federal power throughout the slaveholding states; insurrections would follow. But secession was based on a lot more than fear; it was also based on great confidence in "King Cotton," the belief that the southern economy, based on slave labor and agricultural exports, was strong and stable enough to support an independent nation. This belief also drew on Atlantic history. In the aftermath of the Haitian Revolution and British abolition, Cuba and Brazil became the world's biggest producers of sugar and coffee, respectively, and they had done so with slave labor.[3]

Secessionists combined the fear of abolitionism with a confidence in the economics of slavery that emboldened their strike for independence. But the formation of the Confederacy, its claim to Fort Sumter, and its siege of the fort in the spring of 1861 led to the brutal civil war that ultimately destroyed slavery. Military conflict later contributed to the end of slavery in Cuba and Brazil as well, yet in neither place did the politics of slavery directly provoke war, nor did war act as the principle motor of emancipation. Only in the United States did slavery end as it had in Haiti, through a vicious civil war with massive loss of life. Why? Why did the struggle over slavery lead to the deaths of more than a half million people in the United States, while for its contemporaries that struggle ultimately led to legislation?

Secessionists pointed to Cuba and Brazil as their slaveholding confederates to the south. But when the Union won the Civil War and the Thirteenth Amendment abolished slavery, independent Brazil and colonial Cuba became the last bastions of slavery in the hemisphere. The Union victory isolated the slaveholders of Cuba and Brazil, intensifying their struggles over slavery, which finally ended in the 1880s. This essay compares the political contests over the future of slavery in the United States, Cuba, and Brazil. It is my hope that this comparison can begin to explain not only the exceptionalism of the United States Civil War but also those commonalities in the processes of abolition that shaped the Americas during the nineteenth century.[4]

To do this comparison, we need to follow the histories of two particular aspects of these societies: their economic development and the role of abolitionism in their politics. Because we are considering Brazil, the first American slave society, this history must begin in 1444, when the Portuguese became the first Europeans to purchase slaves on the West African coast. Two hundred and thirty-five captives arrived in Lagos, Portugal, that year, and by 1492, when Columbus crossed the Atlantic Ocean, African slavery had become a fixture in European cities like Lisbon and Seville and the main source of labor in Portugal's growing empire. There were enslaved Africans in Cuba by 1520 and in Brazil by 1580. English colonists in North America and the Caribbean began to purchase enslaved Africans during the 1620s, and by 1700 African slavery was a part of the economy in every colonial society throughout the Americas, from Bahia to Boston.[5]

But there were differences in economic development that would have profound political consequences for later generations. By the eve of the American Revolution, in places like Brazil, the Caribbean, Virginia, and the Carolinas, slaves were employed principally as agricultural laborers on plantations that produced export crops—sugar and gold from Brazil, sugar from the Caribbean, tobacco from Virginia, and rice from South Carolina. These crops were all labor intensive, which meant that slavery became the economic foundation for all of these colonies. Colonial elites emerged that built up significant fortunes that they were able to pass on to their children. For generation after generation, enslaved people labored, fought, and struggled to survive, while slaveholders became wealthy and politically dominant. These were slave societies; slavery shaped everything from the aspirations of the poor to the political calculations of the rich.

In contrast, places like Peru, Pennsylvania, New York, and Massachusetts were also home to slaves and slaveholders, but slavery played a subordinate role in these economies. Enslaved people worked on the docks, on ships, as domestics, on truck farms, or with livestock. Slaveholders tended to be wealthier than others, but their wealth was rooted in a broad diversity of economic endeavor, not in the export of agricultural staples. Slavery thrived, but it was not the foundation of wealth. These were not slave societies; rather, they were societies with slaves.[6]

It is one of the great paradoxes in the history of slavery that the Haitian Revolution—while it inspired slave rebels and terrified slave masters—proved an economic boon to the slave economies of Cuba and Brazil. After thirteen years of war and the massive destruction of lives and property, independent Haiti struggled even to survive; it produced very little coffee or sugar. The prices of these commodities in Atlantic markets rose, and slaveholders in Cuba and Brazil invested more money in slaves than they ever had before. In the decade before the Haitian Revolution (1781–90) the slaveholders of Cuba and Brazil had purchased about 150,000 Africans from slave merchants. In the following decade that number increased to 250,000 captives, and by the late 1830s, Cuban and

Brazilian slaveholders purchased more than forty thousand enslaved Africans every year—forty thousand mothers and sons, fathers and daughters, torn from their homes every year. Sugar plantations spread across the vast central plain of Cuba; coffee production expanded along the Paraiba River valley in south-central Brazil, and both commodities became the everyday items that we know today.[7]

The Haitian Revolution had a similar effect upon the export economy of the United States. From 1793 until 1802 the Haitian army of self-liberated slaves fought the armies of Spain, Britain, and revolutionary France to maintain their liberty in the face of armies that sought to reimpose slavery. When Napoleon realized that he had lost Saint-Domingue forever, his ambitions for a great French empire—with bases in Saint-Domingue and New Orleans—evaporated. So he sold the lands of Louisiana to the United States, doubling that country's territory and creating the space for the American slave economy to expand. And for those few Louisiana planters who had begun to grow sugar along the southern reaches of the Mississippi, the rise in sugar prices provided an impetus to expansion, just as it had for the sugar planters of Cuba and Brazil. By 1803 the Louisiana sugar crop was worth three-quarters of a million dollars annually.[8]

Even more important than sugar was cotton. The relentless expansion of cotton production placed the United States in the same class as Cuba and Brazil as a modernizing slave society. Cotton production had first taken root during the 1780s along South Carolina's coastal plain and quickly spread into the piedmont counties; by 1800 slaveholders planted cotton in Georgia, North Carolina, and parts of Virginia. Cotton production increased from 3,000 bales in 1790 to 178,000 bales in 1810; production doubled by 1816 and doubled again by 1825. By 1830 the United States was the greatest cotton producer in the world.[9]

While the growth of the export economies of Cuba and Brazil had been fueled by the transatlantic slave trade, the economic expansion of the Lower South depended upon the forced migration of enslaved African Americans from the older Atlantic states to the dynamic economies of the new southwest. Every autumn professional slave traders would travel to Virginia, Maryland, and the Carolinas, where they would buy up slaves, who were in demand in the cotton and sugar districts of Georgia, Alabama, Mississippi, Texas, and Louisiana. From 1820 to 1860, 875,000 African Americans were uprooted from the lands of their birth and sold down the river to the slave markets of New Orleans and Natchez. In the 1850s this was twenty-five thousand people every year. Twenty-five thousand mothers and sons, fathers and daughters, torn from their homes. Cotton plantations spread through South Carolina, Georgia, and Alabama; they spread up the Mississippi River valley and then west into Arkansas and east Texas. Cotton became the everyday item we know today, and through this vicious combination of oppression, forced migration, and economic growth, Cuba, Brazil, and the United States became some of the most productive agricultural economies in world history to that point in time.[10]

Now let us turn to politics and abolitionism, for it was the combination of these forces that was distinctive in the United States. Once abolitionism emerged, slaveholders in the United States, Cuba, and Brazil mobilized aggressively to defeat it, and by the end of the 1830s slaveholders in each place had consolidated political power. Political strength facilitated the expansion of slavery that we have seen.[11] Beginning in the 1840s, however, the political struggle over slavery in the United States took on an intensity that did not surface in Brazil or the Spanish Empire until after the U.S. Civil War.

It was not until the 1750s—after more than two thousand years of living with slavery—that writers began to argue that slavery was wrong. Antislavery ideas were first used in political argument during the American Revolution. Famously, in his first draft of the Declaration of Independence, Thomas Jefferson accused the British of forcing the African slave trade upon unwilling colonists. During the war itself, John Laurens of South Carolina, son of the major slaveholder and Revolutionary leader Henry Laurens, recommended the liberation of slaves to fight as soldiers against the British. The rhetoric of liberty was powerful during the Revolution, but the suggestions of both of these men were rejected; the investments in slavery were far more powerful.[12]

But in the northern states, where slavery's roots were shallow, rhetoric trumped investment. Beginning with Vermont in 1777, the northern states began the very gradual abolition of slavery. At the constitutional convention of 1787, delegates like Luther Martin, Rufus King, and George Mason sought to write the end of slavery into the federal compact. Despite their efforts, the constitution that emerged did precisely the opposite. Slaveholders, led by Charles Pinckney and Pierce Butler of South Carolina, demanded that slavery be protected; the alternative, they threatened, was that Georgia and South Carolina would not join the Union. In this first constitutional struggle, slavery won. Simultaneously, slavery gradually dissolved north of the Chesapeake Bay while it found political protection in the nation's founding document. The three-fifths clause, the fugitive slave clause, the pledge of the federal government to suppress rebellion, and the agreement to not consider the abolition of the transatlantic slave trade for another twenty years provided the political foundation for slavery to expand as a national institution, even while it became a sectional one.[13]

In Great Britain, the loss of the North American colonies inspired reformers such as Granville Sharp, James Ramsay, and William Wilberforce to begin agitation against the transatlantic slave trade. By the late 1780s they had fostered the emergence of a widespread popular movement that sent hundreds of petitions to Parliament. The conservative reaction to the French Revolution delayed the abolitionists' victory, but in 1807 Parliament abolished Britain's enormous share of the transatlantic slave trade. This would have serious implications in the Atlantic World, for when Britain emerged victorious from the wars with Napoleon, the abolition of the slave trade would become central to its diplomacy.[14]

It was probably mere coincidence that the United States abolished its slave trade during the same year as Great Britain. An abolitionist movement had not yet emerged in the United States, and representatives from the Lower South were against fulfilling this constitutional possibility. But Thomas Jefferson's Republicans were ascendant, and economically only the planters of the Lower South, a minority even among slaveholders, would have benefited from the lower slave prices the transatlantic slave trade would bring.[15]

But slave trade abolition did nothing to resolve the political tensions over the future of slavery that had been evident during the Constitutional debates. In 1819, when the territory of Missouri applied for statehood, Congressman James Tallmadge of New York proposed that slavery be barred from the new state, defending his position with strong antislavery language. Tallmadge's proposition led to a heated national debate over the future of American slavery that took three years to resolve; Missouri and Maine became states at the same time, one free and one slave, a compromise—the first of many—to maintain the sectional balance.[16]

As the nation's political leaders sought to maintain sectional equilibrium, they drove antislavery opinion out of mainstream politics, and when it emerged again it was far more radical. Free African Americans in the North began to organize against plans to encourage their emigration to West Africa, beginning in 1817 in Philadelphia. Within ten years African Americans published the most radical abolitionist newspaper in the country, *Freedom's Journal* of New York City, and David Walker's famous *Appeal to the Colored Citizens of the World* in 1828 was a militant call to action. The most famous abolitionist, William Lloyd Garrison, depended upon this black community to support his radical newspaper, *The Liberator,* which in 1831 called for the immediate abolition of slavery. Further inspired by British abolition in 1833, American reformers established forty-seven local abolitionist societies by the end of that year, as well as, in Philadelphia, the first national abolitionist society.[17]

In those heady days of the early movement, abolitionists believed they could convince the country that slavery was wrong and that it should be abolished. They compiled lists of southern ministers, printed massive quantities of antislavery literature, and sent it all southward in the post. When the mail arrived in Charleston, a mob of white citizens seized and burned the mailbags from New York—a federal crime—and hanged effigies of William Lloyd Garrison and other abolitionists. Charleston was not alone; there were more than 150 anti-abolitionist meetings throughout the South during the summer of 1835. President

Andrew Jackson supported these meetings, writing to his postmaster, Amos Kendall, that to receive an abolitionist publication was "to subscribe to this wicked plan of exciting the negroes to insurrection."[18]

In December of that year, when Congressman William Jackson of Massachusetts submitted an antislavery petition on behalf of his constituents, James Henry Hammond accused Jackson of attempting "to excite a servile insurrection" through their agitation and demanded that the petition "be not received." Hammond's accusation recalled the Haitian Revolution, the Denmark Vesey conspiracy, and Nat Turner's rebellion, and it would be echoed during the secession crisis. But in 1835 his motion was the first step in the establishment of the gag rule in Congress that disallowed antislavery petitions and thus violated the constitutional rights of Americans who held antislavery views. The gag rule had bipartisan support, a demonstration of the power of slaveholders in the second party system. Each political party—Democrats and Whigs—required support in the South to win national elections and congressional majorities to carry out their policy goals, so neither party could countenance abolitionism. For the next twenty years the second party system kept abolitionism out of mainstream politics and endowed slaveholders with the political stability that facilitated the expansion of the slave economy. In 1835 there were about two million enslaved African Americans in the United States; by 1860 there were nearly four million.[19]

Now we move on to Cuba and Brazil. We can tell these stories together because, despite their differences, their struggles over slavery were not only similar but integrated.[20] Both were colonies in 1808, when Napoleon invaded the Iberian Peninsula. The French occupation forced the abdication of Ferdinand VII of Spain and compelled the royal court of Portugal to flee, en masse, to Rio de Janeiro, which became the Kingdom of Brazil, the new center of the Portuguese Empire. As might be expected, both monarchs received much-needed assistance from Great Britain during these wars with Napoleon. The Portuguese court of Dom João VI was accompanied by four British men of war during its transatlantic crossing and received a significant loan to finance the move. In Spain, French troops provoked a massive war of Spanish resistance, which ultimately drove out the French, though only with the assistance of British troops, led by the Duke of Wellington, in 1812. The British were motivated by their enmity toward Napoleon, but their assistance came with strings attached. Britain had just abolished its slave trade, and in the coming years it would use the debt incurred by Spain and Portugal to suppress their slave trades as well.[21]

It was in the chaos of this moment, when both monarchies were weak, that the slaveholders of Cuba and Brazil first felt abolitionist pressure. In 1811, at the Cortes of Cadiz (formed to govern Spain during the war with France), two delegates, one from Mexico and one from Spain, made proposals to abolish the slave trade. While they received some support, they inspired a fierce response from Cuban planters, who expressed great fear that abolitionist agitation would recreate the Haitian Revolution. The Cuban delegate, Francisco Arrango, argued that the Cortes did not have the authority to abolish the trade and noted that both Britain and the United States had delayed abolition for twenty years after first broaching the issue. The Cortes did consider these proposals but ultimately rejected them because of the overwhelming opposition of Cubans and the important stream of revenue the colony still supplied.[22]

Antislavery views were rare and weak in the Spanish Empire during these years, more so than in Great Britain and the United States, but in Portugal and Brazil they were almost nonexistent. Slavery was not a sectional institution in Brazil, as it was in the United States, nor was Brazil any longer a colony. But Dom João was weak and indebted to Great Britain, which pressed the king to cooperate with its abolitionist agenda. In 1810, 1815, and 1817, Britain signed treaties with Portugal that gave British merchants preferential access to trade in Brazilian ports and took increasingly stronger measures against the slave trade. In the treaty of 1810 Portugal agreed to express its intention to abolish the trade; the treaty of 1815 abolished the trade north of the equator; and the treaty of 1817 gave British warships the right to board and search Portuguese vessels suspected of slaving. Brazilian slaveholders in the northeast resented these treaties, which inhibited their ability to import slaves from the Bights of Benin and Biafra. But slaveholders in the dynamic coffee regions of the central-south were largely unaffected, as most of their captives came from West Central Africa, south of the equator, where the treaty had no jurisdiction.[23]

The transatlantic slave trade to Brazil remained stable during these years at about forty-five thousand captives brought in every year, and the economic expansion under way was unaffected by diplomacy. Indeed, the preferential treatment of Britain in the Brazilian market attracted British capital, which bolstered the Brazilian economy and increased the demand for African slaves. The slave trade policy of Dom João might have offended the patriotic sensibilities of Brazilian slaveholders, but it went easy on their wallets, and it went easy with British merchants as well. Dom João's policy for dealing with the British and the slaveholders while facilitating an economic expansion would become the model for Cuban planters trying to accomplish the same thing.[24]

Britain employed the same strategy in its attempt to suppress the Spanish slave trade, and, for a while, British policies were relatively successful. With British assistance, Ferdinand reclaimed the Spanish throne in 1814 and in 1817 agreed to a treaty with Britain that abolished the Spanish slave trade north of the equator immediately, and abolished that trade south of the equator beginning in 1820. These Spanish treaties were more effective than the Anglo-Portuguese agreements. After 1820 the slave trade to Cuba decreased by almost 75 percent, from about twenty thousand slaves annually to fewer than six thousand.[25]

The difference in the effectiveness of these treaties can be found in merchant confidence in the stability of the economy of slavery. In 1820 a liberal revolution in Spain forced Ferdinand to establish a constitutional monarchy, and there was every reason to believe the liberals would enforce the antislave trade treaty of 1817. Moreover, the Spanish Empire was being ripped asunder by the independence movements that swept across Spanish America, and merchants could not be sure that these movements would not spread to Cuba as well. But in 1823 Ferdinand restored absolutist rule in Spain; he redoubled the military effort to retain Spanish America and in 1825 ordered that Cuba be placed under the authority of a captain-general who would control both political and military power. Through the concentration of power, Ferdinand hoped to maintain Cuba's colonial dependence, and this plan succeeded until 1868. But the dictatorship established also provided the political stability that facilitated the expansion of Cuba's sugar economy and limited abolitionist activity to the metropole. The revenues from Cuba were very important to the Spanish Empire, and, despite the treaties with Great Britain, the Spanish imperial bureaucracy in Cuba knew on which side its bread was buttered. From 1825 until 1866, when the transatlantic slave trade finally ended, merchants brought almost a half million captive Africans to the sugar plantations of Cuba.[26]

British antislavery efforts were an almost total failure in the Spanish Empire, and until 1850 their failure in Brazil was even more dramatic. The liberal revolution of 1820 that had challenged Ferdinand in Spain materialized as well in Portugal, where a Cortes declared its authority to rule Portugal in the absence of the emperor. In 1821 Dom João left Brazil to reassert his authority in Portugal, but, before he left, he crowned his son Pedro king of Brazil. Many Brazilians sought complete autonomy within the empire, much as British colonists in North America had sought autonomy from Britain in the 1760s. When this was denied, in 1822, Pedro unilaterally declared Brazil an independent kingdom. But, like the independence of the United States in 1776, Brazilian independence in 1822 was more aspiration than reality. Independence had to be recognized, and in 1822 only one nation had the power to effectively do this—Great Britain.[27]

It took several years, but British diplomats were able to facilitate a peaceful separation between Portugal and Brazil, and, through a separate treaty in 1826, Britain recognized Brazilian independence. Predictably, Britain secured for its merchants preferential treatment in Brazilian ports and compelled Brazil to agree to abolish the slave trade by 1830. Brazilian slaveholders were aghast, and as soon as the treaty was presented to the Chamber of Deputies, which did not have the power to ratify or reject the treaty, they attacked it. Slave merchants invested in the slave trade as they never had before, hoping to purchase as many captive

Africans as they could before the source of labor was cut off. Slavers had brought about 110,000 captive Africans during the early 1820s, but beginning in 1826 they brought in more than 60,000 every year.[28]

Pedro had many unfortunate qualities, and, rather suddenly, in 1831 he lost the support of the military and was compelled to abdicate and cede power to his son, Pedro II, who was only a boy. Brazil became a regency, governed by a cabinet of three of Pedro's liberal opponents in the Chamber of Deputies who seized power and governed in the name of the boy king. Within a month of Pedro's abdication, the regents ordered that the abolition of the slave trade be enforced. Liberals in the Chamber passed a law that criminalized the purchase of newly arrived Africans, with stiff fines for everyone involved in the transaction—investors, ship captains, and slaveholders. It was clear to all that the liberals intended to abolish the slave trade, and the number of captives brought to Brazil dropped dramatically, to only about two thousand every year, a 97 percent decline.[29]

But these were chaotic years in Brazil. There was partisan violence in Para and Rio Grande do Sul that the regents could not control, and in 1835 a massive slave rebellion in Bahia terrified those who held slaves. The reactionary opposition began to mobilize against the liberals, and the core of what came to be known as the Party of Order materialized. This group made abolition of the 1831 law its central issue and signaled to the slave merchants that if it gained power, it would not enforce it. The slave trade began to increase. In the election of 1837 the reactionaries seized power in the Chamber of Deputies and held power into the 1850s. Between 1837 and 1850, when Great Britain abolished the Brazilian slave trade through naval force, more than seven hundred thousand captive Africans were brought in shackles to Brazil.[30]

The second party system in the United States, the military government of colonial Cuba, and the Party of Order in Brazil forged the political stability that enabled slaveholders to fend off abolitionism and create the most modern slave economies in human history. But in the 1850s the second party system began to crumble, and by the election of 1860 it was completely dead. In contrast, the political systems that supported Brazilian and Cuban slaveholders remained intact for another generation. Slavery persisted in Cuba until 1886 and in Brazil until 1888, and in neither place did slavery end in the brutal violence of civil war. Which brings us back to the key question posed at the beginning of this essay: how can this exercise in comparative history help us understand the near-exceptional abolition of slavery in the United States through brutal civil war, rather than politics?

Let us start this final analysis as we began, with the economy. Of these three economies, the sectional development of slavery in the United States was far more pronounced than in either Cuba or in Brazil. By 1860 slavery had been abolished in all of the states north of Mason and Dixon's line, and it played an increasingly reduced role in the economies of Upper South states such as Delaware, Maryland, Kentucky, and Missouri. Economic development in Cuba and Brazil had rooted slavery more deeply in some regions than others, but abolitionism had played no role in this process. Western Cuba, for example, had far larger slave populations than did the eastern districts of Bayamo, Holguín, Jiguaní, Manzanillo, and Tunas. Brazil also had its plantation belts in the coffee-producing provinces along the Paraiba River valley and the sugar regions surrounding Rio de Janeiro.[31] But nothing like the slaveless North existed in either Cuba or Brazil. The United States South, Cuba, and Brazil were slave societies; slaves were the most important source of labor for the most important branches of the economy. All of the richest men and most of the political leadership were slaveholders. But of these three, only in the United States did slaveholders have to share power with men whose economic interests did not depend upon slavery. The federal system of the United States brought together different economies and forced them to share power. The political leaders of Cuba and Brazil never faced such a challenge.

A second distinction our comparison reveals is in the nature of the abolitionist challenge. Because of the nation's revolutionary founding, abolitionism in the United States emerged as a challenge to slavery much earlier than in colonial Cuba or monarchical Brazil. Abolitionism in the United States also came from a very different place. It emerged from within the national body, whereas in Brazil and Cuba the major abolitionist challenge before 1865 came from without. The Anglo-Atlantic abolitionism that developed in the aftermath of the American Revolution created unprecedented political challenges to slaveholders in the Americas. This powerful movement generated a series of disputes about slavery that punctuated most of the long nineteenth century, shaping the struggle over slavery in the most dynamic economies of the Americas.[32]

The slaveholder response to abolitionism was remarkably similar; each locale developed a political system that effectively neutralized the abolitionist threat. Our brief accounts of Brazil and Cuba suggest that slavery prospered under less than democratic conditions. Cuba remained a colony ruled by a military governor through a bureaucracy that was easily manipulated by the slaveholding elite, allowing that elite to continue the importation of slaves. Citizenship was broad in monarchical Brazil, but it did not spread political power; rather, Brazilian politics were the domain of a small but dispersed elite that exercised hegemonic influence through webs of patronage. In the United States universal white male suffrage became the national norm during the 1820s; it was not a democratic society by twenty-first-century standards, but it was more democratic than anywhere else in the mid-nineteenth century. On the question of slavery, however, the United States was not democratic, as evidenced by the gag rule of the 1830s or the Fugitive Slave Act of 1850, which compelled northerners, regardless of their will, to participate in the capture of runaway slaves. Slaveholders everywhere governed through undemocratic means, but only in the United States did these undemocratic means coexist uncomfortably with a democratic society.[33]

The value of this insight gains explanatory power when we consider how the antislavery movement evolved in the United States. In the 1820s it was an unpopular, radical movement championed by a despised racial minority, but thirty years later the critique of slavery had moved into the mainstream of northern politics, as the cornerstone of the Republican Party. One of the most important factors explaining the broadening of antislavery views was opposition to the undemocratic actions of political leaders invested in protecting slavery, what northerners increasingly called the "slave power." It was the abolitionists who first politicized slavery, who inspired northern leaders such as former president John Quincy Adams to devote his congressional career to overturning the gag rule. But it was far more mainstream northerners, white men like David Wilmot with no special love for black people, who became convinced that the "slave power" had taken over the republic. In 1848 Wilmot proposed in Congress that the lands conquered through the war with Mexico be barred from establishing slavery. His proposal gained bipartisan support, but only in the North, among political leaders concerned with the dominance of the "slave power" in party politics.[34]

Southern slaveholders responded to accusations of a "slave power" with a defense of slavery that was unique in world history. British and French slaveholders had defended slavery from antislavery critiques as early as the 1770s, and Brazilians and Cubans had also defended their rights to hold people as property. But it was the South Carolina senator John C. Calhoun who in 1837 first pronounced that slavery was a "positive good" for southern society. Calhoun and his intellectual disciples argued that black people did not have the intelligence or the discipline to labor consistently; they had to be forced, they had to be enslaved. By the 1850s the Virginian George Fitzhugh even argued that slavery was the most humane way to organize capital and labor in a modern society. The North, he charged, should emulate the South and adopt slavery. Even among secessionists Fitzhugh was extreme; in comparative perspective he was unique.[35]

By the 1850s about a thousand African American slaves were escaping slavery into the North every year. This was not a large percentage of the four million slaves in the South, but they were politically significant in the welcome they received. They found free black communities of radical abolitionists who established systems of support for the fugitives, and in some cities there were even vigilance committees that would fight off slave catchers. In contrast, fugitives in Cuba and Brazil could escape only to the runaway slave settlements known as *palenques* in Cuba and as *quilombos* in Brazil, where they were hunted down by professional slave catchers and their trained dogs. The military struggles with these slave settlements could be quite intense, but the conflicts did not have at stake the future of slavery as an institution. This situation would change in Cuba in 1868 with the onset of the Ten Years War and in Brazil with the emergence of radical abolitionism in the 1880s. But before these developments, runaway slaves in Cuba and Brazil were a problem for slaveholders that did not rise to the level of existential crisis.[36]

The contrast with the United States could not be more stark. Because of growing antislavery sentiment among white voters in the North, many northern state legislatures passed "Personal Liberty Laws" during the 1840s to hinder (and in some cases obstruct) the operation of the federal Constitution, which mandated the return of fugitive slaves. The Fugitive Slave Act of 1850 was a direct response to these laws, a clear demonstration of slaveholder power within the second party system. But northern antislavery opinion grew after 1850, exacerbated by this clear demonstration of "the slave power" at work. During the 1850s, all of the northern legislatures with the exception of Indiana and Ohio passed new and sometimes stronger laws that sought to hinder the new act. Runaways everywhere lived a besieged existence. They fought off slave catchers and dogs and were often killed. But only in the United States did the runaway have a political impact beyond his or her personal freedom. The bold actions of fugitives initiated a political dialectic in the United States that directly contributed to the sectional crisis of 1861; this process had no counterpart in either Cuba or Brazil. By the late 1850s the runaway slave Frederick Douglass could address audiences of thousands of white voters who listened with rapt attention to his denunciations of slavery. And with the Emancipation Proclamation of 1863, thousands of runaway slaves joined the Union army and became a critical factor in the defeat of the slaveholding Confederacy.[37]

In the century-long struggle over Atlantic slavery that began with the Haitian Revolution, the situation in the United States was unique. It was the only society in which the political contest over the future of slavery resulted in a brutal civil war. In the Spanish and Brazilian Empires, interested observers read the news reports from North America and Great Britain with great anticipation. The Confederacy appeared strong at first, and significant numbers of Britons advocated recognition of this new venture couched as a quest for independence. But when federal troops defeated the Confederates at the battle of Antietam, President Lincoln moved to transform civil war into North America's last struggle over slavery. The Emancipation Proclamation ended Confederate hopes of British recognition and enabled Lincoln to raise black troops for the Union armies, tipping the balance of power. Union victory in 1864 and the Thirteenth Amendment in 1865 abolished slavery in the United States, leaving Brazil and Cuba as the last bastions of slaveholding in the Atlantic World.[38]

The American Civil War was also a critical turning point in the struggle over slavery in both Cuba and Brazil. The defeat of the slaveholding Confederacy had a powerful impact upon public opinion in both empires. Many elites and the growing middle classes in both societies had developed political identities that embraced what was called "the civilized world," and many had read translations of Harriet Beecher Stowe's *Uncle Tom's Cabin*. The "civilized world" had condemned slavery, and abolition in the United States was the last nail in the coffin of proslavery respectability. In Spain an abolitionist society formed in 1865, and Spanish legislators raised the question of the future of slavery in the Caribbean. In Brazil, Dom Pedro II suggested to his cabinet that they consider a plan for gradual emancipation; all of these actors explicitly noted the end of slavery in the United States as a principal motivating factor.[39]

With Washington, D.C. no longer acting internationally in the interest of slaveholders, the United States finally cooperated with Great Britain in its decades-long effort to abolish the transatlantic slave trade. The Anglophone nations pressured Spain, which formally abolished its slave trade in 1866. The Spanish government also created the *Junta de Información sobre Ultramar* to consider colonial reforms, including the gradual abolition of slavery. The Junta consisted of Spanish representatives as well as delegations from Puerto Rico and Cuba. Both groups of colonial representatives sought more autonomy within the empire, and while the Cubans were willing to consider gradual abolition, the Puerto Rican delegates sought immediate abolition. The Junta disbanded with few accomplishments, which frustrated the ambitions of colonists and abolitionists alike and laid the seeds of a war for independence that would come.[40]

Spain's actions inspired Dom Pedro to finally make public his desire to see gradual abolition in Brazil. His 1867 address to the newly elected Chamber of Deputies charged them to consider the future of the empire's "servile element" with a view to ending slavery. With small steps, the emperor had already begun to act toward this end. In July 1866 he responded to the petition of a French abolitionist society by observing that emancipation was "nothing more than a question of method and opportunity." In November he granted freedom to government-owned slaves who agreed to serve as soldiers in the Paraguayan War and strongly encouraged private slaveholders to grant manumissions for this same purpose. But slaveholders were Dom Pedro's most powerful supporters, and their interests would not be ignored. These initial steps foundered, but the question of emancipation had been raised, and it did not go away.[41]

In September 1868 a liberal revolution swept the Bourbons from the Spanish throne and in October a group of slaveholding *independistas* in eastern Cuba declared themselves in revolt against Spain. The new liberal government in Madrid included many abolitionists, and the revolutionists in Cuba declared the abolition of slavery to be one of their goals, though they retreated from this stance in order to gain support for their movement. Some slaveholders who supported independence freed their slaves to serve in the rebel army, and the military conflict expanded the opportunities for slaves to escape from their masters. The inclusion of former slaves in the rebel armies infused Cuba's independence movements with strains of antiracism and antislavery sentiment that were unique. The new government in Spain, dedicated to abolition but eager to keep Cuba and Puerto Rico as colonies, sought to preempt the independence movement with a gradual abolition act known as the Moret Law. Passed in 1870, the Moret Law freed the womb; all children born to enslaved mothers after September 18, a date chosen to honor the Revolution, were declared free, though they were compelled to work without pay for their former masters until the age of eighteen. Slaves over the age of sixty-five were also freed. In addition, the law freed all slaves who served in the Spanish armies in the conflict in Cuba, which considerably expanded the emancipatory tendencies of that war. In 1873 the Spanish Cortes also passed legislation abolishing slavery in Puerto Rico, though slaveholders still secured three more years of unpaid labor from those freed. Slaveholders everywhere still retained much influence, and it was those in the weakest political positions who lost slavery first.[42]

Conflict in Cuba and the Spanish government's Moret Law contributed powerfully to Dom Pedro's ability to move the passage of Brazil's own gradual emancipation act in 1871. Known as the Rio Branco Law after the prime minister who secured its passage, the Brazilian legislation emulated Spain's Moret Law, though it did not liberate elderly slaves. The Rio Branco law also established an emancipation fund intended to compensate slaveholders, who were encouraged to manumit their slaves.

The government's action conveyed to most observers that slavery would gradually wither in Brazil; in fact, an internal slave trade expanded that gradually concentrated Brazil's remaining slaves within the coffee-growing regions in the central-south provinces, and the emancipation fund liberated relatively few. Slaveholders still dominated the upper echelons of power in Brazil, and, while they recognized the international potency of antislavery, they carefully protected their interests.[43]

Like the Emancipation Proclamation in the United States, these laws were more important for their symbolic impacts than for the number of enslaved people freed through the formal mechanisms they put in place. It has become commonplace to note that Lincoln's Emancipation Proclamation freed no one, though it did become the pivot of the war that liberated all. Likewise, the Ten Years War for independence had a greater impact upon the erosion of Cuban slavery than the Moret Law. We can see this in the Peace of Zanjon, which temporarily ended the conflict in 1878. Because of the realities of wartime emancipations, Spain was compelled to recognize the liberty of sixteen thousand freedmen who had fought in the armies of the independence movement. The government had little choice. But, for those people not directly affected by the war, especially the mothers of children on sugar plantations that still thrived, the prospect of freedom for their sons and daughters provided life-sustaining hope. The Moret Law accelerated the processes of manumission that had always been a part of Iberian slave systems. In 1880 Spain passed legislation that abolished Cuban slavery, yet established a new legal structure of labor control that transformed slaves into *patrocinados*, who owed their former masters labor until the *Partronato* culminated in eight years. Like the British apprenticeship system that had failed in 1838, the *Patronato* ended abruptly in 1886, two years prior to the intended termination. After 394 years, slavery in Cuba had ended.[44]

In the urban centers of Brazil, which had grown in wealth and sophistication over the past thirty years, the advance of international abolitionism inspired many. Brazil's abolitionist movement took off in the late 1870s when reformer-legislators such as Jeronymo Sodre and Joaquim Nabuco became disenchanted with the inadequacy of the Rio Branco Law and publicly dedicated themselves to immediate abolition. Brazil was the only slave society to have ever generated an abolitionist movement from within. Abolitionism in the British and Spanish Empires had been rooted in the metropoles, and while abolitionism in the United States did have an influence upon the national electorate, it could never extend a public presence south of Philadelphia. The contrast with Brazil is astonishing and can be exemplified by Rio de Janeiro. Rio became Brazil's most dynamic and cosmopolitan port during the nineteenth century because of its deep hinterland that produced both coffee and sugar, Brazil's most lucrative exports. These were precisely the sectors of the economy where slaves had been concentrated after 1850. Yet one of Brazil's first abolitionist societies formed in Rio de Janeiro in 1880. It is very difficult to imagine a comparable development—say, a New Orleans Abolitionist society—in the antebellum South.[45]

Brazilian abolitionism borrowed much from the abolitionist movements that had emerged in Great Britain and then the United States. Brazilian abolitionists organized societies, they held public lectures and debates, they published antislavery pamphlets and newspapers, they linked antislavery politics with musical performances, and, as was true of the movement in the United States, many abolitionist leaders were free blacks from the cities. Jose do Patrocino, son of a slaveholder and a free black market woman, became Brazil's most fervent and influential abolitionist editor from his position at the *Gazeta da Tarde* of Rio de Janeiro. Luiz Gama, also the son of a slaveholder and a free black woman, became an abolitionist lawyer who advocated for those Africans brought to Brazil after 1831 in violation of the law that Brazilian officials had long ignored. Gama freed more than a thousand people through these suits. Gama died when still a young man in 1882, but his work inspired Antonio Bento, whose radicalism and personal demeanor reminded contemporaries of the legendary John Brown. Bento wore a long, black cape and a black hat that shrouded him with an intense religiosity. He surrounded himself with a dedicated group of radical activists who would visit the plantations by night to convince the slaves to flee en masse.[46]

Bento's associates began to deploy these tactics in 1886, and soon an underground railroad developed that surpassed its precursor in the United States. Centered in the antislavery cities and stretching into the plantation belts of their hinterlands, Brazil's underground railroad included real trains with conductors who assisted fugitives to safe houses and employment, usually in the cities. Brazilian abolitionism had a revolutionary impact upon Brazilian society by undermining the very foundations of slavery, the masters' ability to control the slaves. When slaveholders sought the assistance of the military in controlling the flight from the estates, military leaders refused. Twenty thousand former slaves had gained their freedom through military service during the Paraguayan War, and many officers held antislavery views as a result. Moreover, in the lower ranks of the Brazilian army were large numbers of black soldiers sympathetic to the slaves and unlikely to play the role of slave catcher. By early 1888 the slave regime had collapsed in much of Brazil, and in May of that year the Chamber of Deputies passed the "Golden Law," bringing an immediate and unconditional end to almost four hundred years of slavery.[47]

In 1889 the Brazilian military executed a bloodless coup d'état, overthrowing the monarchy that had established Brazilian independence in 1822. Dom Pedro II, having alienated much of the elite through his advocacy of abolition, had no allies to help him defend his crown. In a sense this echoed what had happened in the United States and foreshadowed what would soon occur in the Spanish Empire. In North America, the federal government of the United States as it had been administered since 1789 lost legitimacy because a man with antislavery views had been endowed with executive power. With the Union victory in the Civil War and the Thirteenth, Fourteenth, and Fifteenth Amendments to the national Constitution, the political framework of the United States was completely transformed. What Don Fehrenbacher called the "Slaveholding Republic" had been overthrown. In the Spanish Empire, the interracial independence movement born in the Ten Years War reemerged in 1895, and, after three more years of war, Spain's rule over Cuba was also destroyed.[48]

In the aftermath of the Haitian Revolution and Spanish American independence and in the face of radical abolitionism in Britain and the United States North, the slaveholders of the United States, Cuba, and Brazil established political alliances that protected their investments in the world's most modern slave-based economies. These political arrangements varied considerably, the result of distinctive national and imperial developments, but the struggles over slavery that ensued were interconnected and cumulative. And, with a rapidity that belied slavery's ancient legacy, these struggles destroyed slavery and the governments that supported it.

NOTES

The author would like to thank Angela Alonso, Celso Castilho, Enrico Dal Lago, Simon Lewis, Rafael de Bivar Marquese, Christopher Schmidt-Nowara, and Stuart Schwartz for their insightful comments on this essay.

1. "The Non-Slaveholders of the South: Their Interest in the Present Sectional Controversy Identical with That of the Slaveholders," *DeBow's Review*, January 1861, 75.

2. One of the most powerful interpretations of the Haitian Revolution remains C. L. R. James, *The Black Jacobins: Toussaint L'Ouverture and the San Domingo Revolution* (1938; repr., New York, 1963), but for a more recent account see Laurent Dubois, *Avengers of the New World: The Story of the Haitian Revolution* (Cambridge, Mass.: Harvard University Press, 2004).

3. Edward B. Rugemer, *The Problem of Emancipation: The Caribbean Roots of the American Civil War* (Baton Rouge: Louisiana State University Press, 2008), chap. 2; Matthew Clavin, *Toussaint Louverture and the American Civil War* (Philadelphia: University of Pennsylvania Press, 2010), chap. 3; E. N. Elliott, ed., *Cotton Is King, and Pro-Slavery Arguments* (Augusta, Ga.: Pritchard, Abbott and Loomis, 1860).

4. Previous comparisons of the abolition of slavery that include the United States, Brazil, and Cuba include Seymour Drescher, "Brazilian Abolition in Comparative Perspective," *Hispanic American Historical Review* 68 (August 1988): 429–60; Steven Hahn, "Class and State in Postemancipation Societies: Southern Planters in Comparative Perspective," *American Historical Review* 95 (February 1990): 75–98; Rebecca J. Scott, "Defining the Boundaries of Freedom in the World of Cane: Cuba, Brazil, and Louisiana after Emancipation," *American Historical Review* 99 (February 1994): 70–102.

5. John Thornton, *Africa and Africans in the Making of the Atlantic World, 1400–1800*, 2nd ed. (Cambridge: Cambridge University Press, 1998), chap. 1; Russel R. Menard, *Sweet Negotiations: Sugar, Slavery, and Plantation Agriculture in Early Barbados* (Charlottesville: University of Virginia Press, 2006); Edmund Morgan, *American Slavery, American Freedom: The Ordeal of Colonial Virginia* (New York: Norton, 1975), 105. For a comparative analysis of slavery and economy in Brazil and the U.S. South, see Richard Graham, "Slavery and Economic Development: Brazil and the United States South in the Nineteenth Century," *Comparative Studies in Society and History* 23 (October 1981): 620–55.

6. The distinction between "slave societies" and "societies with slaves" is best described in Ira Berlin, *Many Thousands Gone: The First Two Centuries of Slavery in North America* (Cambridge, Mass.: Harvard University Press, 1998), 8.

7. David Eltis, *Economic Growth and the Ending of the Transatlantic Slave Trade* (New York: Oxford University Press, 1987), 37–40. All slave trade figures in this essay are from the Transatlantic Slave Trade Database, http://www.slavevoyages.org/tast/database/search.faces (accessed February 22, 2011).

8. Adam Rothman, *Slave Country: American Expansion and the Origins of the Deep South* (Cambridge, Mass.: Harvard University Press, 2005); Berlin, *Many Thousands Gone,* 343.

9. Joyce E. Chaplin, "Creating a Cotton South in Georgia and South Carolina, 1760–1815," *Journal of Southern History* 57 (May 1991): 171–200; R. W. Fogel and Stanley Engerman, *Time on the Cross: The Economics of American Negro Slavery* (New York: Norton, 1974), 44; Lewis Gray, *History of Agriculture in the Southern United States to 1860,* 2 vols. (1933; repr., Gloucester, Mass.: Peter Smith, 1958), 2: 1026; Brian Schoen, *The Fragile Fabric of Union: Cotton, Federal Politics, and the Global Origins of the Civil War* (Baltimore: The Johns Hopkins University Press, 2010), 23–60.

10. Steven Deyle, *Carry Me Back: The Domestic Slave Trade in American Life* (New York: Oxford University Press, 2005), 288–89; Walter Johnson, *Soul by Soul: Life Inside the Antebellum Slave Market* (Cambridge, Mass.: Harvard University Press, 1999). Many historians see the expansion of slavery in these regions of the Atlantic world as a "second slavery"; see Dale Tomich, *Through the Prism of Slavery: Labor, Capital, and World Economy* (Lanham, Md., 2004), 56–71; Anthony Kaye, "The Second Slavery: Modernity in the Nineteenth-Century South and the Atlantic World," *Journal of Southern History* 75 (August 2009): 627–34.

11. Rafael Marquese and Tâmis Parron, "The Proslavery International and the Politics of the Second Slavery," paper presented at "The Politics of the Second Slavery: Conflict and Crisis on the Nineteenth-Century Atlantic Slave Frontier," a conference of the Fernand Braudel Center for the Study of Economics, Historical Systems, and Civilizations, Binghamton University, New York, October 15–16, 2010.

12. David Brion Davis, *The Problem of Slavery in Western Culture* (New York: Oxford University Press, 1966); Davis, *The Problem of Slavery in the Age of Revolution, 1770–1823* (New York: Oxford University Press, 1975), 24; Gregory D. Massey, "The Limits of Antislavery Thought in the Revolutionary Lower South: John Laurens and Henry Laurens," *Journal of Southern History* 63 (August 1997): 495–530.

13. Arthur Zilversmit, *First Emancipation: The Abolition of Slavery in the North* (Chicago: Chicago University Press, 1967); Paul Finkleman, "Slavery and the Constitutional Convention: Making a Covenant with Death," in Richard Beeman et al., eds., *Beyond Confederation: Origins of the Constitution and American National Identity* (Chapel Hill: University of North Carolina Press, 1987), 188–225.

14. Christopher Leslie Brown, *Moral Capital: Foundations of British Abolitionism* (Chapel Hill: Published for the Omohundro Institute of Early American History and Culture by the University of North Carolina Press, 2006); James Walvin, *England, The Slaves, and Freedom, 1776–1838* (Jackson: University of Mississippi Press, 1986).

15. Matthew E. Mason, "Slavery Overshadowed: Congress Debates Prohibiting the Atlantic Slave Trade to the United States, 1806–1807," *Journal of the Early Republic* 20 (Spring 2000): 59–81.

16. Robert Forbes, *The Missouri Compromise and Its Aftermath: Slavery and the Meaning of America* (Chapel Hill: University of North Carolina Press, 2007).

17. Timothy Patrick McCarthy, "'To Plead Our Own Cause'": Black Print Culture and the Origins of American Abolitionism," in McCarthy and John Stauffer, eds., *Prophets of Protest: Reconsidering the History of American Abolitionism* (New York: New Press,

2006): 114–44; James Brewer Stewart, *Holy Warriors: The Abolitionists and American Slavery,* rev. ed. (New York: Hill and Wang, 1997), 51–66.

18. Susan Wyly-Jones, "The 1835 Anti-Abolition Meetings in the South: A New Look at the Controversy over the Abolition Postal Campaign" *Civil War History* 47 (December 2001): 289–309; Jackson, quoted in Rugemer, *Problem of Emancipation,* 141.

19. Edward B. Rugemer, "Caribbean Slave Revolts and the Origins of the Gag Rule: A Contest between Abolitionism and Democracy, 1797–1835," in John Craig Hammond and Matthew Mason, eds., *Contesting Slavery: The Politics of Bondage and Freedom in the New American Nation* (Charlottesville: University of Virginia Press, 2011), 94–113; Ira Berlin, *Generations of Captivity: A History of African American Slaves* (Cambridge, Mass.: Harvard University Press, 2003), 275.

20. Márcia Berbel, Rafael Marquese, and Tâmis Parron, *Escravidão e Política: Brasil e Cuba, 1790–1850* (Sao Paolo: Editora Hucitec, 2010).

21. Peter Bakewell, *A History of Latin America,* 2nd ed. (Oxford: Blackwell, 2004), 386–87; Roderick J. Barman, *Brazil: The Forging of a Nation, 1798–1852* (Stanford: Stanford University Press, 1988), 45–46.

22. Arthur F. Corwin, *Spain and the Abolition of Slavery in Cuba, 1817–1886* (Austin: University of Texas Press, 1967), 22–25; Christopher Schmidt-Nowara, *Empire and Antislavery: Spain, Cuba, and Puerto Rico, 1833–1874* (Pittsburgh: University of Pittsburgh Press, 1999), 14–16.

23. Leslie Bethell, *The Abolition of the Brazilian Slave Trade: Britain, Brazil and the Slave Trade Question, 1807–1869* (Cambridge: Cambridge University Press, 1970), 11–22, 42.

24. David Eltis, *Economic Growth and the Ending of the Transatlantic Slave Trade* (New York: Oxford University Press, 1987), chap. 4.

25. Corwin, *Spain and the Abolition of Slavery in Cuba,* 28–29.

26. Corwin, *Spain and the Abolition of Slavery in Cuba,* 36–37; Marquese and Parron, "The Proslavery International," 6–7; Schmidt-Nowara, *Empire and Antislavery,* 16–17; Franklin W. Knight, *Slave Society in Cuba during the Nineteenth Century* (Madison: University of Wisconsin Press, 1970), 90–91.

27. Barman, *Brazil: The Forging of a Nation,* chap. 3.

28. Bethell, *The Abolition of the Brazilian Slave Trade,* 62–66.

29. Barman, *Brazil: The Forging of a Nation,* chaps. 4–5; Bethell, *The Abolition of the Brazilian Slave Trade,* 68–70.

30. Jeffrey D. Needell, *The Party of Order: The Conservatives, The State, and Slavery in the Brazilian Monarchy, 1831–1871* (Stanford: Stanford University Press, 2006), 59–62.

31. Laird W. Bergad, *The Comparative Histories of Slavery in Brazil, Cuba, and the United States* (Cambridge: Cambridge University Press, 2007), 113–31.

32. To be precise, abolitionism generated conflict at the U.S. Constitutional Convention; in the Francophone Atlantic during the French Revolution; during the constitutional moments in both the Portuguese and Spanish Empires; in international deliberations among Britain, Spain, Portugal, and the United States over the transatlantic slave trade; during the Missouri crisis in the United States; in the British Empire over the future of West Indian slavery; with the sectionalization of U.S. politics beginning in the 1830s; and in the Spanish and the Brazilian Empires after the U.S. Civil War.

33. Richard Graham, *Patronage and Politics in Nineteenth-Century Brazil* (Stanford: Stanford University Press, 1990), chap. 2; William W. Freehling, "The Divided South, Democracy's Limitations, and the Causes of the Peculiarly North American Civil War," in Gabor S. Boritt, ed., *Why the Civil War Came* (New York: Oxford University Press, 1996), 125–75.

34. William Lee Miller, *Arguing about Slavery: The Great Battle in the United States Congress* (New York: Knopf, 1996); Leonard L. Richards, *The Slave Power: The Free North and Southern Domination, 1780–1860* (Baton Rouge: Louisiana State University Press, 2000).

35. Edward Long, *Candid Reflections upon the Judgment Lately Awarded by the Court of King's Bench, in Westminster-Hall, on What Is Commonly Called the Negroe-cause* (London, 1772); Barbara Weinstein, "Slavery, Citizenship, and National Identity in Brazil and the United States South," in Don Doyle and Marco Antonio Pamplona, eds., *Nationalism in the New World* (Athens: University of Georgia Press, 2006), 248–71; Robert Brent Toplin, *The Abolition of Slavery in Brazil* (New York: Atheneum, 1972), 131–44; Seymour Drescher, *Abolition: A History of Slavery and Antislavery* (Cambridge: Cambridge University Press, 2010), 309; George Fitzhugh, *Cannibals All! Or, Slaves without Masters*, ed. C. Vann Woodward (Cambridge, Mass.: Harvard University Press, 1960).

36. James Oakes, "The Political Significance of Slave Resistance," *History Workshop Journal* 22 (1986), 19–81; Herbert S. Klein and Fransisco Vidal Luna, *Slavery in Brazil*, (Cambridge: Cambridge University Press, 2010) 195–99; Gabina la Rosa Corzo, *Runaway Slave Settlements in Cuba: Resistance and Repression*, trans. Mary Todd (Chapel Hill: University of North Carolina Press, 2003).

37. James M. McPherson, *Battle Cry of Freedom: The Civil War Era* (New York: Oxford University Press, 1988), 78–80, 769; John Ashworth, *Slavery, Capitalism, and Politics in the Antebellum Republic*, 2 vols. (Cambridge: Cambridge University Press, 1995–2007), 2: 131–33; David Blight, *Frederick Douglass' Civil War: Keeping Faith in Jubilee* (Baton Rouge: Louisiana State University Press, 1989). See also Thomas D. Morris, *Free Men All: The Personal Liberty Laws of the North, 1780- 1861* (Baltimore: The Johns Hopkins University Press, 1974).

38. James M. McPherson, *Crossroads of Freedom: Antietam* (New York: Oxford University Press, 2002), 68–71; Joaquim Nabuco, *Abolitionism: The Brazilian Antislavery Struggle*, trans. and ed. Robert Conrad (1883; repr., Urbana: University of Illinois Press, 1977), 119.

39. Corwin, *Spain and the Abolition of Slavery in Cuba*, 162–63; Schmidt-Nowara, *Empire and Antislavery*, 100–101; Roderick J. Barman, *Citizen Emperor: Pedro II and the Making of Brazil, 1825–91* (Stanford: Stanford University Press, 1999), 195.

40. Drescher, *Abolition*, 340–341; Schmidt-Nowara, *Empire and Antislavery*, 106–108.

41. Barman, *Citizen Emperor*, 215; Robert Conrad, *The Destruction of Brazilian Slavery, 1850–1888* (Berkeley: University of California Press, 1972), 75–77.

42. Schmidt-Nowara, *Empire and Antislavery*, 126–29; Ada Ferrer, *Insurgent Cuba: Race, Nation, and Revolution, 1868–1898* (Chapel Hill: University of North Carolina Press, 1999), chap. 1; Scott, *Slave Emancipation in Cuba*, 54–62; Christopher Schmidt-Nowara,

Slavery, Freedom, and Abolition in Latin America and the Atlantic World (Albuquerque: University of New Mexico Press, 2011), 147–48.

43. Schmidt-Nowara, *Slavery, Freedom and Abolition,* 150–51; Robert Conrad, *The Destruction of Brazilian Slavery, 1850–1888* (Berkeley: University of California Press, 1972), 87, 90–91; Richard Graham, "Another Middle Passage? The Internal Slave Trade in Brazil," in Walter Johnson, ed., *The Chattel Principle: Internal Slave Trades in the Americas* (New Haven: Yale University Press, 2004), 291–324. For the historical background to gradual abolition laws see Stanley Engerman, "Emancipation Schemes: Different Ways of Ending Slavery," in Enrico Dal Lago and Constantina Katsari, eds., *Slave Systems: Ancient and Modern* (Cambridge: Cambridge University Press, 2008), 265–82.

44. Rebecca Scott, *Slave Emancipation in Cuba: The Transition to Free Labor* (Princeton: Princeton University Press, 1985), 71–73, 114–15; Drescher, *Abolition,* 346–47.

45. Needell, *Party of Order,* 14–19; Toplin, *Abolition of Brazilian Slavery,* 66.

46. Angela Alonso, "The Theatricalization of Politics: The Brazilian Movement for the Abolition of Slavery," paper presented at "American Counterpoint: New Approaches to Slavery and Abolition in Brazil," a conference of the Gilder Lehrman Center for the Study of Slavery, Resistance, and Abolition, Yale University, October 2010; Celso Castilho, "Performing Abolitionism, Enacting Citizenship: The Social Construction of Political Rights in 1880s Recife, Brazil," *Hispanic American Historical Review* (August, 2013): 377-409; Toplin, *Abolition of Brazilian Slavery,* 204–5; Conrad, *Destruction of Brazilian Slavery,* 242–44.

47. Toplin, *Abolition of Brazilian Slavery,* 216, 238–39; Conrad, *Destruction of Brazilian Slavery,* 245–47. See also Richard Graham, "Causes for the Abolition of Negro Slavery in Brazil: An Interpretive Essay," *Hispanic American Historical Review* 46 (May 1966): 123–37.

48. Drescher, *Abolition,* 370; Schmidt-Nowara, *Slavery, Freedom and Abolition,* 154–55; Don Fehrenbacher, *The Slaveholding Republic: An Account of the United States Government's Relations to Slavery* (New York: Oxford University Press, 2001); Ferrer, *Insurgent Cuba,* chap. 6.

MATTHEW KARP

King Cotton, Emperor Slavery

Antebellum Slaveholders and the World Economy

As they looked out on the wider world in the 1850s, American slaveholding elites felt more confident than ever in their grasp on international power. The recent conquest of Mexico, organized and commanded disproportionately by southerners, expanded their sense of the nation's possible imperial horizons. Across the Atlantic, European revolutions, reactions, and great power wars—breaking a quarter-century of relative stability—enhanced southerners' belief in the superior fortitude of their own social and political systems. And perhaps most of all, spiking global demand for cotton left the South flush with wealth and ecstatic about the dependence of the entire industrializing world on an item that only southern slaves could produce with profit. Even as antislavery voices gained ground within American domestic life, slaveholders could take solace in their growing stature in an international context.

This confidence left a distinctive mark on national politics between the war with Mexico and the Civil War. The South's insistence on the role of slavery in the western territories; its programs for imperial expansion into Latin America; its belief that "King Cotton" alone could ensure the viability of an independent southern Confederacy—historians are of course familiar with all these phenomena, even if they prefer explanations that rely more heavily on southern anxiety than self-assurance. Scholarly discussions of proslavery imperialism or King Cotton ideology, indeed, frequently see them as large but hollow overcompensations, bursts of desperate arrogance that sought, unsuccessfully, to hide the fact of southern weakness. When the slaveholding South's international self-confidence is taken seriously, it is often understood as something that grew out of—and was ultimately defeated by—domestic politics. Would-be southern expansionism in the Caribbean had as much to do with the composition of the U.S. Senate as anything in the Caribbean itself; the rhetoric of King Cotton was directed at wavering northern moderates or constituents at home, not merchants or manufacturers in Europe. What these explanations have in common is their insistence on the ultimate priority of domestic affairs. Whether a psychological projection or a domestic political tactic, the South's external confidence remains a creature of its internal anxieties.[1]

But there is good reason to focus on the South's international position on its own terms, as a number of scholars have lately begun to do.[2] With transatlantic tariffs falling across the late 1840s, the Western world seemed to be moving decisively in the direction of free trade—an implicit acknowledgment of the primacy of slave-grown agricultural products. The "four articles most necessary to modern civilization," as an essayist in *DeBow's Review* put it in 1851—"sugar, coffee, cotton, tobacco"—provided the indispensable fuel that drove the modern commercial and industrial economy. And these staples, southerners insisted with growing persuasiveness, could be cultivated only by enslaved workers.[3]

From the perspective of imperial economics, British emancipation in the West Indies had been a catastrophic failure: sugar and coffee exports dropped precipitously after 1833, and southerners eagerly culled British periodicals for acknowledgments that Africans were, after all, unfit for freedom. More recently, the French and Danish West Indian emancipations of the late 1840s had produced similarly disappointing results. Underneath the veneer of Europe's cultural inclination toward abolitionism, many slaveholders believed, lay a hardheaded appreciation of slavery's merits as an engine of economic production. "[T]he abolition fever has nearly or quite extinguished itself in Europe," declared James Henry Hammond in 1858. Both Great Britain and France now seemed to understand that the "great agricultural staples" could "never be produced as articles of wide extended commerce, except by slave labor."[4] This essay attempts to reconstruct some of the larger presuppositions that underlay southern commentary on the world economy in the 1850s. The growing appeal and sophistication of King Cotton arguments was the most audible consequence of the South's international confidence. An emphasis on cotton alone, however, cannot fully reflect the broad spectrum of proslavery economic thought or capture the certainty with which many southerners believed the Western world would turn back against "failed" antislavery politics.

The 1840s was the decade in which Great Britain embraced the gospel of free trade. In June 1846, Parliament settled years of contentious debate by abolishing the Corn Laws and opening the home market to foreign grains—a major setback for Britain's landed gentry and a major boost to international advocates of open commerce.[5] For years, southern elites had drawn close connections between Atlantic tariff rates and the politics of slavery. British antislavery sentiment itself, John C. Calhoun and others argued in the early 1840s, was the child of colonial mercantilism: by ending black bondage in the Americas, Britain sought to boost the cotton and sugar exports of its East Indian empire.[6] Yet as early as 1845 many in Calhoun's circle saw reasons to believe that this formula might be changing. Prime Minister Robert Peel's budget for that year offered a reduction in a wide range of import duties—including, significantly, a lowering of the tax on sugar and an elimination of the tax on raw cotton.[7] In March, after the inauguration of the Polk administration and the successful annexation of Texas, Calhoun himself referred approvingly to the "movement of England towards free trade" and predicted more tariff reductions and repeals in the future.[8]

Further developments on the other side of the Atlantic seemed to fulfill Calhoun's prediction. When the Whig leader John Russell replaced Peel as prime minister in 1846, one of his first major proposals was the gradual reduction and eventual repeal of the tariff on imported slave-grown sugar.[9] The decade's final set of dominos to fall were the British Navigation Acts. Part of the same notorious parcel of mercantile regulations that had helped trigger the American Revolution, the Acts prohibited the importation of key overseas goods (including sugar and tobacco) to Great Britain in foreign ships. In 1849, after a prolonged and furious debate in Parliament, Russell's government succeeded in abolishing most of the restrictions.[10] By the early 1850s, southerners eagerly identified the spread of free trade as the dominant economic trend in the Western world. The 1853 annual report of Franklin Pierce's treasury secretary, the Kentuckian James Guthrie, exulted in the sheer number of open markets: "The tables accompanying this report exhibit the free lists of England, France, Belgium, Portugal, Brazil, Austria, Spain, Russia, Cuba, the Zoll Verein, Chili, Netherlands, Hans Towns, Norway, Mexico, and Sweden, and mark the progress of free trade among commercial nations." The principle of "[u]nrestrained commerce," Guthrie declared, "has numerous and increasing advocates in this and other commercial countries."[11]

The decline of transatlantic protectionism in the late 1840s, along with a rapid rise in cotton prices—which climbed from under eight cents per pound to more than eleven cents in 1847 alone—left many southern elites, by the end of the decade, richer and more confident about the global marketplace than they had ever been before.[12] But slaveholders cheered the rise of free trade not merely because it lined their own pockets or because it represented progress toward some grand utopia of unfettered commerce. By 1850, the international embrace of open markets pushed southerners to draw significant practical and ideological conclusions about the future trajectory of the Atlantic economy. The decline of tariff protection on both sides of the ocean, many believed, implied that even industrializing societies recognized the primary economic position of a few key agricultural staples. Cotton, sugar, tobacco, rice, and coffee—perhaps more than any other comparable products—dominated international commerce and tilted the world market toward liberal trade agreements. Almost all of these products were grown in the United States, and all of them, of course, were cultivated with the labor of African slaves.[13]

As they digested these insights, a growing number of southern voices began to argue that the international momentum of free trade therefore represented a shift in world opinion—regarding not only agriculture and commerce but also black slavery itself. The British debate over the Sugar Duties was a particularly fruitful source of evidence for this argument. "[T]he recent discussion of the Sugar question" in Parliament, observed an 1846 essay in the *Charleston Evening News,* reflected Britain's dawning awareness that West Indian slave emancipation was "an almost irremediable blunder." The "equalization of the duties between slave grown and free grown sugar," the article continued, represented an admission that vital tropical staples—"the source of much of the civilization, if not refined luxury, of our times"—could be produced only by bound labor. From his post in Berlin, Andrew Jackson Donelson alerted Calhoun to the ongoing "debates in the British Parliament on the slavery question. . . . England's mistake in this respect is reacting powerfully and concurs with other causes to bring upon her a change of commercial policy." By the end of the decade, Alabama judge and future Supreme Court justice John A. Campbell's long examination of the British West Indies in the *Southern Quarterly Review* concluded that the end of the Sugar Duties represented not only the triumph of free trade but the international vindication of African slavery as an economic system.[14]

The emancipation of the French West Indies in 1848 was, in some sense, a significant defeat for southerners freshly optimistic about the position of slavery in the world economy. Yet, in the favorable commercial environment of the early 1850s, it was not long before confident slaveholders transformed even this new rebuff from a potentially dangerous precedent to another data point in the failure of worldwide abolitionism. The influential editor James D. B. DeBow and other writers made the case that the emancipated workers of Martinique and Guadeloupe simply could not compete with "the organized, well-fed and contented labor" in the nearby slave regimes of Cuba and the United States. The inadequacy of free labor, of course, was defined in terms of the production of staple goods: one essayist brandished statistics that showed a 50 percent drop in French West Indian sugar exports from 1847 to 1848. By 1852, Congressman Charles James Faulkner of Virginia summarized a consensus position when he lumped the French in with the wider failure of Caribbean freedom, denouncing the "ruinous emancipation policy which has marked the course of Denmark, England, and France over their West Indian possessions."[15]

Such a wide range of proofs for the failure of emancipation, southerners argued, only strengthened the international economic position of slavery. The liberalization of commerce all across the Atlantic world was more than just a technical adjustment on the part of world markets; it reflected a larger ideological transformation. The political economy of slavery and free trade had defeated the rival model of abolition and mercantilism. "The whole scheme of a monopoly of raw products . . . based on a colonial system," boasted DeBow's *Commercial Review* in 1850, had "failed" abysmally: "Gradually the British commercial policy has accommodated itself to the fact, that the great staples which keep in operation the workshops of England are slave products, and that that condition of their production cannot be changed. She repeals, therefore, her duties on them, removes her discriminations, and throws open her navigation laws to the vessels of the world . . . and her whole colonial policy becomes changed." Great Britain, the anonymous writer predicted, had begun to "prepare the public mind of England for a toleration of slavery, as the best means of ameliorating the condition of the blacks."[16]

Over the course of the 1850s, this conviction only grew stronger among southern elites. The world economy's reliance on slave-grown products, an increasing number of southerners believed, underpinned the political, social and even scientific developments of the era. Whatever Europeans—and northerners, too—pretended to believe about slavery, they could not escape their dependence on it. The onward march of Western civilization, in fact, proceeded atop a foundation of coercive agriculture.

John C. Calhoun had always been more than usually attentive to the international politics of slavery and abolition. In the two years before his death, in 1850, as the dour South Carolinian brooded on the dangerous growth of northern abolitionism and the diminution of southern power within the Union, he found some hope in signs that Great Britain was altering its position in regard to American slavery. "[A] change of sentiment in England," he informed the Senate in 1848, had "diminished her attachment to abolition." Such confidence in the waning of British abolitionism was buoyed, of course, by the triumph of free trade in general and by Parliament's explicit rejection of antislavery sugar discrimination in particular.[17] Yet there were other signs—less concrete but perhaps even more suggestive—that British opinion was shifting. During the sugar debates, observers on both sides of the Atlantic noted the rise of anti-abolitionist invective in the British press. "The question, *Slavery,* begins to be much better understood," reported the English travel author Sarah Myrtton Maury to Calhoun in 1848. "The London Times which is our most influential organ has most emphatically espoused the cause of the West India Proprietors . . . the effect produced by its taunts against the Abolition party have been powerful in their operation upon the public mind."[18]

Across the 1850s, southern periodicals diligently tracked down and reprinted these taunts for a receptive domestic audience. James D. B. DeBow was especially assiduous in this regard: his *Review* and his multivolume encyclopedia,

The Industrial Resources of the Southern and Western States, repeatedly excerpted long anti-abolitionist essays in the London *Times, Blackwood's Magazine,* and other British publications. The African's congenital unsuitability for freedom, the proven economic failure of multiple West Indian emancipations, the retreat of the "rose-water philanthropy" of "Clarkson and Wilberforce"—these were the notes sounded in the British press that appealed most reliably to southern publishers.[19]

To be sure, slaveholding observers could not be certain that Great Britain or Europe as a whole had abandoned abolitionism. In the early 1850s, the runaway success of Harriet Beecher Stowe's *Uncle Tom's Cabin* generated a fresh round of popular antislavery sentiment in Europe. Slaveholders traveling abroad reported witnessing *Uncle Tom*–inspired public speeches, theatrical performances, and even an art exhibition at a gallery in London.[20] Yet often the same southerners who encountered abolitionist sentiment in the Old World were quick to point out that Europeans nevertheless envied the economic progress of the slaveholding states. "I feel it my duty to say that all Europe is against us," noted Randal McGavock in his 1854 travelogue, *A Tennessean Abroad.* "Ignorant of our peculiar institution . . . they . . . say to us that it is a system unworthy of the age." But Europe's high ground on the slavery question, McGavock insisted, was undercut by its virtual confession that colonial emancipation had failed: "Having ruined and rendered bankrupt the citizens of her colonies by the abolition of slavery, they look with jealousy upon the cotton-growing region of our country." Calhoun's Savannah correspondent Jacob C. Levy offered an even more caustic perspective on the structural weakness of European abolitionism: "You have not failed to notice what a large segment in the circle of European & American industry, the Slave labor contributes—how every increase of wealth but stimulates, and as it were holds out a bounty for the products of Slave labor. . . . The very Moralists who denounce slavery almost in the same breath urge the use of its products." The British antislavery movement, he predicted, could not long thrive in a larger commercial environment whose health was so intimately linked to slave-grown staples.[21]

If Europe's cultural attitudes lagged behind economic truth, many politically influential slaveholders across the 1850s believed that the gap would soon close. James Gadsden, the U.S. minister to Mexico, shared his optimism with Secretary of War Jefferson Davis in 1854: "The statesmen of the world," he declared, "are awakening to the great truths which the Harpers and McDuffies of my little State first foreshadowed as to African slavery." The "rabidness" of abolitionist activism, Gadsden argued, reflected the weakness of its international position. James Henry Hammond, characteristically, was even more grandiloquent in his proslavery confidence. "The anti-slavery feeling is running to seed," he pronounced solemnly in 1853. "England, the originator of the system of slavery, and, from selfish and sinister motives, the very head of the crusade for its extirpation, is sick of the heartless struggle. . . . The grand politico-religious fervour is nearly evaporated, and *slavery, this day, stands on a firmer basis than it has ever done*!" The curators of the Royal Academy and the theaters of the West End might still cherish their sentimental assumptions about the forward progress of free labor, Gadsden and Hammond implied, but international men of affairs knew better.[22]

The sturdiest and most familiar foundation for such proslavery confidence, of course, was the global importance of the southern cotton export. Slaveholders in the 1850s seldom passed up an opportunity to sketch the inexorable syllogism of King Cotton: that the American South produced nearly all the world's usable raw cotton; this cotton fueled the industrial development of the North Atlantic; therefore the advanced economies of France, the northern United States, and Great Britain were ruled, in effect, by southern planters. This was the basic logic, and southerners were not short of statistics to hammer home their case. Charts and tables demonstrated, over and over again, Great Britain's great and growing dependence on southern cotton (76 percent of its imports came from the United States); the enormous amount of national resources involved in cotton production (more than $650 million, according to one estimate); and the almost unfathomable number of human beings who derived their support from the cotton industry (more than three million in Europe, said Alexander Stephens).[23]

The conclusions southerners drew from this King Cotton model were no less grandiose than their premises. DeBow's encyclopedia declared that cotton was the "most beneficent product that commerce has ever transported for the comfort of the human family." Never "in the history of the world" was there "an abundant article raised by which the poor and helpless could be clothed on an extensive scale." The "slaveholder of the South," observed an author in the *Southern Quarterly Review,* "is in fact a great instrument in the hands of Providence, to regenerate and improve the world."[24]

While cotton did its part to civilize the planet, it also served to define the South's indispensable role in world affairs. For the "*slave-holding* states of the Union," DeBow continued, "it is the great source of their power and their wealth, and the main security for their peculiar institutions. It is that which gives us our energy and enterprise under a hot climate, and enables us to command the respect of foreign powers." Just as the Egyptian revered the Nile and the Hindu venerated the lotus, he suggested, "let *us* teach our children to hold the cotton plant in one hand, and a sword in the other, ever ready to defend it as the source of commercial power abroad, and through that, of *independence at home.*" The almighty power of King Cotton, in this view, expressed itself on several different levels. It simultaneously gave structure to the world economy, power to the United States in transatlantic geopolitics, and "independence" to the South in American domestic affairs.[25]

This last prong of King Cotton ideology, of course, proved the most immediately influential in both American and world history. The extent to which global cotton triumphalism guided the course of Confederate foreign policy has long been a subject of interest to Civil War historians; more recently, several scholars have emphasized its significance in shaping the decision to secede from the Union itself. Yet it may be that King Cotton, in his antebellum rather than his Civil War regalia, deserves another examination.[26] One traditional understanding of the phenomenon involves the idea that cotton, with its enormous global value, provided essential economic support for the institution of slavery. If slave labor—already politically controversial on both sides of the Atlantic—were not tied to a commercial product of such obvious importance, slaveholders might well succumb to the pressure piled up against them. This is the line of thought DeBow embraced when he declared that cotton was both the "great source" of the South's wealth *and* "the main security for [its] peculiar institutions." The Cincinnati journalist David Christy, whose 1855 book *Cotton Is King* coined the famous phrase, was also quite explicit about the nature of the relationship between cotton and slavery: "KING COTTON cares not whether he employs slaves or freemen. It is the *cotton,* not the *slaves,* upon which his throne is based."[27]

Yet, for many southerners who dabbled in cotton triumphalism, the inverse proposition seemed at least equally true. In early 1854, the South Carolina novelist and *Southern Quarterly Review* editor William Gilmore Simms surveyed a new book by C. Edwards Lester, an antislavery activist who attacked the international abolitionist movement for its economic naiveté and political ineffectiveness. Until abolitionists mounted a challenge to the southern cotton monopoly, Lester argued—by developing a rival source of production in India or elsewhere—their efforts to undo slavery would be hopeless. In its emphasis on the South's position of strength within the global marketplace, Lester's reasoning emerged from many of the same premises that upheld the King Cotton ideology itself. Simms nevertheless flipped this formulation upside down: "'Cotton is the support of negro slavery,' quoth Mr. Lester. It would read more sensibly to say that negro slavery is the soul of cotton. Take away the latter, and you will have but a flemish account of the former, whether in India or America."[28] Cotton's international importance, Simms argued, could be traced back to immutable facts on both its demand *and* its supply side. If it was true that the West's surging desire for cotton imports gave the product its immense value, it was no less true that the only truly successful cotton export model in existence depended on southern slave labor. Lester's hope that Indian railroads would stimulate exports, Simms noted, neglected the fundamental reality of cotton production: "All right but the last, Mr. Lester. Your dream is like all the rest. . . . Negro slavery is established in the equal necessities of the world. . . . A necessity in social and national affairs, is something stronger than a mere truth. It is a law, with a certain vital principle working restlessly within it, which forbids that it should grow obsolete. . . . The nations cannot part with it. It is their life, and the very soul of the policy which saves."[29]

For many southerners, David Christy notwithstanding, King Cotton's throne was propped up entirely by the labor of African slaves.[30] In 1856, an essayist in *DeBow's Review* observed that "it has grown into a maxim, that 'cotton is the king of the [commercial] world.'" Yet "it is equally notorious that cotton cannot, under present circumstances, be raised in quantities sufficient for the demands of civilization, in any other than a southern latitude, or by any other than slave labor." The two facts were undeniable, and inextricable. Without the miraculous system of slave labor, extensive cotton production—and therefore the growth of the world economy itself—would not be possible.[31]

In 1850, speaking on the eternal question of slavery in the territories, Senator Robert M. T. Hunter of Virginia temporarily abandoned the domestic arena and offered his colleagues a global thought experiment: "Suppose that, in 1833, African slavery had been abolished all over the world—in the colonies of France and Spain, in Brazil, in the United States, wherever, in short, it existed what would have been the consequences to mankind? . . . I ask how such a policy would have operated upon the world at large? No cotton! No sugar! But little coffee, and less tobacco! Why, how many people would thus have been stricken rudely and at once from the census of the world?"[32]

Slavery's empire, as Hunter's speech implied, was far larger than the mere kingdom of cotton. Both British abolitionists and northern free-soilers alike, declared the *Charleston Mercury* in 1852, grounded their "fallacious experiments" in a false theory: "It is the assumption that free labor is cheaper and more effective than slave labor." In fact, "the efficient organization" of the slave system explained the striking success of southern cotton planters—and this efficiency was not confined to cotton alone. "This instance of cotton," the *Mercury* continued, "is only [proof] among many that stare every observer in the face, of the superiority of slave labor." The paper's global survey of bound labor found that "the serfs of Russia produce by far the cheapest wheat in Europe," that the slave economy of Brazil had made "enormous advances in competition with a dozen free labor countries" in coffee production, and that "the same may be said of the sugar culture in Cuba."[33]

In one sense, the international arguments of Simms, Hunter, and the *Mercury* only echoed the formative principles of what might be called slavery development economics, as expounded by Thomas Dew and William Harper back in the 1830s. Dew and Harper, like their heirs twenty years later, toasted the economic efficiency of slavery in all staple-producing regions, from Virginia to Brazil, and contrasted the wealth and vitality of slaveholding areas with the poverty and sluggishness of their emancipated neighbors.[34] But by the 1850s the difference was not merely that such international proslavery arguments had a much wider currency among elite southerners themselves. The most important change, as some saw it, was that wider world was beginning to recognize this principle for the first time. In the eyes of these southerners, Europeans were not merely turning away from the failure of emancipation; they were acknowledging the failure of free labor itself. Beyond mere anti-abolitionism, they contended, the evolution of political economy had arrived at an active proslavery position.[35]

The Virginia social theorist George Fitzhugh was an especially conscientious and enthusiastic reporter of proslavery trends in European political economic thought. His 1854 treatise *Sociology for the South* remarked hopefully that "[s]o far as the slaves are concerned, opinion is fast changing. . . ." As Europeans began to " look more closely at what the slaveholders have been doing since our Revolution, they find that they have been exceeded in skill, enterprise and industry, by no people under the sun." The vast hemispheric wilderness from "the Alleghany to the La Platte," Fitzhugh concluded, had been domesticated and enriched by slave labor; the world could not long resist the conclusion that bondage was a superior system of economic organization. As the decade progressed, Fitzhugh's metaphor shifted, but his confidence remained: he identified "a counter current, or slavery principle," which would soon sweep across Europe. His 1856 book, *Cannibals All!*, contained the most comprehensive evidence of British proslavery yet. Citing the Edinburgh *Review*, the London *Globe*, and the work of the Scottish economist John Ramsay McCulloch, Fitzhugh argued that political economy had already begun to trump cultural prejudice. The collapse of the free West Indies, he argued, along with the continued prosperity of slave regimes in Cuba and Brazil, had convinced the leading British economic thinkers to look favorably on the merits of bound labor.[36]

Of course, southerners were aware that not all European thinkers had abandoned the free-labor critique of slavery as an inefficient economic system. In an 1856 essay for the *Southern Quarterly Review*, the Virginia intellectual George Frederick Holmes reviewed a large batch of European and American works that treated the economics of slavery, including John Stuart Mill's *Principles of Political Economy*. Unlike DeBow and others, he was quite willing to concede the narrow point that free labor was often cheaper than slave labor. Noting that Mill, the French professor Robert du Var, and other political economists continued to deny the efficiency of slave labor, Holmes responded that there were far higher moral and social goals than the optimal accumulation of wealth. Slavery's political strengths as a stabilizing, patriarchal system—one that allowed the South to avoid mass poverty, mob rule, and other "social leprosies"—far outweighed its economic defects. The efficiency of free labor only proved its superior capacity for exploitation and cruelty.[37]

This kind of lofty, conservative paternalism, of course, was a familiar weapon in the proslavery arsenal. "Slavery is a blessing to the negro," Fitzhugh himself put it, but "it is too costly, too humane, and too merciful for France, England, or New England." For many years, scholarly treatments of proslavery discourse centered on such moralistic critiques of the northern free-labor system, but the defense of slavery was in fact a highly elastic and heterogeneous enterprise.[38] For every Holmes who surrendered the economic field to free labor, there was a DeBow on hand to rejoin the battle. Just months after Holmes's essay appeared, the South Carolina essayist Louisa S. McCord flooded the pages of DeBow's magazine with an extended critique of the Virginian's argument. Slavery, she argued, could not turn its back on political economy; indeed, "if free labor is cheaper and more productive than slave labor, slavery is a wrong." Only a truly scientific defense of slavery would suffice, and political economy, being "the science of wealth," was the appropriate tool. Fortunately, this was a comparatively easy task, for slavery's contributions to global wealth were immeasurable: "the wonderful development of this western continent effected only through and by means of slavery—her immense produce scattered all over our globe, carrying food and clothing to the hungry and the destitute; her cotton and sugar sustaining not only herself but the might of Europe's most powerful nations." Slavery, McCord concluded, "which is the negro's protection, is the world's wealth."[39]

Holmes, too, had erred badly when he let John Stuart Mill's "vulgar prejudice" against slavery stand in for all of European political economic wisdom. In fact, "*free trade,* not *free labor*" was the guiding principle of contemporary commercial wisdom. Leading economic lights on both sides of the Atlantic, after all, had rejected the dubious "experiments" of "modern philanthropists." Like Fitzhugh, McCord espied a new phenomenon at work in Europe. "[T]he true principles of Political Economy," she declared, have "carried the day *in favor of slavery,*" in spite of the "strongest prejudice on the part of those who were thus obliged to acknowledge the folly of their own previous action." She did not hesitate to offer proofs of this surging proslavery spirit: they came in the form of excerpts from the Sugar Duties debate in the British Parliament; Gustave du Molinari's recent article on "Esclavage" in a new two-volume *Dictionnaire d[e l]'économie politique,* published in Paris; and an "Address to the People of America from the Citizens of Manchester," which had circulated widely in Britain and the United States. For McCord and other influential thinkers, the South's overall economic position did not depend exclusively on the specific market for raw cotton. It rested, rather, on the much firmer foundations of modern commercial and agricultural science—foundations that upheld not only southern cotton but Cuban sugar, Brazilian coffee, and slave-based staple cultivation across the Atlantic World.[40]

In 1854, an anonymous author in the *Southern Literary Messenger* penned an extensive rebuttal to Charles Sumner's widely reprinted speech on the Kansas-Nebraska Act. Sumner had surveyed the globe and found that slave labor was everywhere confined and retreating: "in effeminate India," he declared, "slavery has been condemned"; "in Constantinople . . . the Ottoman Sultan has fastened upon it the stigma of disapprobation"; even in "despotic Russia," slaves "are never allowed to travel with the flag . . . but carefully restricted by positive prohibition." Trumpeting this "Wilmot Proviso of Russia" and celebrating the global movement toward "the Equality of Men," Sumner noted that only the United States remained tenaciously committed to its slave institutions: "alone in the company of nations does our country assume this hateful championship."[41]

The *Messenger* author, predictably, took issue with the entire premise of Sumner's catalogue. "The Russian, the Turk, the Moor, and the Algerine! Mild, estimable, tender-hearted people, how can we resist the contagion of their example!" There was more than a tinge of white supremacy in the *Messenger*'s dismissal of Sumner's "tawny Wilberforces and saffron Howards," but the rebuttal did not rest on racist derision alone. Rather than examining the supposed philanthropy of worn-out empires on the margins of the modern world, the *Messenger* recommended turning to the recent activity of the "civilized and christian nations." And by this standard, it was racialized slavery, not the "Equality of Men," that was truly on the march.

Great Britain, the writer granted, "rightfully takes rank among the first nations of the earth." And Britain "bitterly repented the emancipation of the negroes in Jamaica," as "[e]ven Blackwood and the London Times confess." Now, "in view of all these facts, she is seeking to repair her own errors by the re-institution of slavery in Jamaica under another designation, and by the silent subjugation of those parts of Africa adapted to the production of the great staples upon which her commerce rests." France, too, "in pursuance of the same policy, is directing her energies to tropical Africa, and preparing for extensive colonization, cultivation and commerce with that fruitful region."[42]

Slavery, then, was not in retreat—in fact, it was advancing all across the Atlantic world, from the Windward Passage to the Cape of Good Hope. According to some observers, it was even tightening its grip on colonial India and Java. By expanding the definition of bondage to include coolie and apprentice labor—and, indeed, Europe's imperial activity in Asia and Africa—slaveholders rejected Sumner's claim that the United States stood alone in its championship of servitude.[43] "Slavery," intoned the *Messenger*, "is now, and must be for years to come, an inexorable necessity." It was necessary not merely to organize southern society, to protect slaveholders' property, or to provide a conservative bulwark against the mad energies of the epoch. It was also the necessary product of modernity—an irresistible, international force that was both a lead driver and an inevitable passenger in the progressive van of civilization.

For all of this wide-ranging confidence, of course, southern elites could not completely banish their own fears about the future of slavery in a world and a nation increasingly divided between free and bound labor. And their vision of an expanding global marketplace regulated by a heroic class of slaveholders did not, in fact, closely resemble the actual course of international economic development in the decades to come. Yet the slaveholding view of the midcentury world economy left its own powerful imprint on history. The elite movement for southern secession in 1860 and 1861, after all, did not emerge purely from a climate of fear or weakness. Slaveholders may have been pushed out of the Union by domestic political anxiety, but they were also pulled into the Confederacy by their own ravenous international ambition. In their embrace of free-trade economics, their celebration of Europe's turn against abolitionism, and their enthusiasm for the global future of slavery, southerners helped convince themselves that their society, grounded in black bondage, could survive on its own in the world. The tangible economic clout of King Cotton surely contributed to this confidence, but, in some ways, the larger ideological power of Emperor Slavery made the entire thought process possible.

NOTES

1. For larger narratives of the era that explain southern imperialism as a phenomenon that grew primarily out of domestic politics, see David Potter, *The Impending Crisis, 1848–1861* (New York: Harper and Row, 1976), 177–98; James M. McPherson, *Battle Cry of the Republic: The Civil War Era* (New York: Oxford University Press, 1988), 91–116; John McCardell, *The Idea of a Southern Nation: Southern Nationalists and Southern Nationalism, 1830–1860* (New York: Norton, 1979), 227–76. Focused analytical treatments of proslavery imperial activity that pay more attention to external issues but still grant interpretive priority to internal politics include Robert E. May, *The Southern Dream of a Caribbean Empire, 1854–1861* (Baton Rouge: Louisiana State University Press, 1973); William W. Freehling, "The Complex Case of Slaveholder Expansionism," in Freehling, *Reintegration of American History: Slavery and the Civil War* (New York: Oxford University Press, 1994), 158–75; C. Stanley Urban, "The Ideology of Southern Imperialism: New Orleans and the Caribbean, 1845–1860," *Louisiana Historical Quarterly* 39 (Winter 1956): 48–73.

2. Some of the most important examples include the essays in L. Diane Barnes, Brian Schoen, and Frank Towers, eds., *The Old South's Modern Worlds: Slavery, Region, and Nation in the Age of Progress* (New York: Oxford University Press, 2011); Brian Schoen, *The Fragile Fabric of Union: Cotton, Federal Politics and the Global Origins of the Civil War* (Baltimore: The Johns Hopkins University Press, 2009); Edward Rugemer, *The Problem of Emancipation: The Caribbean Roots of the American Civil War* (Baton Rouge: Louisiana State University Press, 2008); Gerald Horne, *The Deepest South: The*

United States, Brazil, and the African Slave Trade (New York: New York University Press, 2007); Matthew Pratt Guterl, *American Mediterranean: Southern Slaveholders in the Age of Emancipation* (Cambridge, Mass.: Harvard University Press, 2008); Steven Heath Mitton, "The Free World Confronted: The Problem of Slavery and Progress in American Foreign Relations, 1833–1844," Ph.D. diss., Louisiana State University, 2005.

3. Anonymous [Thomas P. Kettell], "The Future of the South," *DeBow's Review,* February 1851, 137. This proslavery perspective on the international vitality of bound-labor products finds an echo in contemporary scholarship on Atlantic slave economies in the nineteenth century. Southern readers of *DeBow's Review* would not have been surprised by the notion of a "second slavery," peaking between 1830 and 1860, in which the production of slave goods (especially American cotton, Cuban sugar, and Brazilian coffee) rose to meet the spiking demand in the North Atlantic economies while at the same time incorporating and often innovating industrial practices of its own. See, in particular, Dale W. Tomich, *Through the Prism of Slavery: Labor, Capital, and World Economy* (Lanham, Md.: Rowan and Littlefield, 2004), 56–71; Anthony E. Kaye, "The Second Slavery: Modernity in the Nineteenth-Century South and the Atlantic World," *Journal of Southern History* 75 (August 2009): 627–50; Daniel B. Rood, "Plantation Technocrats: A Social History of Knowledge in the Slaveholding Atlantic World, 1830–1865," Ph.D. diss., University of California, Irvine, 2010. On the fundamentally symbiotic relationship between capitalism and slavery in the nineteenth-century Atlantic World, see Walter Johnson, "The Pedestal and the Veil: Rethinking the Capitalism/Slavery Question," *Journal of the Early Republic* 24 (Summer 2004): 299–308.

4. James Henry Hammond, speech at Barnwell Court House, October 29, 1858, in Clyde N. Wilson, ed., *Selections from the Letters and Speeches of the Hon. James H. Hammond, of South Carolina* (Spartanburg, S.C.: Reprint Company, 1978 [1866]), 347–48.

5. On the Corn Laws and the 1840s as a turning point in British commercial policy, see Paul Bairoch, "European Trade Policy 1815–1914," in Peter Mathias and Sidney Pollard, eds., *Cambridge Economic History of Europe* (New York: Cambridge University Press, 1989), 8: 1–160.

6. See, for instance, John C. Calhoun to Duff Green, April 2, 1842, in Clyde N. Wilson et al., eds., *The Papers of John C. Calhoun* (Columbia: University of South Carolina Press, 1959–2003), 16: 209; Anonymous, "East India Cotton," *Southern Quarterly Review* (April 1842): 446–92; Rugemer, *Problem of Emancipation,* 204–8.

7. Peel's 1845 tariff cuts built on the significant reductions in his 1842 budget. Eric Evans, *Sir Robert Peel: Statesmanship, Power, and Party* (New York: Routledge, 1991), 56–58.

8. Calhoun to Robert M. T. Hunter, March 26, 1845; Calhoun to Abbott Lawrence, May 15, 1845, in *Papers of Calhoun,* 21: 447–50, 550. On the long-standing importance of free-trade ideology to Calhoun's political worldview, see Bruno Gujer, "Free Trade and Slavery: Calhoun's Defense of Southern Interests against British Interference, 1811–1848," Ph.D. diss., University of Zurich, 1971, 91–121. On the confidence that northern and southern Democrats alike placed in global free trade and the global commercial power of the United States in the late 1840s, see Thomas R. Hietala, *Manifest Design: American Exceptionalism and Empire,* rev. ed. (Ithaca: Cornell University Press, 2003), 55–94.

9. On the British debate over the sugar duties in the late 1840s, which pitted free traders against an unlikely coalition of abolitionists and West India planters, see Seymour Drescher, *The Mighty Experiment: Free Labor versus Slavery in British Emancipation* (New York: Oxford University Press, 2002), 176–88 Richard Huzzey, "Free Trade, Free Labour and Slave Sugar in Victorian Britain," *Historical Journal*, 53 (2010), 359-79; C. Duncan Rice, "'Humanity Sold for Sugar!' The British Abolitionist Response to Free Trade in Slave-Grown Sugar," *Historical Journal* 13 (September 1970): 402–18. On some southerners' belief that the collective reduction in tariffs "marked an epochal moment in world history," see Schoen, *Fragile Fabric of Union*, 190–91.

10. On the British debate regarding the Navigation Acts, see J. H. Clapham, "The Last Years of the Navigation Acts," *English Historical Review* 25 (July 1910): 480–501, and the same article continued, *English Historical Review* 25 (October 1910): 687–707. For a favorable southern response to Russell's free trade initiatives, see "D. J. M." [David James McCord], Review of *The Anatomy of the Navigation Acts, Southern Quarterly Review* (January 1850): 417.

11. "Report of the Secretary of the Treasury," December 6, 1853, *Congressional Globe*, 33rd Cong., 1st Sess., App. 2. Guthrie's report was quoted approvingly in *DeBow's Review*, February 1854, 176. On the broader spread of free trade in continental Europe after the repeal of the British Corn Laws, see Bairoch, "European Trade Policy," 23–36; C. P. Kindleberger, "The Rise of Free Trade in Western Europe, 1820–1875," *Journal of Economic History* 35 (March 1975): 20–55.

12. For more expressions of the South's international confidence—economic, strategic, ideological—grounded in European free trade reforms, see *Milledgeville* [Ga.] *Federal Union*, March 3, 1846; William Henry Trescot, *A Few Thoughts on the Foreign Policy of the United States* (Charleston: John Russell, 1849), 13–14.

13. Different kinds of southern planters, to be sure, held different kinds of views about both international trade and U.S. commercial policy—cotton planters supported free trade most vigorously, while sugar and tobacco planters were sometimes drawn to protective tariffs. See Brian Schoen, "The Burdens and Opportunities of Independence: The Political Economies of the Planter Class," in Barnes, Schoen, and Towers, eds., *The Old South's Modern Worlds*, 66–84. For all their disagreements about American tariffs, however, the politicians and intellectuals who represented cotton, tobacco, and sugar barons in the 1850s tended to agree that the collapse of *overseas* duties reflected the potency of slave-grown staples.

14. *Charleston Evening News* article reprinted in the *Milledgeville Federal Union*, September 8, 1846; Andrew Jackson Donelson to Calhoun, March 3, 1848, in Wilson et al., *Papers of John C. Calhoun*, 25: 222; "'J.A.C.'" [John A. Campbell], "The British West Indies Islands," *Southern Quarterly Review* (January 1850): 342–77. On Campbell's essay, see Rugemer, *Problem of Emancipation*, 265–66; on the Sugar Duties and the British West Indies, see Thomas C. Holt, *The Problem of Freedom: Race, Labor and Politics in Jamaica and Britain, 1832–1938* (Baltimore: The Johns Hopkins University Press, 1992), 117–25.

15. [James D. B. DeBow], "The West India Islands," *The Commercial Review of the South and West*, May/June 1848, 472–74; "C," "The French Republic," *Southern Quarterly*

Review (July 1848): 233–35; Thomas P. Kettell, "The Future of the South," *DeBow's Review*, February 1851, 132–36; Charles James Faulkner, speech at public dinner, December 16, 1852, Faulkner Family Papers, Box 70, Virginia Historical Society.

16. Anonymous, "Stability of the Union," *Commercial Review of the South and West*, April 1850, 354–56. John Majewski has called attention to the distinctive way in which proslavery advocates understood the structure of world trade. Although they sometimes stood behind the classic free-trade argument "that all nations would benefit from open commerce," slaveholding leaders frequently imagined global trade as "a way in which one nation imposed its will on another." Indeed, the "economic blackmail" of the King Cotton worldview "was at odds with the cosmopolitan openness of free trade doctrines." John Majewski, *Modernizing a Slave Economy* (Chapel Hill: University of North Carolina Press, 2009), 118–19. But, for all the coercive elements of this vision of "free" trade, southern elites nevertheless celebrated the rise of open markets as a vindication of their own slave system.

17. *Congressional Globe*, 30th Cong., 1st Sess., App. 617 (May 10, 1848). See also Gujer, "Free Trade and Slavery," 313–17.

18. Sarah Myrtton Maury to Calhoun, August 15, 1848, Wilson et al., eds., *Papers of John C. Calhoun*, 26: 4. On the negative evolution of British attitudes toward West Indian emancipation in the years between 1833 and 1865, see Holt, *Problem of Freedom*, 278–309; Drescher, *The Mighty Experiment*, 158–230.

19. See, for instance, Anonymous, "A Few Thoughts on Slavery," *Southern Literary Messenger*, April 1854, 203; *Charleston Mercury*, October 24, 1854. DeBow, however, assembled by far the most abundant store of favorable British comments about slavery. During one stretch in 1857, four consecutive issues of *DeBow's Review* featured anti-abolitionist quotations from the London *Times*: see Anonymous, "English Opinions, Cotton, Slave Trade, Etc," *DeBow's Review*, September 1857, 282–84; George Fitzhugh, "Southern Thought," *DeBow's Review*, October 1857, 337 (quotation); P. A. Morse, "Southern Slavery and the Cotton Trade," *DeBow's Review*, November 1857, 480–82; George Fitzhugh, "Wealth of the North and the South," *DeBow's Review*, December 1857, 595. On DeBow and his *Review*, which according to Robert F. Durden achieved "by far the largest circulation of any southern magazine," see Robert F. Durden, "J.D.B. DeBow: Convolutions of a Slavery Expansionist," *Journal of Southern History* 17 (November 1951): 441–61; Ottis Clark Skipper, *J.D.B. DeBow, Magazinist of the Old South* (Athens: University of Georgia Press, 1958); Eric H. Walther, *The Fire-Eaters* (Baton Rouge: Louisiana State University Press, 1992), 195–227.

20. William Henry Trescot attended an *Uncle Tom* stage show in London; Henry Wise's son Obadiah saw paintings based on *Uncle Tom* at "the Royal Gallery" (presumably the Royal Academy). See David Moltke-Hansen, "A Beaufort Planter's Rhetorical World: The Contexts and Contents of William Henry Trescot's Orations," *Proceedings of the South Carolina Historical Association* (1981): 123, 130; Obadiah Jennings Wise to Henry Wise, August 21, 1853, Henry A. Wise Correspondence, Wise Family Papers, Virginia Historical Society. On the popularity of *Uncle Tom's Cabin* in Europe, see Stephen A. Hirsch, "Uncle Tomitudes: The Popular Reaction to *Uncle Tom's Cabin*," *Studies in the American Renaissance* (1978): 303–30; on the continuing potency of cultural

anti-slavery in post-emancipation Britain, see Richard Huzzey, *Freedom Burning: Anti-Slavery and Empire in Victorian Britain* (Ithaca and London: Cornell University Press, 2012), 21-39.

21. Randal William McGavock, *A Tennessean Abroad; or, Letters from Europe, Africa, and Asia* (New York: J. S. Redfield, 1854), 214; Jacob C. Levy to Calhoun, January 29, 1849, in Wilson et al., eds., *Papers of John C. Calhoun,* 26: 251. For useful discussions of elite southern travelers abroad and their varying opinions on Old World labor systems, see Elizabeth Fox-Genovese and Eugene Genovese, *Slavery in White and Black: Class and Race in the Southern Slaveholders' New World Order* (New York: Cambridge University Press, 2008), 121–42; Michael O'Brien, *Conjectures of Order: Intellectual Life and the American South, 1810–1860* (Chapel Hill and London: University of North Carolina Press, 2004), 90–213.

22. James Gadsden to Jefferson Davis, July 19, 1854, in James T. McIntosh et al., eds., *The Papers of Jefferson Davis* (Baton Rouge and London: University of Louisiana Press, 1985), 5: 78–80; "H" [James Henry Hammond], "Maury on South America and Amazonia," *Southern Quarterly Review* (February 1853): 445–47.

23. For the 76 percent estimate, see Anonymous, "The Cotton Trade of Great Britain," *DeBow's Review,* May 1855, 653; for $650 million, see Anonymous, "The Growth and Consumption of Cotton," *Southern Quarterly Review* (January 1848): 121–23; for three million people, see Alexander Stephens, "Speech in Reply to Mr. Campbell, of Ohio," January 15, 1855, in Henry Cleveland, *Alexander Stephens, in Public and Private, with Letters and Speeches, before, during, and since the War* (Philadelphia: National Publishing Co., 1866), 458.

24. James D. B. DeBow, *The Industrial Resources, etc., of the Southern and Western States . . .* (New Orleans: Pudney and Russell, 1852–53), 1: 174–78; Anonymous, "The Growth and Consumption of Cotton," *Southern Quarterly Review* (January 1848): 103–4.

25. DeBow, *Industrial Resources,* 1: 178.

26. In truth, even the privileged position of cotton in the world economy did not justify the arrogance of King Cotton diplomacy, as Confederates learned to their chagrin during the Civil War. Yet the tendency to view cotton triumphalism backward, from the perspective of the 1860s, obscures its centrality to antebellum politics. On cotton, Confederate diplomacy, and Anglo-American relations during the war, see Frank Owsley, *King Cotton Diplomacy* (Chicago and London: University of Chicago Press, 1959 [1931]); Henry Blumenthal, "Confederate Diplomacy: Popular Notions and International Realities," *Journal of Southern History* 32 (May 1966): 151–71; Richard J. Blackett, *Divided Hearts: Britain and the American Civil War* (Baton Rouge: Louisiana State University Press, 2001). On the relationship linking cotton, slavery, and secession, see Schoen, *Fragile Fabric of Union,* 237–59; Nicholas Onuf and Peter Onuf, *Nations, Markets, and War: Modern History and the American Civil War* (Charlottesville and London: University of Virginia Press, 2006), 308–42.

27. DeBow, *Industrial Resources,* 1: 178; David Christy, *Cotton Is King: Or, Slavery in Light of Political Economy,* reprinted in E. N. Elliott, ed., *Cotton Is King, and Proslavery Arguments . . .* (Augusta, Ga.: Pritchard, Abbott and Loomis, 1860), 216.

28. W. G. Simms, "Literary Woolgatherings," *Southern Quarterly Review* (January 1854): 193, 200–203.

29. Simms, "Literary Woolgatherings," 204.

30. The notion that slavery, not cotton, was the truer potentate was not uncommon amid late-antebellum and secessionist rhetoric. As one South Carolina politician avowed in 1860, "Slavery is our king—slavery is our truth—slavery is our divine right." See Manisha Sinha, *The Counterrevolution of Slavery: Politics and Ideology in Antebellum South Carolina* (Chapel Hill: University of North Carolina Press, 2000), 220. Yet most historical discussions of "King Slavery," such as they are, have understood the idea—in contrast to King Cotton—to refer to bondage's central place in southern domestic society. But, of course, slavery, like cotton, possessed an international dominion.

31. Anonymous, "The Black Race in North America, No. III," *DeBow's Review,* March 1856, 305. There were many monarchs in the boosterish rhetorical world of antebellum periodicals: the motto of DeBow's own magazine read, "Commerce is King." But international commerce itself, DeBow and other proslavery leaders believed, could not exist without the agricultural produce of slave labor. See also Walther, *Fire-Eaters,* 199–202.

32. Robert M. T. Hunter, speech in Congress, March 25, 1850, *Congressional Globe,* 31st Cong., 1st Sess., 381. DeBow reprinted Hunter's speech eight years later, calling it "the most thorough vindication of negro slavery ever produced in any deliberative body." "Mr. Hunter on the English Negro Apprentice Trade," *DeBow's Review,* June 1858, 492–502.

33. *Charleston Mercury,* August 25, 1852. For a historical and historiographical discussion of these collective advances in mid-nineteenth-century slave-based agriculture, see Kaye, "The Second Slavery," 631–42.

34. Thomas Roderick Dew, "Professor Dew on Slavery," in *The Proslavery Argument; as Maintained by the Most Distinguished Writers of the Southern States* (Charleston: Walker, Richards, 1852), 485–88; William Harper, "Memoir on Slavery," *Southern Literary Journal and Magazine of the Arts* 3 (January 1838): 241. On Dew, Harper, and southern interest in other slave societies throughout history, see Eugene Genovese and Elizabeth Fox-Genovese, *The Mind of the Master Class: History and Faith in the Southern Slaveholders' Worldview* (New York: Cambridge University Press, 2005), 201–24; O'Brien, *Conjectures of Order,* 606–21, 942–53; Schoen, *Fragile Fabric of Union,* 163–68; Christa Dierksheide and Peter Onuf, "Slaveholding Nation, Slaveholding Civilization," in William J. Cooper and John M. McCardell, eds., *In the Cause of Liberty: How the Civil War Redefined American Ideals* (Baton Rouge: Louisiana State University Press, 2009), 21–23.

35. This does not mean, of course, that southern thinkers believed Europeans would or should commence enslaving their white workers. All but the most zealous proslavery advocates confined their belief in the superior efficiency of bondage to agricultural regions with warm climates and black workers: see, for instance, James Oakes, "The Peculiar Fate of the Bourgeois Critique of Slavery," in Winthrop D. Jordan, ed., *Slavery and the American South* (Jackson: University Press of Mississippi, 2003), 29–48.

Yet Oakes and other domestically focused scholars have largely neglected the confident proslavery view that the products of these warm-weather, black-worker areas all across the Americas occupied a central place in the world economy.

36. George Fitzhugh, *Sociology for the South; or the Failure of Free Society* (Richmond: A. Morris, 1854), 257–61; Fitzhugh, "The Counter Current, or Slavery Principle," *DeBow's Review* July 1856, 90–95; Fitzhugh, *Cannibals All! Or Slaves Without Masters* (Cambridge, Mass.: Belknap, 1960 [1856]), 162, 184–87.

37. George Frederick Holmes, "Slavery and Freedom," *Southern Quarterly Review* (April 1856): 62–95.

38. Fitzhugh, *Sociology of the South,* 253. On the elasticity of proslavery, see Schoen, *Fragile Fabric of Union,* 161. Fitzhugh himself provides a powerful example of this elasticity—he cheerfully embraced slavery as both a paternalistic social institution, in opposition to the abuses of free labor capitalism, *and,* in the right circumstances, a powerfully amoral engine for the generation of raw wealth. "[C]otton, rice, sugar, coffee, tobacco, and other products of slave labor," Fitzhugh boasted, have become "necessaries of life" in the Western world. If slavery were eliminated, Europe and the North would "starve"; conversely, if it were extended, the global economy would flourish. "If all South America, Mexico, the West Indies, and our Union south of Mason and Dixon's line, of the Ohio and Missouri, were slaveholding, slave products would be abundant and cheap in free society: and their market for their merchandise, manufactures, commerce, &c illimitable." Fitzhugh, *Cannibals All!,* 202. For an interesting discussion of Fitzhugh as a "bourgeois thinker" who saw slavery as part of a productive, progressive world order, see O'Brien, *Conjectures of Order,* 972–92.

39. McCord's essay, "Slavery and Political Economy," appeared in consecutive issues: *DeBow's Review,* October 1856, 331–49; *DeBow's Review,* November 1856, 443–67. The entire piece is reproduced in full in Richard C. Lounsbury, ed., *Louisa S. McCord: Political and Social Essays* (Charlottesville and London: University of Virginia Press, 1995), 422–69. For the argument that Britain's political leadership did not in fact abandon their faith in free labor, see Huzzey, *Freedom Burning,* 126-31.

40. McCord, "Slavery and Political Economy," in Lounsbury, ed., *McCord: Essays,* 427, 431, 464–69. On McCord's view of slavery as the economic engine of civilization and for a brief account of her exchange with Holmes, see Robert Bonner, *Mastering America: Southern Slaveholders and the Crisis of American Nationhood* (New York: Cambridge University Press, 2009), 106–13. On southern eagerness to refute sentimental British abolitionism with evidence generated by "the scientific method," see Matthew Mason, "A World Safe for Modernity: Antebellum Southern Proslavery Intellectuals Confront Great Britain," in Barnes, Schoen, and Towers, eds., *The Old South's Modern Worlds,* 47–65.

41. Charles Sumner, speech in Senate, February 21, 1854, reprinted as *The Landmark of Freedom: Hon. Charles Sumner against the Repeal of the Missouri Prohibition of Slavery North of 36° 30* (Boston: John P. Jewett, 1854), 12–13.

42. Anonymous, "A Few Thoughts on Slavery," *Southern Literary Messenger,* April 1854, 193–206.

43. The British economist John Ramsey McCulloch, whose work was cited frequently by George Fitzhugh in both *Sociology for the South* and *Cannibals All!*, claimed in 1850 that "Slave and compulsory labor . . . is indispensable to the production of sugar. . . . In Brazil and Cuba, the planters are furnished with slave labor, and in Java the population, though not enslaved, is subjected to compulsory service." McCulloch, *Dictionary, Practical, Theoretical, and Historical, of Commerce and Commercial Navigation* (London: Longman, Brown, Green, and Longmans, 1850), 1249–51. On the active debate in Britain on the moral and economic relationship between slavery and other "coercive relations" in Asia, Africa, and the Americas, see Drescher, *Mighty Experiment*, 179–237.

HUGH DUBRULLE

"If it is still impossible . . . to advocate slavery . . . it has . . . become a habit persistently to write down freedom"

Britain, the Civil War, and Race

"It is a remarkable fact to reflect upon that we have had the Negro so long before us now, and yet that there is so little agreement as yet upon his intellectual character and capabilities—upon what can ultimately be made of him. The phenomenon is before us, but is not yet explained."

London *Times*, September 5, 1863, p. 8

Perhaps the best measure of changing transatlantic attitudes toward race during the mid-nineteenth century consists of a comparison of the ideas expressed by Fanny Kemble, the prominent British actress, and her daughter, Fan Butler. In December 1838, Fanny Kemble arrived on Butler Island, Georgia, with her husband, Pierce Butler, one of the state's greatest slave owners. Butler and others had led her to believe that his Georgia estates possessed a reputation for enlightened management.[1] Kemble had left the family residence in Philadelphia "prepared to find many mitigations in the practice to the general injustice and cruelty of the system—much kindness on the part of the masters, much content on that of the slaves."[2] Nonetheless, she headed South "prejudiced against slavery," for, as "an Englishwoman . . . the absence of such prejudices would be disgraceful."[3] Kemble believed that the shortcomings of African Americans were caused by their circumstances, not by their race.[4] Anticipating that her time in the South would constitute a test of her principles, she kept a travelogue in the form of letters to Elizabeth Sedgwick (sister-in-law of the novelist Catharine Sedgwick), her intimate abolitionist friend. Kemble would eventually publish these letters in *Journal of a Residence on a Georgian Plantation in 1838–1839* (1863), an extraordinary book that provided far more of an insider's view of slavery than any other work by an antebellum British visitor.

What Kemble saw first on Butler Island and then at Hampton Point on St. Simon's Island only confirmed her views; slavery, not race, accounted for the shortcomings of black slaves.[5] Indeed, one of the main themes of her journal was that the "detestable qualities, which I constantly hear attributed to them [slaves] as innate and inherent in their race, appear to me the direct result of their condition."[6] Although she did not shy away from describing the physical hardships of slavery, it was the moral degradation of the institution that appalled her.[7] Realizing that she was implicated in the slave system, she could not view it as a disinterested spectator. As she explained, "with shame and grief of heart I say it, by their unpaid labor I live—their nakedness clothes me, and their heavy toil maintains me in luxurious idleness."[8] Kemble attempted to reform practices at the estates, but her husband refused to countenance her projects. She drew parallels between herself and the slaves; both were subject to the same master who was unwilling to ameliorate the wretchedness that surrounded them. After Butler refused to accept any more petitions from slaves, Kemble wept with frustration "for them, for myself, for US."[9]

The visit to Georgia dealt a fatal wound to her already troubled marriage.[10] Upon their return to Philadelphia in May 1839, Kemble threatened to leave Butler if he did not cease living upon the labor of slaves. Butler refused, and the marriage staggered onward for several more tempestuous years. In 1845, however, fatigued by her "great energy of will" and "decided preference for her own judgment and opinions," both of which were compounded by her vision of marriage as a "companionship on equal terms," Butler finally ejected her from the household.[11] Four years later, a Philadelphia court granted him a divorce.

In March 1866, Butler and one of his daughters by Kemble, Fan, headed back to his Georgia estates to repair his fortunes. These properties had fallen into decay under federal occupation, but many of his former slaves—now freedmen—had wandered back to the Sea Islands looking for work. Fan became Butler's indispensable helpmate until his death, in 1867, when she took over management of his Sea Island farms. Like her mother, Fan eventually published an account of her experience, *Ten Years on a Georgia Plantation since the War* (1883), based mainly on contemporary letters that sought to serve as an antidote to her mother's account.

For almost a decade, Fan waged an unremitting struggle against flood, drought, labor troubles, lack of capital, armyworm, fluctuating rice prices, and an uncertain political situation to save her patrimony and livelihood. In the end, the struggle proved too much for her, and in 1876, she and her husband, James Leigh, an English clergymen, abandoned the properties, left their oversight to an agent, and moved to Britain. In retrospect, Fan partly blamed her black laborers for her failure. Initially, she had sought to perpetuate the indulgent paternalism that she believed traditionally characterized the Butler estates. Such a policy not only served as a kind of tribute to her father but also accorded with her view (based on "hard ethnological facts") of blacks as "children" by "nature and character."[12] Yet these views became unsustainable in the long run as it became clear that her workforce had taken advantage of her paternalism to gain the upper hand in a test of wills.[13] Frustrations with her freedmen led Fan to yearn for greater authority over her workforce. She eventually inclined toward a defense of slavery stripped of sentimentality. She confessed that she was "utterly unable to understand them [her black workers], and what God's will is concerning them, unless He intended they should be slaves."[14]

As one observer who knew both women commented, Kemble believed slavery accounted for all the South's problems, while Fan thought blacks were responsible for the region's difficulties.[15] Where Kemble attributed the behavior of blacks to their status as slaves, Fan claimed that their race determined their nature. Their differing experiences highlight the dramatic shift in racial attitudes that occurred within the Anglo-American world during the mid-Victorian years.[16] Kemble wrote her journal during the heyday of abolitionist sentiment in Britain, when sympathy for the black slave was at its height, and many believed slaves could be inculcated with British values.[17] Fan wrote in an era when disappointment with emancipated slaves was palpable and growing, leading to increasing doubts about the capacities of black people and the belief that they were fundamentally different from whites. Although she was somewhat unusual in defending slavery, Fan's assumption that blacks absolutely required white guidance had become increasingly prevalent. In the thirty years that passed between Kemble's and Fan's stays in Georgia, American and British attitudes toward people of color had begun to move closer.

Undoubtedly, a number of sources contributed to the increasing strength of British racism throughout the mid-Victorian era. During the antebellum period, the United States played a major role in this process by shaping British images of African Americans. As we shall see, these images were conflicted and often unsatisfactory, for they obscured even as they appeared to clarify. America's significant role continued during the Civil War, which helped crystallize existing British views of African Americans without resolving their fundamental contradictions. If anything, the war created an environment that helped confirm existing British racism and provided an opportunity for its expression rather than inspiring new contributions to racist discourses.

"Sympathies . . . Multiple and Perverse": *Antebellum British Visions of African Americans*

Scholars have long recognized that changes in racial attitudes exercised a significant influence on British opinions toward the Civil War. For instance, as early as

1925, Ephraim Douglass Adams hazily referred to "a decay of general humanitarian sentiments" that took place after 1850.[18] Yet Adams never paid much attention to this issue, and succeeding historians of British opinion toward the Civil War have experienced some difficulty in discussing how British racism played a role in shaping responses to the American conflict. To his credit, R. J. M. Blackett recognizes the increasing prevalence of racism in Britain during the 1850s.[19] His interests, however, revolve around reform and abolitionism, while his story concerns itself with the way in which class, religious, and political affiliations influenced British attitudes toward the conflict.[20] Because he views the topic from this perspective, Blackett does not fully integrate racism into his narrative. Meanwhile, Duncan Andrew Campbell admits that by the 1860s "Britain was beginning to emulate American views on race," but he seems determined to minimize the extent and intensity of racist feeling in Britain during the conflict. According to Campbell, the "decisive incident" in the development of British racial thinking occurred only after the Civil War, with the Jamaican Rebellion of 1865. Nonetheless, in the course of this discussion, he drops the aside that "ideas usually take time before they become widespread," an inadvertence that suggests that racist feelings had gained momentum in Britain well before 1865. The main difficulty with Campbell's treatment of this subject is that, while pursuing the thesis that slavery constituted "the millstone around the neck of the Confederacy" in Britain, he conflates attitudes toward race with those concerning slavery; if Britons were hostile to slavery, so his argument goes, they could not have been very racist.[21]

In Britain, the rise of racism and the decline of abolitionism were thoroughly intertwined in many different ways; it is impossible to understand one without the other. An animus toward slavery, however, was not synonymous with color blindness. Because they were looking through a lens that picked up only various intensities of abolitionism, scholars of British opinion during the war have not always detected these different hues of racism. Whatever the case, emphasizing British attitudes toward race during this period is fraught with difficulty. If students of British opinion toward the war have frequently avoided fully coming to terms with the question of race, scholars of race have often gone to the other extreme. As Douglas Lorimer has complained, contemporary scholarship, particularly postcolonial discourse, has a tendency to "colonize" the mid-Victorians as a racist "Other." In an attempt to define themselves against this racist past, these academics have tended to drain it of nuance and complexity.[22] British thinking about race during the mid-Victorian period, however, was characterized by conflict, ambiguity, and change.

As soon as racism emerged in Britain, it immediately found itself challenged from without and contested within. From without, the Christian humanitarian discourse associated with abolitionism perpetuated the belief in "particularism-generalism"—that all men were different but nonetheless brothers in the eyes of God.[23] Interwoven with British national identity and the evangelical movement, this discourse proved immensely strong.[24] At the same time, as Peter Mandler has argued, the evangelicalism that served as a foundation for abolitionism also contributed (along with Scottish conjectural history) to the emergence of a "civilisational perspective" that stressed the extent to which all people—regardless of their nationality or race—could progress toward civilization.[25] Such attitudes were buttressed by the sciences, particularly the ethnology associated with James Cowles Prichard, who emphasized the common origin of men, attributed their variety to environmental factors, and stressed linguistic and cultural differences rather than physical ones.[26]

At the same time, racial theorists were badly divided. As George Fredrickson, one of the leading historians of race, has lamented, for all the modern discussion of the topic, the word "racism" has long been unstable and ill defined.[27] The mid-Victorian period was no different, with James Hunt, the controversial founder of the London Anthropological Society, famously pointing out in his 1863 inaugural address that there were "hardly two persons [who used] such an important word as 'race' in the same sense."[28] Discussions of race were invariably complicated through their intersection with discourses concerning gender, class, nation, and empire.[29] Proponents of the new race science also employed concepts that differed from those used by common people, and British writers not only dismissed American scientific racism but remained ignorant of developments in French racial theory.[30] It is not surprising, then, that racists like Thomas Carlyle and Anthony Trollope did not see eye to eye on very important issues.[31] Moreover, individual racists often felt much ambivalence about the subject. For instance, William Thackeray's attitude toward blacks was inspired by conflicting elements: English abolitionism, an Indian upbringing, and a reaction against his mother's evangelicalism. To quote Deborah Thomas, these elements inspired in Thackeray "powerful and contradictory" attitudes towards blacks and slavery.[32]

Regardless of these challenges and difficulties, racism clearly grew more powerful in Britain throughout the 1850s. Carlyle's "Occasional Discourse on the Negro Question" (1849) might have been the product of a cranky maverick, but Trollope's *The West Indies and the Spanish Main* (1859), in which he referred to West Indian blacks as members of a "servile race" and as an "inferior species," cannot be so easily dismissed.[33] The abolitionist idea of a man and a brother—a passive supplicant who suffered from heathenism but was nonetheless a man and a brother for all that—was slowly but surely faltering before a new vision of an incorrigible alien and inferior. The mid-Victorians themselves were well aware that their views had changed and commented upon this phenomenon extensively. In 1862, the *Saturday Review* claimed that a "great revolution" in British attitudes toward blacks had taken place in the previous generation: "Interest in our 'black brother' continued some time after his emancipation but gradually began to die away, and finally was to some extent replaced by contemptuous indifference and indignant depreciation."[34]

To some extent, abolitionists themselves were to blame for this revolution. Some members of the movement displayed patronizing attitudes toward blacks and reduced them to passive subjects who required British assistance.[35] Widespread abolitionist propaganda also inadvertently led the British public to identify blacks with slavery. As an 1853 essay in *Fraser's Magazine* put it, "there is some cloudiness in the perception of John Bull which induces him to consider every man with a black face is a slave, and one entitled to his, Mr. Bull's, especial protection."[36] This association of African Americans with slavery and degradation facilitated the habits of mind that automatically linked blackness and debasement. Indeed, abolitionist images and tropes often became unmoored from their original context and served sinister ends. Meanwhile, abolitionists and other reformers did not achieve their overly ambitious goals of promoting improvement overseas. Perceived failures in these areas, particularly in the West Indies, led many Britons to question the abilities of people of color.[37]

Various domestic social and cultural developments also contributed to the rise of racism. Lorimer has posited that as social mobility slowed and widespread poverty refused to succumb to the progress of the age, Britons' attitudes toward class became more exclusive. As a more tough-minded disposition toward the lower orders emerged and blacks became automatically associated with these lower orders, elites proved less susceptible to appeals based on sentimental humanitarianism and more inclined toward authoritarianism.[38] Catherine Hall has also suggested that as Dissent moved from the peripheries to the center of political power, it became less inclined to identify with other outsiders—such as blacks overseas—to form part of a universal brotherhood. Instead, Dissenters' identity was increasingly defined by a discourse of exclusion that revolved around white, independent manliness.[39] Both deliberately and unconsciously, a variety of mass media also helped promote racism. Several scholars have drawn a link between the information explosion of the mid-nineteenth century and the growth of racism.[40]

American slavery also figured prominently in British discussions of race. This contribution to British discussions about race was complex and difficult to interpret, largely because it was filtered through a series of discourses associated with the Anglo-American relationship, national identity, the meaning of freedom, and the worth of democracy. As Sidney Smith's famous 1820 rant in the *Edinburgh Review* suggests, attacks on American slavery were often linked to assaults on American claims to distinction and pretensions to liberty.[41] It was in this context that minstrelsy constituted the single most important American influence on British representations of African Americans during the antebellum era.

Undoubtedly, this form of popular culture did incalculable harm in Britain to the image of the American slave by depicting him as lazy, happy, mischievous, sly, careless, irresponsible, impulsive, pretentious, uneducated, sentimental, and inferior.[42] The extent and nature of this harm, however, remains difficult to ascertain. Michael Pickering has made a strong case that minstrelsy provided Britons with a black "Other," a subterranean self that helped define English national identity and justify imperial expansion overseas.[43] Yet several factors probably blunted minstrelsy's pernicious racial influence. As many scholars have argued, Britons embraced the form, made it their own, modified it according to their own traditions, and drained it of racial content.[44] Even more important is the question of minstrelsy's fundamentally ambivalent and contested nature. Contemporary students of minstrelsy are unanimous in arguing that while the form denigrated African Americans, it simultaneously used blackface as a shield from behind which to engage in social protest—a way "to laugh at social pretension, posturing and pomposity, and to mock the holders of authority and power."[45] Minstrelsy, as Eric Lott has asserted, carnivalized race, which meant that its "ideological production became more contradictory, its consumption more indeterminate, its political effects more plural than many have assumed."[46] Impossible to control, minstrelsy, like British racism, was never "monolithic or simply hegemonic."[47]

Harriet Beecher *Stowe's Uncle Tom's Cabin; or, Life among the Lowly* (1852), which was widely read in Britain and relied extensively on minstrelsy for its dialog and characterizations, also exerted an unpredictable and contradictory influence on British race thinking. Readers of the novel, as Sarah Meer claims, "could harbor sympathies as multiple and perverse as those of any blackface audience."[48] It is easy to see how the "plethora of tie-ins and spin-offs" associated with Tom-mania led to a "fragmenting and diversifying" of the public's understanding of the book.[49] Meer claims that the combination of blackface, sentimentality, patriotism, and antislavery attitudes that characterized *Uncle Tom*–inspired plays "made for a very strange cocktail" in which audiences "wept for stage slaves, cheered at their rebellions, reflected smugly on the superiority of British laws and attitudes, and also laughed at images of dim, deceitful, and inherently comical blacks."[50]

While it is almost impossible to measure the impact of these American imports, they clearly changed British attitudes for the worse and exposed the risks inherent in Britain's postcolonial relationship with the United States; while Britain felt obliged to engage with cultures under its sway, it ran the risk of becoming contaminated by the values of these other cultures. Frederick Douglass recognized this dynamic in 1860 when he spoke to a Newcastle audience about the "reciprocal influence" between the two nations. Globalization had brought these two countries ever closer, and the "proximity to and intercourse with the

United States . . . endangered the high moral purity of England on the question of slavery." Where once Britain had been color-blind, Douglass now found "American prejudice" in "nearly all" of Britain's "commercial towns."[51]

The extent to which Americans could control the representation of their slaves within this relationship indicated how much power they exercised in relation to Britain. Americans made it very difficult for British visitors to report on the nature of the African American slave. Southerners carefully controlled access to slaves, while British visitors were reluctant to criticize the slave owners whose hospitality had made visits to the South possible in the first place. Consequently, as Fanny Kemble pointed out, "it is morally impossible for any Englishman going into the Southern states except as a *resident,* to know any thing whatever of the real condition of the slave population."[52] In any event, many travelers clearly did not want to witness slavery firsthand because they found it too distressing.[53] Instead of undergoing such an ordeal, it was much easier, like Thomas Colley Grattan, to "consider slavery as an abstract moral question" because such a stance made close observation of slaves unnecessary.[54] For these reasons, travel literature was filled with discussions of the slave system and its political, social, and economic consequences, but it rarely examined slaves themselves. A British metropolitan population that rarely encountered black people, let alone African Americans, was left to form its image of the slave from literature, lectures, and popular entertainment.[55]

The African American lecturers who toured Britain throughout the antebellum period constituted the great exception to this rule. They were popular, accomplished, and, especially after the passage of the Fugitive Slave Act, in 1850, numerous. As Blackett claims, they possessed a "legitimacy" and "authenticity" that made them "bona fide" representatives of the more than three million black Americans who remained in chains. Few of these lecturers, however, sought to counter British racism because they feared such a tack would distract from their main mission, which consisted of building a moral cordon around the United States. Meanwhile, it is not clear what British audiences learned from these encounters. That British newspapers in one issue could praise lectures by Douglass and William Lloyd Garrison and in the next encourage readers to visit a traveling minstrel show indicates that Britons possessed a far-from-straightforward attitude toward African American slaves.[56]

British reactions to John Brown's raid in 1859 provide an interesting means of gauging this complex stance toward slaves on the eve of the Civil War. Initially, newspapers portrayed the raid as a servile insurrection, conjuring up images of slave rebellions in ancient Rome and more recent outrages in Haiti. From this perspective, black slaves played the role of vengeful savages prepared to commit the worst atrocities in a fight to the finish against their masters. When it became clear that Brown's plans had failed, the image of the slave reverted to the passive and harmless creature who, enervated by slavery, required white guidance. Attention subsequently focused on Brown, the man who had attempted to mislead them. British reporting of the incident indicates, as Seymour Drescher argues, that the image of the slave was "sharply bifurcated."[57] This bifurcation was partly a result of the many discourses that collided in any discussion of African Americans. As *The Times* pointed out, the events at Harper's Ferry were connected with "the growth of cotton in India or West Africa, with the instincts of the Anglo-Saxon race, with the intellectual powers of the African, with the principles of self-government, with the theory of the American Constitution."[58] Clearly, imperial concerns were never far from British considerations of American slaves.[59]

When the Civil War broke out, British views of African Americans—as well as of all people of color—were contradictory and increasingly negative. Lorimer has rightfully referred to "the many-sided stereotype of the Negro" that portrayed African Americans simultaneously as children and as savages.[60] They could play the roles of passive Christian martyr and untamed heathen. They could serve as vehicles for critiques of bourgeois values and justifications for imperialism. They could be objects of pity and of fear. They could be the paradoxical "Other" that served as an object against which to define national identity while also acting as a "subterranean self." What is more, they could be all of these things at once.[61] W. T. Lhamon has likened the reception of minstrelsy to the curious sensation associated with Ludwig Wittgenstein's "duck-rabbit," and it appears that in mid-Victorian Britain, African Americans themselves partook of this curious creature.[62]

Moreover, with the Civil War's outbreak, a number of intelligent British observers realized that racism was increasingly an "Anglo-Saxon" problem rather than a uniquely American one; it had become an imperial issue that faced all of Greater Britain. In 1862, as he discussed northern racism, Edward Dicey, correspondent for both *Macmillan's Magazine* and *The Spectator*, referred to the treatment of the "native Irish," the "Chinese in Australia," the "New Zealanders by the colonists," and the "Hindoos under the Company's rule" while arguing that Anglo-Saxons had "shown an uniform intolerance of an inferior race." In so many ways, America was "the complement of England," and on race, as on other issues, "the national virtues of the New World are very much those of the mother country, developed on a different and a broader scale."[63]

"A Flood of Light upon the Condition of American Slaves": *British Difficulties Associated with Discussing Race during the Civil War*

It would seem that the war ought to have clarified British thinking about African Americans. As Northern forces penetrated Confederate territory and outsiders enjoyed unprecedented opportunities for unimpeded views of slaves, there was a sense in Britain that the true nature of African Americans would finally become apparent. John Malcolm Forbes Ludlow, the prominent Christian Socialist, argued in an 1864 pamphlet that before the war, the British public had to rely on "the representations of masters and of their friends," the "overcharged" accounts of abolitionists, and the depictions of escaped slaves whose knowledge "was at best local and limited, presumably tinged with passion, resentment, habits of falsehood, [and] likely to represent only extreme cases." Now, he wrote, Northern armies had overrun "the domain of the slave-power . . . well nigh from end to end," and "what the white man may have failed to see, the black man has told." These circumstances had "cast a flood of light upon the condition of the American slaves."[64]

These opportunities, however, produced more smoke than light, partly because the topic of slavery inspired a series of powerful related and yet contradictory discourses. Abolitionism still retained great power in Britain during the war, and a postcolonial discourse led Britons to believe they had a special role to play in the resolution of the "negro question" in America.[65] Yet, as the foregoing indicates, Britons who discussed slavery and the capacities of African Americans were also involved in an imperial discourse that focused on questions concerning the labor and raw materials on which British commerce and industry depended. From the beginning of the American crisis until its end, British commentators fretted about how it would affect the labor force that produced cotton for Lancashire's mills. This concern inclined many British observers against anything that might throw southern society into turmoil and disrupt the production of cotton—including secession and sudden emancipation.[66] Belonging as they did to a great empire that relied on cheap, disciplined labor, British observers of the American scene felt they had another important interest in the outcome of the secession crisis: they wondered if a new labor system might emerge in the South after the war that might serve as a model for British possessions. Indeed, in this context, the South was discussed as if it were a part of the British Empire. In a survey of secession's origins that he wrote for the *Edinburgh Review* in April 1861, Sir George Cornewall Lewis, then the home secretary, explored this imperial dimension of the "negro question." According to Lewis, the Anglo-Saxon race thrived in "temperate regions" but proved less successful in "hot countries." In these latter areas, the Anglo-Saxon had been "forced to avail himself of the labour of an inferior race." Three different arrangements had been employed to extract that labor: "One is the negro slavery of the Southern United States; another is the free labour of negroes in the British West India Islands; the third is the system of British India, by which the ownership and cultivation of the soil remain in the hands of the natives, and the entire governing power is vested in Englishmen temporarily resident in the country." None of these arrangements, Lewis argued, was entirely satisfactory, and he hoped events in America might point the way to a better labor system.[67] As Lewis's statements indicate, the empire had a great stake in defining "inferior" peoples and contriving to make those people serve British economic interests more effectively. These interests limited what British observers were willing to approve of in America.

Throughout the war, these competing abolitionist and imperial discourses sat uneasily with each other. British journals demanded more than nominal liberty for the slave but were unwilling to countenance freedom from some type of disciplined regime. If these discourses created some ambivalence about African Americans, the manner in which British partisans of either belligerent conducted their debates—particularly with respect to slavery—led to a neglect of race. Abolitionists did not refer much to race and never made a concerted effort to convince the British public that African Americans were their equals. Abolitionists partly took this tack because they found the point irrelevant: slavery was wrong or pernicious regardless of African Americans' capabilities.[68] At the same time, abolitionists probably refrained from discussing race because there was a great diversity of opinion among them on the topic; many abolitionists, including Dicey, were racists.

Supporters of the South tended to neglect the topics of slavery and race, either because they earnestly believed the institution had nothing to do with the conflict or because they sought to avoid what they saw as an embarrassing topic. Pro-South Britons could maintain this pretense largely because the federal government was initially unwilling to declare a war of emancipation. John Worden explained British confusion regarding slavery's relationship to the war as part of a semantic problem. Britons did not regard slavery as relevant to the conflict because they instinctively identified a "slavery question" as an "abolition question," but since the federal government had initially refused to embrace emancipation, many Britons assumed that slavery was not a significant factor.[69] Southern sympathizers, then, could plausibly portray the war as a fight over tariffs, a political battle, or a clash of cultures—anything but a struggle originating in slavery. This stance, however, involved much dissembling. As *The Spectator* charged, British supporters of the Confederacy suffered from the disadvantage that they could not "display the focus of their case at all" because "they are obliged to keep it as decently out of sight as may be."[70]

The intensity of the debate between Southern and Northern sympathizers also led to the spinning of information about African Americans if not outright obfuscation. During the Civil War, the supercharged atmosphere in which discussions took place led British reviewers and journalists to embrace an overt partisanship, discard all pretensions of antebellum objectivity, and discredit their opponents by making dishonest charges of partiality. The *Saturday Review* made a great show of evenhandedness by claiming that "it is not enough to take the testimony of the advocates of slavery who depict [the slave] as little better than a brute beast, or that of Abolitionists of the *Uncle Tom* stamp, who paint him as rather lower than the angels."[71] By drawing a specious equivalence between caricatured positions, this statement provided cover for a very skewed discussion of African Americans.[72] For instance, when *The Spectator* praised Frederick Law Olmsted's *Journeys and Explorations in the Cotton Kingdom* (1861) as an impartial and accurate piece of reportage, the *Saturday Review* described this classic work as "clever pleading" akin to a "political pamphlet" in which the author's facts deserved as much credence as those presented by "a first-class Old Bailey barrister retained for the defence of a wealthy client on trial for his life."[73]

Finally, the fundamental question British commentators posed about African Americans contributed to great difficulties: was the slave degraded because of his condition or his race? As the *Saturday Review* put it in 1861, "Undoubtedly, the negroes in the Slave States are lower in the scale of being than the Anglo-Saxon race. This might be owing to a natural inferiority; but it may quite as reasonably be attributed to the fact of their being slaves."[74] To ask such a question just as slaves were emerging from centuries of bondage needlessly prejudiced the issue; it was impossible for British travelers to separate the effects of environment from race when studying slaves or newly emancipated African Americans. Moreover, the fact that so many observers—regardless of their opinions concerning abolition—claimed that the slave was degraded limited the conversation about race that could take place in Britain. Even abolitionists could not argue otherwise unless they wished to risk legitimizing slavery. When Harriet Martineau suggested in an 1864 *Edinburgh Review* essay that slaves had inadvertently received a "training for freedom" over the previous "one or two generations," the *Saturday Review* gleefully retorted that slavery could not be all bad since in a short time it had, according to Martineau, "elevated the negroes to a condition which their African ancestors had never approached during thousands of years of indigenous freedom."[75]

From "Contraband of War" to "Domestic Life in South Carolina": *British Representations of African Americans during the Civil War*

At least initially, difficulties associated with the British discussion about American slavery and race prevented the emergence of any definitive evidence or arguments. As Lorimer argues, the British did not possess "an intimate knowledge of race relations in the South." For that reason, British discussions about race showed much continuity with antebellum fantasies.[76] James Spence's *The American Union; Its Effect on National Character and Policy, with an Inquiry into Secession as a Constitutional Right, and the Causes of the Disruption* (1861) is a good expression of these continuities. The book turned Spence, a small-time dealer in "plate and iron repair commissions" from Liverpool, into a mainstay of the Confederate propaganda effort in Britain. Spence attributed all of the Americans' political and social ills to the federal union and dismissed slavery as a cause of the war. Having brought up slavery, however, he defended it through a number of traditional means—slaves were well treated, they fared better than coal miners and agricultural laborers in Britain, and the steady growth of the slave population indicated they were neither "ill-used" nor "overtaxed."[77]

Spence denied that slavery had degraded African Americans because "the amount of degradation resulting from any cause must be limited by the height from which there was room to fall." Indeed, the "African" was already degraded because of his race. In other words, the African was a born slave and found such a position natural.[78] Under these circumstances, "it is difficult to see what injury has been inflicted upon the negro by taking him from slavery to a savage in Africa, to place him under a civilized master in America." Spence wanted slavery abolished, but he clearly desired "laws carefully devised" that would compel blacks to work and keep them under white control in a postemancipation world.[79]

Overall, *The American Union* proved successful because it employed a number of traditional ideas with which the British public was already familiar. The case was no different when Spence discussed race. Much of his argument was grounded in a partisan reading of important antebellum works of travel literature (including Tocqueville, Martineau, and Stirling), leaned on old ideas associated with white-labor slavery and critiques of "telescopic philanthropy" that had appeared most famously in Charles Dickens's *Bleak House* (1852), and relied on Carlyle's ideas about nature and hierarchy while engaging in the same kind of reckless generalization. Almost all of Spence's notices conceded the force of his work, even if reviewers did not agree with his thesis. Few took *The American Union* to task for its racist, proslavery views. Even *The Economist,* which disagreed with Spence, admitted that few books had "done more to mould into definite form the floating mass of public opinion on the right or wrong-doing of the Southern States in the matter of Secession."[80]

The racist views espoused by Spence, however, were conflicted. Although Spence and likeminded observers wrote with confidence about the slave, they experienced great difficulties fixing his character, and nowhere was this problem more evident than in discussions about the potential for servile insurrection in the Confederacy, especially after the promulgation of the Emancipation Proclamation.[81] British commentators stressed the savage nature of slaves, but they did not always clarify whether this savagery was due to slavery or race.[82] Lurid thoughts on the topic were clearly inspired by the great Caribbean slave revolts of the early nineteenth century as well as the Indian Mutiny. Richard Cobden was not the only observer to see events unfolding in America "à la St. Domingo," while *The Standard* believed, like many others, that the Emancipation Proclamation sought "to make a Cawnpore of Charleston [and] a Delhi of New Orleans."[83] The influence of antebellum travel literature was also responsible for stoking such fears. Tocqueville, whom many British writers followed, had intimated that a race war was a likely event in the South's future.[84] Racism was often associated with these kinds of forecasts, and journals frequently mentioned the significance of "differences of race and color" (or the pitting of "a lower race against a higher") in contributing to the ferocity of such conflicts.[85]

These visions were difficult to reconcile with other prevalent images of African Americans, such as the carefree, improvident figure or the simple, devout slave. In defending the slave from charges that he would engage in atrocities, the *Morning Star* used the familiar picture of the passive and religious supplicant. "If the negro be the harmless, docile, faithful creature his masters have sought to make us believe he is," it surmised, he would shed little blood. Instead, he would "lift up eyes of gratitude and hope to heaven—rejoicing" that he was free.[86]

Various commentators struggled mightily to assemble these contradictory images of the slave into a coherent whole. At the beginning of the war, the *Saturday Review* claimed that the only way to reconcile the conflicting evidence from planters and abolitionists about slaves was to conclude that "the character of the coloured race is one of astonishing plasticity," but such a statement only revealed the extent to which that journal's own views—as well as those of many others—were inconsistent.[87] Like many other observers, George Alfred Lawrence, the novelist (and a visitor to the United States during the war), produced incongruous images of the slave, writing that immediate emancipation would turn "a quaint, simple, childish creature—prone to mirth, and not easily discontented if his indolence be not taxed too hardly, susceptible, too, of strong affection and fidelity to his master . . . —into a sullen, slothful insolent savage, never remembering the past, except as a sort of vague excuse for the present indulgence of his brutal instincts."[88]

The art of Frank Vizetelly strikingly illustrates the same phenomenon that characterized these discussions of race: the difficulty of combining discordant antebellum ideas in a harmonious fashion during the war. An experienced draftsman, Vizetelly served as the American correspondent and graphic artist for the *Illustrated London News* from 1861 to 1865. Initially a supporter of the North, he eventually became a Confederate sympathizer and smuggled himself into the South in the fall of 1862.[89] Relying mainly on themes associated with minstrelsy, Vizetelly portrayed African Americans in a variety of conflicting ways that served different needs.

Minstrelsy clearly exerted a great influence on Vizetelly's depiction of slaves. In describing the conversation of one "aunty" as she awaited the federal naval assault against Charleston in April 1863, Vizetelly rendered her speech in typical minstrel style: "Lor-a-mussy, boss! Is dem cussed bobolitionists gwine to shoot dar big guns mongst us women folk? . . . Praise de Lord be joyful, I'se ready to die, but I ain't no way fixed to go de long road to hebbun, and dat's what's

"The Civil War in America: 'Contraband of War.'—From a Sketch by Our Special Artist." *Illustrated London News,* July 27, 1861, 83.

"Night Amusements in the Confederate Camp—From a Sketch by Our Special Artist." *Illustrated London News,* January 10, 1863, 10.

"The War in America: Negroes at Work on the Fortifications at Savannah—From a Sketch by Our Special Artist." *Illustrated London News*, April 18, 1863, 433.

de matter."[90] The same tradition supplied Vizetelly with ideas for his sketches, most obviously in "Contraband of War" (July 1861) and "Night Amusements in the Confederate Camp" (January 1863). In the former illustration, one can spot a number of characters associated with minstrelsy—the carefree Jim Crow, the dandy Zip Coon, and the hapless Uncle Ned. Their features are exaggerated and remind one of illustrations found in Victorian works on physical anthropology. Milling in disorder with their tattered finery, they provide a striking contrast to the stern and elegant federal sentry who assumes a contrapposto like a classical statue. The escaped slaves appear as an exotic Other literally requiring direction from white authority, but would an audience familiar with the subversive nature of minstrelsy have also seen a joke at the expense of the federal soldier's amour propre? "Night Amusements in the Confederate Camp" (January 1863) must have confirmed to British readers that minstrelsy was an authentic American folk art. The dancing slave appears in a pose conventionally associated with depictions of Jim Crow. He plays the role of a carefree Other on exhibit before a sedated-looking audience.[91]

In other illustrations, references to minstrel themes in Vizetelly's captions appear at odds with his illustrations. "Plantation Negroes Working on the Defenses of Savannah" (April 1863) presents a disciplined and efficient workforce operating in ranks. Yet Vizetelly claimed they did "as little for their living as any class of men I ever saw."[92] In "Slaves at Worship on a Plantation in South Carolina" (December 1863), Vizetelly reports that one of the slaves' outstanding characteristics was their "deep, simple fervent piety." This commendable, Tom-like religiosity, however, is compromised somewhat by Vizetelly's description of the black minister, whose extemporaneous sermons were "marred by his predilection for high-sounding phrases and long words (not always appropriate)." This supposed tendency among blacks who gave themselves "airs" (especially in the guise of a minister) was a common theme of minstrel shows.[93]

Vizetelly could dispense with minstrelsy humor to produce a serious statement, yet, even in such cases, contradictions inevitably arose. In "Domestic Life in South Carolina" (May 1863), "old negro servants" tend to a planter's children. Aside from skin color, there is no real distinction between blacks and whites in this engraving, and there are no caricatured physiognomies as in "Contraband of War." The scene is redolent of bourgeois domesticity, for, as the caption informs us, children raised by "negro domestic servants" showed as much affection for these slaves as for their own parents. Vizetelly intended this scene to serve as a defense of slavery, but by portraying slaves as equals in a bourgeois domestic family scene, he raises the question of why they should be enslaved at all.[94]

"Family Worship in a Plantation in South Carolina."
Illustrated London News, December 5, 1863, 561.

"Domestic Life in South Carolina—From a Sketch by Our Special Artist." *Illustrated London News*, May 23, 1863, 552.

In Vizetelly's work, the ambivalence of minstrelsy became the means by which he attempted to depict what could not be depicted—the paradoxical Other. It seems curious that an intelligent observer with direct experience of a people would subscribe to problematic discourses regarding their nature, but a number of factors pushed visitors like Vizetelly in that direction. Antebellum racist discourses inculcated a "habit of mind," to use Lorimer's phrase, that increasingly led British society to interpret differences between people in racial terms.[95] Clearly, the physical appearance of African Americans contributed to a profound sense of difference that served as a foundation for racism. The significance of these differences is evident in William Howard Russell's account of a slave for auction in Montgomery. A sincere opponent of slavery, the famous correspondent for *The Times* felt compelled to point out that the slave's expression "was by no means disagreeable, in spite of his thick lips, broad nostrils, and high cheek bones," while "on his head was wool instead of hair." The slave's appearance filled Russell with ambivalence about where African Americans stood in relation to whites, for the journalist immediately produced the following ambiguous assessment: "no sophistry . . . could persuade me the man was not a man—he was indeed, by no means my brother, but assuredly he was a fellow-creature."[96] In other words, the slave was human but not an equal.

Uniquely personal factors also influenced stances on race, as the case of George Augustus Sala, *The Daily Telegraph's* American correspondent from 1863 to 1864, demonstrates. Peter Blake points out that his rejection of "telescopic philanthropy," protest against "white slavery" at home, and acceptance of scientific racism meant Sala was very much a product of his time, even if the journalist's ideas were "not completely representative" of British opinion. Sala's racism also helped satisfy both professional and personal needs. Blake argues convincingly that Sala sought to "forge his own journalistic identity" through a bald advocacy of racism and defense of slavery. This strategy was part of an attempt to create a new public persona closely bound with the sensationalism of his newspaper.[97] At the same time, Sala's work also revealed his need for an Other, an underground self against which he could project his undesirable traits so that he could take his place among the respectable. Sala experienced depression, suffered from erratic work habits, drank too much, mismanaged his finances, frequented brothels, and wrote a great deal of pornography.[98] In light of his difficulties, Sala's description of African Americans is most interesting: "He will always . . . be lazy, indolent, slovenly, good-natured and kind-hearted, but subject to inexplicable fits of caprice, sulkiness, obstinacy, and perversity:—willing and obedient only when he fears the eye or the hand of his master; inconceivably vain, trivial, and puerile, always as lecherous as a monkey and often as savage as a Gorilla, and finally totally unconscious of or indifferent to the moral laws."[99]

One also cannot discount the influence of white Americans on British visitors, particularly in the South. It would have been difficult for British travelers, many of whom had little previous experience of black people, to avoid succumbing to the ideas of their white American hosts, who claimed superior familiarity with the topic. In some cases, Britons were intimidated or tricked by their hosts. In a private letter to William Gregory, Frank Lawley, *The Times*'s Southern correspondent from 1862 to 1865, complained that he could not really address issues "calculated to ruffle the amour propre & awaken the jealousies of one of the most susceptible people & Governments on earth."[100] In other cases, British visitors sought congenial company. After spending no more than a few days in New York, Sala fell in with well-known Copperheads who confirmed his racist views.[101]

Finally, American slavery and racism had placed many African Americans in a position where they would undoubtedly fail to impress British visitors already predisposed to judge them harshly. In the South, Britons found the slave, on average, uneducated, badly used, and exploited. In the North, they found free blacks very frequently shunned, scorned, and condemned to menial occupations. Kemble pointed out that slavery had "debased and degraded" southern blacks while, in the North, blacks were "pariahs" who suffered under a regime similar to that of the "Hebrew lepers of old." "Stamped with a badge of infamy of Nature's own devising," they lost their self-respect and became repulsive in the eyes of whites.[102] As Handel Cossham, the colliery owner and Liberal politician, argued: "It is one of the sad . . . evils resulting from slavery that if you degrade a race by oppression, you make them odious in the eyes of their oppressors."[103]

Under these circumstances, when they contemplated the question of whether the slave was degraded because of his condition or his race, British visitors frequently inclined to the latter answer. Their encounters with African Americans during the Civil War, then, frequently confirmed what British visitors already believed. These experiences formed part of a self-reinforcing cycle, becoming a cause and a consequence of those "habits of mind" that Lorimer saw as the basis of racism.

As we have seen, it was ideas, discourses, and dynamics that initially emerged during the antebellum period that waxed during the war years and bridged the gap between British and American racial attitudes during the Civil War. The conflict, however, witnessed one unprecedented development that hastened this process: the South mounted a serious effort to influence British opinion. That effort depended largely on Henry Hotze, who introduced many Britons to a racial science with which most of them were unfamiliar.

Hotze is best remembered as a Swiss-born Southern propagandist in London who sought to obtain recognition for the Confederacy, founded *The Index,* a pro-Confederate weekly, and miraculously extended his influence throughout much of the metropolitan press.[104] Realizing that slavery was proving a major obstacle to obtaining British public approval, Hotze concluded that the Confederacy's path to respectability involved making racism and the subordination of inferior races acceptable. In pursuing these ends, Hotze exploited the British taste for social hierarchy and commitment to imperial rule. He also sought to link the Confederate cause with progress by associating it with the new race science, particularly physical anthropology, which had hitherto exerted little influence in Britain. While living in Alabama before the war, Hotze had produced the first English translation of Arthur de Gobineau's *Essay on the Inequality of the Human Races* (1853–55), to which he added a one-hundred page introduction.[105] During his stay in London, he became an associate of James Hunt, president of the London Anthropological Society, and sat on the society's council.[106] As it became clear that the Confederacy would fail to obtain recognition and also lose the war, Hotze began to reconceive his mission: *The Index* would serve as a transatlantic mediator in resolving the "negro question." "Emancipation," he asserted, "settles no question," because it did not define African Americans' position in society or explain how they would be cared for. Once political equality had been established, Anglo-Saxons on both sides of the Atlantic would have to discover the "average amount of liberty which can, consistently with social order, attach to the common citizenship of enfranchised Africans and Anglo-American freedmen."[107]

Assessing Hotze's significance is difficult partly because he exercised influence behind the scenes among a wide number of politicians and journalists. His ideas appeared to obtain traction among several British commentators, who earnestly began to study the "negro question."[108] However, as a naturalized Southerner, Hotze held views on race that were considerably harder than those of British partisans of the Confederacy, and they led to his well-known rift with James Spence. For all its flaws, the old abolitionist tradition still had "currency," as Blackett puts it, and this force prevented many Britons from fully embracing the racism that Hotze promoted. Despite these limitations, Hotze is an important transitional figure whose activities, Robert E. Bonner argues, not only "represented a late episode in the history of New World slavery" but also "anticipated an early chapter of a darker, more modern story" of racialism.[109]

Empire, "Greater Britain," and the "Negro Question"

The great material interests that always shape discourses largely determined the extent to which racism was both powerful and limited in Victorian Britain. Britons were reluctant to embrace the full implications of race thinking because it sometimes ran counter to British interests. For instance, the project to separate white Americans into different races (usually along sectional lines) failed to obtain much traction partly because such a project would have promoted Anglo-American disharmony and undermined British influence in North America.[110] Arguing, like John Roebuck, for instance, that southerners were Anglo-Saxons and northerners were mongrels would have placed many Americans outside Britain's cultural empire. For all their mixed feelings, Britons preferred to see all white Americans in the same manner as John Bright did—as part of a "Transatlantic English nation."[111] In fact, by war's end, Britons looked forward to hearty cooperation with America on the basis of their common Anglo-Saxon culture and race. In 1865, William Forster, the prominent Radical MP, told his constituents in Bradford that, despite important wartime differences, he did not "despair of a close alliance and friendship" with the "English-speaking race on the other side of the Atlantic." Such an alliance would serve as a "pattern to the world" and "teach the nations peace by the majesty of its success."[112]

As Forster indicated, a transatlantic reconciliation would help consolidate Anglo-Saxon leadership of other peoples, and it is in this context that Hotze's ideas seemed much more congenial. The assumption that blacks required subordination had become widespread, but the destruction of slavery had removed the tools that made such subordination possible. By 1865, many Britons had reached a point where, as Charles Dilke put it in *Greater Britain: A Record of Travel in*

English-Speaking Countries, during 1866–1867 (1868), "if it is still impossible . . . to advocate slavery. . . it has . . . become a habit persistently to write down freedom."[113] The precise design of a new social order depended on a knowledge of black capacities, and these remained opaque; black Americans were still mysterious figures in Britain. As *The Times,* which had uncritically embraced Spence's confident assertions about the slave, admitted in 1863, "we have had the Negro so long before us now," but "there is so little agreement as yet upon his intellectual character and capabilities."[114]

The same imperial attitudes that sought to subordinate this figure also account for his elusiveness. The experiences of Fanny Kemble and her daughter, Fan Butler, illustrate the difficulties associated with this endeavor. Writing from relatively privileged positions, both women found it hard to understand their black subjects. Kemble may have sincerely empathized with the slaves on the Butler estates, but she possessed the power to represent their thoughts and ambitions in a way that they could not. In a more aggressive fashion, Fan frequently interjected herself between blacks and her audience, providing conflicting interpretations of their actions that justified her racist views. Meanwhile, both women participated in an imperial discourse that sought to change others while remaining unchanged themselves. Each rejected the southern social order she confronted so that she could remake black people according to a different template. Kemble subscribed to a British model that sought to turn slaves into yeoman farmers.[115] Inspired by Lost Cause nostalgia, Fan wanted to produce docile dependents.

These struggles provided both women with the means to define themselves against blacks, who served as surrogate selves. Kemble's attempts to reform her slaves by wiping away filth, ignorance, and laziness served as a means of insulating herself from her own bondage to her husband. Fan's insistence on the superiority of her race permitted her to avoid recognizing that she now shared a common status of freedom with her laborers. In both cases, the widespread miscegenation that had taken place on the Butler estates made blacks there a particularly subversive Other—especially when they claimed privileges on account of their white blood.

As an Other frequently characterized by hybridity, these African Americans inevitably became both known and unknowable. Kemble was confident that blacks would act like whites if provided with similar incentives, but, not having been "born among slaves," she admitted she could neither understand them nor accustom herself to slavery.[116] Fan wrote with more ostensible confidence about the nature of the black Americans in her employ. Yet her categorical statements about her black workers were constantly balanced by repeated expressions of surprise at their behavior, revelations that they had misled her, and admissions that her judgments were characterized by contradiction.

Fanny Kemble and Fan Butler differed in many ways, but both women were engaged in imperial projects. The very nature of these projects, however, denied them the confidence in their judgment that they sought. Despite their experiences and all they had "learned," they, like other Britons, found African Americans inscrutable. As Dicey wrote, they remained "a race apart—a strange people in a strange land."[117]

NOTES

1. Rebecca Jenkins, *Fanny Kemble: A Reluctant Celebrity* (New York: Simon and Schuster, 2005), 441–42.

2. Frances Kemble, *Journal of a Residence on a Georgian Plantation in 1838–1839* (New York: Harper and Brothers, 1864), 15–16.

3. Jenkins, *Fanny Kemble,* 441–42.

4. Kemble, *Journal,* 11–12.

5. Deirdre David follows Christopher Mulvey in claiming that Kemble was "unusual in the force of her rejection of Southern claims to civilisation . . . but she was not unusual in her acceptance of certain attitudes, beliefs, and responses that would be identified as racist in the twentieth century." While twentieth-century Americans might find some of her descriptions and metaphors offensive, Kemble's oft-repeated conviction that the deficiencies of black slaves had everything to do with their circumstances as slaves rather than their blackness is a striking assertion that does not place her at all in the same category as Bird, Murray, Thackeray, and Trollope, all of whom subscribed much more clearly and ardently to racial typologies. See Deirdre David, *Fanny Kemble: A Performed Life* (Philadelphia: University of Pennsylvania Press, 2007), 162–63, 310.

6. Kemble, *Journal,* 263.

7. Ibid., 23–24, 255–56.

8. Ibid., 73.

9. Ibid., 183.

10. Margaret Armstrong, *Fanny Kemble: A Passionate Victorian* (New York: Macmillan, 1938), 448–50; David, *Fanny Kemble,* 171.

11. Pierce Butler, *Mr. Butler's Statement: Originally Prepared in Aid of His Professional Counsel* (Philadelphia: J. C. Clark, Printer, 1850), 12–13.

12. Ibid., 70–71, 228.

13. Ibid., 83, 148.

14. Ibid., 147.

15. Catherine Clinton, *Fanny Kemble's Civil Wars* (New York: Oxford University Press, 2001), 255.

16. Although David insists that Fan identified herself primarily as an American, the fact that she married an English clergyman and moved to Britain rather than remain in the United States—let alone live on the old Butler estates—speaks to her fundamentally transatlantic nature. See David, 247.

17. Christine Bolt, *Victorian Attitudes to Race* (London: Routledge and Kegan Paul, 1971), 46.

18. Ephraim Douglass Adams, *Great Britain and the American Civil War* (New York: Russell and Russell, 1958), 1: 32.

19. R. J. M. Blackett, *Divided Hearts: Britain and the American Civil War* (Baton Rouge: Louisiana State University Press, 2001), 36–47. See also R. J. M. Blackett, *Building an Antislavery Wall: Black Americans in the Atlantic Abolitionist Movement, 1830–1860* (Baton Rouge: Louisiana State University Press), 155.

20. Blackett, *Divided Hearts*, 3–5, 88.

21. Duncan Andrew Campbell, *English Opinion and the American Civil War* (Rochester: Boydell Press/Royal Historical Society, 2003), 126–27.

22. Douglas Lorimer, "Reconstructing Victorian Racial Discourse: Images of Race, the Language of Race Relations, and the Context of Black Resistance," in Gretchen Holbrook Gerzina, ed., *Black Victorians/Black Victoriana* (New Brunswick, N.J.: Rutgers University Press, 2003), 187.

23. Edward Beasley, *The Victorian Reinvention of Race: New Racisms and the Problem of Grouping in the Human Sciences* (New York: Routledge, 2010), 159.

24. Linda Colley, *Britons: Forging the Nation 1707–1837* (New Haven: Yale University Press, 1992), 354–59.

25. Peter Mandler, "'Race' and 'Nation' in Mid-Victorian Thought," in Stefan Collini, Richard Whatmore, and Brian Young, eds., *History, Religion and Culture: British Intellectual History 1750–1950* (Cambridge: Cambridge University Press, 2000), 226–27.

26. George W. Stocking, *Victorian Anthropology* (New York: Free Press, 1987), 49–53. See also H. F. Augstein, *James Cowles Prichard's Anthropology: Remaking the Science of Man in Early Nineteenth-Century Britain* (Atlanta: Rodopi, 1999).

27. George Fredrickson, *The Comparative Imagination: On the History of Racism, Nationalism, and Social Movements* (Berkeley: University of California Press, 1997), 77–87; George Fredrickson, *Racism: A Short History* (Princeton: Princeton University Press, 2002), 1.

28. James Hunt, "Introductory Address on the Study of Anthropology," *Anthropological Review* 1 (May 1863): 5, 13. As J. W. Barrow has pointed out, "the diversity of interests," "the loose terms of reference," and the "fluid state of scientific opinion in many fields" meant that the Anthropological Society was often the "stamping-ground of cranks and exhibitionists of every description." J. W. Barrow, "Evolution and Anthropology in the 1860's: The Anthropological Society of London, 1863–1871," *Victorian Studies* 7 (1963): 147. See also Edward Beasley, *The Victorian Reinvention of Race: New Racisms and the Problem of Grouping in the Human Sciences* (New York: Routledge, 2010), 9–11.

29. See Catherine Hall, *Civilising Subjects: Metropole and Colony in the English Imagination 1830–1867* (Chicago: University of Chicago Press, 2002).

30. Michael Banton, *Racial Theories* (New York: Cambridge University Press, 1998), xiii–xiv; Beasley, *Victorian Reinvention of Race*, 14, 69–70.

31. Hall, *Civilising Subjects*, 214.

32. Deborah Thomas, *Thackeray and Slavery* (Athens: Ohio State University Press, 1993), 4–16.

33. Anthony Trollope, *The West Indies and the Spanish Main* (London: Chapman and Hall, 1859), 63, 61, 60, 56.

34. *Saturday Review*, January 18, 1862, 62.

35. Douglas Lorimer, *Colour, Class and the Victorians: English Attitudes to the Negro in the Mid-Nineteenth Century* (New York: Holmes and Meier, 1978), 33–37.

36. "Concerning the Free British Negro," *Fraser's Magazine* (January 1853), 121.

37. Martin Lynn, "British Policy, Trade, and Informal Empire in the Mid-Nineteenth Century," and Andrew Porter, "Trusteeship, Anti-Slavery, and Humanitarianism," in Andrew Porter, ed., *The Oxford History of the British Empire: The Nineteenth Century* (New York: Oxford University Press, 1999), 3: 107, 109, 213–14.

38. Lorimer, *Colour, Class, and the Victorians,* 109–14, 200.

39. Hall, *Civilising Subjects,* 427, 432–433.

40. Beasley, *Victorian Reinvention of Race,* 15, 157–58. See also Marcus Wood, *Blind Memory: Visual Representations of Slavery in England and America 1780–1865* (New York: Routledge, 2000). Of particular interest is Wood's discussion (pp. 143–81) of George Cruikshank's illustrations for John Cassell's edition of *Uncle Tom's Cabin*—probably Britain's most elegant pirated edition of the work.

41. H. C. Allen, Great Britain and the *United States: A History of Anglo-American Relations (1783–1952)* (New York: St. Martin's Press, 1955), 148.

42. Lorimer believes minstrelsy "reinforced rather than caused" the "growth of English racial conceit." The growth of racism, he believes, can "best be explained by the social changes and stresses within English society itself." See Douglas Lorimer, "Bibles, Banjoes, and Bones: Images of the Negro in the Popular Culture of Victorian England," in Barry M. Gough, ed., *In Search of the Visible Past: History Lectures at Wilfrid Laurier University 1973–1974* (Waterloo, Ont.: Wilfrid Laurier University Press, 1975), 45.

43. Pickering recognizes, however, that "imperialist discourse" was not "monolithic" and that there was nothing "fixed or rigid" about it. At the same time, he also admits that "minstrelsy was not simply or wholly subsumed by racial and imperialist discourse." See Michael Pickering, "Mock Blacks and Racial Mockery: The 'Nigger' Minstrel and British Imperialism," in J. S. Bratton, ed., *Acts of Supremacy: The British Empire and the Stage, 1790–1930* (New York: St. Martin's Press, 1991), 185, 188–96, 208.

44. See, for instance, Michael Pickering, "White Skins, Black Masks: 'Nigger' Minstrelsy in Victorian England," in J. S. Bratton, ed., *Music Hall: Performance and Style* (Philadelphia: Open University Press, 1986), 76; George F. Rehin, "Harlequin Jim Crow: Continuity and Convergence in Blackface Clowning," *Journal of Popular Culture* 9 (June 1975): 682–701; George F. Rehin, "Blackface Street Minstrels in Victorian London and Its Resorts: Popular Culture and Its Racial Connotations as Revealed in Polite Opinion," *Journal of Popular Culture* 15 (February 1981): 19–38. See also J. S. Bratton, "English Ethiopians: British Audiences and Black-Face Acts, 1835–1865," *Yearbook of English Studies* 11 (1981): 138.

45. Pickering, "White Skins," 88.

46. Eric Lott, *Love and Theft: Blackface Minstrelsy and the American Working Class* (New York: Oxford University Press, 1993), 20.

47. Ibid., 234.

48. Sarah Meer, *Uncle Tom Mania: Slavery, Minstrelsy and Transatlantic Culture in the 1850s* (Athens: University of Georgia Press, 2005), 44.

49. Ibid., 7.

50. Ibid., 157.

51. *The Frederick Douglass Papers, Series 1: Speeches, Debates, and Interviews,* ed. John W. Blassingame (New Haven: Yale University Press, 1985), 3: 335–36.

52. Kemble, *Journal,* 304.

53. Basil Hall, *Travels in North America in the Years 1827 and 1828* (Edinburgh: Cadell, 1830), 3: 39.

54. Thomas Colley Grattan, *Civilized America* (London: Bradbury and Evans, 1859), 2: 181.

55. Lorimer, *Colour, Class, and the Victorians,* 17.

56. Blackett, *Building an Antislavery Wall,* 169, 195, 155, 157, 159, 188, 190, 160.

57. Seymour Drescher, "Servile Insurrection and John Brown's Body in Europe," *Journal of American History* 80 (September 1993): 506, 509, 513–15.

58. *The Times,* December 19, 1859, 8.

59. For an interesting discussion of what *The Times* was willing to countenance and why, see *The Times,* December 28, 1859, 6.

60. Lorimer, *Colour, Class, and the Victorians,* 166.

61. Ibid., 90.

62. W. T. Lhamon, *Raising Cain: Blackface Performance from Jim Crow to Hip Hop* (Cambridge, Mass.: Harvard University Press, 1998), 138.

63. Edward Dicey, *Spectator of America* (Athens: University of Georgia Press, 1989), 52.

64. J. M. Ludlow, *American Slavery* (London: Emily Faithfull, 1864), 1–3.

65. See, for example, *The Times,* January 30, 1861, 6; Frederic Seebohm, *The Crisis of Emancipation in America, Being a Review of the History of Emancipation, from the Beginning of the American War to the Assassination of President Lincoln* (London: A. W. Bennett, 1865), 40.

66. For an example of how British commentators worried about how sudden changes in the status of the South or of slaves would affect commercial opportunities, see *The Economist,* January 26, 1861, 88.

67. [Sir George Cornewall Lewis], "Election of President Lincoln and Its Consequences," *Edinburgh Review* 113 (April 1861): 566, 584–85.

68. For evangelicals and dissenters reared in the antislavery tradition, the slave was a brother in Christ, and slavery was a sin. For those classical political economists who employed a free-labor critique of slavery, the system was, as *The Economist* put it, "an economic blunder," "a social stain," "a moral wrong," and "detestable" because of its pervasive social effects. For many others, it was simply a violent, barbarous, and intolerable system. Edward Dicey described slavery as a "gigantic . . . attempt to reduce oppression to a system, and to establish a social order of which the misery of human beings is to be a fundamental principle." London *Daily News,* December 25, 1861, 4; *The Economist,* July 6, 1861, 732; Edward Dicey, *Six Months in the Federal States* (London: Macmillan, 1863), 1: 66–67.

69. John Worden, *The Plain English of American Affairs* (London: Alfred E. Bennett, 1863), 20.

70. It was for this reason that Francis William Newman accused the Southern Independence Association of "want of frankness" and dared it to defend slavery with the brazenness that the Confederate leadership displayed. *The Spectator,* June 21, 1862, 691;

Francis William Newman, *Character of the Southern States of America: Letter to a Friend Who Had Joined the Southern Independence Association* (Manchester: Union and Emancipation Society, 1863), 11–12.

71. *Saturday Review,* February 2, 1861, 106.

72. The *Saturday Review*'s founder and owner, A. J. B. Beresford-Hope, was a member of the London Southern Independence Association.

73. The *Spectator,* October 12, 1861, 1123; *Saturday Review,* November 2, 1861, 460.

74. *Saturday Review,* February 16, 1861, 160

75. [Harriet Martineau], "The Negro Race in America," *Edinburgh Review* 19 (January 1864): 204; the *Saturday Review,* February 20, 1864, 221.

76. Lorimer, *Colour, Class, and the Victorians,* 164–65, 166.

77. James Spence, *The American Union; Its Effect on National Character and Policy, with an Inquiry into Secession as a Constitutional Right, and the Causes of the Disruption* (London: Richard Bentley, 1862), 121, 122, 125, 129.

78. Ibid., 126–27.

79. Ibid., 163.

80. *The Economist,* June 21, 1862, 680.

81. Earl Russell's 1862 mediation plan was premised on the fear that the proclamation would "excite the passions of the slave" and culminate in "acts of plunder, of incendiarism, and of revenge." *British Documents on Foreign Affairs: Reports and Papers from the Foreign Office Series C, Confidential Print, Part 1: From the Mid-Nineteenth Century to the First World War,* ed. Kenneth Bourne and D. Cameron Watt (Frederick, Md.: University Publications of America, 1984–1987), 1: 95.

82. *The Standard* claimed the slaves were not ready for immediate emancipation because they still lived in a "semi-savage state, unaccustomed to provide for themselves or one another" and remained "strangers to the restraint of lust and passion." An insurrection waged by such people would include "murder, arson, [and] outrages of every kind describable and indescribable." The origins of their "semi-savage state" remained unclear in this explanation. *The Standard,* October 7, 1862, 4; *The Standard,* October 8, 1862, 4.

83. Cobden to Bright, January 7, 1862, Cobden Papers, British Library, Add. Mss. 43652; *The Standard,* October 8, 1862, 4..

84. Alexis de Tocqueville, *Democracy in America* (New Rochelle: Arlington House, 1965), 1: 372–75.

85. *Army and Navy Gazette,* February 14, 1863, 97; *The Economist,* October 25, 1862, 1178.

86. *Morning Star,* January 1, 1863, 1.

87. *Saturday Review,* February 2, 1861, 106.

88. George Alfred Lawrence, *Border and Bastille* (New York: W. I. Pooley, 1863), 297. For other examples of the same phenomenon, see *The Times,* October 9, 1862, 9; *Saturday Review,* October 11, 1862, 437; *The Economist,* October 25, 1862, 1178.

89. *Illustrated London News,* July 26, 1862, 111; [Frank Vizetelly], "Underground to Richmond," *All the Year Around* 17 (February 16, 1867), 172–78.

90. [Frank Vizetelly], "Charleston under Fire," *Cornhill Magazine* 10 (July 1864), 100–101.

91. *Illustrated London News,* January 10, 1863, 44.

92. Vizetelly's reference in the caption to their song "I Don't Like the Lowland Gal" (whose lyrics look much like those associated with minstrelsy) is particularly interesting. Some years after the war, while writing an essay about smuggling himself into the Confederacy, Vizetelly had a crew of six African Americans row him across the Patuxent River in Maryland; as they rowed, they sang . . . "I Don't Like the Lowland Gal." Apparently, from Vizetelly's perspective, all African American songs had a kind of generic quality that made them interchangeable. *Illustrated London News,* April 18, 1863, 432; [Frank Vizetelly], "Underground to Richmond," 175.

93. *Illustrated London News,* December 5, 1863, 561.

94. *Illustrated London News,* May 23, 1863, 552.

95. Lorimer, *Colour, Class, and the Victorians,* 210–11.

96. *The Times,* May 30, 1861, 10.

97. Evidence suggests that Edward Lawson, the owner, and Thornton Hunt, the editor, had a good understanding of what kind of correspondence Sala would supply to the *Daily Telegraph.* According to Sala, "frequent and protracted were the conferences between the proprietors of the *Daily Telegraph* and myself as to how my mission to America in the midst of war was to be carried out. They knew perfectly well that as the son of a West Indian lady and the grandson of a West Indian slave-owner, my sympathies were on the side of the South." George Sala, *The Life and Adventures of George Augustus Sala* (New York: Charles Scribner's Sons, 1895), 2: 19.

98. Ralph Straus, *Sala: The Portrait of an Eminent Victorian* (London: Constable, 1942), 138, 140.

99. George Augustus Sala, *My Diary in America in the Midst of War* (London: Tinsley Brothers, 1865), 1: 39.

100. Lawley to Gregory, March 26, 1863, Gregory Family Papers, Mss. 624, Box 24, Folder 3, Emory University Special Collections. On the basis of incidents he related in *Down South; or, An Englishman's Experience at the Seat of the American War, The Economist* was certain that Samuel Phillips Day, southern correspondent for the *Morning Herald,* had been fooled by his hosts. See Samuel Phillips Day, *Down South, or, an Englishman's Experience at the Seat of the American War* (London: Hurst and Blackett, 1862), 2: 167–68; *The Economist,* April 19, 1862, 1–2.

101. George Augustus Sala, *Things I Have Seen and People I Have Known* (London: Cassell, 1894), 1: 218.

102. Kemble, *Journal,* 10–13.

103. Handel Cossham, *The American War: Facts and Fallacies* (Bristol: H. J. Mills, Gazette Office, 1864), 22.

104. The most significant recent work linking the Civil War to the development of racist attitudes in Britain consists of essays focusing on the activities of Hotze. See Robert J. C. Young, "Egypt in America, the Confederacy in London," in *Colonial Desire: Hybridity in Theory, Culture, and Race* (New York: Routledge, 2000); Robert E. Bonner, "Slavery, Confederate Diplomacy, and the Racialist Mission of Henry Hotze," *Civil War History* 51 (September 2005): 288–316.

105. Lonnie A. Burnett, *Henry Hotze, Confederate Propagandist: Selected Writings on Revolution, Recognition, and Race* (Tuscaloosa: University of Alabama Press, 2008), 3–5.

106. Bonner, "Slavery," 289–90, 295, 303, 305.

107. Hotze to Benjamin, July 29, 1864, Hotze Papers, Library of Congress; *The Index*, April 27, 1865, 264.

108. James Fitzjames Stephen conceded that "slavery is a wretched institution" but echoed Hotze's sentiments in claiming that "it does after a way solve the fearful problem of getting an inferior and superior race to live together somehow in nearly equal numbers." [James Fitzjames Stephen], "England and America," *Fraser's Magazine* 68 (October 1863), 437.

109. Bonner, "Slavery," 316.

110. This failure was also partly a result of the tremendous problems inherent in such a project and the fact that the Britons and Americans who promoted these ideas subscribed to very different racial mythologies. See Robert Bonner, "Roundheaded Cavaliers? The Context and Limits of a Confederate Racial Project," *Civil War History* 48 (January 2002): 34–59; Jan C. Dawson, "The Puritan and the Cavalier: The South's Perception of Contrasting Traditions," *Journal of Southern History* 44 (November 1978): 597–614.

111. See Bright's December 4, 1861 dinner speech at Rochdale in John Bright, *Speeches of John Bright on the American Question* (Boston: Little, Brown, 1865), 11. See also Christine Bolt, *The Anti-Slavery Movement and Reconstruction: A Study in Anglo-American Co-operation* (New York: Oxford University Press, 1969), 141–46.

112. *The Times*, January 13, 1865, 7.

113. Charles Dilke, *Greater Britain: A Record of Travel in English-Speaking Countries during 1866 and 1867* (London: Macmillan, 1868), 31.

114. *The Times*, September 5, 1863, 8.

115. Indeed, Pierce Butler complained that Kemble "constantly indulged" in a "spirit of unwise comparison . . . between my country and her own." "Almost every thing which she found different from what she was accustomed to," he wrote, "was pronounced inferior and wrong." Pierce Butler, *Mr. Butler's Statement: Originally Prepared in Aid of His Professional Counsel* (Philadelphia: J. C. Clark, Printer, 1850), 21–22.

116. Kemble, *Journal*, 171.

117. [Edward Dicey], "Notes of a Tour through the Border States," *Macmillan's Magazine* 6 (June 1862), 139.

JAMES M. MCPHERSON

"Two irreconcilable peoples"?

Ethnic Nationalism in the Confederacy

Ethnic nationalism is one of the most powerful forces in the modern world. It broke up Yugoslavia into Slovenia, Croatia, Serbia, Bosnia, Montenegro, and Kosovo and caused sometimes deadly conflict among these ethnic nations. It shattered the Soviet Union into a bewildering checkerboard of ethnic nations that can scarcely be said to live in peace with one another or with Russia. It split Czechoslovakia in two and threatens to do the same to Belgium. At one time it appeared that Canada might follow the same path. Kurdish nationalists fight in vain to carve out their own nation from portions of Turkey, Iraq, and Iran. Ethnic and religious conflict have kept Ireland, Nigeria, and Sudan embroiled in violent conflict or on the verge of it numerous times over the years, and it recently split Sudan into two nations. Distrust and violence between Jews and Arabs in Israel and the West Bank have so far prevented either a one-state or a two-state solution to the problem of Palestine. Sunni and Shiite Muslims war with each other in several Arab nations. Tribal, religious, and ethnic conflicts threaten to undermine or erode some of the democratic and nationalist aspirations of the uprisings of the "Arab Spring" in 2011. Even in the United Kingdom, the British government has recognized ethnic nationalism by devolving a degree of sovereign power to the Scottish and Welsh parliaments.

From these and other examples one could cite and from the work of numerous scholars who have studied nationalism, we can derive a definition of ethnic nationalism as the sense of identity and loyalty shared by a group of people united among themselves and distinguished from others by one or more of the following factors: language, religion, culture, and, perhaps most important but also most nebulous, a belief in the common genetic descent of the group. As one student of nationalism explains, because "there are very few groups in the world today whose members can lay any claim to a known common origin, it is not actual descent that is considered essential to the definition of an ethnic group but a belief in a common descent."[1] This quotation points up an important element in any kind of nationalism, ethnic or otherwise: it is self-defined. As two other scholars have noted, nationalism "is first and foremost a state of mind"; it "is subjective and consists of the self-identification of people with a group."[2]

Ethnic nationalism is far from unique to our own time. Revolts and civil wars that involved the Dutch against Spain or Scots and Irish against English rule were examples of such nationalism in the seventeenth and eighteenth centuries. In the nineteenth century, violent as well as nonviolent movements of ethnic nationalism included the Greeks against Turkey, Hungary versus the Hapsburgs, Poland against Russia, Norway against its union with Sweden, and some of the German states against Napoleon. The ethnic nationalism of the nineteenth century originated in part from the response of German intellectuals and cultural leaders to the French Revolution and to Napoleon's conquests. They constructed the concept of a German *Volk* whose blood ties should unite all Germans against French domination. This idea of the *Volk* grew more and more powerful until Otto von Bismarck, who urged Germans to " think with your blood," united most German-speaking peoples into a single state in 1871. This model of ethnic nationalism was a top-down creation constructed by intellectuals and diffused into the culture through literature, music, art, and, eventually, political discourse to support the struggles of Germans, Greeks, Hungarians, Poles, Norwegians, and other ethnic nationalities for independent nationhood.[3]

Ethnic identity is not the only form of nationalism. Another powerful current in the modern world is civic nationalism. The example closest to home is the United States. What binds Americans together is not ethnic solidarity but common citizenship and collective allegiance to a set of legal and political institutions forged by historical experience. There is no American *Volk*. The origins of American civic nationalism can be traced not to descent from an ancient bloodline but to the Declaration of Independence, the flag, the Constitution, and the shared history of a victorious struggle for independent nationhood.

Almost from its founding the United States was a multiethnic nation. Although English language, law, and culture predominated, nearly two-fifths of the white population in 1790 came from non-English stock: Scots, Irish, Germans, Dutch, French, and other European groups. Even if the Scots and Irish are lumped with the English, more than one-fifth of the white population was non-British. That percentage grew over time with heavy immigration of non-British peoples, especially after 1840. American civic nationalism became identified not only with citizenship but also with ideas of liberty, republicanism, manhood suffrage, equality of opportunity, and the absence of rigid class lines. As a Norwegian immigrant wrote to a friend back in Norway, "I have learned to love the country to which I emigrated more sincerely than my old fatherland. I feel free and independent among a free people, who are not chained down by any class or caste systems." This immigrant's choice of words defined the difference between ethnic nationalism ("my old fatherland") and civic nationalism ("a free people . . . not chained down").[4] As with so many other things, perhaps Abraham Lincoln said it best. In 1858 he pointed out that half of all white Americans had no ancestral ties to the generation of the Founders. "If they look back through this history to trace their connection with those days by blood, they find they have none," said Lincoln, "but when they look through that old Declaration of Independence . . . they feel that the moral sentiment taught in that day evidences their relation to those men. . . . That is the electric cord in that Declaration that links the hearts of patriotic and liberty-loving men together."[5]

There was, of course, a glaring exception to the equal citizenship that was the centerpiece of American civic nationalism: the slaves. The Supreme Court's *Dred Scott* decision in 1857 declared that even free blacks, as the descendants of slaves, were not citizens. One-seventh of the population was thus defined out of American nationality. This egregious violation of civic nationalism helped fuel the antislavery movement. As Lincoln expressed it in 1854, "the monstrous injustice of slavery deprives our republican example of its just influence in the world" and "enables the enemies of free institutions, with plausibility, to taunt us as hypocrites."[6]

For a time in the 1850s the political movement known as "nativism" also threatened to turn the United States in the direction of ethnic nationalism. American-born Protestants who resented the large influx of Irish and German Catholic immigrants founded the American Party in 1854 and won control of several state legislatures. Branded "Know-Nothings" by their opponents, movement adherents set as their goal to limit the influence of foreign-born voters and to lengthen the waiting period for immigrants to become naturalized citizens from five to twenty-one years.

Although some leaders of the new antislavery Republican Party were tempted to form alliances with the American Party, most opposed this "organized scheme of bigotry and proscription," in the words of a prominent Indiana Republican. Since "we are against Black Slavery, because the slaves are deprived of human rights," declared others," we are also against [this] system of Northern Slavery to be created by disfranchising Irish and Germans."[7] It should come as no surprise that Lincoln penned the clearest indictment of nativism as contrary to the ideals of civic nationalism. "Our progress in degeneracy appears to me to be pretty rapid," he wrote in 1855. "As a nation, we began by declaring that 'all men are created equal.' We now practically read it 'all men are created equal, *except negroes.*' When the Know-Nothings get control, it will read 'all men are created equal, except negroes, *and foreigners, and Catholics.*' When it comes to this I should prefer emigrating to some country where they make no pretense of loving liberty—to Russia, for instance, where despotism can be taken pure, and without the base alloy of hypocrisy."[8]

By 1860 the looming crisis of civil war drove nativism into the shadows, from which it continues to emerge periodically to challenge the tenets of civic nationalism. The greatest threat to American nationalism, however, came not from nativism but from Confederate nationalism. At first glance, it may seem perverse to label the Confederacy as a form of ethnic nationalism. After all, southern whites shared the same language with other Americans, the same Judeo-Christian and mainly Protestant religious tradition, the same predominantly British heritage, a common memory of the struggle for independent nationhood, and a common allegiance to the Constitution and the political institutions that had grown up under it, which they had played a major role in shaping.

Yet these commonalities coexisted with a widespread and growing conviction that northern and southern whites were two peoples with increasingly hostile interests. William Gilmore Simms, a leading southern novelist and editor of the *Southern Quarterly Review* in the 1850s, described residents of the slave states as "a people, a nation" possessing such different "national characteristics" from Northerners "in essential, moral, and physical respects" that their destiny as "a separate political community" was inevitable.[9] In 1861 the son of a wealthy Georgia planter, Charles C. Jones Jr., described northern and southern whites as "two races which, although claiming a common parentage, have been so entirely separated by climate, by morals, by religion . . . that they cannot longer coexist under the same government. Oil and water will not commingle. . . . The sooner we separate the better." Congressman Alfred Iverson of Georgia agreed that there was "an enmity between the northern and southern people that is deep and enduring, and you can never eradicate it—never!"[10]

European visitors to the United States echoed these observations. Alexis de Tocqueville commented as early as 1835 on the "marked differences" between northerners and southerners who had "sprung from the same stock."[11] A Scottish visitor described southerners as "quite a distinct race from the 'Yankees,'" while an Englishman added that South Carolina planters despised Northerners as "an inferior race of men. . . . There is nothing a Southern man resents so much as to be called a Yankee."[12]

What explained this hostility between peoples who, as Tocqueville noted, had "sprung from the same stock"? Tocqueville's own answer was that "almost all the marked differences in character between northerners and southerners have their roots in slavery."[13] The peculiar institution was indeed the wedge that split the two sections farther and farther apart. In 1858 William H. Seward described an "irrepressible conflict" between rival social orders founded on free labor and slave labor. It was this conflict, said Abraham Lincoln the same year, that made the United States a house divided against itself.[14] In March 1861 the new vice president of the Confederacy, Alexander Stephens, said in a speech at Savannah that the conflict over slavery was "the immediate cause" of secession. Stephens pronounced one of the charters of American civic nationalism, the Declaration of Independence, with its ringing affirmation that all men are created equal, to be false. "Our new government is founded on exactly the opposite idea," said Stephens. "Its cornerstone rests upon the great truth that the Negro is not equal to the white man; that slavery . . . is his natural and moral condition. This, our new Government, is the first in the history of the world based on this great physical, philosophical, and moral truth."[15]

Stephens's description of slavery as the cornerstone of the Confederacy was a truism. But was it an expression of ethnic nationalism? Not precisely, though it was related to a southern consciousness of ethnic distinctiveness in both obvious and subtle ways. But the South Carolina planters who were said to consider Northerners "an inferior race" and Charles C. Jones, who referred to northerners and southerners as "two races," were not referring to Caucasian and Negro. They meant that northern and southern whites belonged to different ethnic groups—or races, as ethnic groups were usually described in the nineteenth century. That is also what a North Carolina newspaper editor meant when he declared in May 1861 that "blood is thicker than water" and that his state must therefore join the Confederacy, because the blood ties of white people in slave states were stronger than their watery ties of civic nationalism to the people of the free states.[16]

Confederate nationalists drew on the examples of European ethnic struggles for independent nationhood. Like the Greeks against Turkey, Hungarians against the Hapsburgs, and Poland against Russia, declared the *Richmond Enquirer* during the Civil War, "we are fighting for the idea of race . . . against that crushing, killing union with another nationality."[17] Southerners also drew on traditions closer to their own culture. The extraordinary popularity of Sir Walter Scott's novels can be explained, in part, by the resonance among southerners of Scott's romantic portrayal of Scotland's efforts to express its cultural nationalism vis-à-vis England. Southerners acquired the term "Southron" from Scott. This was an archaic Scottish word for "southerner," meaning the English people on Scotland's border. Whether aware of the irony or not, southern whites transposed this vaguely contemptuous Scottish term into a term of southern pride to distinguish themselves from "Yankees."

An even greater irony inhered in the particular popularity in the South of Scott's novel *Ivanhoe*. Set in the twelfth century, the novel portrays a struggle between descendants of Norman conquerors and the vanquished Anglo-Saxons for the soul of England. Most of Scott's Norman protagonists are cruel, arrogant, and overbearing, while the novel's hero and heroine, Ivanhoe and Rowena, are Anglo-Saxons. Southern readers seem to have missed the point. Their enthusiasm for the novel coincided with the rise of the central myth of southern ethnic nationalism: the idea that southern whites, or at least the planter class, were descended from the English Cavaliers of the seventeenth century, who in turn were descended from the Normans, while Yankees were descended from the "Saxon churls" by the way of the seventeenth-century Puritans who migrated to New England when the Cavaliers migrated to Virginia.

This belief gained a remarkable currency among the southern cultural elite. By 1860 it had become diffused into the discourse of southern nationalism. One of the fullest expressions of this ethnic nationalism appeared in the *Southern Literary Messenger* in June 1860, just as the crucial presidential election campaign was warming up. Published in Richmond, the *Messenger* was the principal outlet for southern writers. This article boldly declared the sectional conflict to be "a contest of race . . . between the North and the South. . . . The people of the Northern States are more immediately descended of the English Puritans" who "constituted as a class the common people of England . . . and were descended of the ancient Britons and Saxons. . . . The southern States were settled and governed . . . by . . . persons belonging to that stock recognized as Cavaliers . . . directly descended from the Norman Barons of William the Conqueror, a race distinguished in its earliest history for its warlike and fearless character, a race in all times since renowned for its chivalry, honor, gentleness, and intellect. . . . The southern people come of that race."[18]

The South's leading writer on political economy, James B. D. DeBow, subscribed to this Norman-Cavalier thesis and helped to popularize it in his influential journal published in New Orleans, *DeBow's Review.* As the states in the Lower South seceded one after another during the winter of 1860–61, *DeBow's Review* carried several long articles justifying this separation on the grounds of irreconcilable ethnic differences between southern and northern whites. "The Cavaliers, Jacobites, and Huguenots, who settled the South, naturally hate, contemn, and despise the Puritans who settled the North," proclaimed one such article written by George Fitzhugh, the South's foremost proslavery intellectual. "The former are a master-race—the latter a slave race, the descendants of Saxon serfs. . . . Cavaliers and Jacobites are of Norman descent, and the Normans were of Roman descent, and so were the Huguenots. The Saxons and Angles, ancestors of the Yankees, came from the cold and marshy regions of the North, where man is little more than a cold-blooded, amphibious biped."[19]

DeBow's Review proudly contrasted the South's ethnic nationalism with the civic nationalism of the North. "The two distinct peoples" of North and South, another article declared, had been forced into an alliance in 1776 by the mutual cause against Britain. But the union they formed was an experiment doomed to failure. The South was now recovering its "independent destiny," according to this writer, by repudiating the failed experiment of civil nationalism that had sought "to erect one nation out of two irreconcilable peoples."[20]

These ideas percolated into the southern popular press. A Louisville newspaper acknowledged that until Lincoln's election in 1860 the South had controlled the national government just as "our Norman kinsmen in England, always a minority, have ruled their Saxon countrymen." Southern states departed when Lincoln came in, this editorial continued, because "the Norman Cavalier of the South cannot brook the vulgar familiarity of the Saxon Yankee."[21] The *Richmond Dispatch,* with the largest circulation of any newspaper in the Confederacy, published frequent editorials analyzing "the incongruous and discordant elements out of which the framers of the Constitution [in 1787] sought to create a homogenous people. . . . The great wonder is not that the sections have fallen asunder at last, but that they held together so long. . . . The dissimilarities between moral constitutions, habits of thought, breeding and manners of the Cavalier and Roundhead must necessarily run in the blood for generations, and defy all the glue and cement of political unions." And the Confederacy's poet laureate, Henry Timrod, celebrated the formal creation of the Confederate States of America as "a nation among nations" in a poem with the significant title "Ethnogenesis."[22]

Proponents of the Norman-Cavalier genealogy of southern whites readily incorporated slavery into this ideology. After all, the Normans were a ruling race and therefore had "an affinity with the institution of slavery," according to articles in the *Southern Literary Messenger* and *DeBow's Review.* In contrast, the subordinate Saxons—who became Puritans and then Yankees—did not possess "that combination of dignified greatness and natural command, so necessary to the proper control of slavery." As a consequence, the Yankees developed "an insane philanthropy for the Negro" while the "conservative, bold, chivalrous, and commanding" Norman Southrons, with "their peculiar capacity for *executive control,*" were "the only people on this continent who can properly control . . . this peculiar institution of slavery." Thus it became "the mission of the Norman blood of this country "to exercise the power and charm of slavery."[23]

This Norman-Cavalier thesis, on the face of it, is little short of ludicrous. Modern scholars have shown it to have scarcely any foundation in reality. Relatively few southerners in 1860 were descended from Cavaliers, and even fewer Cavaliers could claim unmixed descent from those Norman barons of William the Conqueror. But these facts are irrelevant to a consideration of ethnic nationalism. As almost every student of this phenomenon has noted, ethnic nationalism is much more a subjective than an objective reality, an "invented tradition," an "imagined community," an instrumental construction of genealogy to serve cultural or political ends. This does not mean, however, that southerners who embraced the Norman-Cavalier myth did not believe it. Many of them appear to have been true believers. Like other myths at other times, it became a credo that defined the reality by which they lived.[24]

American civic nationalism was also constructed of symbols and myths. The most potent of them were associated with the generation that invented the republic in 1776, won its independence in 1783, and formed its government in 1789. In the eyes of most northerners in 1861, the breakup of the Union by southern secession threatened to destroy these achievements. Shortly after the Confederate attack on Fort Sumter, a Vermont newspaper published an editorial titled "What Is Our Government Worth?" "If one wishes to have even a faint idea of what this government cost," the editor declared, "let him go to Lexington and Concord, to [Bunker] Hill and Saratoga . . . Bennington and Yorktown . . . where the blood of our fathers flowed like water, as the price which was paid not simply for our liberty, but chiefly for our *Law,* for our Government."[25] In his first inaugural address, Lincoln invoked this heritage of civic nationalism in an appeal to southerners. "We must not be enemies," he said. "Though passion may have strained, it must not break our bonds of affection. The mystic chords of memory, stretching from every battlefield, and patriot grave, to every living heart and hearthstone, all over this broad land, will yet swell the chorus of the Union, when again touched, as surely they will be, by the better angels of our nature."[26]

The inventors of Confederate nationalism feared the power of such invocations of the South's own important share in those mystic chords of memory. To counter that appeal, they attempted to appropriate these memories and symbols for their version of ethnic nationalism. Judah P. Benjamin, the Confederacy's secretary of state, proposed "'a cavalier' copied from the equestrian statue of George Washington" in Richmond for the great seal of the Confederacy. "The cavalier or knight is typical of chivalry, bravery, generosity, humanity," wrote Benjamin, "and . . . is eminently suggestive of the origin of southern society, as used in contradistinction to Puritan." After the battle of Chancellorsville, in 1863, the Confederate envoy in Brussels boasted of the "invincible cavaliers" of the South "whose heroism overpowered three times their number of semi-barbarian Yankees" descended from Saxons and Puritans.[27] "The present conflict in America is not a *civil* strife, but a war of *Nationalities,*" proclaimed a Louisiana writer, "a war of alien races. . . . Cavalier and Roundhead no longer designate parties, but *nations,* whose separate foundations were laid on Plymouth Rock and the banks of the James River." The "warrior race" of Cavaliers "will found an empire, illustrious in arms, as renowned in arts, and show the Cavalier blood to be still worthy of its origins," declared another southern intellectual. When the "*inferior race*" of Saxon Yankees was "whipped, and *well whipped,*" the "Norman race [will] record, in America, what, with strong hand and ten centuries of dominion and power, it has written on the civilization of Europe."[28]

In the rhetoric of white Southerners, the word "Yankee" became an ethnic slur. A South Carolina woman frequently referred to "the calculating, money worshipping, cowardly Yankee race" as the essence of everything "dirty, low, cruel, wicked, mean."[29] The Anglo-Saxons of England, noted another southerner in 1863, had sprung from the Goths and Vandals of Europe who had destroyed the Roman Empire. By the similar behavior of Union soldiers in the South, he wrote, we see how "the terms Goth and Vandal" have been "condensed in the synonym Yankee."[30]

Most of the derogatory terms used by Southern journalists, political leaders, and Confederate soldiers to demonize the Yankee enemy carried ethnic overtones. They were not only Goths and Vandals; they were also "hordes of Northern Hessians," as numerous as the "hordes of Alaric the Visigoth and Attila" the Hun.[31] An educated sergeant in a Louisiana regiment, a schoolmaster before the war, managed to compare the Yankees with two different ethnic groups when he wrote of his "absolute hatred of the hyperborean vandals with whom we are waging a war for existence. . . . The Thugs of India will not bear a comparison. . . . I expect to murder every Yankee I ever meet when I can do so with impunity if I live a hundred years."[32]

In contrast with these ethnic terms, northerners demonized the enemy in words consistent with civic nationalism. They were "rebels," "traitors," an arrogant "aristocracy" of "miserable despots who are trying to destroy our country."[33] As General William T. Sherman's army entered South Carolina in 1865, one of the Union soldiers voiced contempt for the self-styled Carolina aristocrats who "can talk of nothing but purity of blood of themselves & their ancestors. . . . Their cant about aristocracy is perfectly sickening. . . . If you hear any condemning us for what we have done, tell them for me and for Sherman's army, that 'we found here the authors of all the calamities that have befallen this nation . . . and that their punishment is light when compared with what justice demanded.'"[34]

When General Robert E. Lee's surrender at Appomattox ended the Confederacy's bid to create a new nation, victorious northerners assumed that defeat would also put an end to southern claims of ethnic superiority grounded in alleged Norman-Cavalier ancestry. Secretary of the Navy Gideon Welles blamed the previous four years of slaughter on "the diseased imagination" of southerners "who some thirty or forty years since studied Scott's novels, and fancied themselves cavaliers. . . . They came ultimately to believe themselves a superior and better race, knights of blood and spirit. Only a war could wipe out this arrogance and folly."[35] Six years later, during the Franco-Prussian War, when France claimed to fight for something called the "Latin Race," the German-born American political scientist Francis Lieber ridiculed this claim as the same nonsense professed by southerners who claimed Norman descent. "Races are very often invented from ignorance, or for evil purposes," Lieber wrote in a passage that seems strikingly modern. "The rebels told us and each other again and again that they were a race totally different from the race of the North." This "pitiful attempt," declared Lieber, consisted of nothing more than "arbitrary maxims, vague conceits or metaphorical expressions."[36]

Vague and arbitrary it may have been, but such thinking did not disappear. On June 17, 1865, the seventy-two year-old Virginian Edmund Ruffin, an original secessionist who claimed to have fired the first gun against Fort Sumter, made a final entry in his diary, vowing "unmitigated hatred . . . to the perfidious, malignant, & vile Yankee race." He then put the barrel of a rifle in his mouth and blew out his brains.[37] Most Southrons did not respond so drastically to the bitter truth that the illustrious warrior race supposedly descended from Normans could not whip those churlish Saxon Yankees after all. Rather, they followed the advice of Edward Pollard, wartime editor of the *Richmond Examiner.* Pollard wrote the first history of the Confederacy, whose title, *The Lost Cause,* gave a label to the romantic glorification of those Cavaliers of 1861–65 that is still with us today. "There may not be a political South," Pollard acknowledged in 1866, but there can be "a social and intellectual South. . . . It would be immeasurably the worst consequence of defeat in this war that the South should lose its moral and intellectual distinctiveness as a people and cease to assert its well-known superiority in civilization over the people of the North."[38]

Few people think this way anymore. The outcome of the Civil War placed civic nationalism on a firm footing in the American polity and culture. But what of the "monstrous injustice of slavery" that violated the central tenet of civic nationalism—inclusive citizenship? Union victory abolished the institution and brought forth the "new birth of freedom" that Lincoln invoked at Gettysburg. In 1868 the Fourteenth Amendment to the Constitution remedied the most blatant defect in American civic nationalism with the words that "all persons born or naturalized in the United States" are citizens and that no state can "abridge the privileges or immunities of citizens" or "deny to any person within its jurisdiction the equal protection of the laws."

These phrases of the Fourteenth Amendment have had a profound impact on the course of civic nationalism in the United States. They provided the constitutional basis for desegregation decisions by the Supreme Court and for the civil rights legislation by Congress since the 1950s. They have also blunted the recurrent extrusions of ethnic nationalism that seek to deny citizenship to various categories of immigrants, including illegal immigrants, by ensuring that their children born in the United States would automatically become citizens.

Despite these achievements, the contest between civic and ethnic nationalism has obviously not ended—in the United States or elsewhere in the world. In the second decade of the twenty-first century, the words that Lincoln spoke in the middle of the nineteenth are as relevant today with respect to convictions of racial or ethnic superiority as they were then with respect to slavery: they deprive "our republican example of its just influence in the world" and enable "the enemies of free institutions, with plausibility, to taunt us as hypocrites."

NOTES

1. Paul R. Brass, *Ethnicity and Nationalism: Theory and Comparison* (Newbury Park, Cal.: Sage, 1991), 69.

2. Hans Kohn, *The Idea of Nationalism: A Study of Its Origins and Background* (New York: Macmillan, 1944), 10; Walker Connor, *Ethnonationalism: The Quest for Understanding* (Princeton: Princeton University Press, 1994), 4.

3. Michael Ignatieff, *Blood and Belonging: Journeys into the New Nationalism* (New York: Farrar, Straus and Giroux, 1993), 85–89; Eric J. Hobsbawm, *Nations and Nationalism since 1870* (Cambridge: Cambridge University Press, 1990), 12; John Hutchinson and Anthony D. Smith, eds., *Nationalism* (New York: Oxford University Press, 1994), 5.

4. Quoted in Liah Greenfeld, *Nationalism: Five Roads to Modernity* (Cambridge, Mass.: Harvard University Press, 1992), 435. See also Roy P. Basler, ed., *The Collected Works of Abraham Lincoln,* 9 vols. (New Brunswick, N.J.: Rutgers University Press, 1952–55), 2: 499–500.

5. Basler, *Collected Works of Lincoln,* 2: 499–500.

6. Ibid., 255.

7. Republicans quoted in Hans L. Trefousse, *The Radical Republicans: Lincoln's Vanguard for Racial Justice* (New York: Knopf, 1969), 86; Richard H. Sewell, *Ballots for Freedom: Antislavery Politics in the United States, 1837–1860* (New York: Oxford University Press, 1976), 269; Michael F. Holt, *The Political Crisis of the 1850s* (New York: John Wiley, 1978), 171.

8. Basler, *Collected Works of Lincoln,* 2: 323.

9. Quoted in John McCardell, *The Idea of a Southern Nation: Southern Nationalists and Southern Nationalism, 1830–1860* (New York: Norton, 1979), 170–71.

10. Charles C. Jones Jr., to Charles C. Jones, Jan. 28, 1861, in Robert Manson Myers, ed., *The Children of Pride: A True Story of Georgia and the Civil War* (New Haven: Yale University Press, 1972), 648; Iverson speech in Congress, 1860, *Congressional Globe,* 36 Cong., 2nd Sess. (1860–61), 12.

11. Alexis de Tocqueville, *Democracy in America,* trans. George Lawrence, ed. J. P. Mayer (New York: Harper and Row, 1966), 378.

12. A Scot quoted in Grady McWhiney, *Cracker Culture: Celtic Ways in the Old South* (Tuscaloosa: University of Alabama Press, 1988), 1; Englishman quoted in Rollin G. Osterweis, *Romanticism and Nationalism in the Old South* (New Haven: Yale University Press, 1949), 141. For more on parallels between Europe and southern nationalism see Paul Quigley, *Shifting Grounds: Nationalism and the American South, 1848–65* (New York: Oxford University Press, 2011), 16–49.

13. Tocqueville, *Democracy in America,* 348.

14. George E. Baker, ed., *The Works of William H. Seward* (New York: Redfield, 1861), 4: 289–92; Basler, *Collected Works of Lincoln,* 2: 461.

15. *Augusta Daily Constitutionalist,* March 30, 1861.

16. *Raleigh Register,* May 10, 1861.

17. *Richmond Enquirer,* March 16, 1863, November 2, 1864.

18. *Southern Literary Messenger,* June 1860, 404–5, 407.

19. *DeBow's Review,* February 1861, 162.

20. *DeBow's Review,* January 1861, 45–51.

21. Quoted in Osterweis, *Romanticism and Nationalism,* 101.

22. *Richmond Daily Dispatch,* February 7, March 23, 1863; Henry Timrod, "Ethnogenesis," in William Gilmore Simms, ed., *War Poetry of the South* (New York: Richardson, 1867), 7–11.

23. *Southern Literary Messenger*, 30 (June 1860), 403, 409; 31 (November 1860), 349; 33 (July 1861), 19 ; (August 1861), 106; *DeBow's Review*, 31 (October-November 1861), 393.

24. Eric J. Hobsbawm and Terence Ranger, eds., The *Invention of Tradition* (Cambridge: Cambridge University Press, 1983; Benedict Anderson, *Imagined Communities: Reflections on the Origin and Spread of Nationalism* (London: Verso, 1983). Robert B. Bonner, "Roundheaded Cavaliers? The Context and Limits of a Confederate Racial Project," *Civil War History* 48 (March 2002): 34–59, argues that the Norman-Cavalier theme faded in Confederate writings in 1863 and after. But Ritchie Devon Watson Jr., *Normans and Saxons: Southern Race Mythology and the Intellectual History of the American Civil War* (Baton Rouge: Louisiana State University Press, 2008), sees it persisting to the end of the war and, in some respects, even afterward. See also Michael T. Bernath, *Confederate Minds: The Struggle for Intellectual Independence in the Civil War South* (Chapel Hill: University of North Carolina Press, 2010), 57–60.

25. *Vermont Watchman and State Journal,* April 26, 1861, in Howard C. Perkins, ed., *Northern Editorials on Secession,* 2 vols. (New York: D. Appleton-Century Co., 1952), 2: 751–53.

26. Basler, *Collected Works of Lincoln*, 4:271.

27. Judah P. Benjamin to Clement C. Clay, January 22, 1863; A. Dudley Mann to Judah P. Benjamin, June 25, 1863, *Official Records of the Union and Confederate Navies* (Washington, D.C.: Government Princeton Office, 1894–1922), ser. 2, vol. 3, 668–69, 819.

28. *Southern Literary Messenger*, 33 (July 1861), 21; *DeBow's Review*, 31 (July 1861), 72, 73, 75; 32 (Jan.–Feb. 1862), 9, 19.

29. C. Rebecca Burkmyer to Cornelius L. Burkmyer, July 10, 1863, November 4, 1864, Charlotte R. Holmes, ed., *Burkmyer Letters, March 1863–June 1865* (Columbia, S.C.: The State Co., 1926), 75–76, 413.

30. *Southern Literary Messenger,* November–December 1863, 686.

31. *New Orleans Bee,* May 1, 1861, in Dwight Lowell Dumond, ed., *Southern Editorials on Secession* (New York: The Century Co., 1931), 513; *DeBow's Review,* 30 (May–June 1861), 681.

32. Edwin H. Fay to Sarah Fay, June 27, September 19, 1863, Bell Irvin Wiley, ed., *"This Infernal War": The Confederate Letters of Sgt. Edwin H. Fay* (Austin: University of Texas Press, 1958), 286–87, 329.

33. A. D. Pratt to Charles C. Murdock, February 16, 1863, Murdock Papers, Illinois State Historical Library.

34. George M. Wise to John Wise, March 13, 1865, Wilfred W. Black, ed., "Civil War Letters of George M. Wise," *Ohio Historical Quarterly* 46 (April 1957): 193.

35. Howard K. Beale, ed., *Diary of Gideon Welles*, 3 vols. (New York: Norton, 1960), 2: 276–77, entry for April 7, 1865

36. Francis Lieber, "The Latin Race," letter published in the *New York Evening Post*, 1871, reprinted in Lieber, *Contributions to Political Science* (Philadelphia: Lippincott, 1881), 108–9.

37. William K. Scarborough, ed., *The Diary of Edmund Ruffin* (Baton Rouge: Louisiana State University Press, 1989), 3: 946.

38. Edward A. Pollard, *The Lost Cause: A New Southern History of the War of the Confederates* (New York: E. B. Treat, 1866), 751.

DAVID T. GLEESON

Proving Their Loyalty to the Republic

English Immigrants and the American Civil War

On April 23, 1861, the members of the long-established St. George's Society of New York City were holding their annual banquet in honor of their patron, St. George, at the St. Nicholas Hotel. The society represented the elite of their immigrant community in New York, and the distinguished guests included Her Majesty Queen Victoria's consul and the Episcopal (Anglican) vicar of Trinity Church in Manhattan (where founding father George Washington had worshipped). As usual, toasts were made to the day they celebrated, to Queen Victoria, and to their homeland across the Atlantic Ocean. Despite the title of the article covering this event, "The English Feeling," this year it had more of an American tone. The Reverend Alexander Hamilton Vinton of Trinity Church gave a hint of the difference by arriving at the dinner with, "like many others, the badge of the Union" on his lapel.[1]

The banquet was taking place less than two weeks after the firing on Fort Sumter, and the English attendees were keen to show their loyalty to the Union in its hour of need. The normally perfunctory toast to the president of the United States was made extraordinary this time. There were "nine cheers" in response to the toast to Lincoln, "our illustrious President." The chairman of ceremonies recognized that the president was taking "office in no times of ordinary difficulties" but added that "every American and loyal British heart will be with him in this crisis." In response to the toast, the Reverend Vinton went further, stating that the "present contest" was a "conflict of civilizations; the one the travail of generations that had come before us, coming from England in revolutionary times, and transmitted by the ancestors of the Queen, whose image we have before us . . . transmitted again by our fathers in the constitution of the United States of America." The division was deeper than American and English heritage, however. Vinton continued: "The Word of God had proclaimed to man that by the sweat of his brow he should eat bread; but the inauguration of the present rebellion which was threatening the Union was based on the notion instigated by the Prince of Darkness, that man should not eat bread by the sweat of his own brow, but by the sweat of others." Southerners thus had "no power to sustain their mechanical arts"; they would have "to look abroad for support and could get it only by piracy at sea and fraud on land." Vinton concluded: "All Europe would join in the toast to President Lincoln" and oppose "secession as a demoniac idea which should be overthrown at once." Vinton's reply, according to the correspondent recording the meeting, was met with "immense applause," and the band struck up "Yankee Doodle."[2]

There was one discordant note, however, when a former president of the society, one Dr. Beale, while "agreeing heartily with all the sentiments of the previous speakers on the crisis," also "condemned the introduction of political matter [to] the festive board" and noted that in "thirty years he had never heard American politics discussed at the St. George's dinner." Beale's intervention caused some debate, with some supporting but others "hissing" his comments. The sitting president and the first vice president of the society attacked Beale's negativity, pointing out that "no Englishman with his inherent love of liberty could sit tamely still and not allude to a subject so vital to their interests as American residents."[3] The situation was too serious to sit on the fence.

Despite Beale's protest, American politics had always been a part of English lives in America. The United States had defined itself in opposition to Great Britain from its founding. The attack on the early Federalists, for example, and what eventually destroyed them was their perceived closeness to Britain and British values.[4] Later, during the Jacksonian period, the president for whom the era was named had entered the national scene after "killing 2,500 Englishmen" at the Battle of New Orleans in January 1815. His anti-English feeling ran deep, as his Irish mother (according to his official campaign biographers) regaled him with stories of Britain's poor treatment of Ireland, including the sufferings of his "grandfather, at the siege of Carrickfergus [County Antrim], and the oppressions exercised by the nobility of Ireland over the labouring poor."[5] "Anglophobia" played an important role in the politics of Jacksonian America.[6] Tensions between America and Britain rose to a new height in the 1840s over Texas and particularly Oregon, although the crisis over the latter was eventually settled in 1846 by treaty rather than force. Nevertheless, attacking Britain remained a popular element of American politics, especially in the press, throughout the antebellum era.[7] The leading Whig and, later, Republican politician William Henry Seward, for example, expressed a feeling held by many that Britain "was the greatest, the most rapacious, and the most grasping" nation on the earth.[8] The fact that English societies made toasts to a foreign sovereign, a sovereign who did not accept any disavowal of loyalty and whose government refused to recognize foreign naturalization, only called into question the true loyalty of English immigrants to the United States.[9] Unfavorable coverage of the United States by English stalwarts such as Charles Dickens exacerbated the differences between the two countries, and English establishment opinion could still be condescending toward the American republic and its "governmental inadequacy."[10]

It should be no surprise, then, that English immigrants, just like the Irish and others and perhaps even more markedly, needed the sectional conflict to confirm their bona fides as Americans. Scholars, though, have in general downplayed and discounted English ethnicity in the United States. Even on the precipice of World War II, when new histories emphasizing the importance of foreign contributions to the United States were written as the country looked to unify after the anti-immigrant hysteria of the 1920s, the English could be left out of the story. Carl Wittke in his popular *We Who Built America,* published in 1939, deliberately omitted the English because they were the original settlers and thus ignored the later immigrants who came after American independence. The English, according to Wittke and others, created the American society into which others assimilated. New English immigrants thus found American culture very compatible with their own. Modern scholars of ethnicity have continued the theme, despite work by the likes of Rowland Berthoff, Charlotte Erickson, and William Van Vugt, who examined British immigrants in America and illustrated the difficulty many had in integrating.[11] Specialists on the history of ethnicity, for example, argue that ethnicity in the United States was defined by foreign immigrants in an attempt to negotiate with "the dominant ethnoculture, in this case, the Anglo American." According to this narrative, the whole process of American ethnic identity originated in the "interactions" between immigrants and the "Anglo American culture," which could be competitive, cooperative, or conflictual and perhaps a combination of all three. These encounters "are seen as essential components of the process of ethnic group formation and definition." English culture, immigrant or otherwise, is thus considered integral to, not apart from, the hegemonic host culture. Ultimately, for the nineteenth century, the main period of ethnic formation in America, scholars have perpetuated the notion that the "English had no ethnicity in American eyes."[12]

Those few who have recognized some English ethnicity usually found it in working-class movements in mill towns, such as Fall River, Massachusetts. English workers who arrived in the antebellum United States often brought with them skills gained through work in the well-established Industrial Revolution back home in England. During economic downturns, thousands of industrial workers left for the nascent industries of the northeastern United States, attracted by the demand for their skills, better opportunities to buy property, and the potential to become mill operators or even owners. Exploiting mercantile connections between the United States and the north of England (particularly Lancashire and Yorkshire), some English mill workers achieved extraordinary success. The Dobson brothers, who arrived in Philadelphia in the 1850s armed with little more than their experience of having worked in a Lancashire mill since childhood, quickly became overseers and, later, partners in and owners of what would become the Imperial Woolen Company.[13] Those who did not meet with immediate success or who found the unregulated nature of American industrial capitalism too much turned to labor reform to fix the new situations. Complaints echoed those made by a Yorkshire migrant, Thomas Moseley, to a Pennsylvania state government investigation committee that "the operation of the factory system upon persons employed is more oppressive in this country than in England. In the first place, they work longer hours here; in the next place, the climate here is not so congenial to health."[14]

Many had also experienced the turmoil of the various political reform movements such as Chartism and were used to protesting what they saw as unjust conditions. English workers were thus often at the forefront of movements organizing unions and campaigns for the ten-hour day. They used techniques honed in England when setting up cooperatives, going on strike, and so on in their new positions in America. Influenced by their English experiences, they were in some ways expressing an English ethnic heritage. The reality of organized working-class movements in the United States was, however, that they needed to be multiethnic in character to succeed. The New England mill towns, for example, had English, Irish, Scottish, and native-born workers. To be successful, then, you could not be too explicit in promoting a purely "English" movement. Ethnic chauvinism would doom any labor effort to failure. In an 1848 strike in Fall River, for example, English labor organizers made sure that they appealed to all the ethnicities working in the mills, seeking supporters to appeal to their respective kinsmen and women. Unions that might have begun as ethnically exclusive organizations realized quickly when a new ethnic element came into the workforce that if they could not be excluded through bans on immigration, they would have to be absorbed into the labor movement.[15]

Ultimately, then, English ethnicity remained muted. As David Gerber, the historian of ethnic groups in Buffalo, New York, has put it, English immigrants, if they ever did express ethnicity in their correspondence, did so "more in terms of difference from others (and strong disapproval of those differences), rather than in terms of affirmations of affiliation or peoplehood; the latter nonetheless remained implicit in these judgments." Englishness, therefore, was a negative rather than a positive ethnicity. "To work at discovering who one is not suggests at some level a simultaneous effort to define identification for oneself. In this sense, their ethnicity was less an encompassing way of life, as it was for latecomers such as Poles or Italians, who were significantly culturally distinctive from the founding British-Canadian and Anglo-American populations, than a subtle process of difference among peoples and an appreciation of what was one's own."[16]

It is easy, then, for scholars to subscribe to the idea that "the English had no ethnicity in American eyes."

This hidden nature of English ethnicity was present during the Civil War in industrial cities, where Englishness was not as conspicuous as in the St. George Societies. Charles Schofield, a textile mill owner in Manayunk, Pennsylvania, and an immigrant from Oldham in Lancashire, for example, twice organized companies of soldiers to protect his adopted state from attack by Confederate forces (during General Robert E. Lee's Maryland and Gettysburg campaigns in 1862 and 1863, respectively). His patriotism was matched by his workforce, which also included English immigrants, who sewed large American flags for him. The local newspapers covered these displays of patriotism but described them as examples of the local support from the textile businesses for the war effort rather than as an English effort. The English aspect of the story had become lost. Even the scholar who discovered this episode analyzes it in terms of transference of British industrial paternalism to the United States and not as an example of English immigrants' attempt to fit into the United States.[17] Again, Englishness seemed to blend into Americanness.

Yet the English who could not easily submerge their English ethnicity under an American one were those who were part of English societies. English ethnic societies expressed not just a negative version of ethnicity through private correspondence but an open and positive version of Englishness in very public ways. These societies were dedicated to St. George, the patron saint of England, whose flag, the St. George's Cross, is England's flag and its representative on the Union Jack. A study of the reaction to the outbreak of the Civil War of English associations like the St. George's Society of New York counters the view that the English had no explicit/public ethnicity and also that they assimilated easily.[18] Indeed, they may have had more trouble integrating into the American mainstream than some of their fellow European immigrants, if not in a cultural sense, then definitely in a political one. Embracing Englishness at the beginning of the Civil War could be problematic. The British consul in New York, Edward Archibald, provides evidence of an open hostility to Englishness at the beginning of the war. Although sympathetic to the Union cause, he claimed just after the war began that it was safe to describe oneself as "Scots, Irish or Welsh but not British or English."[19]

Along with the traditional use of England/Britain as the "other" in the United States' image of itself as a republic, Queen Victoria's call in May 1861 on behalf of her government for the United Kingdom to remain neutral in the conflict (in the process granting belligerent status to the Confederacy) increased anti-English feeling. The neutrality proclamation was a very disappointing outcome for the U.S. government, which had hoped that Britain would acknowledge the conflict as merely an illegal insurrection. One prominent New York newspaper saw the queen's declaration and the possibility that Great Britain would break a federal blockade of southern ports as a de facto *"casus belli."* Only a few months earlier, the same newspaper had recognized the St. George's Society meeting described earlier as an "'enthusiastically American' gathering" where "the rebellion of the South was strongly and eloquently denounced." The Reverend Vinton's comments drew particular notice, especially his description of secession as a "demoniac idea" that had to be "overthrown at once." Thus, after an auspicious start in which they were recognized as "enthusiastic 'Americans,'" the English based in the North found their lives quickly becoming particularly difficult as popular opinion there began to assume that the British government was on the side of the Confederacy.[20]

The neutrality declaration caused other potential problems for the English in America. It forbade all British subjects to take a side in the conflict, especially in a military sense. As already mentioned, Britain did not recognize the naturalization of its subjects in the United States, and thus all British subjects in the United States, no matter how long they had lived there and whether or not they had become American citizens, were not to join any army. The queen's Irish subjects and some Scots, however, seem to have ignored the admonition and formed specific units in both armies.[21] Some English did try to form an English company in Massachusetts, but nothing came of it. A more formal effort happened in New York, but the "British Regiment" failed to take off, and its couple of English-dominated companies merged into the Thirty-Sixth New York Infantry, along with some Irish companies. This failure was the result of active discouragement by the British government; sympathetic though he was to the Union cause, Edward Archibald opposed efforts to form a specific British unit.[22]

Although individual Englishmen in the Thirty-Sixth were recognized as valuable officers who had served in the "English army," the regiment was never seen as a purely English unit. The regiment served for two years, acting with particular distinction (in the local press's eyes anyway) at the Seven Days battles in the summer of 1862 and at the Battle of Chancellorsville in May 1863. Its soldiers mustered out, having completed their two-year service in the summer of 1863. Inside the unit, the Englishness of some of the companies was well known, leading to conflicts between the Irish and the English soldiers. The conflict became so intense that some English soldiers went to the Seventy-Ninth New York "Highlander" Infantry, finding the Scottish regiment a better home than the "British" Thirty-Sixth. Apart from the acknowledgment of the English experience of some of the officers, the regiment never gained the ethnic cachet of Thomas Francis Meagher's "Irish Brigade" or the "German" Eleventh Corps in the Army of the Potomac or, indeed, of the "Highlanders." Beyond these unsuccessful efforts in New York and Massachusetts, English immigrants elsewhere in the North, unlike their "British" cousins in Scotland and Ireland, seem to have taken the queen's order seriously and did not form any specific ethnic companies. (The St. George's Society in Cleveland, it seems, did inquire into the recruitment rules, forming a committee "to learn the particulars and laws that govern military organizations of the State," but nothing concrete seems to have come from the inquiry.) Military service, a key component to citizenship in nineteenth-century America, allowed other ethnic groups to claim an American identity equal to that of natives. The absence of specifically English units meant that English immigrants lacked an important tool for integration.[23]

The public effort to prove English immigrants' loyalty to the United States without actually serving would fall, then, to the English societies. The Philadelphia Sons of St. George Society, for example, took advantage of the death of Colonel E. D. Baker at the Battle of Ball's Bluff in October 1861. The battle and Baker's death in it were a severe shock to the nation and led to serious congressional oversight of the war effort with the foundation of the Joint Committee on the Conduct of the War. Baker had lived in Philadelphia and raised a regiment there when war broke out. On his death, the state of Pennsylvania allowed his body to lie in state in Independence Hall, and the city made a major effort to commemorate the fallen hero. The Society was quick to remind everyone, however, that Baker had been born in "merry England." It adopted a series of resolutions and had them read into the minutes of the City Council. In these the Society's members acknowledged the grief they felt at the loss of their "fellow countryman" who had died in a "heroic charge against the rebels." The members also recognized the loss his death inflicted on his fellow troops. Finally, they sent their condolences to his family. They also believed that his sacrifice had a much wider significance. Baker was a "practical illustration of the superior opportunities afforded by the democratic institutions of this country to every naturalized citizen to attain the highest honors—after the Presidency itself—in the gift of the government and people of the United States." Ultimately the life and death of Baker, "in the dark hour of his adopted country's peril, merits the honor and emulation of his surviving fellow citizens."[24]

The fact that Baker had moved to America at about age four and spent only nine years of his childhood in Philadelphia before moving west with his family (he eventually made it to California) did not matter. He was an English role model for all Americans, native or not.[25] He was a son of England who had died in the American cause of liberty, and the Philadelphia English were only too glad to claim him. Other English societies that could not claim famous naturalized heroes instead held benefits and dances to collect money for soldiers' aid societies to highlight their support for the cause.[26] These early demonstrations of solidarity had some effect, helping to separate English Americans from the policy of their government across the Atlantic.

Immigrant Baker's heroics, however, were not of much use to English immigrants when Great Britain and the United States almost came to war over the *Trent* Affair in December 1861. In November the USS *San Jacinto* had stalked and intercepted a British mail packet, the *Trent,* on its way from Cuba to Britain and arrested two Confederate agents on board, James Mason and John Slidell. Britain protested the firing upon and boarding of the *Trent* and declared the seizure of the Confederate commissioners illegal. Her Majesty's government demanded the release of the southerners. To back up their protest, Britain sent troops to Canada and halted saltpeter sales to the United States. War fever gripped the United States, and Irish Americans, as well as Irish nationalists in Ireland, were certainly excited about it.[27]

Armed conflict was eventually averted, but it must have been difficult to be a member of one of the various St. George Societies during this period.[28] Toasting the queen and singing "God Save the Queen" and "Rule Britannia" would not have been a safe thing to do anymore. It was, nonetheless, the English associations that had the opportunity to restore English reputations in America at their next St. George's Day celebration, in 1862. The Cleveland St. George's Society, for example, added a religious element to its celebrations for the first time. The members gathered at Trinity Episcopal Church, where, along with collecting money for soldiers and their families, the resident pastor, one T. A. Starkey, sought to minimize the recent tensions between the English and Americans. He reminded the congregants of the inherent compatibility between the English and the Americans. He spoke of their "great similarities in race, manners, religion, literature, habits, and tones of thought." They had the "same Bible, read the same authors, acknowledge[d] the same principles of Common Law, and even sang the same lullabies to their children." Indeed, Starkey believed: "No two nations in the world so resembled each other in nearly every important particular as Great Britain and America." He concluded that Americans and Englishmen were "brethren" and "they should be brethren in love." This love, of course, had not existed just four months earlier, and Starkey acknowledged this fact and tried to explain the incongruity. "The estrangement that frequently exists between the Americans and the English in this country [the United States] arises from the fact that the English are a particularly domestic people having their affections centred on home, no matter what the conditions of that home." Thus, English immigrants were fussy when they came to America, "extremely sensitive to everything that was different from what they have been accustomed to, feeling annoyed by it, and shrinking from further contact with it." While "no people in this country are more free from combination in political matters, no people isolate themselves so thoroughly socially." The only solution was for English immigrants to mix more with their American neighbors, to "cross the threshold of

American houses, and make themselves more acquainted with American home life." If they did so, they would lose some of their "prejudices," and "at the same time they would be better understood by Americans."[29] Starkey had recognized that the English, despite their lack of political organization, still felt like an ethnic minority. They needed to get over their personal ethnic feelings if they were to integrate fully into American society.

Later that evening, at the social event of the day, the attempted rapprochement continued. The flag of the United States and the flag of England flew together outside the event site. In a speech in answer to the usual toast of "the queen," the Reverend C. C. Cooley, another Anglican minister from the city, spoke of the similarities between Magna Carta and the Declaration of Independence. "The Charta, which was English, was the germ, and the bold declaration that 'all men are born free and equal,' which was the outgrowth of the germ, was American." Thus, almost fifty years before Rudyard Kipling's charge to the United States to take up the "white man's burden," Cooley believed that England and America had to spread their values of "liberty," "Christianity," and "civilization" to the world, "England in the East—America in the West." England needed to keep its "monarchical" government as it took on the "mighty task of bringing the effete empires of the Old World under her more liberal and Christian rule." America too could keep its republican system, and it was "*entirely true* that on *this* Western continent, where men are flocking from all parts of the world, the war cloud which seemed a little while ago arousing between the two countries suddenly disappeared and they are at perfect peace." English Americans it seems, had gotten over the incident, even if England had not. The *Trent* affair, which was never directly mentioned throughout the day, was a mere family spat that had been solved with ease.[30]

The English citizens of Cleveland therefore wanted to reestablish signs of their loyalty to the republic just a few months after their two countries had almost gone to war. In this effort they had a trump card in their integration pack—their support for emancipation. Loyalty to the queen almost automatically meant loyalty to her government's policy ending slavery in British colonies and enforcing the slave-trade ban along the African coast. Now that "perfect peace" had been established between the United Kingdom and the United States, the English in America could help their native neighbors in establishing "peace at home." How would they achieve the end of war? By "the *final removal* of the cause of our terrible fratricidal war." The English Americans of Cleveland called for "the unchaining of all *God's yeomen*."[31] These immigrants were putting themselves at the forefront of the movement for emancipation.

At the beginning of the war President Lincoln had forbidden any attempts at immediate emancipation and, to the frustration of many abolitionists such as Frederick Douglass, seemed to be ignoring what the war was about. In August

1861, for example, he chastised and then eventually removed General John C. Fremont, his predecessor as the Republican nominee for the presidency and the federal commander in Missouri, for proclaiming the emancipation of slaves there. The reality of the war, however, soon forced the issue as slaves began to run away to Union forces in the South. Congress responded with the Confiscation Act, which made runaway slaves from Confederate owners contraband of war and the property of the federal government. Congress strengthened the act in March 1862, forbidding any military officers to return slaves to their owners (which some had been doing). The writing seemed on the wall for slavery, but, as late as May 1862, Lincoln's official position was against emancipation when he reversed General David Hunter's order emancipating slaves on the Union-occupied Sea Islands near Beaufort, South Carolina.[32] English Americans in the North, however, seemed clear on the role of slavery in the war. The conflict was not just about the Union but about something much larger, as the Reverend Vinton of New York had stated just after Fort Sumter in his Manichean description of the two sides. The English hoped that "England and America [would] shake hands over an emancipated race they both helped to enslave and refreshed with a new and *unfettered* spirit of liberty, [and would] go on in their own spheres to the accomplishment of their *one* great mission—to advance and perfect civil and religious liberty all over the world."[33]

The emphasis on words like "final removal," "unfettered," and "one" (in reference to the great mission of spreading liberty) highlights that English leaders in America saw themselves and their homeland as elements in fulfilling America's destiny. Their ethnic heritage connected them directly to the heightened civic nationalism of the United States in the Civil War. The Constitution and various compromises since independence had not ended slavery. Indeed, the "peculiar institution" had flourished and had now torn the country apart. England, rather than being the other to which America was always contrasted, was really an ally of the republic and its raison d'être, liberty. Lincoln's Emancipation Proclamation, in September 1862, seemed to vindicate this vision of an Anglo-American world dedicated to its version of Anglo-Saxon liberty. In 1863 the St. George's Society of Cleveland felt that England's example had finally been taken up by America. "Greater than the victories of Waterloo and Trafalgar," one speaker noted, "were those victories over selfishness and oppression, the emancipation of her slaves and Colonial freedom." He then linked the greatness of England to the growing greatness of America: "The highest and proudest boast that England could possibly make is that the shackles fall from the slave whenever he touches British soil." He reminded America: "Let a nation boast of its greatness and power, but let that greatness and power be tempered with liberty and justice." England's "proudest boast," of course, referred to the 1772 decision made by Justice Lord Mansfield in the *Somersett* case, which had declared freedom the natural condition of man and described slavery as "odious." The United States had finally recognized this truth in the Civil War, and it went hand in hand with its "greatness and power."[34]

By 1863 the English associations had become full members of the war effort, and the *Trent* affair was forgotten (at least in public). The Milwaukee society, for example, felt comfortable inviting General John Pope, now commander of Union forces in the West (after his poor performance at the Second Battle of Manassas in August 1862). Pope could not attend but sent his best wishes. The society's members, and other English immigrants in the United States, also sought to preempt any other potential troubles between the mother country and their new home. The Milwaukee group, for example, held collections to ease the "cotton famine" in Lancashire. The Confederacy's cotton embargo and the blockade had hit the textile mills of northwest England hard, resulting in thousands of workers losing their jobs and facing severe hardship. Confederates hoped that the economic troubles in the textile industry would force Britain to recognize their new nation and break the Union blockade of southern ports. Union supporters among the English and natives alike worried about it, too, and collected food and money in the eastern cities of the United States.[35] St. George Societies had traditionally collected and distributed funds to immigrants in distress in America. But, along with aiding their compatriots at home, there was an American motive to their philanthropy. The Milwaukee call for help concluded: "Let us remember that every dollar contributed and every barrel of flour to our distressed brethren across the water, are more powerful arguments in dissipating prejudice and shaming the evil disposed, than the finest words of eloquence or the most convincing logic." Actions spoke louder than words. They would help the American cause in Britain, and the society forwarded the money it collected to the international relief committee in New York for transmission across the Atlantic.[36]

This aid sent to Britain definitely had an effect and led to prominent speeches in the mill districts in favor of the United States, helping restore the positive view of the country that some English reformers had lost in the 1840s because, even though "American labour had gained its own voice and press," it "had refused to condemn slavery."[37] To the English in Britain, it seems that, as the St. George's Society of Cleveland had indicated, the United States was finally living up to its rhetoric of liberty. Their loyalty to the Republic seemed secure, too. The Cleveland society felt confident enough in 1864 to sing the English "Our National Defences." The chorus went: "Then rally round the standard—that ne'er has conquered been—St. George, for merry, merry England—our altar, and the Queen." The rather rousing chorus, however, was overshadowed by the first verse, which warned those who listened about "Our national defences, but traitors are they—Who dare assert that Britain's power had passed or waned away—While peace shed her blessing, and commerce claim her right—Old England still has manly hearts to guard her in the fight." One could not see this song being safely sung in late 1861 or early 1862 in the shadow of conflict between Britain and America. The Cleveland toast to "England and America" celebrated the differences between the "trim hedge-rows" of England and the "open prairies" of America. The latter was more expansive, and that was a good thing. One speaker mentioned that he was the "expansive" American "by day" and an Englishman "at night" when he dreamed of "the pleasant home of his childhood in England." American growth would continue, and one day "the dear old flag of the United States might soon again wave over every inch of its territory." This sentiment was followed with a toast to William Shakespeare and then one to the "City of Cleveland, our adopted home." The response to the latter included the singing of a military song, "Strike While the Iron Is Hot." "Strike while the iron is hot, put the matter through" the chorus went; "Up with the bonny flag, the Red, White, and Blue." It also called on people to remember "Vicksburgh [*sic*] and Gettysburgh [*sic*] bright and glorious days—To the heroes of each, Grant the Meade of praise—On till the struggle's o'er, traitors know their doom—Strike, strike in freedom's name, and end the matter soon."[38]

The English Ohioans, then, did not advocate compromise with the Confederacy, like many in the southern part of their adopted state, but continued prosecution of the war. Ohio was a center of "Copperheadism" and the home of its leading exponent, Clement Vallandigham. Vallandigham and his supporters had violently opposed the Emancipation Proclamation and the war effort. The English of Cleveland were therefore more supportive of the war and of President Lincoln and his Republican administration than many natives were.[39] At war's end they could proudly claim to have supported the Union cause to the hilt, and they took an active part in the official mourning for Abraham Lincoln. They had proved their loyalty to the republic and integrated their Englishness into American society.[40]

Are these displays of American patriotism by the elite members of St. George Societies representative of a larger English feeling? English mill operatives in Fall River, Massachusetts, joined some of their Irish colleagues in the Union Guard company for U.S. service even though they received a much smaller signing bonus and less support than predominantly native-born companies did. They served as part of the Seventh Massachusetts Infantry, which became, according to one chronicler, "one of the best regiments in the army," serving in the eastern theater of the war until their three-year term expired in July 1864.[41]

Assessing motives, however, is difficult. Were Englishmen inspired to join the Union army by the federal government's move to emancipation? Robert Bower, a mill worker from Lawrence, Massachusetts, may have been. A native of Cheshire, he had worked in the Lancashire textile mills from age seven, emigrating in his twenties to Massachusetts. He was something of a radical, having been involved in labor agitation back in England. In 1862, perhaps inspired by the added focus on ending slavery, he joined the Fiftieth Massachusetts, even though wages were high in the Lawrence mills during the war. Instead of working at home in Massachusetts, he found himself fighting in the swamps and bayous of the Lower Mississippi River valley and south Louisiana. After serving through the war (beyond his regiment's mustering out of service in August 1863), he returned to Massachusetts with an even greater zeal for reform and became a prominent advocate of the ten-hour-day, supporting strikes to achieve it and workers' rights in general.[42]

The Emancipation Proclamation may also have inspired other Englishmen already in service. Francis Patrick, a native of Willerby, Yorkshire, enrolled in the Union army in January, 1864, serving in the Second New York Heavy Artillery at the siege of Petersburg the following summer. Although he wanted "this thing [the war]" to end as soon as possible, as it had "run long enough," nonetheless he was going "to vote for old [A]be again" even though a victory by George McClellan in the November presidential election would have ended the war immediately.[43]

Evidence of a hegemonic role for the avidly English bourgeoisie of the St. George Societies, as has been claimed for the respectable Irish middle classes in America, is scanty.[44] The societies represented the elite of the English community, made up mostly, it seems, of merchants and professionals. They did dispense a lot of charity and usually helped hundreds and even thousands in their benevolent efforts. The "Sons of St. George" may have been more representative than their relative numbers suggest.[45] For the purposes of this essay, however, their existence and their experience are more important than their exact role as ethnic leaders. They were very visible members of the English community, with their portraits of the queen and their British flags hanging from the awnings of their places of celebration. Thus, this examination into the English in America around their day of celebration gives an invaluable insight into the ethnic lives of English immigrants in the United States. Wars hone senses of national identity and give foreign elements a great opportunity to show their allegiance publicly to their host country.[46] The English in America did not fit seamlessly into the "Anglo-American" norm and had to work at integration. They did not have the advantages of the Irish, for example, who had abandoned their allegiance to a foreign power and embraced American politics. It was easier to toast an Ireland in bondage than an England that had a queen and a government that seemed to be the antithesis of American republicanism. The near outbreak of military hostilities between England and America in 1861 only heightened the differences. The fact that well-off immigrants who were well connected in their host cities felt the need to celebrate their Englishness and to find a niche for it in American society indicates how necessary it was for all English to make themselves acceptable in the American republic.

What the war did, however, was allow the middle-class immigrants of the St. George Societies to reclaim an English political connection with the United States. From an initial ethnic standpoint they forged a strong link to America's civic nationalism. Therefore, the Philadelphia St. George men could in 1863 toast "England—the land of our birth," not for its differences from the United States in terms of political system or economic power but as the "the land of religious and civil liberty," a land of "liberty" just like the United States. They had no problem in, as usual, recognizing Queen Victoria (though she appeared later in the order of toasts this year) but also toasting the "memory of [George] Washington" as well as the "Army and Navy of the United States." Washington and the U.S. military were cast not as destroyers of the empire and British power but as "noble, daring" men to whom "freemen everywhere shall weave chaplets of their fame."[47] There was nothing incongruous in being both English and American, not because of a common language or because English people were automatically Americans but because the trials of war had reestablished the political heritage that defined "Englishmen" specifically (and differently from their Celtic compatriots in the United Kingdom) as lovers of liberty, just like Americans.

In conclusion, the Civil War gives scholars a great opportunity to examine American immigrant integration and highlights the fact that wars do not automatically mean an easy path to acceptance in a host society. These global issues of ethnicity, immigration, and assimilation, examined through the prism of America's bloodiest conflict, indicate that integration of immigrants can ebb and flow as circumstances change. At the beginning of the conflict the English were suspect and needed to highlight their support for the cause in visibly public ways. As the focus of the war shifted toward emancipation, however, English Americans could lead in the embrace of the cause, far more so, for example, than the Irish. Irish Americans' reaction to emancipation was generally very negative, and even though Englishmen may have been reluctant to join the army, at least they did not oppose the war effort as the Irish of New York City did in the infamous draft riot of July 1863. The actions of the rioters, particularly against blacks, sullied the reputation of the Irish among Union supporters and considerably reduced the goodwill generated by noteworthy Irish sacrifices on the battlefield.[48] Indeed, English political traditions around Magna Carta and in support of political reform could be the key to understanding English integration into American society. While toasts to the queen may have seemed incompatible with being a true American, belief in political progress and support for the end of slavery could reestablish the transatlantic affection broken by the American Revolution and decades of England baiting. Further study into English-American ethnic associations and their members will only deepen our knowledge of English ethnicity in America and help us understand better the nature of American national identity itself in the mid-nineteenth century.

NOTES

1. *New York Herald,* April 30, 1861.

2. Ibid.

3. Ibid.

4. Gordon S. Wood, *An Empire for Liberty: A History of the Early Republic, 1783–1815* (New York: Oxford University Press, 2009), 53–54, 84, 243–46, 692–96.

5. Quoted in Jon Meacham, *American Lion: Andrew Jackson in the White House* (New York: Random House 2008), 11.

6. Sam W. Haynes, *Unfinished Revolution: The Early American Republic in a British World* (Charlottesville: University of Virginia Press, 2010), chapter 5.

7. See Howard Jones and Donald A. Rakestraw, *Prologue to Manifest Destiny: Anglo-American Relations in the 1840s* (Wilmington, Del.: Rowman and Littlefield, 1997); Frederick Merk, *The Oregon Question: Essays in Anglo-American Diplomacy* (Cambridge, Mass.: Harvard University Press, 1967); Martin Crawford, *The Anglo-American Crisis of the Mid-Nineteenth Century: The Times and America, 1850–1862* (Athens: University of Georgia Press, 1987).

8. Quoted in Howard Jones, *Blue and Gray Diplomacy: A History of Union and Confederate Foreign Relations* (Chapel Hill: University of North Carolina, 2010), 22.

9. For a good synopsis of the controversy over British nonrecognition of American naturalization see Christian G. Samito, *Becoming American under Fire: Irish Americans, African Americans, and the Politics of Citizenship during the Civil War Era* (Ithaca: Cornell University Press, 2009), 172–216. This policy led, among other things, to the impressment of American sailors into the British navy and Irish American nationalists being charged with "treason" against the Crown.

10. Louie Crew, "Charles Dickens as a Critic of the United States," *Midwest Quarterly* 16 (October 1974): 42–50; Martin Crawford, ed., *William Howard Russell's Civil War: Private Diary and Letters, 1861–1862* (Athens: University of Georgia Press,), xxviii–xix.

11. Carl F. Wittke, *We Who Built America: The Saga of the Immigrant* (New York: Prentice Hall, 1939); Rowland Berthoff, *British Immigrants in Industrial America, 1790–1950* (Cambridge, Mass.: Harvard University Press, 1953); Charlotte Erickson, *Invisible Immigrants: The Adaptation of English and Scottish Immigrants in Nineteenth-Century America* (London: Weidenfeld and Nicolson, 1972); William E. Van Vugt, *Britain to America: Mid-Nineteenth-Century Immigrants to the United States* (Urbana: University of Illinois Press, 1999); Van Vugt, *British Buckeyes: The English, Scots, and Welsh in Ohio, 1700–1900* (Kent, Ohio: Kent State University Press, 2006); Van Vugt, *British Immigration to the United States, 1776–1914,* 4 vols. (London: Pickering and Chatto, 2010).

12. Kathleen Neils Conzen, David A. Gerber, Ewa Morawska, George E., Pozzetta, and Rudolph J. Vecoli, "The Invention of Ethnicity: A View from the U.S.A," *Journal of American Ethnic History* 12 (Fall 1992): 5–7.

13. Mary H. Blewett, *Constant Turmoil: The Politics of Industrial Life in Nineteenth-Century New England* (Amherst: University of Massachusetts Press, 2000), 81. For more information on the extraordinary careers of the Dobsons see Philip Scranton, *Proprietary Capitalism: The Textile Manufacture at Philadelphia, 1800–1885* (New York: Cambridge University Press, 1983), 63.

14. Quoted in Scranton, *Proprietary Capitalism,* 153.

15. Blewett, *Constant Turmoil,* 86; John H. M. Laslett, *Colliers across the Sea: A Comparative Study of Class Formation in Scotland and the American Midwest, 1830–1924* (Urbana: University of Illinois Press, 2000), 137–38. Laslett, a labor historian, for example, has studied a Scottish mining union branch (made up of immigrants from southwest Scotland) in Illinois that, for "pragmatic reasons," accepted new eastern European immigrants in the late nineteenth century and thus "succeeded in creating both an organizational structure and a union philosophy that . . . largely defused the ethnic issue." For the multiethnic nature of early American industrial towns see Donald B. Cole, *Immigrant City: Lawrence, Massachusetts, 1845–1921* (Chapel Hill: University of North Carolina Press, 1963), and Brian C. Mitchell, *The Paddy Camps: The Irish of Lowell, 1821–1861* (Urbana: University of Illinois Press, 1987).

16. David A. Gerber, *Authors of Their Lives: The Personal Correspondence of British Immigrants to, North America in the Nineteenth Century* (New York: New York University Press, 2006), 20.

17. Scranton, *Proprietary Capitalism,* 66.

18. I am not attempting here to get into the debate on the reality of ethnicity or to what extent it was invented. Invented, imagined, and/or based on real differences, as long as it existed for the English, then, they, like other minorities in America would have to "fit in" to the dominant American culture. For a good definition of ethnicity in America see the various works of Milton George. I accept his definition of ethnicity as "a group with a shared sense of peoplehood." The English associations displayed this "shared sense." Milton M. George, *Assimilation in American Life: The Role of Race Religion, and National Origins* (New York: Oxford University Press, 1964), 24. For the significance of associations in lives of immigrants and their ubiquitous nature across place and time see Jose C. Moya, "Immigrants and Associations: A Global and Historical Perspective," *Journal of Ethnic and Migration Studies* 31 (September 2005): 833–64. In terms of their very important role in immigrant integration see Marlou Schrover and Floris Vermeulen, "Immigrant Organizations," *Journal of Ethnic and Migration Studies* 31 (September 2005): 823–32.

19. Amanda Foreman, *A World on Fire: An Epic History of Two Nations Divided* (London: Allen Lane, 2010), 116.

20. Jones, *Blue and Gray Diplomacy,* 101–3; *New York Herald,* April 24, June 10, 1861.

21. Jones, *Blue and Gray Diplomacy,* 44; Ella Lonn, *Foreigners in the Union Army and Navy* (repr., Westport, Conn.: Greenwood Press, 1969), 130, 236; Susannah Bruce and David T. Gleeson, "Irish Rebels, Southern Rebels: The Irish Confederates," in *Civil War Citizens: Race, Ethnicity, and Identity in America's Bloodiest Conflict,* ed. Susannah J. Ural (New York: New York University Press, 2010), 133–56; Susannah Ural Bruce, *The Harp and the Eagle: Irish American Volunteers and the Union Army, 1861–1865* (New York: New York University Press, 2006).

22. William I. Burton, *Melting Pot Soldiers: The Union's Ethnic Regiments* (New York: Fordham University Press, 1998), 57. Some English militia units were formed in the Confederacy, but only when federal forces threatened local areas. Ella Lonn, *Foreigners in the Confederacy* (repr., Chapel Hill: University of North Carolina Press, 2002), 496, 498.

23. *Daily Cleveland [Ohio] Herald,* April 26, 1861. For significance of military service to ethnic groups and American citizenship, see Samito, *Becoming American under Fire;* Bruce, *The Harp and the Eagle;* and Christian Keller, *Chancellorsville and the Germans: Nativism, Ethnicity, and Civil War Memory* (New York: Fordham University Press, 2010).

24. *Philadelphia North American and United States Gazette,* November 8, 1861.

25. "Baker, Edward Dickinson," *Biographical Directory of the United States Congress,* http://bioguide.congress.gov/scripts/biodisplay.pl?index=B000059 (accessed February 10, 2011).

26. See, for example, *Daily Cleveland Herald,* April 18, 1862, and *Cleveland Morning Daily Herald,* April 25, 1862.

27. Jones, *Blue and Gray Diplomacy,* 83–112. See also Norman B. Ferris, *The* Trent *Affair: A Diplomatic Crisis* (Knoxville: University of Tennessee Press, 1977).

28. See, for example, *Dublin Irishman,* December 1, 1861.

29. *Cleveland Morning Daily Herald,* April 25, 1862.

30. Ibid.

31. Ibid.

32. Steven Hahn, *A Nation under Our Feet: Black Political Struggles in the Rural South from Slavery to the Great Migration* (Cambridge, Mass.: Harvard University Press, 2003), 68–73 ; David Herbert Donald, *Lincoln* (New York: Simon and Schuster, 1996), 314–17, 363; William S. McFeely, *Frederick Douglass* (New York: Norton, 1995), 212–14.

33. *Cleveland Morning Daily Herald,* April 25, 1862.

34. *Daily Cleveland Herald,* April 24, 1863. For the Somersett decision see Stephen M. Wise, *Though the Heavens May Fall: The Landmark Trial That Led to the End of Human Slavery* (Cambridge, Mass.: Da Capo Press, 2006).

35. R. J. M. Blackett, *Divided Hearts: Britain and the American Civil War* (Baton Rouge: Louisiana State University Press, 2001), 171–73.

36. *Milwaukee Daily Sentinel,* January 24, March 2, 1863.

37. Jamie L. Brownstein, "From the Land of Liberty to the Land of Monopoly: The United States in a Chartist Context," in *The Chartist Legacy,* ed. Owen Ashton, Robert Fyson, and Stephen Roberts (Woodbridge, England: Merlin Press, 1999), 147 [147–70]. I am grateful to my colleague Dr. Joe Hardwick for this reference.

38. *Daily Cleveland Herald,* April 26, 1864.

39. Jennifer L. Weber, *Copperheads: The Rise and Fall of Lincoln's Opponents* (New York: Oxford University Press, 2008), 3, 17, 76–77, 98–100, 112–14, 150.

40. *Milwaukee Daily Sentinel,* April 21, 1865; *Daily Cleveland Herald,* April 26, May 2, 1865.

41. Blewett, *Constant Turmoil,* 100–101; Phineas Camp Headley, *Massachusetts in the Rebellion: A Record of the Historical Position of the Commonwealth* (Boston: Walker, Fuller and Company, 1866), 193–98.

42. Blewett, *Constant Turmoil,* 104–105, 129–30, 197; Headley, *Massachusetts in the Rebellion,* 436–37; Donald B. Cole, *Immigrant City: Lawrence, Massachusetts, 1845–1921* (Chapel Hill: University of North Carolina Press, 1963), 118, 130.

43. Francis Patrick to [wife], October 14. 1864, Francis Patrick Letters, Civil War Miscellaneous Collection, U.S. Military Institute, Carlisle, Pennsylvania; Francis Patrick Pension File, National Archives and Records Administration, Washington, D. C. I am very grateful to Ian Delahanty of Boston College for providing me with these sources. For possibilities of a negotiated end to the war if McClellan won see John C. Waugh, *Reelecting Lincoln: The Battle for the 1864 Presidency* (Cambridge, Mass.: Da Capo Press, 1997), 26–27, 324–25, 342.

44. Kerby A Miller, "Class, Culture, and Immigrant Group Identity in the United States: The Case of Irish American Ethnicity," in *Immigration Reconsidered: History, Sociology and Politics,* ed. Virginia Yans-McLaughlin (New York: Oxford University Press, 1990), 96–129.

45. Annual Report for 1877, 6, St George's Society of New York Collection, New York Public Library, New York. See also *New York Times,* April 25, 1853. I am grateful to my colleague Dr. Tanja Bueltmann for her calculations on the extent of the New York society's charitable efforts.

46. Bruce, *Harp and Eagle,* 51–53, 62.

47. *Philadelphia Inquirer,* April 24, 1863.

48. Bruce, *Harp and Eagle,* 121. For more on the draft riots see Iver Bernstein, *The New York City Draft Riots: Their Significance for American Society and Politics in the Age of the Civil War* (New York: Oxford University Press, 1990).

ALEXANDER NOONAN

"A new expression of that *entente cordiale?*"

Russian-American Relations and the "Fleet Episode" of 1863

It was a most extraordinary situation: Russia had not in mind to help us but did render us distinct service; the United States was not conscious that it was contributing in any way to Russia's welfare and yet seems to have saved her from humiliation and perhaps war. There is probably nothing to compare with it in diplomatic history.

Frank A. Golder "The Russian Fleet and the Civil War."
American Historical Review 20 (July 1915): 812

Upon its arrival at the harbor of New York in mid-September 1863, the Russian frigate *Osliaba* became the center of intense public speculation. Though foreign warships in the Union's ports were not an unusual sight, even during the Civil War, the Russian visit was unprecedented. Newspapers in the city were quick to supply an interested public with tales of a formidable fighting force, crewed by well-trained men and led by gallant officers fluent in both English and French. At the same time, the press hinted at a mystery: the *New York Times* reported that the *Osliaba*'s crew was enthusiastic about the anticipated arrival of several other warships under the command of an admiral, though which ships and which admiral were unknown.[1] The Russian crew did not wait long. Two more large steam-frigates—the *Alexander Nevskii,* flagship of the recently promoted Rear Admiral Stepan Lisovskii, and the *Peresviet*—appeared off the coast of Stonington, Connecticut, on September 21 and anchored in Flushing Bay the evening of September 23. That same day, the Russian minister, Edouard Stoeckl, notified the American secretary of the navy, Gideon Welles, of the fleet's imminent arrival. In a written response, excerpts of which were published in the *New York Times,* Welles placed the services of the Brooklyn Navy Yard at the fleet's disposal and expressed gratification at learning "that a squadron of Russian war vessels had arrived at New York for the purpose, *it is supposed,* of visiting that city."[2] Under the circumstances, supposition was necessary because the Russian officers remained silent regarding the reasons for their arrival. On September 26, two additional clippers—the *Variag* and the *Vitiaz*—joined the growing Russian force, and, fifteen days later, the small clipper *Almaz* rounded out the fleet.[3] In early October, a smaller squadron under the command of Rear Admiral Andrei Popov arrived in San Francisco. For the next seven months, these naval forces were a widely reported presence, and their sudden departure in April 1864 hardly diminished the enduring impact of their stay.

Over the years, popular and scholarly understanding of the visit, which became a disputed topic within the complex history of the two countries' diplomatic relations, has undergone a significant evolution. In the earliest American accounts, though the specific circumstances often differed, the prevailing sentiment was that when fears of foreign intervention in the Civil War were at their height, Tsar Alexander II dispatched the fleets as a gesture of friendship and that the action successfully restrained the British and the French.[4] At the same time, however, those responsible for these tales often struggled to account for what General Rush Hawkins described as "the friendly relations that have always existed" between two countries "so completely opposed in form of government."[5] In 1915, using the records of the Russian Ministry of the Marine as well as articles from *Morskoi Sbornik,* Frank Golder revealed what he believed were "the real motives of the expedition."[6] For the first time in English, Golder discussed the fifteen-point order issued by Adjutant General Nikolaii Krabbe, in which the Russian force was charged with conducting naval operations against "Western powers [Britain and France]" in the event of war over the "Polish question."[7] For Golder, an appreciation of the end result—which, he argued, unintentionally benefited both states—was something that escaped the understanding of observers on both sides.

With the orders revealed, subsequent generations of scholars examined the visit as part of a larger discussion of Russian-American relations and turned their focus away from Golder's narrative of mutual, if incidental, benefits. William Nagengast argued that in the public debate, contemporaries quickly adopted what became known as the "bottling up" thesis. According to this reasoning, Americans understood that, fearing war over Poland, the Russian government dispatched the fleets to the United States in order to avoid their being trapped in port by the British and French navies in a repeat of the Crimean War.[8] Two years later, Thomas Bailey attacked Nagengast's conclusions and, after surveying a more diverse collection of newspapers—though, crucially, for only the first two weeks after the Russian arrival in New York—identified no fewer than a half dozen possible explanations for the visit, including its being undertaken as an exercise in Russian-American friendship, as a practice cruise, and as a threat to the French position in Mexico.[9] Though Russian scholars were less quick than their American counterparts to downplay the naval visits' place in the broader narrative of Russian-American relations, they focused primarily on the diplomatic balance in Europe and argued that the potential threat to the sea trade of the Western powers posed by the fleets was critical to the relaxation of political tensions over the Polish Uprising of 1863.[10]

Though scholars' evolving appreciation for the impetus behind—and American understanding of—the Russian visit has opened up important lines of inquiry, these examinations have also obscured the important role contemporaries assigned to Russian-American relations. Though the 1863–64 visit of the two Russian squadrons was not, as was rumored, the harbinger of a formal alliance between the two countries, parties on both sides played up the appearance of compatible interests, similar circumstances, and close relations in order to take full advantage of the visit. "A fortunate decision in the political sense," Prince Alexander Gorchakov, the Russian minister of foreign affairs, wrote of the event, which "was carried out in an exemplary fashion."[11] Individuals from both countries hotly debated, deliberately manipulated, and occasionally exaggerated the cordial relationship between the two states while demonstrating their understanding that the belief in Russian friendship, both at home and abroad, was critical for both countries to exploit the squadrons' arrival for political gain. The balls and formal dinners held in honor of the Russian officers and sailors were a public forum in which the debate over Russian-American cooperation and shared circumstance, ideas perceived to be at the heart of the visit, played out. Rather than being ill informed or intentionally misled, those who adopted a position that the visit was the logical extension of Russian friendship did so on the basis of their awareness of each country's recent diplomacy, common interests, and potential to affect the political balance with other European powers.

Locating the Russian visit in the context of global diplomatic questions stands at odds with how American foreign relations during the Civil War and mid-nineteenth century Russian-American relations have traditionally been perceived. In studies on international dimensions to the Civil War, Russia has been consistently relegated to the periphery.[12] Scholars of the war's international dimensions have concentrated, as David Crook writes, "unrepentantly, upon the interplay which took place between the American contestants and the 'great powers' of the day: Great Britain and France. Lesser powers, like Spain, Austria, Russia, merely flit across the stage." Even in Howard Jones's *Blue and Gray Diplomacy*, an integrated study of Union-Confederate diplomacy, Russia's influence on European interventionist plans is "shadowy," and the country remains on the margins.[13] Where the Russian government's sympathetic attitudes and policies toward the Union receive detailed attention, such as in Nina Kiniapina's work, Richard Jensen writes off Russia's diplomatic interest in the United States as "marginal."[14]

The underlying belief in what the Russian visit represented—an appreciation of cordial relations, if not perfectly shared interests—was dismissed as myth; the possibility that contemporaries adroitly exploited such perceptions was treated as misguided.[15] Yet this attitude, heavily influenced by Cold War geopolitical considerations, mistakenly gives credence to the erroneous belief that Russian-American relations were of "secondary importance," that closer contact brought increased conflict, that American diplomats were uniquely ineffective or misled, or that, in cooperating, Russian and American leaders were out of step with public sentiment.[16] While Russian and American scholars alike have gradually moved beyond the traditional "either-or" narratives of "forgotten friendships" or "age-long hostility" and begun to portray a more nuanced relationship demonstrating "the possibility of overcoming" differences, attention to the Russian visit has remained on the margins.[17] In their respective examinations of the Russian visit, Norman Saul treats the experience as a passing episode in the two countries' long history while Victoria Zhuravleva examined how later interpretations of the visit were dependent on political considerations.[18] The visit of the Russian naval squadrons illustrated how closely intertwined Russian-American relations were with each country's foreign relations, and the manner in which the visit was exploited reveals a contemporary awareness of how those relations were perceived. The Russian visit's import is a reflection, in no small part, of the growing ties between people and states: in 1905, Oscar Straus argued that Russian actions toward the Union were moves made "upon the chessboard of European diplomacy."[19] What Straus and others have overlooked is that Russia's relationship with the Union had just as much to do with those moves.

Russian Soirées and Contested Meaning

Following the Russian fleets' arrivals in New York and San Francisco, local leaders organized public ceremonies to celebrate the officers, while newspaper accounts injected the festivities into a larger debate on the nature of Russian-American friendship. In New York, the Committee of the Common Council passed a series of resolutions honoring Admiral Lisovskii and his officers, threw a parade in their honor, held a reception with Mayor Opdyke, and sponsored two large, formal banquets. As the *Philadelphia Inquirer* reported, the "courteous conduct of the Russian naval officers" when meeting Mayor Opdyke prompted a delegation of British officers to try to do the same. The mayor, however, was unavailable, and "it was understood the reception to be given to the Russian officers will not be extended to the officers of any other nation."[20] When Lisovskii's fleet moved south in the winter, the ships stopped in Washington, D.C., where Secretaries

Welles and Seward along with members of Congress honored the fleet with official visits. In San Francisco, the celebrations were more subdued—in part because Russian naval vessels were more familiar—yet Admiral Popov hosted a banquet onboard the *Bogatir* that was attended by Governor Leland Stanford.[21] Such public celebrations, parades, and official visits deliberately highlighted the different treatment received by Russians and by other foreign representatives. "The splendid Russian banquet in New York has a far greater significance than such festivals can usually claim," the *Philadelphia Inquirer* declared. "It is at once municipal, national and international."[22]

In New York, where the first galas were thrown, press reports emphasized the national and international significance of the Russian presence. The highlight of the first ball, held at the Metropolitan Hotel on October 1, occurred when the band played "Yankee Doodle" and "The Star Spangled Banner" alongside "God Save the Tsar." The evening's speeches by Admiral Lisovskii, General Wallbridge, and a Mr. Mitchell focused on domestic turmoil and emphasized shared political sympathies. Lisovskii, who addressed the assembly first, toasted Tsar Alexander II as "the Delight of Mankind," offered a toast to President Abraham Lincoln, and expressed "deep interest" and "sorrow" at "the trials through which you [the citizens of the United States] are passing." Mitchell, who spoke next, alluded to the squadron's stay in New York when he suggested that "We might have the gratification of seeing the squadron here not only for weeks and months, *but until the fight was over.*" Going next, Wallbridge honored the "memory of Peter the Great, the founder of the Russian Empire, and of George Washington, the founder of the American republic—may their memories be immortal." Cheers interrupted Lisovskii's second speech when he declared, "I believe it to be the duty of every people to defend its integrity either to live as a nation or to die. There is no middle ground."[23] *Harper's Weekly,* in an article describing the parade to the Metropolitan and the ensuing ceremony, opined that the crowds treated the event, "which amounted to little less than an international demonstration," with appropriate somberness.[24]

As prominent public figures injected themselves into the discussion over the national and international importance of these events, they did so within the context of concurrent national crises: the Civil War and the Polish Uprising. Just as the debate over the expansion of slavery exacerbated sectional divisions within the United States and Lincoln's election in 1860 pushed the first of the southern states to declare their secession from the union, Nicholas Riasanovsky argues, Alexander II's "great reforms" opened the door for Polish unrest because the government struggled to "resolve the fundamental dilemma of change: where to stop."[25] For the tsar, Russia's defeat in the Crimean War provided the impetus for long-overdue reforms, including the restoration of Polish autonomy. Yet Poland's new status failed to satisfy ardent nationalists who wanted complete independence and, following the government's efforts to quell small demonstrations, initiated a guerrilla campaign in January 1863 that was supported by the French, British, and Austrian governments. When, during the banquet at the Metropolitan, Secretary of State William Seward's toast to the Russian officers was read, the political parallels between the crises faced by the two countries were made evident to contemporaries. "A banquet specially honoring that Empire," the *Philadelphia Inquirer* pointed out, "means further that Gortschakoff's [*sic*] stratagems of statesmanship, so annoying to France and England, are endorsed by our Government, and that our present course is one of cordial alliance with and support to Russia in her continental imbroglio."[26] Understood in this light, Lisovskii's second speech from that same evening about a people's obligation to defend their country's territorial integrity resonated in both circumstances.

The theme of parallel domestic insurrections was also present in both the private diplomatic correspondence and the public statements of American officials. Four months before the Russian squadrons appeared in Union harbors, Seward politely refused French entreaties to join a proposed intervention in Poland, citing a reluctance to intervene "in the political affairs of sovereign states." Despite the appeal of the Polish cause to Seward, as well as to the American people, the secretary of state noted that such a policy of nonintervention "could not be wisely departed from at this moment, when the existence of a local, although as we trust only a transient disturbance, deprives the government of the counsel of a portion of the American people, to whom so wide a departure from the settled policy of the country must in any case be deeply interesting."[27] Gorchakov was elated by Seward's position and, with the active encouragement of the American minister to the Russian court, Cassius Clay, received permission to publish the diplomatic note.[28] Less than two weeks before the Russian arrival in September 1863, Senator Charles Sumner gave a speech in New York that reiterated the Union government's attitude toward foreign intervention and also served as a warning to the British and French governments. "Nations are equal in the eye of international law," Sumner declared, "so that what is right for one is right for all. . . . Therefore, should our cases be reversed, there is nothing England and France now propose, or may hereafter propose, which it will not be our equal right to propose when Ireland or India once more rebels, or when France is in the throes of its next revolution."[29]

Despite the largely positive attention garnered by the Russian squadrons, press reports were not uncritical of the receptions accorded the Russians, nor were they overly carried away by the symbolism of the visit. Following a second gala in New York, at the Academy of Music on November 5, a split emerged between those who continued to trumpet the importance of the Russian visit and those who expressed regret over such public displays. Some of the best evidence of this debate appeared in *Harper's Weekly,* whose articles frequently swung from praising the Russian presence to bemoaning or dismissing the celebrations as frivolous—often on the same page. On one hand, news coverage hailed the "Soirée Russe" as "undoubtedly the greatest ball ever given in the country, without excepting the ball to the Prince of Wales."[30] Writers for *Harper's Weekly* scoffed at "John Bull" for mocking the "splendor" of the reception given to the Russian officers. Rather than being "bamboozled by the Russian compliments," Americans understood the Russian presence was a matter of political convenience; just as French sympathy during the American Revolution stemmed from "a hatred of England," the Russian presence was tied to mutual concerns over English and French threats, the paper explained.[31] At the same time, other editorials publicly fretted over the "Diamond Ball" and asked, if "a million of dollars' worth of diamonds were worn at the Russian Ball . . . could the jewels be put to a nobler use" by providing clothing and food for wounded soldiers?[32]

While the American press concentrated on the welcome bestowed on the visitors, the actions of the Russian sailors offered examples of direct engagement in American domestic affairs. Though the Russian Atlantic fleet garnered most of the public's attention, it was the Pacific fleet, led by Rear Admiral Popov, that most clearly, as Adamov delicately writes, "went somewhat ahead of the Russian diplomacy."[33] Three weeks after the Pacific fleet's arrival in San Francisco, Russian crewmen manning buckets and pumps played a crucial role in extinguishing a damaging blaze in the city's financial district.[34] A second, more notable intervention took place after rumors circulated that Confederate ironclads, the *Sumter* and the *Alabama,* were coming to attack the city. Though a Confederate attack never materialized, Popov publicly committed his forces "to assist the authorities of every place where friendship is offered them, in all measures which may be deemed necessary by the local authorities, to repel any attempt against the security of the place." When word of this declaration reached Stoeckl in Washington, D.C., and Foreign Minister Gorchakov in St. Petersburg, they were dismayed. In a letter dated March 13, 1864, Stoeckl emphasized that Russia had no right to interfere in the internal affairs of another nation and that Popov should intervene only in the event of a direct threat to the city "in the name of humanity, and not for political reasons, to prevent this misfortune." In other words, Popov was barred from intervening on behalf of the Union in what Russian officials deemed a matter of national interest.[35]

Though the private concern over Popov's declaration can be interpreted as emblematic of the insincerity of Russian sympathy for the Union, it is more accurate to see it as fully consistent with the view that the Civil War—like the Polish Uprising—was a purely internal matter. From the onset of hostilities, Stoeckl urged against taking sides: preservation of the Union was strongly preferable, and, though he felt it important not to antagonize the Confederates in the event they were successful, any recognition of the Confederacy should be withheld until a permanent settlement was achieved.[36] Despite the fear that the ongoing struggle would leave the country divided and too weak to resist "hostile powers," conversations between American representatives and Gorchakov as well as Stoeckl's commentaries on the reaction to foreign intervention and possible Russian mediation continued to be contingent upon both sides accepting—with an understanding that the Union would not allow such a circumstance.[37]

Between the arrival of the fleets in fall 1863 and heightened fears of foreign intervention over the Civil War and uprising in Poland, the symbolic value of the Russian naval presence and the nature of Russian friendship was a matter of intense debate. On October 5, shortly after the ball at the Metropolitan hotel, Philipp von Brunnow, the Russian minister to Britain, sent an anxious letter to Foreign Minister Gorchakov expressing his concern over the attention the Russian visit was drawing in the British government and press. Von Brunnow was further dismayed by the report of Wallbridge's speech and the possible message of open hostilities that the English navy could read into the Russian fleet's maneuvers.[38] In contrast to the cautious tone of von Brunnow's letter, a telegram from the Black Sea naval station of Nicolayoff was quite positive: in a telegram forwarded by Stoeckl to the mayor of New York, the citizens of the town expressed their deep gratification "for feelings of sympathy evinced to their countrymen in New York."[39] The Russian presence in New York and San Francisco was neither incidentally beneficial nor solely a picturesque fiction. Instead, the American public and Russian officials debated and worried over the significance of the visit, at least partially aware of the international ramifications of the unprecedented display of Russian naval power.

An Expression of Friendship?

The earliest accounts of the "Russian Fleet Myth" were dramatic and rich with popular appeal, and it is precisely these fanciful, often implausible tales that have provided so many reasons to dismiss the squadrons' visit as inconsequential. In one famous retelling, Thomas Harris linked the Russian presence with the *Trent* Affair, which arose when, in November 1861, the USS *San Jacinto* intercepted the British mail steamer *Trent* and seized the Confederate envoys James Mason and John Slidell. According to Harris, "a few weeks" after this incident, the two Russian fleets appeared in New York and San Francisco. In a meeting between Admiral Lisovskii and Rear Admiral David Farragut at Astor House, the former supposedly divulged that the fleets were under sealed orders, to be opened only in the event of "a contingency which has not yet occurred"; he later admitted that the contingency was British and French recognition of the Confederacy.[40] Though colorful, the story was impossible, as the Russian fleets arrived nearly two years after the *Trent* Affair.[41] Another popular version came from George Pierce, a Philadelphia lawyer, who retold a story he claimed to have heard from

Governor Andrew Curtin after the latter's tenure as minister to Russia. According to this rendition, before Curtin left St. Petersburg in 1872, Prince Gorchakov revealed to him three letters: the first, from Napoleon III, inviting Tsar Alexander II to join with Britain and France in recognizing the Confederacy; the second, from the tsar, declining the invitation and pledging aid to the United States in the event of foreign intervention; and the third, also from the tsar, instructing Lisovskii to place his fleet at President Lincoln's command in the event of war.[42] The common theme running through these accounts was the idea that in the darkest hour of the American republic, Alexander II had dispatched the two fleets as a gesture of friendship between the two nations and that his action successfully restrained British and French intervention.

Though the stories were false, the belief in a close relationship between the Russian and the Union governments was not unwarranted. For more than fifty years preceding the visit, Russian tsars and their foreign ministers often viewed their diplomatic objectives as compatible with those of the United States and saw in the latter a useful check on English influence. In his letters appointing representatives to the United States, Tsar Alexander I repeatedly portrayed the United States as a counterweight to England and stressed the compatibility of Russian and American interests.[43] While his successor, Nicholas I, would declare, "where once the Russian flag has flown, it must not be lowered again," it was under his rule that the Russian-American Company authorized the abandonment and sale of the settlement at Fort Ross, now part of Sonoma County, California, to Johann Sutter.[44] Seemingly at odds with the Russian government's policy of expanding in the Pacific, selling the area around Fort Ross made political and economic sense. The decimation of the area's marine animal population caused by the unrestricted fur trade and an agreement with the Hudson's Bay Company to provide food for the Alaskan colonies made Russian California a financial liability and a drain on the already precarious holdings in Alaska. Selling the territory removed a point of Russian-American tension and secured America as a rival to British influence in the Pacific. After Russia's 1856 defeat in the Crimean War powerfully demonstrated the military gap between Russia and the Western powers, the new tsar, Alexander II, continued his predecessors' policy of promoting America as a rival to Britain.[45]

One of the main points of Russian-American cooperation intended to deliberately counter British power centered on the proposed creation of a trans-Pacific telegraph line. Joint Anglo-American efforts to lay a transatlantic telegraph cable achieved brief success in August 1858, though it took five mostly unsuccessful attempts between 1857 and 1866 before a reliable connection was established.[46] This cable was of great interest to the Russian government because telegraphic cables radically changed the speed at which information traveled. With the active participation of both the Russian and the American ministers,

Russian representatives observed the setting of the Atlantic cable from the American steamer *Niagara.* In his letter of introduction to Captain Hudson, Minister Thomas Seymour emphasized that Russia, despite its distance, was "not indifferent to the sublime work in which you are about to engage" and that the Russian presence was "gratifying proof of the friendly relations" between the emperor of Russia and the United States.[47] Yet a transatlantic cable was not the only proposed solution; following his successful journey down the nearly 2,700-mile length of the Amur River, the first American to manage the feat, Perry McDonough Collins, used the success following the publication of his account to lobby on behalf of a Pacific cable.[48] Charles Vevier argues that Collins's travels captured a unique historical moment in the territorial expansion of both the United States and Russia: as California was to the United States, contemporaries saw the Amur as a potential "food base for Russian development" and believed that the region could provide an impetus and direction for Russian expansion. Similarly, for the United States, contemporaries argued the telegraph would aid in the development of California by easing the burden of communication and offering new opportunities for American commerce.[49]

Contemporaries saw three principal advantages in constructing an overland telegraph line between the American Pacific Coast, Russian Alaska, and across the Bering Strait, where it would connect with the Russian telegraph line running from the mouth of the Amur River seven thousand miles west to Moscow. First and foremost, because only the forty-mile stretch of the Bering Strait would require a submarine cable, there would be fewer logistical difficulties with a Pacific line than with the transatlantic cable.[50] Second, it made financial sense: the estimated cost of the cable was $3 million to construct, plus annual costs estimated at around $750,000, whereas the cable would generate annual revenue of $1.5 million.[51] Third, as Clay communicated to Seward, "the Russian government will not fail to see how much the United States, as well as Russia, are interested in not having the telegraphic intelligence of the world confined to the Atlantic line, in the sole possession of the British nation."[52]

When the Russian squadrons arrived in 1863, many American observers and diplomats explicitly linked their presence to the proposed Pacific telegraph. One contemporary editorial argued, as part of a larger case for a formal diplomatic alliance arising from the visit of the Russian fleets, that "the world has kept on moving since Washington's time" and that steam, telegraphs, and railroads meant an end to the United States' isolation from the rest of the world.[53] In a series of letters to Seward, Clay outlined the diplomatic implications, explicitly linking Russian friendship, support of the Union in the Civil War, and the proposed Russian-American Telegraph Company. Aware of how Russian-American relations were perceived, a dispatch dated June 17 commented on the public reception following the *St. Petersburg Journal*'s publication of Seward's letter to

Dayton on the "Polish Question" and American intervention before moving on to discuss the telegraph charter that Alexander II "deigned to grant." In an October dispatch, written after the Russian fleet's arrival in New York, Clay attacked Senator Charles Sumner for his defense of Poland and again linked Russian support for the telegraph to support for the Union.[54]

As the telegraph was stimulating closer cooperation between the two states, similar developments in ship design and naval doctrine also generated closer ties as the Russian government tried to modernize in the wake of the Crimean War. That contest had clearly demonstrated Russian weakness vis-à-vis its western rivals, and, upon his ascension to the throne, Alexander II embarked on a rigorous program of domestic reform.[55] In the navy, even after the increasing utilization of steam power in the early 1850s, most Russian vessels were based on designs from the turn of the century. Though victorious in the Russo-Turkish War of 1853, the navy became "nearly non-existent" after the Crimean War.[56] In addition to an institutional reorganization, the Russians increasingly concentrated on the development of screw-propelled warships and, subsequently, ironclads—a focus that intensified in the mid-1860s. In describing the naval arms race, Adolph Hoehling writes, "The U.S.S. *Monitor* revolutionized war at sea, adding 'turret,' 'armor,' and quite a bit more to the international naval lexicon. As the world's first all-iron fighting ship, she demolished forever the 'wooden walls' of the fleets of oak and billowing canvas."[57] In an article titled "The 'Monitor' Panic," *Harper's Weekly* captured the spirit of the age, quoting an article in the London *Times* that declared that England could not allow "'any other nation a moment's start' in obtaining the 'greatest force of invulnerable vessels,' and that 'all other things are secondary to this.'" France, where an iron-plated gunboat had been in development for more than a year, and Russia, whose tsar had caught "the disease" and was "determined to save every ruble possible in order to apply the money for the fitting out of an iron-plated fleet," also joined the naval arms race.[58]

The Russian government's efforts to modernize the navy created opportunities for greater collaboration between American shipbuilders and Russian representatives. Though during the Crimean War Russian interest in American involvement was generally concerned with neutral shipping rights, the restoration of peace had led to a remarkable collaboration between the Russian navy and the United States' foremost shipbuilder, William H. Webb.[59] Two of the 135 ships Webb produced over his career saw service in Russia by the mid-1850s: just prior to the First War of Schleswig in 1848, the Russian government purchased the first side-wheel steamship built in Webb's shipyard, the *United States,* while the *Astoria,* Webb's only screw steamship, was later renamed *Alexander II* and served the Russian government's commercial interests.[60] The vessel most critical to making Webb's international reputation, however, was the *General Admiral.* Though construction was delayed for four years because of the Crimean War, the

Webb Shipyard began building the *General Admiral* in 1857, a year when a severe depression forced many of New York's shipyards to close due to lack of business.[61] Designed as the flagship for Grand Duke Constantine Nikolaevich, General Admiral of the Imperial Russian Navy and Alexander II's younger brother, the *General Admiral* was, at 327 feet long and more than six thousand tons, the largest warship in the world and, in tonnage, the largest wooden-hulled ship built in the United States.[62]

Though the Russian navy replaced the ship in 1873, from the time the keel was laid through the arrival of the Russian squadrons in 1863, the *General Admiral* was emblematic of close Russian-American relations. The launch on September 21, 1858—exactly one year after the keel was laid and the birthday of the grand duke—drew one of the largest crowds ever for such an occasion, and the more than three thousand people on board to participate in the launch included a number of the ship's Russian crew.[63] When the completed vessel was delivered to Kronstadt in 1859, after crossing the Atlantic in a mere eleven days, Tsar Alexander II praised Webb's "skill and intelligence" and bestowed gifts on both Webb and the vessel's American captain.[64] The praise heaped on the *General Admiral,* one of two warships built for the Imperial Russian Navy during this period, helped Webb secure an agreement with the newly unified Kingdom of Italy for two warships based on the same design.[65] The Russian government's endorsement of Webb helped counter the criticism of rival British shipbuilders also vying for the contract with the new Italian government and was useful in securing permission from the federal government to build warships for a foreign power during the Civil War.[66] Such enthusiasm was not lost amid the arrival of the Russian squadrons in 1863. At the "Soirée Russe," the second grand gala held to honor the Russian Atlantic squadron in November, a model of the *General Admiral* was suspended at the center of the first tier of viewing boxes at the Academy of Music bearing the signal code for "Welcome Russia."[67]

While the proposed Russian-American telegraph line and the *General Admiral* were tangible examples of close Russian-American relations, public comparisons of Tsar Alexander II and President Lincoln, the "Tsar Liberator" and the "Great Emancipator," further enlivened the debate over the Russian visit. On its face, such a comparison seems strained. After all, it was Lincoln who, in his oft-quoted 1855 letter to Joshua Speed, lamented the growing influence of the Know-Nothings and their attitudes toward slavery, saying, "When it comes to this [the prospect of the Know-Nothings gaining power], I shall prefer emigrating to some country where they make no pretense of loving liberty,—to Russia, for instance, where despotism can be taken pure, and without the base alloy of hypocrisy."[68] At the same time, Stoeckl's correspondence with Prince Gorchakov revealed important criticisms and doubts about Lincoln and the American democracy.[69] Yet, from the moment Alexander II announced his intention to end serfdom in Russia, support for the imperial regime began to come from the abolitionist presses in the United States. In contrasting Russian sympathy for the Union with British "selfishness and indifference," the *Christian Recorder* stated, "the significance of the liberal and reforming Emperor's allusion to American liberty can hardly be lost upon any of our readers."[70] Once the questions of serfdom and slavery became intertwined, proponents of abolition argued, "The very time in which we live offers to those two countries a true and strong inducement for mutual sympathy."[71] When word spread that Alexander II sped up the process by emancipating twenty-one million crown serfs, the *Christian Recorder* declared the end of "the most gigantic and most baneful relic of barbarism that infested Europe."[72]

Diplomatic representatives from each country also expressed the idea that Alexander II and Lincoln were confronting similar circumstances. In a letter authorizing Taylor to congratulate Gorchakov on the establishment of an independent, impartial judiciary in the wake of the tsar's emancipation of the serfs, Seward wrote, "It is calculated to command the approval of mankind. It seems to secure to Russia the benefit without the calamities of a revolution. . . . Constitutional nations which have heretofore regarded the friendship which exists between Russia and the United States as wanting a foundation in common principles and sentiments must hereafter admit that this relation is as natural in its character as it is auspicious to both countries in its results."[73] A year after Seward's letter, the American consular officer in St. Petersburg, Edwin Phelps, wrote to the secretary of state, informing him that "it is well known that His Majesty the Emperor is anxious to introduce, as rapidly as possible, those great reforms [trial by jury and the writ of habeas corpus], in his civil and criminal codes, which are the basis of Constitutional Governments."[74] Like his American counterpart, Gorchakov also expressed a notion of shared destiny, writing: "Both countries carried out a struggle for emancipation, both had to face disagreements and foreign intrigues."[75]

From his diplomatic post in Russia, Cassius Clay wrote a series of letters back to Seward that implicitly linked the uprisings facing each country. In a stunning twist, given traditional American sympathies toward Poland, Clay repeatedly avowed that the Russian government was acting liberally before the outbreak of violence. In an August dispatch, Clay quoted at length from a London *Times* article—repeating "The Poles of the Kingdom had representative institutions, a Polish administration, and . . . religious freedom before the insurrection broke out"—to offer support for his contention. "Here is proof, from an enemy, of what I said long ago," Clay crowed, "that the Emperor Alexander had granted, or was disposed to grant Poland all things short of independence." Clay did not find fault with the Polish people, instead placing blame on "the Catholic religion" and "Polish Conservatism with avowed anti-democratic institutions." Turning his wrath on supporters of the Polish Uprising, Clay asserted, "Their cause is as bad as their methods are repugnant to the just sentiments of mankind and violative of the laws of God and every 'progressive' the world over should rejoice in the steady overthrow of both."[76]

Not only were both Russia and the Union—in Clay's eyes—acting liberally when confronted with domestic insurrections but also, as the dispatches between August and October 1863 made clear, both states had to be wary of foreign intervention. Though, as of early September, Clay reported that war in Europe seemed unlikely, he was increasingly concerned with French actions in North America. Napoleon, Clay charged, had deceived him like so many others and was seeking "new strength in the Catholic reactionary elements of all the world"; Clay predicted that the French seizure of Texas was "imminent" if the Union did not take proper precautions, as Russia had. "It seems to me," he wrote, "that the time has come for all America [the republics of the Americas] to unite in a defensive alliance to sustain the Monroe Doctrine."[77] In early October, responding to what he perceived to be an anti-Russian speech by Charles Sumner, Clay sent off one of his more strident defenses of Russian-American relations. After recalling the on-the-record support for the Union by both Gorchakov and the tsar, negotiations over a bilateral treaty of maritime rights, and the importance of the Russian-American telegraph, Clay reached the heights of his rhetoric. "When the maritime powers were stirring up strife, and threatening armed intervention in Poland, Russia was asked to join them in their combined crusade against the existence of the Republic. What did Russia do?" Clay asked. "Sell us out for her own safety? No, but with a magnanimity which characterizes that greatest liberator of men, Alexander II spurned the proposal and sets himself to work in defense."[78] How, Clay indignantly wondered, could anyone question Russian sympathy and sincerity?

While the proposed telegraph, models of the *General Admiral,* and the much-discussed parallels between slavery and serfdom were intimately tied to the debate over Russian-American cooperation, a separate diplomatic crisis at the time of the Russian fleets' visit illustrated just how differently American statesmen viewed their Russian and British counterparts. Confronted by the Union's naval superiority, Confederate diplomats had come to depend on the shipyards of England and France for vessels that could be used as blockade runners and commerce raiders.[79] As the Russian fleets lay at anchor in New York and San Francisco, a rumor began to circulate that Russian subjects were selling merchant ships to British and French representatives who, Clay alleged, would then turn them over to be equipped as blockade runners or privateers for the Confederacy.[80] Yet, rather than lead to deterioration in Russian-American relations, the rumor moved Clay to write to Gorchakov to lobby for the tsar's direct, personal intervention. Instead of citing neutrality laws, Clay preferred to rely "upon the friendship of his Imperial Majesty"; if only the tsar was made aware of his subjects' actions, he would take prompt action to suppress the sales.[81]This backchannel and personal approach was a dramatic departure from the debate surrounding neutrality laws in the very public discussions over the British government's reluctant efforts to detain the Laird Rams.[82] Such a sharp difference in America's responses to similar crises involving the provision and arming of ships for the Confederacy was traced, in part, to Russia's conduct as a friendly power.[83]

Ultimately, the same ideas that came through in the embellished accounts of Harris or Pierce were also present in the contemporary debates over Russian friendship that erupted during the squadrons' visit. Official discussions about the future of the Russian-American telegraph or the presence of a model of the *General Admiral* at the Russian ball reveal a sophisticated understanding of the two countries' shared interests and the potential of each to affect the other's political balance with the other great powers. Such attitudes were not accepted uncritically or without debate, however. In commenting on the launch of the *General Admiral,* the *New York Times* wryly commented that the two-headed eagle, symbol of Imperial Russia, was "said to be emblematic of her partiality for China tea and cold Turkey."[84] Following the outbreak of the Civil War, the press hinted at the "cheap character" of American sympathy for Russians. The *Christian Recorder* stated, "It will come to an end, as soon as the Russians shall be in our way . . . and it is not very distant. The locality will be the Pacific, and the coasts of Eastern Asia and Western Africa." In some ways, no article appearing

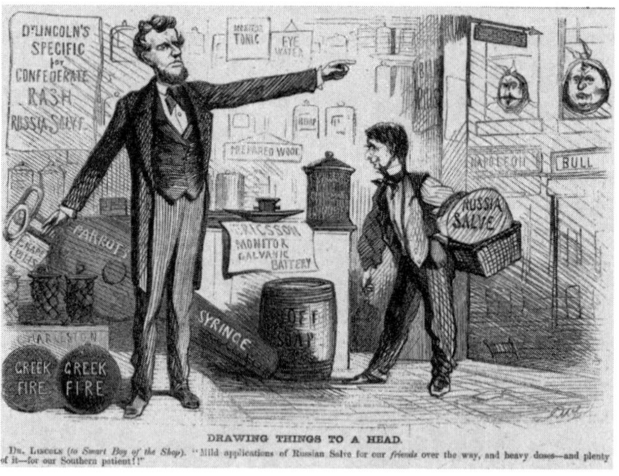

Like a soothing balm, the Russian presence was a circumstance to be used for diplomatic effect. In *Harper's Weekly,* November 28, 1863, drawn by John McLenan.

in American newspapers at this time was more representative of the competing strains of thought regarding Russian-American friendship: one paragraph disparaged any notion of similarities, while a subsequent paragraph explicitly connected the abolition of serfdom and slavery, declaring, "May God speed the Emperor!"[85] An editorial cartoon in *Harper's Weekly* from late November clearly expressed the popular opinion of what the fleets represented: in a shop, whose windows were adorned with the heads of "Napoleon" and "Bull," shopkeeper Lincoln directs that "Russian salve" should be applied in mild doses to the "*friends* over the way" while reserving "heavy doses—and plenty of it—for our Southern patient."[86]

An Expression of National Self-Interest?

The idea of the "Russian fleet myth" gained traction after the 1950s because it appealed to how scholars and the public wanted to depict Russian-American relations and fit with the narrative of American foreign relations during the Civil War. The essence of the myth was contemporaries' naïve belief that the Russian presence was a sign of the tsar's sympathy for the Union cause and that Russia would act as a bulwark against possible intervention by France and England. "The two systems of government were antipathetic in the highest degree," Bailey says to refute such an idea, "and the Czar, as was perfectly natural, exploited us openly in promoting his own ambitions."[87] This argument obscures contemporary reality on two fronts: it ignores important shared interests and circumstances that were the foundation of the cordial relations between the two countries at the time; more important, by advancing the argument that Russian actions deceived many Americans, Bailey fails to consider how figures from both states were able to exploit the widespread perception of the two countries' cordial relations to embellish the visit's significance.[88]

In the Union, the anti-Russian sentiments of many prominent figures were a matter of public record, yet officials from Lincoln on down demonstrated a willingness to twist the ambiguity behind the visit to suit national goals. As senator, Lincoln publicly supported the Hungarian revolutionary Louis Kossuth during his visit to the United States and criticized Russian autocracy; as president, Lincoln requested that Bayard Taylor offer up "a good lecture or two on Serfs, Serfdom and Emancipation" that would coincide with Lisovskii's visit to Washington, D.C., in order to foster a better understanding of Russia.[89] In his memoirs, Frederick Seward, assistant secretary of state and son of William Seward, referred to Russia as "a steadfast friend" and argued in favor of the friendly intent behind the Russian naval visit because "Gortschakoff [*sic*] was a sagacious diplomatist."[90] Secretary of State Seward, far more cautious in his official dispatches on Russian-American relations, commented to Taylor, "In regard to Russia, the case is a plain one. She has our friendship in every case in preference to any other

European power simply because she always wishes us well and leaves us to conduct our affairs as we think best."[91] Seward, however, thought the visit could be used to direct effect. "The welcome . . . was an unprompted act of the American people. It was, I believe, as universal as it was spontaneous," he expressed to Clay in December, assuring the minister that "The President has earnestly desired that their reception at the Capitol might reflect the cordiality and friendship which the nation cherishes towards Russia."[92] As Henry Clews argues, Seward, rather than being misled, demonstrated in his correspondence that he "was astute enough to see that this visit . . . might seem to be what it was not, particularly to foreign eyes."[93]

Accounts of the Russian fleet often cite Gideon Welles's diary entry in which he exclaimed, "God bless the Russians" in order to show how the appearance of the Russian fleets misled American policymakers. Yet, when examined as a whole, the passage demonstrated a sophisticated understanding of the impact of the fleets' visits. Upon learning of the arrival of the Russian fleet in New York, Welles confided to his diary that the reason for the visit was to prevent the fleet from being "confined in the Baltic by a northern winter." Yet he also observed, "In sending them to this country at this time there is something significant. What will be its effect on France and the French policy we shall learn in due time. It may moderate; it may exasperate. God bless the Russians." While the last phrase has been taken as an example of how Americans were led astray, in a subsequent entry around the time of the Atlantic fleet's sojourn to Washington, D.C., in December, Welles wrote, "The Russian government has thought proper to send its fleets into American waters for the winter. . . . It is a politic movement for both Russians and Americans, and somewhat annoying to France and England."[94]

Senator Charles Sumner was an outspoken opponent of Russian actions in Poland as chairman of the Foreign Relations Committee, but even he used the symbolic value of the Russian visit to suit the ends of the Union. With public anxiety over British and French intervention running high, Sumner wrote a letter to the liberal British statesman John Bright, which mentioned "the hobnobbing at New York with the Russian admiral" and how "England and France must retrace their steps."[95] Sumner went further by pointing out the paradox that France and Britain supported liberal institutions in Poland while simultaneously engaging in the Chinese civil war and in Mexico.[96] Taken at face value, Sumner could appear deceived by the Russian presence. Yet it was Sumner who famously declared that the United States had but one friend—Switzerland—in Europe. Sumner's speech, which prompted the ire of Clay—whose longest letters during this period involve harsh attacks on Sumner—took place *after* the Russian fleet had arrived in New York.[97] Such political maneuvering was the act of a skilled politician keenly aware of how the Russian visit could be seen by outside observers, the British and French governments in particular, and Sumner echoed Seward,

Welles, and Lincoln in manipulating how the visit and Russian-American relations were perceived.

The Russian government also used their fleet's mysterious arrival in New York to send strategic and political signals. According to Krabbe's orders, "the aim of the undertaking of the squadron . . . in the event of a war at present foreseen with the Western powers is to act with all the possible means available to you against our opponents."[98] The phrase "all the possible means" included both commercial raids on the shipping lanes and attacks on weakly defended colonial territories. As such, the order was influenced by lessons learned during Russia's bitter defeat during the Crimean War: as in that conflict, the technological and numerical superiority of the British and French navies made it seem imperative that Lisovskii have unfettered access to the open seas.[99] At the time, James Buchanan made a connection between the privateer threat to Britain's trade and sharp increases in insurance rates.[100] As part of the government's analysis of the war, Stoeckl composed a memo back to the Russian Foreign Ministry on the country's trade with the United States that stressed both the importance of American commerce, particularly cotton, to Russian industry and the disruptions to Russian trade caused by British and French action during the Crimean War.[101] In 1863, Mikhail Katkov, a reactionary newspaper editor, commented on the relative weakness of the Russian navy vis-à-vis those of the British and French and argued that greater benefit was to be derived from a few ships with open access to the ocean where they—or their potential Union allies—could pose a greater threat to the overseas trade of England and France.[102]

The threat to the sea trade and colonial possessions of England and France has been a central focus of Russian accounts of the fleets' 1863 visit, yet often overlooked is the fact that the threat's credibility stemmed from the appearance of strong Russian-American diplomatic ties.[103] Indeed, the Russian government had learned how the naval threat could be parlayed into political advantage from the British and French naval forces during the Crimean War—where the presence of their fleets in the Black Sea prevented the Russian navy from conducting effective operations and forced the country to acquiesce to the provisions of the Treaty of Paris.[104] In one of his letters to Gorchakov, Stoeckl commented on the public receptions and remarked, "It was not without a degree of envy that the English and the French observed the attention of which our sailors were the object, and they even expressed some displeasure in this connection."[105] It was logical for Russian representatives, alarmed at the prospect of foreign intervention, to underscore the country's cordial relations with the Union while emphasizing the domestic character of both insurrections. A report from the Russian Ministry of the Marine to Alexander II described the diplomatic effect: "This sudden appearance of Russia's Naval squadrons in the ports of the American Union was the more impressive because no one expected anything of the kind, coming at the very moment when an alliance was on the eve of being concluded between two of the greatest maritime Powers."[106] Having their fleets based in American ports from which they could operate against British and French interests gave the Russian government a powerful bargaining tool—a tool that relied on an explicit connection between Russian and American interests to be effective.

Conclusion:
The Legacy of the Fleet Episode in Russian-American Relations

A cursory glace at the visit of the Russian squadrons can lead to the easy conclusion that it had little direct effect on the affairs of the day. Certainly the actions of the sailors of the Pacific squadron in extinguishing a fire that ravaged parts of San Francisco and the Atlantic fleet's donation in the name of poor relief in New York City helped reinforce notions of friendship between the two states. In subsequent years, American diplomats in Russia like Jeremiah Curtin and Eugene Schuyler traced their first efforts to learn Russian all the way back to Lisovskii's mission to New York.[107] Yet a rumored alliance between the two countries never took place and, with the relaxation of European tensions over Russian actions in Poland, the Russian fleets in New York and San Francisco received orders to return to Russia in early 1864. In the United States, Union victories helped reverse the tide of the Civil War, and, with the benefit of hindsight, it became obvious that the likelihood of direct foreign intervention had passed by the time the Russian fleets arrived.[108] In Europe, when the British government surrendered to both domestic and international pressure and ordered the detention of the Laird Rams, one of the most serious points of Anglo-American tension gradually diminished.

Despite the rather limited direct effects on Russian-American relations of the fleets' extended stay in the United States, their presence was often invoked as a powerful example of the relationship between the two powers. When the American press reported the unsuccessful assassination attempt on Alexander II on April 16, 1866, newspapers reminded the public of "the friendly and unselfish favors shown by the Czar Alexander during our civil strife," and the United States was one of the first countries to respond with a note of congratulations. In June of that year, two American ships, the ironclad *Miantonomoh* and the side-wheel steamer *Augusta,* sailed for Russia, carrying an American mission led by Assistant Secretary of the Navy Gustavus Fox.[109] Fox's mission was treated to a lavish reception and a personal audience with the tsar, and in 1867 Admiral Lisovskii hosted a reception in honor of Admiral Farragut during the latter's visit to Kronstadt.[110] In September 1871, Grand Duke Alexis, son of Alexander II, made a prolonged visit to the United States, where he was presented with a portrait of Admiral Farragut, went on a buffalo hunt, and enjoyed ample toasts dedicated to the continued "peace and good will of the United States and Russia."[111] In March 1881, the American press greeted news of the assassination of Tsar Alexander II with dismay and an outpouring of public sympathy. Echoing the earlier parallel between the tsar and Lincoln, the *New York Times* described Alexander II as "a man of liberal instincts"—as evinced by his "emancipation of the serfs and in his warm admiration of, and intimate sympathy with, popular institutions as they exist in the United States. Undoubtedly he meditated the establishment of representative government in Russia as the crowning glory of his reign."[112] In New York, important dignitaries and the city's leading citizens jammed a small Greek chapel for a memorial, and the Senate passed a resolution denouncing the assassination and "cherishing with satisfaction the relations of genuine friendship that have always existed between the people and Governments of Russia and of the United States."[113]

Beyond these public assertions of friendship, the fleet episode was also invoked at key moments in the highest circles of government. Though the American government's interest in Russian Alaska predated the Crimean War, when the treaty negotiating the sale of the territory was completed between Secretary Seward and Minister Stoeckl in March 1867, the Russian naval visit was cited in support of the agreement. In his Senate speech on April 9, Charles Sumner exploited the memory of the Russian fleets. In providing reasons for Russia's willingness to surrender the vast territory, Sumner framed the decision in terms of Napoleon's sale of the Louisiana territory: as France had done earlier, now Russia was addressing the European balance, and the sale would "establish forever the power of the United States, and give to England a maritime rival that would sooner or later humble her pride." Sumner went on to call the treaty "a new expression of that *entente cordiale* between the two powers which is a phenomenon of history" and used as evidence Russian mediation in the War of 1812, the Russian-American telegraph, and "the visit of the Russian fleet in the winter of 1863, intended by the Emperor, and accepted by the United States, as a friendly demonstration."[114] Sumner certainly saw economic potential in the territory, but it is telling that he put aside his past support for Poland to craft an argument on behalf of the treaty around the character and history of Russian friendship.

Rather than a case of one-sided manipulation or mutually beneficial but incidental support, the Russian fleet episode demonstrated how both sides selectively embellished the visit to suit their own ends set against a public tradition of cordial relations. In dismissing the sincerity of the apparent cordiality of Russian-American relations, Thomas Bailey remarked that in international friendships, results, not motives, are what matter.[115] Russian and American authorities, separately understanding the maneuver through the lens of national self-interest, demonstrated a sophisticated awareness of and alarm over the fleets' symbolic value precisely because of the popular perception of friendly relations between the two states. In light of the renewed popular and scholarly interest in Russian-American relations during the mid-nineteenth century, the reception for and the reaction to the visit of the Russian fleets challenge conventional evaluations of Russia's significance to the diplomacy of the American Civil War and illustrate how the two states utilized diplomatic connections and popular perceptions of their close relations to influence larger diplomatic questions.[116]

NOTES

1. See, for example, "The Russian Fleet," *New York Herald,* September 26, 1863, 7; "Russian Frigates," *New York Times,* September 23, 1863, 1; "A Russian Fleet Coming into Our Harbor; Their Arrival," *New York Times,* September 24, 1863, 2.

2. "Our Naval Visitors," *New York Times,* September 26, 1863, 5, emphasis added.

3. Lisovskii's squadron boasted roughly 170 guns and 2,400 men. It was rumored that three additional vessels would also arrive, bringing the total force to around 300 guns and 5,000 men, but these reinforcements were not sent. See "The Russian Squadron—Eastern Russia—Russian Commerce," *New York Times,* September 30, 1863, 4.

4. See, for example, Thomas W. Balch, *The Alabama Arbitration* (Philadelphia: Allen, Lane and Scott, 1900), 28–32; James M. Callahan, "Russo-American Relations during the American Civil War" (Morgantown: Department of History and Political Science, West Virginia University, January 1908), 2–4, 11–13; Thomas L. Harris, *The Trent Affair* (Indianapolis: Bobbs-Merrill, 1896), 207–10.

5. General Rush C. Hawkins, "The Coming of the Russian Ships in 1863," *North American Review,* April 1904, 539.

6. Golder, "The Russian Fleet and the Civil War," 801.

7. Goncharov and White, who were the first to make use of the official records, had previously affirmed the primacy of European concerns when they discussed the orders in a compendium commemorating the fiftieth anniversary of the 1863 visit. In subsequent work, E. A. Adamov—apparently working without being aware of Golder's 1915 article—reiterated this claim and published the order itself in 1930. See E. A. Adamov, "Documents Relating to Russian Policy during the American Civil War," *Journal of Modern History* 2 (December 1930): 603–7; E. A. Adamov, "Russia and the United States at the Time of the Civil War," *Journal of Modern History* 2 (December 1930): 586, n. 2.

8. William E. Nagengast, "The Visit of the Russian Fleet to the United States: Were Americans Deceived?" *Russian Review* 8 (January 1949): 46–55.

9. Thomas A. Bailey, "The Russian Fleet Myth Re-Examined," *Mississippi Valley Historical Review* 38 (June 1951): 85. For additional explanations, see Robin Higham, "The Russian Fleet on the Eastern Seaboard, 1863–1864," *American Neptune* 20 (January 1960): 49–61; Howard I. Kushner, "The Russian Fleet and the American Civil War: Another View," *Historian* 34 (August 1972): 633–49; Earl S. Pomeroy, "The Myth after the Russian Fleet, 1863," *New York History* 31 (April 1950): 169–76; Albert A. Woldman, *Lincoln and the Russians* (Cleveland: World Publishing Co., 1952), 140–66.

10. Adamov, "Russia and the United States at the Time of the Civil War"; V. Arsen'ev, "Amerikanskaia Ekspeditsiia Russkogo Flota v 1863–1864 gg.," *Morskoi sbornik* (1995): 72–76; Nikolai N. Bolkhovitinov, "Istoriki v Poiskakh Istiny: Vizit Russkogo Flota v SSHA v 1863–1864," *Amerikanskii Ezhegodnik* (1994): 194–207.

11. Arsenev, "Amerikanskaia Ekspeditsiia Russkogo Flota v 1863–1864 gg.," 72; Nina S. Kiniapina, "Russia and the U.S. Civil War," in *Russian-American Dialogue on Cultural Relations, 1776–1914,* ed. Norman E. Saul and Richard D. McKinzie (Columbia: University of Missouri Press, 1997), 105.

12. Tom Delahaye, "The Bilateral Effect of the Visit of the Russian Fleet in 1863," *Loyola University Student Historical Journal* 15 (Spring–Fall 1984): 33–42; C. Douglas Kroll, *Friends in Peace and War: The Russian Navy's Landmark Visit to Civil War San Francisco* (Washington, D.C.: Potomac Books, 2007); Norman E. Saul, *Distant Friends: The United States and Russia, 1763–1867* (Lawrence: University of Kansas Press, 1991), 339–54.

13. David P. Crook, *The North, the South and the Powers, 1861–1865* (New York: John Wiley, 1974), vi; Howard Jones, *Blue and Gray Diplomacy: A History of Union and Confederate Foreign Relations* (Chapel Hill: University of North Carolina Press, 2010), 4. Other influential accounts of Civil War diplomacy frequently treat the Union and the Confederacy separately; Ephraim Douglass Adams, *Great Britain and the American Civil War* (New York: Longmans, Green, 1925); Bruce Catton, *The Civil War* (Boston: Mariner Books, 2005); James T. de Kay, *The Rebel Raiders: The Astonishing History of the Confederacy's Secret Navy* (New York: Ballantine Books, 2002); Edwin De Leon, *Secret History of Confederate Diplomacy Abroad,* ed. William C. Davis (Lawrence: University Press of Kansas, 2005 [1867]); James M. McPherson, *Battle Cry of Freedom: The Civil War Era* (repr., New York: Oxford University Press, 2003); Frank J. Merli, *The Alabama, British Neutrality and the American Civil War,* ed. David M. Fahey (Bloomington: Indiana University Press, 2004); Frank Lawrence Owsley, *King Cotton Diplomacy: Foreign Relations of the Confederate States of America* (Tuscaloosa: University of Alabama Press, 2008 [1931]).

14. Ronald J. Jensen, "Comment," in *Russian-American Dialogue on Cultural Relations, 1776–1914,* ed. Norman E. Saul and Richard D. McKinzie (Columbia: University of Missouri Press, 1997); Kiniapina, "Russia and the U.S. Civil War."

15. Bailey argued that the belief in Russian friendship at the core of the fleet myth endured because of the visit's "opportune timing, its emotional impact, and its picturesque quality," rather than because of any mutually derived benefit. Thomas A. Bailey, *America Faces Russia: Russian-American Relations from Early Times to Our Day* (Ithaca: Cornell University Press, 1950), 93.

16. Thomas A. Bailey, *Probing America's Past: A Critical Examination of Major Myths and Misconceptions* (Lexington: Heath, 1973); John Lewis Gaddis, *We Now Know: Rethinking Cold War History* (New York: Oxford University Press, 1997), 2–4; Max M. Laserson, *The American Impact on Russia: Diplomatic and Ideological, 1784–1917* (New York: Macmillan, 1950), 162, 70; David Mayers, *The Ambassadors and America's Soviet Policy* (New York: Oxford University Press, 1995), 11, 30–32, 35–40.

17. Nikolai N. Bolkhovitinov, *The Beginnings of Russian-American Relations, 1775–1815,* trans. Elena Levin (Cambridge, Mass.: Harvard University Press, 1975), 355, 362. See also David S. Foglesong, *The American Mission and the "Evil Empire": The Crusade for a "Free Russia" since 1881* (Cambridge: Cambridge University Press, 2007); Hugh Seton-Watson, *The Decline of Imperial Russia, 1855–1914* (Boulder, Colo.: Westview Press, 1985); Nikolai V. Sivachev and Nikolai N. Yakovlev, *Russia and the United States,* trans. Olga Adler Titelbaum (Chicago: University of Chicago Press, 1979).

18. Saul, *Distant Friends,* 336–54; Victoria I. Zhuravleva,. "Eho Grazhdanskoi Voini 1861–1865 gg. v Rossiiskoi-Amerikanskii Otnosheniah," in *Avraam Linkol'n: Uroki Istorii i Sovremennost',* ed. Victoria I. Zhuravleva (Moscow: Russian State Humanities University, 2010), 173, 191. For examples and discussions of how interpretations of events in Russian-American relations have been shaped by contemporary political agendas, see A. A. Arustamova, "Amerikanskaia Tema v Kurse Russkoi Slovesnosti XIX-nachala XX veka," in *Russia and the United States: Mutual Representations in Textbooks,* ed. Victoria I. Zhuravleva and Ivan I. Kurilla (Volgograd: Volgograd State University, 2009), 68–83; Hiroo Nakajima, "The Monroe Doctrine and Russia: American Views of Czar Alexander I and Their Influence upon Early Russian-American Relations." *Diplomatic History* 31 (June 2007): 439–63; Victoria I. Zhuravleva and Ivan I. Kurilla, "Obrazi Rossii na Stranitsah Amerikanskih Shol'nih Uchebnikov Istorii XIX-nachala XX veka," in *Russia and the United States: Mutual Representations in Textbooks,* ed. Victoria I. Zhuravleva and Ivan I. Kurilla (Volgograd: Volgograd State University, 2009), 16–67.

19. Oscar S. Straus, "The United States and Russia: Their Historical Relations," *North American Review* (August 1905): 243.

20. "General News," *Philadelphia Inquirer,* October 1, 1863, 4.

21. Admiral Popov had made two previous visits to San Francisco, in 1859 and 1862, and had many friends in the city. The corvette *Novik,* one of the six vessels of Popov's fleet, had visited the city as recently as January 1860.

22. "Russia and America," *Philadelphia Inquirer,* October 29, 1863, 4.

23. "Banquet to the Russian Officers," *Chicago Tribune,* October 2, 1863, emphasis supplied.

24. "Our Russian Visitors," *Harper's Weekly,* October 17, 1863, 662.

25. Nicholas V. Riasanovsky, *A History of Russia* (New York: Oxford University Press, 2000), 378. For the United States and the question of slavery's expansion, see Glenn M. Linden, *Voices from the Gathering Storm: The Coming of the American Civil War* (Wilmington: Rowman and Littlefield, 2001), 236; McPherson, *Battle Cry of Freedom,* 241–53.

26. "Russia and America," *Philadelphia Inquirer,* October 29, 1863, 4.

27. Seward to Clay, May 11, 1863, cited in Harold E. Blinn, "Seward and the Polish Rebellion of 1863," *American Historical Review* 45 (July 1940): 830–31. See also "No. 9, Official: Mr. Clay to Mr. Seward, 7 June 1863," U.S. Department of State (hereafter RG 59), M35; "Despatches from United States Ministers to Russia, 1808–1906," Roll 20 (March 13, 1863–December 28, 1865), National Archives Records Administration, Washington, D.C. (hereafter NARA). On the importance of Poland more generally, see François Charles-Roux, *Alexandre II, Gortchakoff et Napoléon III* (Paris: Plon-Nourrit et cie, 1913), 315–16; John Kutolowski, "The Effect of the Polish Insurrection of 1863 on American Civil War Diplomacy" *Historian* 27 (August 1965): 560–77; Laserson, *The American Impact on Russia,* 179; Sergei S. Tatishchev, *Imperator Aleksandr II, ego zhizn' i tsarstvovanie* (St. Petersburg: A.S. Suvorina, 1911), 1: 487; Benjamin Platt Thomas, *Russo-American Relations, 1815–1867* (Baltimore: The Johns Hopkins University Press, 1930), 136–37.

28. Though ostensibly private diplomatic correspondence, such exchanges were occasionally published to reinforce public opposition to foreign intervention. See, for

example, the annexes to "N. 29—Stoeckl to Gorchakov, 14 April 1863" and "N. 55—Stoeckl to Gorchakov, 2 July 1863," Folder 2, Box 2, Record Group 49, Central Archive, Moscow, Russia, Foreign Affairs, Library of Congress Manuscript Division, Washington, D.C. (hereafter RG 49).

29. Quoted in Moorfield Storey, *Charles Sumner* (Boston: Houghton, Mifflin, 1900), 251.

30. "The Great Russian Ball," *Harper's Weekly,* November 21, 1863, 746.

31. "The Lounger: The Russians," *Harper's Weekly,* October 24, 1863, 674; "The Lounger: The Ball," *Harper's Weekly,* November 21, 1863, 738.

32. "The Russian Ball," *Harper's Weekly,* November 21, 1863, 738. Picking up on the contrast between Russian autocracy and the American republic, other papers publicly expressed dismay that anyone would conflate the names of Peter the Great and George Washington. See "The Russian Reception at New York," *The Liberator* (Boston), December 4, 1863.

33. Adamov, "Russia and the United States at the Time of the Civil War," 602. One way in which the Atlantic squadron actively engaged the community of New York City was through the voluntary collection of $4,700 from the officers before their departure. In donating the money to the mayor, Lisovskii requested that the money be used to benefit the city's destitute. "Magnificent Gift to the Poor of New York by the Russian Officers," *Daily Evening Bulletin* (San Francisco), January 4, 1864, 5.

34. Kroll, *Friends in Peace and War,* 78–81.

35. Golder, "The Russian Fleet and the Civil War," 809.

36. "N. 3—Stoeckl to Gorchakov, 9 January 1861," Folder 4, Box 3, RG 49. In contrast to the way other Confederate representatives were received in Europe, the envoy to Russia, Lucius Q. C. Lamar, was spurned by Gorchakov and was eventually recalled. Undoubtedly, part of Stoeckl's reticence with regard to the Confederacy stemmed from the many friends he had on that side of the struggle, his generally high opinion of Jefferson Davis and the Confederate generals, and his low estimation of the institutions of democracy—though not the American people. See "N. 11—Stoeckl to Gorchakov, 13 February 1861," Folder 3, Box 2; "N. 27—Stoeckl to Gorchakov, 15 April 1861," Folder 3, Box 2; "N. 61—Stoeckl to Gorchakov, 11 September 1863", Folder 2, Box 2; "N. 74—Stoeckl to Gorchakov, 22 November 1863," Folder 2, Box 2; "N. 81—Stoeckl to Gorchakov, 19 December 1863," Folder 7, Box 3, RG 49.

37. See "N. 29—Stoeckl to Gorchakov, 14 April 1863," Folder 2, Box 2, RG 49; Taylor's letters to Seward, excerpted in Marie Hansen-Taylor and Horace E. Scudder, eds., *Life and Letters of Bayard Taylor* (Boston: Houghton, Mifflin, 1884), 1: 397–402; Woldman, *Lincoln and the Russians,* 134–37.

38. See Adamov, "Documents Relating to Russian Policy during the American Civil War," 608.

39. The article concluded with, "From other sources it is known that the reception of the Russian naval officers in the United States has produced much enthusiasm throughout Russia." "Cordial Acknowledgement," *New York Times,* December 18, 1863, 4.

40. Harris, *The Trent Affair,* 207–10; Thurlow Weed, *Life of Thurlow Weed, Including His Autobiography and a Memoir,* ed. Harriet A. Weed and Thurlow Weed Barnes (Boston: Houghton Mifflin, 1884), 2: 346–47.

41. Woldman, *Lincoln and the Russians,* 153–55.

42. See Balch, *The Alabama Arbitration,* 28–32; Callahan, "Russo-American Relations during the American Civil War," 4, 11–13; Hawkins, "The Coming of the Russian Ships in 1863."

43. "No. 5—Instructions to Count Pahlen by Alexander I, Washington, 1809"; "No. 24—Instructions to Baron Tuyll by Alexander I, Washington, 1817," Box 1, RG 49.

44. Hugh Seton-Watson, *The Russian Empire, 1801–1917* (Oxford: Clarendon Press, 1967), 297. See also Barbara Jelavich, *A Century of Russian Foreign Policy, 1814–1914* (Philadelphia: Lippincott, 1964), 125–27; Seton-Watson, *The Decline of Imperial Russia, 1855–1914;* Thomas, *Russo-American Relations, 1815–1867,* 9–10.

45. Francis Henry Skrine, *The Expansion of Russia* (Cambridge: Cambridge University Press, 1915),125.

46. For a description of the difficulties experienced laying the cable as well as the benefits of this transatlantic communication, see "The Ocean Telegraph," *New York Times,* August 31, 1857, 1.

47. "The Great Atlantic Telegraph," *New York Times,* June 26, 1858, 1.

48. Collins's account was one of two that appeared at roughly the same time. Published in 1858, *Oriental and Western Siberia: A Narrative of Seven Years' Explorations and Adventures in Siberia, Mongolia, the Khirgis Steppes, Chinese Tartary, and Parts of Central Asia* was the travel journal of the British artist Thomas Atkinson. Collins's own account, with an equally verbose title, appeared first in 1860 and then, in expanded form, in 1864. That year the *New York Times* revealed that Atkinson's account was "borrowed" from a Russian chronicle. For reviews of each, see, respectively, "Another Great Travel Book; Uniform with Livingstone's Travels—Atkinson's Siberia," *Harper's Weekly,* March 6, 1858, 159; "New Books," *New York Times,* August 8, 1864, 2.

49. "The Russian Squadron—Eastern Russia—Russian Commerce," *New York Times,* September 30, 1863, 4; Perry McDonough Collins, *Siberian Journey: Down the Amur to the Pacific, 1856–1857,* ed. Charles Vevier (Madison: University of Wisconsin Press, 1962 [1860]), 35–36.

50. "Foreign News: England: Is the Atlantic Telegraph a Failure?" *Harper's Weekly,* October 9, 1858, 646.

51. "The International Telegraph," *Christian Recorder,* November 9, 1861. For a complete account of the construction project, see Perry McDonough Collins and Western Union Telegraph Company, *Statement of the Origin, Organization and Progress of the Russian-American Telegraph Western Union Extension, Collins' Overland Line, via Behring Strait and Asiatic Russia to Europe* (Rochester: Evening Express Printing Office, 1866).

52. "No. 5, Official: Mr. Clay to Mr. Seward," in U.S. Department of State, *Message of the President of the United States, and Accompanying Documents, to the Two Houses of Congress, at the Commencement of the First Session of the Thirty-Eighth Congress* (Washington, D.C.: U.S. Government Printing Office, 1863), 2: 870.

53. "A Russian Alliance," *Harper's Weekly,* October 17, 1863, 658.

54. See, respectively, "No. 10, Official: Mr. Clay to Mr. Seward," June 17, 1863 and "No. 24, Official: Mr. Clay to Mr. Seward," October 7, 1863, RG 59, M35, Roll 20. Though

the plan received the early support of President Lincoln, a series of unexpected hardships and the success, in 1866, of the transatlantic telegraph line caused the entire enterprise to be abandoned. On the line's failure, see "New Cable Laid in Record Time," *New York Times*, October 7, 1928, 20; U.S. Department of State, *Message of the President of the United States to the Two Houses of Congress at the Commencement of the Third Session of the Thirty-Seventh Congress* (Washington, D.C.: U.S. Government Printing Office, 1862), 1: 6.

55. In his study of Russian naval modernization in the wake of the Crimean War, Jacob Kipp highlights the importance of the defeat and the technological revolution, rather than just the personality of Grand Duke Constantine Nikolaevich. See Jacob W. Kipp, "Consequences of Defeat: Modernizing the Russian Navy, 1856–1863," *Jahrbücher für Geschichte Osteuropas* 20 (June 1972): 211–13, 224–25; Riasanovsky, *A History of Russia*, 368–78; Saul, *Distant Friends*, 237–39; Skrine, *The Expansion of Russia*, 175.

56. In describing the scuttling of the Black Sea fleet to block the harbor of Sevastopol, Fred Jane calls the Russian action "suicide." Fred T. Jane, *The Imperial Russian Navy: Its Past, Present, and Future* (London: W. Thacker, 1899), 151.

57. Adolph A. Hoehling, *Thunder at Hampton Roads* (New York: Da Capo Press, 1993), ix. For studies and contemporary commentary, see "The Second Trip of the 'Merrimac' [*sic*]," *Harper's Weekly*, May 3, 1862, 278, illustration on 277; James L. Nelson, *Reign of Iron: The Story of the First Battling Ironclads, the Monitor and the Merrimack* (New York: William Morrow, 2004). Philip Van Doren argues against the significance of the clash, writing that "it proved nothing more than the obvious fact that iron is harder to penetrate with shot and shell than wood." James D. Bulloch, *The Secret Service of the Confederate States in Europe; or How the Confederate Cruisers Were Equipped* (New York: Thomas Yoseloff, 1959), 1: v.

58. "Foreign News," *Harper's Weekly*, May 3, 1862, 275. Built in England, the ironclad *Pervenetz* was launched in 1863; that March, the Russian government appropriated four million pounds sterling for the construction of a fleet of ironclads. See "The Russia Frigate Osliaba," *Harper's Weekly*, October 3, 1863, 635.

59. For a discussion of the rights of neutrals, see "Letter from Marcy to Stoeckl," April 14, 1854, RG 59, M99, Roll 82. For an extensive discussion of American ties to Russia during the Crimean War, see Saul, *Distant Friends*, 198–236. The *New York Herald* praised Webb as "The very first naval architect in this country" while the *New York Times* named him the foremost shipbuilder in the world. "Crown of W. H. Webb's Life," *New York Times*, May 6, 1894.

60. "William H. Webb Dead," *New York Times*, October 31, 1899, 7; Edwin L. Dunbaugh and William duBarry Thomas, *William H. Webb: Shipbuilder* (Glen Cove, N.Y.: Webb Institute of Naval Architecture, 1989), 204–5.

61. "Marine Matters," *New York Times*, June 27, 1857, 1.

62. There is a discrepancy in the ship's description, as it is listed at 327 feet in the text and 313 feet 7 inches in the Appendix. See Dunbaugh and Thomas, *William H. Webb*, 78, 201.

63. "Sea and Ship News," *New York Times*, September 6, 1858, 8; "Sea and Ship News: Launch of the Russian Frigate, Yesterday," *New York Times*, September 22, 1858, 5.

64. "Excursion of the General Admiral," *New York Times,* May 19, 1859, 8; "Russian Acknowledgements of American Skill," *New York Times,* July 11, 1860, 2; Dunbaugh and Thomas, *William H. Webb,* 201.

65. Webb's other ship for the Russian navy was the steam corvette *Japanis* (sometimes referred to as *Japanese*), built under a contract with Captain Crown for use on the Amur River. "The Russian Corvette and the Egyptian Yacht," *Harper's Weekly,* March 27, 1858, 200, 202.

66. The rivalry between English and American shipbuilders was evident in English naval critics "abusing the Russian frigate *General Admiral*" and in the vigorous defense mounted by American news correspondents in St. Petersburg. "The Trip of the General Admiral Frigate to England, 29 September 1859," *New York Times,* November 18, 1859, 1. See also Dunbaugh and Thomas, *William H. Webb,* 90–91.

67. "The Great Russian Ball," *Harper's Weekly,* November 21, 1863, 746.

68. Letter from Abraham Lincoln to Joshua F. Speed, August 24, 1855, in Abraham Lincoln, *Letters and Addresses of Abraham Lincoln,* ed. Mary Maclean (New York: Unit Book Publishing Company, 1907), 91.

69. See, for example, "No. 60, Stoeckl to Gorchakov," December 23, 1860 (Old Style), Folder 3, Box 2; "No. 74, Stoeckl to Gorchakov," November 22, 1863 (Old Style), Folder 2, Box 2, RG 49; A. R. Tyrner-Tyrnauer, *Lincoln and the Emperors* (Bristol: Western Printing Services, 1962); Woldman, *Lincoln and the Russians.*

70. "Varieties: Russia and America," *Christian Recorder,* September 14, 1861.

71. See respectively, "Emancipation in Russia—12 January 1861," *Christian Recorder,* February 9, 1861; "Russia and America," *Christian Recorder,* February 22, 1862.

72. "Emancipation in Russia—12 January 1861," *Christian Recorder,* February 9, 1861.

73. "No. 6: Letter from Mr. Seward to Mr. Taylor," November 24, 1862, RG 59, M77, Roll 136.

74. "Letter from Mr. Phelps to Mr. Seward," December 19, 1863, RG 59, M81, Roll 06.

75. Quoted in Kiniapina, "Russia and the U.S. Civil War," 98.

76. "No. 17, Letter from Clay to Seward," August 5, 1863, RG 59, M35, Roll 20.

77. "No. 21, Official: Mr. Clay to Mr. Seward," September 19, 1863. For Clay's sentiments on the European situation, see "No. 19, Official: Mr. Clay to Mr. Seward," September 2, 1863, RG 59, M35, Roll 20.

78. "No. 24, Official: Mr. Clay to Mr. Seward," 7 October 1863, RG 59, M35, Roll 20.

79. For accounts of Confederate efforts, see Bulloch, *The Secret Service of the Confederate States in Europe;* De Kay, *The Rebel Raiders;* De Leon, *Secret History of Confederate Diplomacy Abroad;* Jones, *Blue and Gray Diplomacy,* 191–201; Merli, *The Alabama, British Neutrality and the American Civil War.*

80. For unsuccessful Confederate efforts to sell the *Alexandra* to Russian officials, see "James H. North to J.M. Mason, 26 June 1863" and "James H. North to Navy Department, 10 July 1863," in *Official Records of the Union and Confederate Navies in the War of the Rebellion* (Washington, D.C.: Government Printing Office, 1922), 3: 443, 57–59 (hereafter referred to as ORN).

81. "No. 31, Official: Mr. Clay to Mr. Seward," November 19, 1863, RG 59, M35, Roll 20; "Letter from Mr. Phelps to Mr. Seward," September 29, 1863, RG 59, M81, Roll 06.

82. "Additional from Europe," *New York Herald,* October 27, 1863, 4; "Affairs in England," *New York Times,* November 7, 1863, 1; "The Anglo-Rebel Rams," *Harper's Weekly,* October 17, 1863, 661; "Foreign News: England: The New Rebel Rams, England Alarmed at Her New Naval Doctrine," *Harper's Weekly,* September 19, 1863, 595; "Foreign News: England: The Neutrality Law," *Harper's Weekly,* August 15, 1863, 515; "Foreign News: England: A Speech from Earl Russell," *Harper's Weekly,* October 24, 1863, 675; "French Rams," *Harper's Weekly,* November 21, 1863, 739; "Our Transatlantic Cousins," *Harper's Weekly,* October 31, 1863, 690.

83. This does not mean, however, that there was no tension. As late as June 1864, Confederate representatives were still considering using Russians to help transfer vessels purchased in Europe. Further, at the same time that stories of the Laird Rams were dominating news reports related to England, the Russian legation in Washington, D.C., was protesting the federal government's response to Japan's interests in a dispute with Russia over Sakhalin Island. The Russian letters were concerned with the possibility of perceived differences between the two countries. See "Stoeckl letter to Department of State," September 22, 1863, RG 59, M39, Roll 3; "Bulloch to Mallory, 3 June 1864," in *ORN,* 2: 661.

84. "New York City: Sea and Ship News," *New York Times,* September 6, 1858, 8.

85. "Russia and America," *Christian Recorder,* February 22, 1862.

86. "Drawing Things to a Head," *Harper's Weekly,* November 28, 1863, 768.

87. Bailey, *America Faces Russia,* 2.

88. Howard Kushner's article, which appeared a year before Bailey's, examined the deception and argued, "The conscious policy of the Administration and its allies, and not Russian deception, created the popular and scholarly confusion over Russia's intentions." While more sophisticated than Bailey's argument—by acknowledging Union attempts at deception—it also failed to consider how successfully manipulating the visit's purpose for political ends depended on a shared belief in close Russian-American relations and fails to attribute any lasting impact to the visits. Kushner, "The Russian Fleet and the American Civil War: Another View," 649.

89. Abraham Lincoln, *Uncollected Letters of Abraham Lincoln,* ed. Gilbert A. Tracy (Boston: Houghton Mifflin, 1917), 237.

90. Frederick W. Seward, *Reminiscences of a War-Time Statesman and Diplomat, 1830–1915* (New York: G. P. Putnam's Sons, 1916), 218.

91. "No. 10: Letter from Mr. Seward to Mr. Taylor," December 23, 1862, RG 59, M77, Roll 136.

92. "No. 52: Letter from Mr. Seward to Mr. Clay," December 8, 1863, RG 59, M77, Roll 136.

93. Henry Clews, "England and Russia in Our Civil War," *North American Review* (June 1904): 816.

94. Gideon Welles, *Diary of Gideon Welles, Secretary of the Navy under Lincoln and Johnson* (New York: Norton, 1960), 443, 80.

95. Edward Lillie Pierce, ed., *Memoir and Letters of Charles Sumner* (Boston: Roberts Brothers, 1877), 4:146.

96. Charles Sumner, *The Works of Charles Sumner* (Boston: Lee and Shepard, 1870–83), 7: 397.

97. "No. 24, Official: Mr. Clay to Mr. Seward, 7 October 1863," RG 59, M35, Roll 20.

98. Adamov, "Documents Relating to Russian Policy during the American Civil War," 603.

99. "Letter from Mr. Phelps to Mr. Seward, 31 December 1863," RG 59, M81, Roll 07; "Foreign News," *Harper's Weekly,* May 3, 1862, 275. As part of a program of crash modernization, in March 1863 the Russian government appropriated four million pounds sterling for the construction of a fleet of ironclads. See "The Russia Frigate Osliaba," *Harper's Weekly,* October 3, 1863, 635.

100. From *The Works of James Buchanan,* vol. 9, cited in Frank A. Golder, "Russian-American Relations during the Crimean War," *American Historical Review* 31 (April 1926): 465.

101. « No. 652—Mémoire sur le commerce de la Russie avec les États Unis d'Amérique, Washington, 1854, » Box 1, RG 49.

102. Katkov, Mikhail N. *1863 God,* Vol. 2. Detroit: UMI Press, 1971 [1887], 961–62. See also "S.R. Mallory to C.M. Conrad, 10 May 1861," in Office, United States Naval War Records. Navy Department Correspondence, 1861-1865, with Agents Abroad. Vol. II, Official Records of the Union and Confederate Navies in the War of the Rebellion. (Washington D.C.: Government Printing Office, 1921), 67–69.

103. Kutolowski, "The Effect of the Polish Insurrection of 1863 on American Civil War Diplomacy," 571; Laurence J. Orzell, "A 'Favorable Interval': The Polish Insurrection in Civil War Diplomacy, 1863," *Civil War History* 24 (December 1978): 332–33.

104. Sergei G. Gorshkov, *Red Star Rising at Sea,* ed. Colonel Herbert Preston, USMC, Ret., trans. Theodore A. Neely Jr. (Washington, D.C.: U.S. Naval Institute, 1974), 27–28; Kipp, "Consequences of Defeat: Modernizing the Russian Navy, 1856–1863," 214, 24 n. 63.

105. Quoted in Sivachev and Yakovlev, *Russia and the United States,* 12.

106. Alexandre Tarsaïdzé, *Czars and Presidents: The Story of a Forgotten Friendship* (New York: McDowell, Obolensky, 1958), 214.

107. Norman E. Saul, *Concord and Conflict: The United States and Russia, 1867–1914* (Lawrence: University Press of Kansas, 1996), 13–16.

108. Jones, *Blue and Gray Diplomacy,* 253–84.

109. J. F. Loubat, who chronicled the Fox mission, wrote of Russian-American relations: "The friendship . . . between Russia and the United States . . . was cemented anew when our ancient ally, alone of the governments of the old world, sent to us words of sympathy when we were believed by our enemies to be in the throes of dissolution." Upon the arrival of the Russian fleets, "we welcomed them as friends and allies," Loubat wrote, "and tried to prove by deeds all that our words expressed." While the congressional resolution to Alexander II after his attempted assassination was "unique" and contained "fitting expressions" of shared sympathy and friendship, so too was Gorchakov's speech at a banquet honoring the Fox delegation in September 1866. See J. F. Loubat, *Narrative of the Mission to Russia, in 1866, of the Hon. Gustavus Vasa Fox,* ed. John D. Champlin (New York: D. Appleton, 1873), 20–22, 436–39.

110. "Admiral Farragut's Reception at Cronstadt," *Farmers' Cabinet* 66, no. 8: 2; "Beaumont's Russian Trip," *New York Times,* August 7, 1882, 5.

111. "The Coming Russian," *New York Times,* July 18, 1871, 6; "Grand Duke Alexis," *New York Times,* December 3, 1871, 1.

112. "What the Nihilists Have Done," *New York Times,* March 14, 1881, 4.

113. "Expressions of Sympathy," *New York Times,* March 15, 1881, 2; "In Memory of the Czar," *New York Times,* March 21, 1881. Another mass was held in Washington, D.C., on the first anniversary of the assassination. Presiding over that mass was Father Nicholas Bjerring, who also served the mass in New York in 1881.

114. Sumner, *The Works of Charles Sumner,* 11: 200–01, 28–30.

115. Bailey, *America Faces Russia,* 2.

116. Much of the renewed interest can be tied into popular efforts to "reset" relations with Russia as well as interest stemming from the 150th anniversaries of the Civil War and, subsequently, Lincoln's Emancipation Proclamation. In February 2011 a new exhibit, "The Tsar and the President, Alexander II and Abraham Lincoln: Liberator and Emancipator," opened at the State Archive of the Russian Federation. At the opening, the American ambassador stated, "Maybe because we all remember very well the years of the Cold War, sometimes we mistakenly think that the spirit of ideological confrontation between Russia and America is characteristic of our relations, but this is a mistake." See Sophia Kishkovsky, "Russia Links Lincoln with the Freedom of Serfs," *New York Times,* February 23, 2011, http://www.nytimes.com/2011/02/24/world/europe/24iht-lincoln.html (accessed November 13, 2012). Additionally, academic conferences examining global aspects of how Lincoln is remembered and international perspectives on the Civil War have been held at Oxford (2009), at the Russian State University for the Humanities (2009), and at the College of Charleston (2011).

NIELS EICHHORN

The Rhine River

The Impact of the German States on Transatlantic Diplomacy

On January 19, 1859, Emperor Napoleon III of France and the Piedmont-Sardinian prime minister Camillo Benso, Conte di Cavour, concluded a formal alliance aimed at ending the Habsburg Empire's hold on northern Italy and to bring about Italian unification.[1] In the treaty, Piedmont-Sardinia agreed to cede Nice and Savoy to France as compensation for French assistance in gaining the Austrian provinces of Trentino, Lombardy, and possibly Venetia. The exchange was confirmed in yet another secret treaty, signed on March 12 and 14, 1860, and shortly thereafter, the two territories changed sovereigns.[2]

These two provinces gained Napoleon a natural frontier on the southeastern flank of his imperial realm; however, the annexation had another unintended effect on diplomacy. Along the Rhine River, in the German states, in the Low Countries, and even in Great Britain, concerns emerged about the French emperor's future plans concerning the eastern frontier. It was an open secret that Napoleon wanted to rearrange the European state system, which had been created by the Congress of Vienna in 1815. Alan J. P. Taylor wrote in his 1954 classic, *The Struggle for Mastery in Europe,* "Thanks to the annexation of [Nice and] Savoy, the British government, which had cheerfully worked with Napoleon in his adventurous days, were incurably suspicious just when he had become pacific and conservative." Taylor goes on to quote Britain's prime minster, John Henry Temple, Lord Palmerston: "The whole drift of our policy is to prevent France from realizing her vast schemes of expansion and aggression in a great number of Quarters."[3] The situation in Europe at the outbreak of the American Civil War was one of mistrust and explosive tensions, at the center of which was the Rhine River.

The following discussion uses the Rhine River problem to show how European issues drew the attention of the European great powers during the American Civil War. The Euro-centric approach, which does not follow the usual state-to-state narrative often used in diplomatic history, is intended to move Civil War diplomacy out of the confines of the "Anglo-bubble." Because of the heavy focus on Great Britain, historians tend to deal extensively with the legal issues of war and to start their works with the outbreak of hostilities instead of observing the *longue durée* of international relations. Many Civil War diplomatic historians would most likely agree with Howard Jones, who recently said that "French, Russian, and, to some extent, Spanish, Austrian, and Prussian diplomacy, became ancillary to the decisions made in London. British, Union, and Confederate diplomacy provided the vital heart of the interventionist question."[4] This essay, in contrast, maintains that those relations did matter in determining British policy. The Rhine River problem illustrates the complicated nature of Europe during the Civil War and suggests an additional reason for Great Britain's policy of strict neutrality.

As the major nation that could alter the balance of power by its mere diplomatic interaction, Great Britain could not risk a war with the United States at any time during the Civil War. A war in North America would have distracted Great Britain and would have given Napoleon free rein to reorganize the continental state system to his liking. Often these concerns were mere illusions, but in historic events perceptions sometimes matter more than fact, and the mere rumor of a French army on the Rhine River affected Great Britain's policymakers as much as an army could have done. Therefore, the Rhine River problem shows that European powers, especially Great Britain, prioritized the volatile situation in Europe and delegated the developments in North America to lower priority.[5]

The British anxiety about French ambitions concerning the Rhine River is entirely absent from Civil War diplomatic scholarship, as are most of the continental crises of the period. Recent studies like Phillip Myers's *Caution and Cooperation,* Jay Sexton's *Debtor Diplomacy,* and even the many works by Howard Jones tend to present the diplomatic relations between Great Britain and the United States as if there were few European issues of concern.[6] Yet, as Sexton has acknowledged, "A truly international history of the war years should consider not only the diplomacy of the Union, the Confederacy, and the European powers, but should also explore how the war shaped international events and how events outside of the United States influenced the war."[7] The latter issue is of concern here. Alexander DeConde made a similar argument forty years earlier, when he asked historians to broaden their understanding and to present diplomatic relations in an international context.[8] So far, only David P. Crook has tried to present this broader framework for the Civil War.[9] An international history of the mid-nineteenth century or the Civil War has still to see the light of day.[10]

Of course, a presentation of Civil War diplomacy based largely on developments in Europe faces the charge of being European history by another name.

However, recalling that DeConde once said that "most of the scholars who did the best works in American diplomatic history, essentially the deepest and soundest research, were those who were interested primarily in the history of Europe," it seems essential to understand the impact of European events in order to understand European reactions vis-à-vis North America.[11] Unfortunately, contemporaries have left scant evidence that connect the European, North American, and imperial crises. The foreign office's policy is partly to blame. For example, Henry Richard Charles Wellesley, Lord Cowley sent up to five different reports a day to London elaborating on specific questions. While this may give the impression of disunity, the governments of the various European countries had to consider all these questions when making policy decisions. The volatile situation in Europe and North America made a war in Europe or North America undesirable because of its incalculable repercussions. Complete neutrality was the best option.

The Rhine River had featured prominently as a natural boundary in Europe since Roman times. In that day and age, the Rhine River was the border between the civilized Roman Empire and barbaric Germanic tribes. Its location continued to make the Rhine a central feature in European conflicts. Geographically, the Rhine River winds its way 820 miles from its sources in the Swiss Alps to its mouth on the Dutch North Sea coast. In 1860, the Rhine was the border between France and the German duchy of Baden in the southwest. Within the German Confederation, the river crossed through or bordered Baden, the Bavarian Palatinate, Hesse-Darmstadt, Nassau, and Prussia. The last stretch was solely in the Netherlands. The German states and France long struggled over control of the riverbanks, especially the western bank.

The historian Hermann Oncken argued almost a century ago that French schemes on the Rhine River developed by Louis XIV were threefold in purpose. Beyond the acquisition of all territory west of the Rhine, *le Roi Soleil* wanted to be able to influence domestic affairs in the German states and continental leadership. The French monarchy desired nothing less than hegemony along the Rhine.[12] Louis's successors shared this dream. Napoleon Bonaparte temporarily achieved it, until the Congress of Vienna redrew the borders in Europe. After 1815, Prussia assumed the "Watch on the Rhine."[13] Despite its defeat, France continued to see the Rhine as a natural frontier.[14] In 1828–29, during a crisis surrounding the Eastern Question, French politicians tried unsuccessfully to play Austria and Great Britain in order to reclaim it.[15] When Napoleon Bonaparte's nephew, Louis Napoleon Bonaparte, overthrew the short-lived Second Republic and recreated the French Empire, the Rhine frontier appeared once again in danger. French territorial ambitions would complicate European diplomacy for the next eighteen years as the world experienced a series of conflicts and insurrections.

Because the German states had a special role in this cold war, the perception of the second largest periodical in the German states, *Kladderadatsch,* seems a good starting point.[16] On April 8, 1860, the weekly published a cartoon titled "Unnecessary Fear," which has to be understood with the satirical undertone of the paper in mind. Napoleon III is out for dinner. He has just finished his bowl of "Savoy." His Swiss tablemate is concerned about his cheese and asks cautiously, "You still have not had enough! Now you would like to eat my cheese? That is not going to happen!" Undeterred, Napoleon replies, "Do not scream that loud! I have no intentions yet to close my stomach."[17]

The image is not only a good illustration that the Swiss worried about Napoleon's intentions after his annexation of Nice and Savoy.[18] The Swiss cheese, which likely represented the Dappenthal, Neuchatel, or another border canton, was joined by a bottle labeled "Rhine." The British government and its representatives in Europe were keenly aware of the danger the French desire for the Rhine River posed to European peace.[19] In contrast to the united front presented by Great Britain and France towards the United States in the Civil War, Great Britain's prime minister perceived it as possible that aggression by France to overthrow the Vienna System could mean war between the two traditional rivals. By mid-1860, the Rhine River problem had become an explosive European diplomatic controversy. Long before the election victory of the Republican Party candidate, Abraham Lincoln, triggered the secession of the southern states, Europe had turned inward.

Another indication of the French ambitions appeared only two months later in the same newspaper. By then, the European powers had become preoccupied with the situation in Syria, where in mid-July 1860 marauding Muslims had sacked the Christian quarter of Damascus and killed scores of people.[20] As the death toll continued to rise and Russia appeared interested in taking the opportunity to break out of its semi-isolation, the European powers met for a small conference in Paris. The envoys agreed to send an investigation to the Levant, which would be accompanied by a detachment of French troops.[21] The dangerous Eastern Question had returned. Despite the restrictions placed on the mission, the European powers worried that France might take the opportunity to establish a more permanent outpost in the region.[22] *Kladderadatsch* again captured this growing European concern about the French emperor's ambitions. In a cartoon called "Political Three-Horse Carriage," Napoleon's cart is drawn by three horses, each representing one of his ambitious goals—Italy, the Orient, and the Rhine.[23] However, Napoleon's ambitions were not the only concerns Europeans had.

A number of events preoccupied Europeans in 1861. The death of the Prussian king Friedrich Wilhelm IV allowed speculations about Wilhelm I's "liberal 'new era'" to rise. In France, Napoleon appreciated his free-trade agreement with Great Britain, and, since he had "no pressing worries" in domestic affairs, he was disinclined to engage in diplomatic or military adventures. Napoleon's annexation of Nice and Savoy had made Great Britain suspicious. In southern Europe,

Italian unification was largely complete, but Austria had an interest in "undoing the unification of Italy," which threatened Austria's remaining Italian territory—Venetia. However, Austria could do nothing as relations with Prussia started to deteriorate in April 1861.[24]

Queen Victoria mentioned many of these events in her opening speech to the British Parliament in February 1861. The queen stressed European and imperial issues. Italy received primary attention, followed by Syria. Third came China, where British and French forces had successfully concluded the Second Opium War. Even the Maori insurrection in New Zealand and the desolate Indian financial situation came before the pending conflict in North America.[25] Many of the points made by the queen are mirrored in the correspondence London received at the time and in the concerns expressed by the members of Her Majesty's cabinet.[26] In these early months of 1861, then, the Civil War had to contest for attention with a half dozen or more European and imperial issues. The Rhine River was an underlying and often unstated issue in many of these European questions, which saw France and the German states on opposing sides.

While in North America secession conventions voted state after state out of the Union and brought the country closer to civil war, Europe had its own problems to deal with. In January 1861, the new kingdom of Italy had taken shape, and the king of Piedmont-Sardinia, Victor Emmanuel, became king of Italy. However, two thorns remained in the flesh of Italian national pride, the most important for the discussion here being Austrian-controlled Venetia.[27] On January 14, 1861, the U.S. consul in Frankfurt, Samuel Ricker, informed Washington that bankers in Frankfurt and Europeans in general feared that war could break out between Austria and the newly established Italian kingdom.[28]

The fear was not far-fetched, and an invasion of Venetia by Garibaldi's guerrilla troops could have brought about a war.[29] Because of the intricate treaty system, a war between Austria and Italy could have forced both the German Confederation and France to participate. As a result, Prussia had to anticipate a French invasion of its Rhine province. The Prussian minister in Brussels reported that while the realignment of the French frontier in Italy had not created much enthusiasm, an advance on the Rhine would certainly do so.[30] The fate of the small Italian-speaking province of Venetia had implications for the Rhine frontier, and the Prussians felt compelled to work for the maintenance of peace.[31] Italy would remain a problem until the late 1860s.

In contrast to Civil War diplomatic scholarship, which sees the distractive influence as starting only in 1863, Poland and Schleswig-Holstein already occupied European attention prior to the outbreak of violence and at a time when Europe had to define its policy toward the Civil War. On February 25, 1861, a demonstration occurred in Warsaw. After Russian troops fired on the crowd, the demonstration broke up. The event quickly became known as the "Warsaw

Massacre."[32] Rumors soon spread about secret dealings between Napoleon and Russia that involved a rearrangement of the European balance of power, including a new state of Poland.[33] In Prussia, rumors that Napoleon wanted to establish an independent Polish state in alliance with France posed an unacceptable threat to Prussia.[34]

A different situation existed in Schleswig-Holstein. The new complications came about because Holstein, the southern and largely German-populated duchy, considered two recent Danish laws, which also applied to the duchy, illegal because the Holstein states had not approved them. In addition, many stipulations of the Protocol of London of 1852 were still unimplemented.[35] Since there was already talk of punishing the Danes for their lack of progress in Holstein with a federal execution, Lord Russell wondered whether such an action on the part of the German Confederation or Prussia might not bring a French army to the Rhine.[36]

By December 1860, a number of British representatives from across central Europe voiced their concern about the impasse between Denmark and the German Confederation. They feared that a federal execution, authorized by the German Confederation, into Holstein could cause a wider conflict.[37] As in Great Britain, the German states worried that Napoleon would aid Denmark and support the Danes militarily against the German Confederation. The best way to do so would have been an invasion on the Rhine.[38] The Earl of Ellenborough indicated a similar concern during a debate in the House of Lords on March 18, 1861, when he noted that a federal execution would bring a French invasion on the Rhine.[39] Thus, in early 1861, a series of European issues occupied the European powers. Furthermore, many of these issues were directly or indirectly related to the Rhine River problem and peace and stability in Europe. It is therefore not surprising that Great Britain adopted a policy of strict neutrality in relation to the Civil War.

While the United States and Great Britain debated neutrality and the Declaration of Paris, the Rhine River problem continued to receive attention. On October 12, 1861, *The London Review* discussed the recent French pamphlet "Le Rhin et la Vistule." On the one hand the pamphleteer wanted to discourage Prussian fears about French ambitions, but on the other hand he argued that Prussia should be more concerned about Russia, against which only an independent Poland could provide safety.[40] The *Review* disagreed. As much as the partition of Poland was a crime, the journal argued that a new Polish state would arouse the wrath of Austria and Russia. The Rhine, not the Vistula, received most of the attention. It was assumed that the natural frontier of the Rhine was a "heresy of political geography," since, "in military theory, no river can afford a strong defensible frontier." The article pointed to the fact that Germans inhabited both banks and that therefore no clear-cut French-German national divide existed.

Despite the apparently peaceful overtone of the pamphlet, the *Review* wondered if Prussia could really feel secure about its Rhine province. The pamphlet had stressed that a portion of the territory, Landau and Sarre Louis, should be returned to France. As a result, the author wrote, "In short, when once a beginning is made in the course of disregarding treaties and redistributing the map of Europe, who can tell when and where such a proceeding is to stop!" He wondered whether Belgium was also in danger of being annexed by France and warned that any such move could throw all Europe into conflict.[41] The *Review* article illustrates the extent to which European developments in Poland and Italy and, for that matter, nearly all European issues were connected with the Rhine River problem and how concerned Great Britain was about developments on the continent, where peace and stability were no longer guaranteed.

Furthermore, the foreign office was well supplied by Lord Cowley and others with these kinds of French pamphlets and newspapers that pointed to the duplicity of France. Even the new U.S. minister to Great Britain, Charles F. Adams, was aware of the situation when he wrote his son in early September:

> Great Britain always looks to her own interest as a paramount law of her action in foreign affairs. She might deal quite summarily with us, were it not for the European complications which are growing more and more embarrassing. There are clouds in the north and in the south, in the east and in the west, which keep England and France leaning against each other in order to stand up at all. The single event of the death of Napoleon, perhaps even that of Lord Palmerston, would set everything afloat, and make the direction of things in Europe almost impossible to foresee. Hence we may hope that these two powers will reflect well before they inaugurate a policy in regard to us which would in the end react most fatally against themselves.[42]

Adams's letter provides a rare piece of evidence that ties developments in Europe to those in North America.

Only a month after Adams's letter, Lord Palmerston too sent a lengthy foreign policy analysis to his foreign secretary, elaborating on some of the most pressing issues. Most of the letter was devoted to the difficulties in southern Europe. Both the Roman and Venetian Questions received Palmerston's attention. He clearly understood that either one had the potential to escalate. He suggested that Italy perhaps wanted to purchase Herzegovina from the Ottoman Empire and trade the province for Venetia. After also dealing with the possible impact on the Ionian Islands, Palmerston turned to the United States. He noted that no reason for an intervention existed; not even a cotton shortage was enough to put neutrality into question. He stated that Great Britain had, because of its possession of Canada, more to fear from a rupture of relations than France. Connecting the American Civil War with recent European revolts, he stressed the unique nature of the war and that European precedents would not apply.[43] The European powers could not escape their continental responsibilities, which, if war broke out, would require all their strength and require that they not allow North America to divert their attention. As 1861 drew to a close, the *Trent* Affair illustrated this last point.

On November 8, 1861, the sloop of war USS *San Jacinto,* commanded by Charles Wilkes, stopped the British mail packet RMS *Trent* and forcibly removed two Confederate envoys, James Mason and John Slidell, as "embodiment of dispatches." Wilkes neither searched nor seized the *Trent,* and he allowed the ship with the correspondence of the Confederate envoys to proceed to Great Britain.[44] The United States had twisted the lion's tail, and a big roar was to come.

Wilkes received a hero's welcome in the United States. After the bleak battlefield reports of the summer and fall, a Union commander finally had achieved a victory against the rebels. However, in Great Britain, news of the events in the Bahamas Canal created a public outcry.[45] On the basis of the recommendations of its legal advisers, the Palmerston government demanded the release of the prisoners and an apology. The usual consultation with the monarchy resulted in Prince Albert softening the language of the message, which then went with additional conciliatory instructions by special messenger to Lord Lyons in Washington.

On December 18, Russell's instructions reached Washington, and Lyons unofficially informed Seward of their content. On Seward's request and in conformity with Russell's instructions, Lyons waited until December 23 before delivering the ultimatum. In the following days, additional news and private letters from Europe indicated the perceived severity of the incident. News of Britain's defensive preparations, including troop deployments in Canada, reached the United States at about the same time, giving the impression of coming hostilities. On Christmas Day, the Lincoln cabinet deliberated, and by the next day Seward's views had prevailed. The prisoners had to be released in order to avoid war with Great Britain. By the end of the year, Lyons and Seward had agreed on the release of Mason and Slidell.

Historians have retold this well-known account of the *Trent* Affair numerous times. Each historian bends the story to fit his or her argument. However, few historians have taken into account the continental European dimension of the episode, and none has explored its connection to the Rhine River.[46] Central to this issue are the Franco-Prussian rivalry and its impact on European and transatlantic diplomacy. To understand both, the so-called "French" and "Prussian" notes deserve close attention.

The French note has received little attention in recent scholarship. The major work on the subject remains Lynn Case and Warren Spencer's *The United*

States and France, in which Case argues that the timely arrival of the French note aided in the peaceful resolution of the maritime incident.[47] In the note, Antoine Edouard Thouvenel, the French foreign minister, stressed the lack of reliable information that had reached Europe about the *Trent* Affair before pointing to the paradox that the United States, as upholder of international law, had grossly violated it. After engaging in a lengthy discussion of the *Trent* Affair's legal issues, Thouvenel concluded that "the Federal government would be showing a just and lofty attitude if it deferred to" the British demands for an apology and the release of the prisoners. A break between Washington and London was in nobody's interest.[48] Proponents of the French note's importance see the moral support given by France to Great Britain as the final push that turned the Lincoln administration toward peace.

After sending the note to Washington, Thouvenel also sent copies to the French ministers at the various European courts. The reason is unclear but might have to do with rampant rumors in Europe concerning French intentions. One of the copies went to Berlin, and the French minister, La Tour d'Auvergne, presented the note to the Prussian foreign minister, Albrecht Graf von Bernstorff. According to the French minister, Bernstorff reacted favorably and expressed his intention of sending a similar message of his own.[49]

Bernstorff started his note with a different premise. The capture of Mason and Slidell had confirmed fears that an infringement of international law might have occurred. According to Bernstorff, the Prussian government had waited so long to comment because it desired more information about the incident in order to determine whether the captain of the *San Jacinto* had acted on instructions from Washington or on his own initiative. Bernstorff cautioned that if the order for the seizure had come from Washington, Berlin would be obligated to see the incident as an attack upon neutral rights. The Prussian government, he said, was "convinced that no conditions have been made by England by which the dignity of President Lincoln could have reasonably been hurt." The minister stressed that Prussia desired to assist in any way the peaceful resolution of the conflict.[50]

The French and Prussian messages differed only slightly in content, but their tone was different. The Prussian note indicates that Bernstorff was not as well versed in questions of maritime law as his French counterpart. Also, while France referred to the two persons of Mason and Slidell and thus avoided the issue of naming the Confederacy, the Prussian note indicated the ambiguous status of the southern states from the German perspective.

Of course, the Prussian note arrived far too late to have any decisive impact.[51] At first, Seward understood the note as a sign of friendship and an acknowledgment of the long-advocated rights of neutrals during war. By the end of January, Seward had changed his mind about the note. Bremen's minister Rudolph M. Schleiden noticed that Seward had become upset and bitter, saying that Prussia "had been whipped" by England into sending the message.[52] However, it is the European side that is under scrutiny here and the question of what influenced Prussia to send a note.

Only twice has the Prussian note received scholarly attention. As a result, the argument advanced by the historian Gordon Warren, indicating that France and Great Britain pressed Prussia to send the note, continues to prevail.[53] Unfortunately, Warren uses only French and German secondary sources to back his argument. In turn, the German historian Enno Eimers added only one letter from Vienna to Berlin to further Warren's argument.[54] The argument is also based largely on perceptions in Washington, as the Seward-Schleiden exchange indicates. However, the undoubted international pressure is not the question here. What Warren did not tell his readers and what Eimers only hints at is the importance of the Rhine River. Consulting the Franco-Prussian rivalry adds an additional dimension that permits a more logical explanation.

On the one hand, Prussia appears to have wanted to prevent a complete shutdown of international trade that a war between Great Britain and the United States would have precipitated.[55] However, territorial integrity trumped even trade interests. If Great Britain became engaged in a war with the United States, it could no longer watch over European affairs, and Prussia would become vulnerable to French territorial ambitions. This was particularly important as Prussia had drawn closer to Great Britain over the past years. Taylor argues for a related reason: "With Austria unyielding and Russia friendly to France, [closeness to Great Britain] seemed the only means of security on the Rhine" for Prussia.[56] Therefore, it is plausible, in the light of the volatile European situation, that Prussia felt compelled to send a note in order to foster peace and to remain on good terms with Great Britain, which Prussia perceived as necessary to protect the Rhine River frontier.

Contemporaries were well aware of the relationship between the *Trent* Affair and the Rhine. It was important for Prussia's territorial integrity that Great Britain's attention not be drawn away from European affairs, which would have allowed Napoleon III to rearrange Europe to his liking. On December 29, *Kladderadatsch* published an image illustrating the paper's take on the international ramifications of the *Trent* Affair, which might be one of the best illustrations of the *Trent* affair's international implications. The image shows the two warring sections of the United States, impersonated by the brothers Jonathan, shooting at each other. On the ocean, Charles Wilkes searches the *Trent*. Great Britain, focused on North America and away from the European continent, screams angrily at the United States. The important part of the image is in the background. With Great Britain's attention turned away from Europe, Napoleon III appears uninterested but reaches behind himself to grasp the Dappenthal, a region in Switzerland that French troops had recently occupied.[57]

"Der Fischer im Trüben," *Kladderadatsch,* Berlin, December 29, 1861.

The image illustrates that any distraction that drew Great Britain's attention away from Europe could have serious consequences for French neighbors. After Napoleon's annexation of Nice and Savoy, the Swiss worried that their territory would be next.[58] *Kladderadatsch* does not refer to the long-standing Prussian fear about French interests to realign the Franco-German border in order to create a natural frontier along the Rhine River. However, the fear that Napoleon might use a war between Great Britain and the United States to reorganize the French frontier, especially in Switzerland or on the Rhine, was not unique to the artists and editors of *Kladderadatsch.* The rumor mill was continuously providing new material to keep that fear alive.

The Prussian ambassador in France, Heinrich VII, Prince von Reuss, reported to Berlin that Napoleon desired a break between Great Britain and the United States.[59] Reuss's statement confirmed the rumors that bothered the French minister in Berlin, La Tour d'Auvergne. According to La Tour d'Auvergne, the rumor was that France wanted to take advantage of a war between Great Britain and the United States for its own ambitions. It appears that many in Berlin viewed French intentions with skepticism and mistrust.[60] However, La Tour d'Auvergne perceived that his presentation of the French note, supporting the British position on the *Trent* Affair, had alleviated some of the mistrust.[61] Nevertheless, long-held mistrust died hard, and, on January 1, 1862, U.S. Consul Henry Boernstein, in Bremen, informed Seward that Napoleon wanted a war between the United States and Great Britain. Such a war would allow the French emperor to be the sole reorganizer of Europe. As a result, Great Britain could ill afford to get involved in a long-term struggle with the United States.[62]

Even in Whitehall, the rumor mills worked overtime, although not all the rumors directly referred to the French ambitions on the Rhine. Lord Russell expressed concern that Napoleon could attack Austria in Venetia or advance the French frontiers on the Rhine if Great Britain allowed the *Trent* Affair to cause a transatlantic war.[63] Members of the cabinet and Lord Cowley mentioned the situation in Mexico and Italy, which required French attention at the time.[64] Napoleon's ambitions were well known in Europe, and it should therefore come as no surprise that during a transatlantic crisis like the *Trent* Affair his ambitions played a role in the decision-making process. As a result, concerns surrounding the Rhine River problem played a role in settling the *Trent* Affair peacefully as Great Britain could not afford a distant, distracting, and unpredictable war.

With the *Trent* Affair settled in January 1862, Europe did not, as some historians imply, calm down. Napoleon's ambitions lingered on. For example, the Roman and Venetian problems in Italy continued to keep the peninsula on the verge of war.[65] More important, the Schleswig-Holstein question still plagued European ministries, which expected a war between Denmark and the German Confederation at any time.[66] The fear increased with a leadership change at the top of the Prussian government. While the constitutional conflict escalated, King Wilhelm finally agreed to give Otto von Bismarck a chance. With Bismarck, a new policy of realpolitik entered Prussian politics and paved the way for the Wars of German Unification.

The fall of 1862 was overall extremely volatile. Howard Jones has underscored the dangerous diplomatic situation that followed Union general George B. McClellan's retreat from the James River peninsula and the defeat of Union troops at Manassas Junction. Jones illustrates how these battles and the huge casualty figures that resulted gave the appearance of a military stalemate and allowed for a cabinet debate on intervention in Great Britain. Stirred up by Chancellor of the Exchequer William Ewart Gladstone's Newcastle speech on October 7, 1862, the cabinet exchanged a series of written opinions on the matter over the next month. Lacking widespread endorsement in the cabinet and lacking support for a joint intervention in France and Russia, the intervention proposal died. The perceived Union victory at the Battle of Antietam and Lincoln's Emancipation Proclamation did not allow for any intervention.[67]

It is ironic that just at a time when a forceful French push for mediation could have had a favorable reception in Great Britain, Napoleon was preoccupied with a cabinet crisis of his own, when Thouvenel, the foreign minister, resigned in protest over the emperor's Italy policy. The two strongly disagreed on the question of if and for how long French troops should remain stationed in Rome and protect the Pope. The cabinet crisis was accompanied by the usual war scares.[68] On the surface, the issue suggests that the Rhine River problem moved to the background, but, as indicated earlier, a Franco-Austrian conflict in Italy could escalate quickly and threaten the German frontier. Therefore, European issues indirectly impacted the October 1862 cabinet debate.

However, the cabinet debate concerning some form of intervention was a sideshow for Great Britain. By the time the cabinet officially met on November 11 and 12 and discussed the matter of an intervention, support had waned and a new issue loomed. On October 23, the day of the unofficial cabinet meeting, King Otto of Greece was deposed. As a result, old fears associated with the Crimean War reemerged. The British cabinet devoted much attention to the search for a new Greek monarch. Most important was to forestall the acceptance of a Russian candidate. The Eastern Question continued to haunt Palmerston's government.[69] It was not until March 1863 that the new king, George I, formerly Prince Vilhelm of Denmark, was crowned. The Balkans contributed another destabilizing factor when the garrison in Belgrade mutinied against the Ottoman rulers. The situation raised further concerns about an intervention that could bring about a second Crimean War.[70] The Civil War was disappearing from the cabinet's agenda.[71]

Almost all historians of Civil War diplomacy argue that European events in 1863, notably the Polish Insurrection, drew attention away from the Civil War. However, they focus narrowly on the Russian fleet's visit to the United States and the insurrection's general impact on the relations between Great Britain and the United States.[72] More attention needs to be paid to why Great Britain focused on these European events, since that would help explain why Great Britain remained neutral prior to 1863 when similar issues already existed. The Rhine River again plays an illustrative role. The insurrection took on Europe-wide implications because of a diplomatic blunder by the new Prussian Minister President Otto von Bismarck.[73] Concerned about the developments in Russian or Congress Poland, Bismarck believed it necessary to support the Russians in their effort to subdue the Poles. On February 1, 1863, he authorized the adjutant general of the Prussian king, General Gustav von Alvensleben, to go to St. Petersburg and make two offers: Prussian military assistance and an open frontier for Russian troops in pursuit of fleeing rebels.[74] Russia reluctantly accepted and signed the convention.[75] The convention, negotiated in two days, lasted for less than four weeks, during which Prussia and France came to the brink of war.[76] According to the Bismarck historian Otto Pflanze, Napoleon trained "his diplomatic artillery on Berlin."[77] For more than two months, the Alvensleben Convention kept the European powers occupied, and, as in any war scare between Prussia and France, the Rhine Province was perceived threatened.

European diplomacy moved quickly in late February 1863 as France, Great Britain, and Austria tried to agree on the contents and destination of a protest note. On February 24, Robert Heinrich Ludwig von der Goltz reported from Paris that France had sent a draft note protesting Prussian involvement to Great Britain. Goltz suggested that diplomatic measures should be taken to soften or prevent a British reply. He suggested that the best answer by Great Britain would be "let us wait until the first intervention" occurs.[78] In London, Bernstorff talked with Lord Russell about the British reaction. Bernstorff emphasized that the Alvensleben Convention was unlikely to be used, which did not change Russell's skepticism. Bernstorff nonetheless noted that Great Britain appeared concerned about a French intervention, which could have wide-ranging implications.[79] Russell confirmed this in a letter to Cowley, expressing the hope that nothing would happen if the Alvensleben Convention was not actually implemented. Otherwise, France might use the opportunity on the Rhine.[80] As a result, British attention focused on Europe, much as in previous scares.

The foreign ministry in Vienna voiced similar concerns. Graf von Rechberg suspected that Napoleon could use the situation in Poland for one of his plans to alter the European balance of power. The main concern was that Napoleon might change the frontiers of France.[81] The Prussian Rhine Province appeared to be the most likely target of Napoleon's ambitions.[82] Thus, at a very early stage in the diplomatic reaction to the Polish Insurrection, Napoleonic ambitions to alter the French frontiers placed an important check on the diplomatic reaction by the European powers to protest the Alvensleben Convention and Russian actions in Poland. The problem that had haunted European diplomacy since the outbreak of the Civil War and made European diplomacy turn inward remained.

The most disturbing news for the Prussian Rhine Province soon appeared, and it tied the entire North Atlantic world together. Napoleon had made a special offer to the Habsburg court that involved one of his wildest schemes yet for rearranging the European state system. Through informal diplomatic channels, he had offered Austria the leadership role in restructuring the German states. Further, he wanted to create an independent Polish kingdom using the Polish provinces of Austria, Prussia, and Russia. To win Austria's support for the idea, he suggested that an Austrian archduke become king of the new Poland. For his special project, Italy, Napoleon wanted Austria to cede Venetia in return for one of the Danubian principalities. In return for Austria's territorial adjustment, Napoleon wanted Austria's silent approval for his plan to extend the French frontier to the Rhine River.[83]

Even before Napoleon proposed the plan, his wife, Empress Eugénie, had broached the idea to Richard Klemens, Fürst von Metternich-Winneburg, the Austrian minister in Paris. Her grand scheme was slightly different. France, of course, was to gain the Rhine Province. In contrast, Austria was to gain Silesia, Bosnia, Herzegovina (the latter two occupied since 1861), and everything south of the Main River. Prussia was to gain everything north of the Main. The plan had one highly intriguing aspect for the Americas, which illustrates how closely connected the Atlantic World had become. The dethroned European princes were to receive new thrones in the New World, where they would "civilize and monarchize" the republican governments.[84] These two variants illustrate how much the Rhine River problem was part of all the European questions and the global extent of these questions. The Rhine, Mexico, and the Civil War were used in the same breath by many Europeans, which explains Great Britain's reluctance to get involved in the American war when such a volatile situation existed on the European continent.

While Bismarck searched for a way out of his dilemma, Great Britain received more disturbing intelligence. In mid-April, the British minister in St. Petersburg reported that nationalism was on the rise in Russia. Polish aggression and rumors of foreign intervention had united the Russians.[85] Great Britain continued to receive information that Napoleon planned to concentrate troops along the eastern border of France for an intended march through the German states to Poland. If the German states denied Napoleon the right to cross their territory, he could then blame them for his failure to assist the Poles, invade the German states, and take what he always had wanted—the Rhine Province. The concentration of French troops along the Rhine concerned King Wilhelm, as well. He expected that once the troops were mobilized and in the field, they would not return to their barracks without having done something. Well aware of Great Britain's interest in maintaining the European status quo, the king expected Great Britain to do everything in its power to prevent the mobilization of the French army.[86]

Lord Russell assured the Prussian foreign minister, Bernstorff, that Great Britain would not tolerate a change in the map of Europe. It was in Prussia's interest that Great Britain help Prussia watch over France and prevent a war. In a sense, Great Britain joined the Prussian "Watch on the Rhine" against French intrigue and ambitions, thus tying Great Britain ever closer to Europe. In the context of the Civil War, a note King Wilhelm wrote on Bernstorff's letter is highly illustrative. "We must put all our effort to the task, that Great Britain, even if the American question takes her attention, never allows France to start a war against Germany, i.e. Prussia."[87] Wilhelm was not too far off in this respect. Only a month later, Russell confided to Cowley, after dealing with Poland, "The Alabama + Oreto are causing great discontent in America, but I shall do all I can to keep the peace."[88] It is rare to find such a clearly stated connection, but in the minds of these European leaders, Great Britain, the Civil War, and the French threat to the Rhine were intimately connected; British distraction was a dangerous specter.

The war scare that had gripped Europe was not receding. In Russia, the chancellor, Prince Alexander Mikhailovich Gorchakov, expected war with France unless Great Britain prevented it. In order to prevent Great Britain from perceiving Russia as the aggressor, as during the Crimean War, Russia informed Great Britain that Russian armaments were for defensive purposes only.[89] As the situation deteriorated, Great Britain remained the decisive factor despite its military inability to force its will; Palmerston and his government still had the nominal power to decide war and peace in Europe. Russia was not ready to call Great Britain's bluff as Bismarck would a year later. With the old warmonger and Crimean War fighter Palmerston at the helm of Her Majesty's government, Great Britain kept up the diplomatic pressure on Russia on the assumption that Russia was too weak to put down the Polish Insurrection.[90] Palmerston based his assumptions on reports he received from the British consul in Warsaw, who constantly stressed the Russian troops' incompetence to mount an effective offensive against the insurgents.[91] However, Great Britain's main concern was to prevent Prussia from bringing about a French attack on the Rhine. In order to prevent that, Britain tried to scare Prussia and thus prevent Prussian assistance to Russia. Her Majesty's government informed Bismarck that a rumored French landing in the Baltic was totally acceptable to Great Britain.[92]

While the Polish question occupied the European powers and the continent struggled over the question of war and peace, the Russian fleet paid a visit to the United States. The visit has attracted much attention by historians and is seen frequently as a sign of Russia's moral support of the United States. The ulterior motive, however, was to obtain a secure base for commerce raiding in case of war.[93] The visit so dominates the discussion of the Polish Insurrection in Civil War diplomacy that the larger European concerns faced by Great Britain are rarely mentioned. In addition, historians focus on Napoleon's new, futile attempt to bring about a joint Anglo-French intervention in the Civil War. The use of William S. Lindsay and John A. Roebuck backfired when Palmerston's steadfastness thwarted their motion in the House of Commons. The other major incident surrounded the so-called Laird Rams, which the Confederate commissioner James Bulloch had ordered from the Laird shipyards. This time, the U.S.

representatives did not fumble, and the British government was keen to prevent a dangerous precedent in stopping the Confederate ships from leaving. Historians often argue that because of the Polish insurrection's impact on British diplomacy, the Civil War became less important. However, this ignores the complexity of the European context, which included concerns over French ambitions that could be fulfilled in a war over Poland.

As the Polish insurrection moved slowly into the background, an old/new dilemma emerged—Schleswig-Holstein. While Poland is at least subject to some Civil War diplomatic scholarship, few scholars mention Schleswig-Holstein. Many European diplomats had hoped never again to deal with the Schleswig-Holstein question after its settlement by the Protocol of London of 1852. However, the protocol left unresolved a number of questions about the royal succession and the status of the duchies. Denmark's unwillingness to implement the protocol fully created the threat of a federal execution and, with it, the potential for war. In May 1863, Bernstorff, in London, wondered whether France had pushed Denmark in the direction of a new constitution, which would have allowed France to get involved against Germany and satisfy France's desire for a natural frontier on the Rhine.[94] As the German Confederation prepared a federal execution, the British minister in Berlin asked Bismarck about the situation. He responded that it was entirely up to the Confederation Diet to determine the future course of action concerning the Schleswig-Holstein question. Austria and Prussia, as individual states, no longer had anything to do with the decision.[95] Bismarck was at his best, misleading the British minister Andrew Buchanan about his real intentions.

Behind the scenes, Bismarck already planned for war. He anticipated protests from Great Britain and France against a federal execution; therefore, two smaller states would send troops into Holstein and not the two major German states.[96] Bismarck benefited from a series of fateful errors made by Denmark's king. In late 1863, Frederick VII tried to integrate the duchy of Schleswig into the Danish kingdom under the auspices of a new constitution. Bismarck seized upon this opportunity and pushed a federal execution against Denmark in the Confederate Diet. With the death of the old king, the succession question, and the new constitution, Denmark and the German states drew increasingly closer to war.

In Great Britain, the government viewed the development in Schleswig-Holstein in January 1864 with growing concern. Officially, the ministry saw no reason, based on the Protocol of London, to get involved in the question. However, the Palmerston government actively supported the Danish side. Bernstorff noticed that Lord Palmerston and some members of his cabinet denied the German states the right to go to war with Denmark based on nonfulfillment of the Protocol of London. Palmerston appeared willing to go to war with the German states in case of a Dano-German war, though how much beyond verbal belligerency he was willing to go is hard to say. Bernstorff cautioned that the true concern of Great Britain was not a war between Denmark and the German states but the possibility that France might assist Denmark and start a war with the German states, which would again involve the Rhine River.[97]

The German states, especially Prussia, were aware of the danger. In case of a Confederation victory, Napoleon could ask for an expansion of French territory on the Rhine to balance the extended northern frontier of the German states. The concern was based on Napoleon's known interest in expanding the French frontier. As a result, a war between France and the German states because of the Dano-German conflict appeared likely.[98] Such a war was not in Great Britain's interest. There was also the possibility that France could be used to create diplomatic pressure. A demonstration of force by France along the Rhine might push Austria and Prussia towards a negotiated solution of the Schleswig-Holstein question.[99] However, because of the danger of tempting Napoleon into such an adventurous move, the idea was quickly dismissed and not taken up again.

British diplomacy aimed to prevent a French take over of the Rhineland and Belgium. Great Britain became increasingly disinclined to support Denmark against the German Confederation, as to do so would likely mean a fight with France about French territorial expansion.[100] Palmerston noted that Great Britain was not interested in becoming involved in the Dano-German conflict alone. He argued that it could provide France with an excuse to satisfy its territorial ambitions.[101] Great Britain had a difficult choice to make. It was in the nation's interest to find a negotiated solution to maintain the balance of power and remain true to its noninterventionist policy.[102]

As the danger of war became a reality in late January 1864, Palmerston's belligerency increased as well. He wanted Denmark to have time to reconsider its moves and decisions. If such an extension was not given by the German states, then the German powers would be solely responsible for the war. Palmerston was adamant that as long as Prussia and Austria restricted their demands to Holstein or the new Danish Patent, he would see their claims as justified but that any extension would be provocative. Again, Palmerston's concern was not so much the war arising from the Schleswig-Holstein question as what the ambitious French emperor would do. Palmerston feared Napoleon might use the occupation of Schleswig to advance the French frontier to the Rhine. If Napoleon did that, Great Britain could do almost nothing militarily to prevent French territorial expansion.[103] Great Britain was militarily weak, and, with Bismarck in power, it was only a question of time until the bluff of British strength would be called.

In accordance with Queen Victoria's position, Palmerston emphasized that Great Britain favored the German side in the conflict and therefore wished to prevent a war between Prussia and France, in which he feared Great Britain could not side with the Prussians.[104] Palmerston's decision to keep Great Britain out of the war was likely not a wholehearted choice. According to Bernstorff, Palmerston went on a verbal crusade upon being told that Bismarck believed that the Protocol of London would be abrogated by war. Palmerston said, “It was the most unprovoked aggression and most villainous act known to history and that all responsibility for blood shed in this unjust war would only and solely be on the two powers that had undertaken the war.” He continued to threaten that should the war continue until spring, Great Britain would lend assistance to Denmark.[105] Palmerston hoped that France would cooperate with him against the German states.[106] The British policy concerning the war in the duchies was ambiguous but favored nonintervention. French ambitions were a major reason for the uncertainty. As a result, Great Britain remained focused on Europe.

Many in Europe shared the concern that Napoleon might use German distraction with the two duchies to the north to advance his interest on the Rhine. A cartoon in *Kladderadatsch* illustrates this perception. The image shows Napoleon pushing a fence entitled “neutral Rhineland” farther into the German states and across the Rhine, while Prussia and Austria are occupied on the Jutland Peninsula. The caption satirically tells the reader that Napoleon wants to create a neutral Rhineland only to protect France against Prussian aggressions.[107] The Rhine River again played an important role in the diplomatic developments surrounding the outbreak of the Dano-German War.

Diplomats continued to work, but the fate of Schleswig-Holstein was decided on the battlefield. Another London Conference failed due to Prussian and Danish

“Phantasiestück,” *Kladderadatsch*, Berlin, March 20, 1864.

stubbornness. It also became increasingly evident that the seeds of discontent sowed among the European powers during the Crimean War and fostered ever since prevented a joint effort by Great Britain and France in Schleswig-Holstein. With the mounting military success of the Union, diplomatic efforts by the Confederacy in Europe were becoming increasingly rare and unlikely to succeed. The situation on the continent eliminated any last hopes the Confederacy might have had to gain European recognition. When France, forced by Union demands, shut down the Confederate shipbuilding program, all hope for European support was lost. The European situation and the Rhine River problem had a lot to do with the failure of Confederate diplomacy. And as both continents settled down in late 1864 and early 1865, further problems loomed on the horizon. The immediate danger to the Union posed by a European power had disappeared as the war came to a close, in April 1865. In Europe, however, the Rhine River problem continued to plague the Franco-German relations for another century.

Overall, historians of Civil War diplomacy have come to acknowledge that European developments in 1863 made European involvement in the Civil War unlikely. However, scholars need to look deeper and consider the situation in Europe more fully. Not only were many of the issues that distracted European powers in 1863 already there in 1861, but also many of the issues were connected with a major river in western Europe—the Rhine River. When the war in North America broke out, in April 1861, European issues—Italy, Schleswig-Holstein, Poland—already dominated the minds of European politicians. In all of these issues the Franco-German rivalry was most likely to find a military solution along the Rhine. As the Civil War continued, Europe continued to be plagued with important and threatening questions that kept the continent on the verge of war. Great Britain, still seen as the important power broker in Europe, looked with increasing concern to the continental developments. On many of the issues, Great Britain was more concerned about forestalling French ambitions and protecting the status quo on the continent than with protecting Poles or Danes. It appears logical that the ambitions of its main rival—France—were of more importance to Great Britain than a conflict on the North American continent. This does not mean that Civil War diplomacy was unimportant; it means only that historians need to look beyond Great Britain and France to explain the two powers' policies during the Civil War and embrace a more global look in research and writing. Historians of Civil War diplomacy need to broaden their understanding of European diplomacy and give more attention to European developments and their underlying causes, which will help to explain European policies, from neutrality to the detention of the Laird Rams and the failure of the Kenner mission. The volatile situation on the European continent and French ambitions toward the Rhine River demanded British attention. Even more, they demanded that

Britain keep out of a conflict in North America at all costs. Neutrality was the only way to accomplish this balancing act and assist Prussia in "The Watch on the Rhine."

NOTES

1. I wish to thank Dr. Daniel E. Sutherland and Dr. Donald Rakestraw for their helpful comments.

2. John A. S. Grenville, *Europe Reshaped, 1848–1878* (London: Fontana Press, 1976), 249, 254.

3. Alan J. P Taylor, *The Struggle for Mastery in Europe: 1848–1918* (New York: Oxford University Press, 1954), 127.

4. Howard. Jones, "Author's Response," H-Diplo Roundtable Review on *Blue and Gray Diplomacy*, H-Diplo, H-Net Reviews, July 2010.

5. For a similar argument see John Darwin, *The Empire Project: The Rise and Fall of the British World-System, 1830–1970* (Cambridge: Cambridge University Press, 2009).

6. Howard Jones, *Union in Peril: The Crisis over British Intervention in the Civil War* (Lincoln, NE: Bison Books, 1997); Jones, *Abraham Lincoln and a New Birth of Freedom* (Lincoln: University of Nebraska Press, 1999); Jones, *Blue and Gray Diplomacy: A History of Union and Confederate Foreign Relations* (Chapel Hill: University of North Carolina Press, 2010); Phillip E. Myers, *Caution and Cooperation: The American Civil War in British-American Relations* (Kent, Ohio: Kent State University Press, 2008); Jay Sexton, *Debtor Diplomacy: Finance and American Foreign Relations in the Civil War Era, 1837–1873* (Oxford: Clarendon Press, 2005).

7. Jay Sexton, "Towards a Synthesis of Foreign Relations in the Civil War Era, 1848–1877," *American Nineteenth Century History* 5 (Fall 2004): 66.

8. Alexander DeConde, "What's Wrong with American Diplomatic History," *SHAFR Newsletter*, May 1970.

9. David P. Crook, *The North, the South, and the Powers 1861–1865* (New York: John Wiley, 1974).

10. This would exclude Eric Hobsbawm, *The Age of Capital 1848–1875* (London: Weidenfeld and Nicolson, 1962), which presents an international history of the period but is heavily focused on economic and social issues and as a result provides little in respect of diplomacy. The same applies to Jürgen Osterhammel, *Die Verwandlung der Welt: Eine Geschichte des 19. Jahrhunderts* (Munich: C. H. Beck, 2011).

11. DeConde, "What's Wrong," 3.

12. Hermann Oncken, *Napoleon III and the Rhine: The Origin of the War of 1870–1871*, trans. Edwin H. Zeydel (New York: Knopf, 1928), 3–5.

13. Max Schneckenburger, "Die Wacht am Rhein," 1840. In response to a French attempt to take over the Rhine province in 1840, Nikolaus Becker composed the "Rheinlied," which called for a defense of the west bank of the river. Max Schneckenburger then composed the more patriotic "Die Wacht am Rhein," which called on people to defend the Rhine Province against France. The song was part of a new set of patriotic music that embraced German nationalism and unity. Thomas Nipperdey, *Germany from Napoleon*

to Bismarck, 1800-1866, trans. Daniel Nolan (Princeton, NJ: Princeton University Press, 1996), 272-273.

14. Oncken, *Napoleon III and the Rhine,* 6, 8–9.

15. Ibid., 12.

16. *Kladderadatsch,* which developed during the revolution of 1848, was based on the idea of Albert Hofmann and David Kalisch. On May 7, 1848, the first issue appeared, and the paper quickly developed a readership. After the 1848 revolutions failed, *Kladderadatsch* survived the conservative counterrevolution but remained within the boundaries of middle-class respectability. The circulation of *Kladderadatsch* increased from 6,000 copies in 1851 to 22,000 seven years later, which made *Kladderadatsch* the second most popular periodical in Germany after *Die Gartenlaube* (which in 1867 boasted a circulation of 215,000). See Ann Taylor Allen, *Satire and Society in Wilhelmine Germany:* Kladderadatsch *and* Simplicissimus, *1890–1914* (Lexington: University Press of Kentucky, 1984).

17. *Kladderadatsch* (Berlin), April 8, 1860, 4, Ruprecht-Karls-Universität Heidelberg, http://www.ub.uni-heidelberg.de/helios/digi/kladderadatsch.html (accessed September 12, 2007).

18. Brian Connell, *Regina v. Palmerston: The Correspondence between Queen Victoria and Her Foreign and Prime Minister 1837–1865* (London: Evans Brothers, 1962), 312.

19. Russell to Cowley, May 4, 1860; Russell to Cowley, May 31, 1860, PRO 30/22/104, Russell Papers, National Archives, Kew, United Kingdom (hereafter NAUK).

20. Lynn Case implies that the Syrian problem had been an issue only during 1860; however, the continued French military presence and the frequent mentions of the Syrian involvement by Lord Cowley suggest that it took until May for the situation to resolve. See FO 27/1340–1351, FO27/1383–1390, NAUK; Lynn M. Case and Warren F. Spencer. *The United States and France: Civil War Diplomacy* (Philadelphia: University of Pennsylvania Press, 1970), 17; Salo Baron, "The Jews and the Syrian Massacres of 1860," *Proceedings of the American Academy for Jewish Research* 4 (1932–1933): 3–5.

21. Protocol of a Conference held at Paris, August 3, 1860, *British and Foreign State Papers 1860–1861* (London: William Ridgeway, 1868), 51: 278–79 (hereafter *BFSP*).

22. Cowley to Russell, February 11, 1861, FO 27/1385; Cowley to Russell, May 2, 1861, FO 27/1390, NAUK. The two letters are examples of the French trying to use various arguments that would leave the French troops in Syria; every time, the arguments are dismantled by Cowley.

23. *Kladderadatsch* (Berlin), June 3, 1860, 4.

24. Taylor, *The Struggle for Mastery in Europe,* 123–28.

25. Speech of the Queen [Victoria], on the Opening of the British Parliament, Westminster, February 5, 1861, *BFSP 1860–1861,* 51: 1–3.

26. Russell to Palmerston, December 31, 1860, GC/RU/644, Broadlands Papers, Hartley Library, University of Southampton, Great Britain (hereafter Broadlands).

27. For an example of the British concerns see Russell to Palmerston, May 18, 1860, PRO 30/22/30, NAUK.

28. Ricker to Cass, January 14, 1861, Roll 11, Dispatches from U.S. Consul in Frankfurt on the Main, Germany, 1829–1906, M161, Diplomatic Records, National Archives and Records Administration, Washington, DC (hereafter NARA).

29. Werther to Schleinitz, undated, *Die auswärtige Politik Preussens 1858–1871* (Oldenburg, Germany: Gerhard Stalling Verlag, 1945), s. 2, 2: 149–51 [hereafter *APP*]; Ricker to Cass, January 21, 1861, Roll 11, M161, NARA.

30. Redern to Schleinitz, January 31, 1861, *APP,* s. 2, 2: 154–56.

31. Loftus to Russell, March 16, 1861, *APP,* s. 2, 2: 241–50; Taylor, *The Struggle for Mastery in Europe,* 123.

32. Ricker to Cass, March 4, 1861, Roll 11, M161; Schleinitz to Thérémin, March 11, 1861, *APP,* s. 2, 2: 241–50.

33. Ricker to Cass, March 18, 1861, Roll 11, M161, NARA; Russell to Cowley, March 15, 1861, PRO 30/22/104, NAUK.

34. Schleinitz to Bismarck, March 11, 1861, *APP,* s. 2, 2: 241–50.

35. Paget to Russell, January 19, 1861, *BFSP 1860–1861,* 51: 813–14; Schleinitz to Bernstorff, December 29, 1860, *APP,* s. 2, 2: 61–63; Russell to Palmerston, February 8, 1861, PRO 30/22/30, NAUK.

36. Russell to Cowley, April 6, 1861, PRO 30/22/104, NAUK.

37. The concern arose because of the unclear border between Schleswig and Holstein. Denmark claimed that the border was on the south bank of the Eider, while the German Confederation argued that it was on the north bank. As a result, especially of the unclear status of the fort at Rendsburg, the occupation of Holstein by Confederation troops acting under the Federal Execution could result in a clash between German and Danish troops and result in war. Howard to Russell, January 26, 1861, *BFSP 1860–1861,* 51: 824–25.

38. Crowe to Russell, March 7, 1861, *BFSP 1860–1861,* 51: 838–39.

39. *Hansard Parliamentary Debates,* 3d ser., vol. 161 (1861), 2136–40.

40. *Le Rhin et la Vistule* (Paris: Amyot, Editeur des Archives Diplomatiques, 1861), 13–16.

41. "The Rhine and the Vistula," *The London Review,* October 12, 1861, 445–46.

42. Charles F. Adams to Charles F. Adams, Jr., September 7, 1861, *A Cycle of Adams Letters, 1861–1865* (New York: Houghton Mifflin, 1920), 1: 39.

43. Palmerston to Russell, October 10, 1861, GC/RU/1139, Broadlands.

44. Gordon H. Warren, *Fountain of Discontent: The* Trent *Affair and the Freedom of the Seas* (Boston: Northeastern University Press, 1981), 16–18.

45. For the legal debate see Alice O'Rourke, "The Law Officers of the Crown and the *Trent* Affair," *Mid-America* 54 (July 1972): 160–62; Warren, *Fountain of Discontent,* 98.

46. Niels Eichhorn, "The *Trent* Affair Revisited: Great Britain and Rhine River Problem in a Transatlantic Context," Annual Conference of the Association of British American Nineteenth-century Historians, Liverpool, October 8–10, 2010.

47. Case and Spencer, *The United States and France,* 201.

48. Thouvenel to Mercier, December 3, 1861, *The War of the Rebellion: A Compilation of the Official Records of the Union and Confederate Armies* (Washington, D.C.: U.S. Government Printing Office, 1886–1922), ser. 2, vol. 2, 1116–18 (hereafter *O.R.*). Also reprinted in Case and Spencer, *The United States and France,* 202–4.

49. Case and Spencer, *The United States and France,* 206.

50. Bernstorff to Gerolt, Berlin, December 25, 1861, *O.R.*, ser. 2, vol. 2, 1176–77.

51. Ralph H. Lutz, *Die Beziehungen zwischen Deutschland und den Vereinigten Staaten während des Sezessionskrieges* (Heidelberg: Carl Winter's Universitätsbuchhandlung, 1911), 215.

52. Schleiden to Heinrich Smidt, January 24, 1862, Schleiden Papers, Archive of the Hanseatic City of Bremen.

53. The idea for the international pressure originated with Gordon Warren and was used later by Enno Eimers. Eimers does not bring any new evidence for the pressure from the Prussian side. Eimers, Enno *Preussen und die USA 1850 bis 1867* (Berlin: Dunker and Humblot, 2004), 494–95; Warren, *Fountain of Discontent*, 160–61.

54. Eimers, *Preussen und die USA*, 494–95. He also mentions a newspaper article's comment, but no detail is provided.

55. Ibid., 492.

56. Taylor, *The Struggle for Mastery in Europe*, 123.

57. *Kladderadatsch* (Berlin), December 29, 1861, 8.

58. Connell, *Regina v. Palmerston*, 312.

59. Eimers, *Preussen und die USA*, 492.

60. La Tour d'Auvergne to Thouvenel, December 15, 1861, *APP*, s. 2, 2: 530–532.

61. Case and Spencer, *The United States and France*, 206.

62. Boernstein to Seward, January 1, 1862, Roll 12, Dispatches from U.S. Consul in Bremen, Germany, 1794–1906, T184, NARA.

63. Warren, *Fountain of Discontent*, 157.

64. Palmerston to Russell, December 2, 1861, PRO 30/22/21; Cowley to Russell, December 15, 1861, FO 27/1400, NAUK.

65. Russell to Cowley, March 29, 1862, PRO 30/22/105; Cowley to Russell, March 4, 1862, FO 27/1434; Cowley to Russell, April 11, 1862, FO 27/1437, NAUK.

66. Cowley to Russell, February 28, 1862, FO 27/1434; Cowley to Russell, April 11, 1862, FO 27/1437, NAUK.

67. Jones, *Union in Peril*, chaps. 6–10; *Abraham Lincoln and a New Birth of Freedom*, chaps. 4–7; *Blue and Gray Diplomacy*, chaps. 6–8.

68. Russell to Cowley, October 6, 1862; Russell to Cowley, November 1, PRO 30/22/105, NAUK; Case and Spencer, *The United States and France*, 343–346; Lynn M. Case, *Franco-Italian Relations 1860–1865: The Roman Question and the Convention of September* (New York: AMS Press, 1932), 207–14.

69. Palmerston to Russell, October 26, 1862, PRO 30/22/14D, NAUK; David F. Krein, *The Last Palmerston Government: Foreign Policy, Domestic Politics, and the Genesis of "Splendid Isolation"* (Ames: Iowa University Press, 1978), chap. 9.

70. Napier to Russell, June 29, 1862; Russell to Cowley, July 3, 1862; Russell to Lord Napier, July 10, 1862; Russell to Cowley, August 7, 1862, *British Documents on Foreign Affairs: Reports and Papers from the Foreign Office Confidential Print. Part I: From Mid-Nineteenth Century to the First World War. Series B: The Near and Middle East, 1856–1914. Vol. 6: The Ottoman Empire in the Balkans, 1856–1875*, ed. David Gillard, Kenneth Bourne, and D. Cameron Watt (Frederick, Md.: University Publications of America, 1984), 191–92, 199–200, 209, 241–42.

71. Cabinet Report to the Crown, November 11/12, 1862, British Royal Archives, Windsor, Great Britain. The November 1862 discussion was the last of four cabinet debates devoted to the American Civil War. The other three were on June 12, 1861, and January 9, 1862, and in November 1861.

72. Crook, *The North, the South, and the Powers,* 284.

73. Robert H. Lord, "Bismarck and Russia in 1863," *American Historical Review* 29 (October 1923): 24–48.

74. Bismarck to Alvensleben, February 1, 1863, *APP,* 3: 222–24.

75. Werther to Bismarck, February 25, 1863, *APP,* 3: 313–14.

76. Lord, "Bismarck and Russia in 1863," 28, 30.

77. Otto Pflanze, *Bismarck and the Development of Germany: The Period of Unification 1815–1871* (Princeton: Princeton University Press, 1963, 1990), 1: 195.

78. Goltz to Bernstorff, February 24, 1863, *APP,* 3: 308.

79. Bernstorff to Bismarck, February 25, 1863, *APP,* 3: 312.

80. Russell to Cowley, February 26, 1863; Russell to Cowley, March 27, 1863, PRO 30/22/105; Cowley to Russell, March 3, 1863, FO 27/1487, NAUK.

81. Werther to Bismarck, February 25, 1863, *APP,* 3: 313–14.

82. Goltz to Bismarck, February 26, 1863, *APP,* 3: 317–18.

83. The rumor that France intended to create an independent Polish state was confirmed a couple weeks later by Bernstorff and Goltz (March 26, 3: 423 and March 26, 3: 427). Herzog von Leuchtenberg was mentioned as a possible king for Poland. Werther to Bismarck, March 3, 1863; Usedom and Wilhelm I, March 27, 1863, *APP,* 3: 355, 433.

84. Pflanze, *Bismarck and the Development of Germany,* 1: 195–96.

85. Napier to Russell, April 15, 1863, *BFSP 1862–1863,* 53: 888–89.

86. Bernstorff to Bismarck, April 20, 1863, *APP,* 3: 489.

87. Bernstorff to Wilhelm I, April 20, 1863, *APP,* 3: 489–90.

88. Russell to Cowley, May 20, 1863, PRO 30/22/105, NAUK.

89. Werner E. Mosse, "England and the Polish Insurrection of 1863," *English Historical Review* 71 (January 1956): 39.

90. Ibid., 41.

91. Stanton and Russell, February 6, 1863, *BFSP 1862–1863,* 53: 780–82.

92. Mosse, "England and the Polish Insurrection," 42.

93. Frank A. Golder, "The Russian Fleet and the Civil War," *American Historical Review* 20 (July 1915): 801–12.

94. Bernstorff to Bismarck, May 23, 1863, *APP,* 3: 584–86.

95. Russell to Cowley, December 26, 1863, PRO 30/22/104, NAUK; Buchanan to Russell, May 30, 1863, *APP,* 3: 595–86.

96. Bismarck to Sydow, October 16, 1863, *APP,* 4: 70–74.

97. Pamerston to Russell, October 19, 1863, PRO 30/22/22, NAUK; Willissen to Bismarck, January 17, 1864, *APP,* 4: 448–49.

98. Willissen to Bismarck, January 17, 1864, *APP,* 4: 448–49.

99. Russell to Palmerston, February 15, 1864, GC/RU/846, NAUK.

100. Bernstorff to Bismarck, December 2, 1863, *APP,* 4: 252–55.

101. Palmerston to Russell, February 24, 1864, PRO 30/22/23, NAUK.

102. Russell to Cowley, February 8, 1864, PRO 30/22/106, NAUK.

103. Palmerston to Russell, October 19, 1863, PRO 30/22/22, NAUK; Bernstorff to Bismarck, January 28, 1864, *APP,* 4: 486–89.

104. Bernstorff to Bismarck, January 28, 1864, *APP,* 4: 486–89.

105. Bernstorff to Bismarck, February 3, 1864, *APP,* 4: 511. There is a similar, but less violent statement in Palmerston to Russell, January 19, 1863, PRO 30/22/23, NAUK.

106. Bernstorff to Bismarck, February 8, 1864, *APP,* 4: 529.

107. *Kladderadatsch* (Berlin), March 20, 1864, 4.

AARON SHEEHAN-DEAN

Lex Talionis in the U.S. Civil War

Retaliation and the Limits of Atrocity

The U.S. Civil War claimed an enormous number of victims, more than all other American conflicts up until Vietnam combined. But this domestic frame of reference distorts the nature of the conflict and its place in history. Any discussion of violence and mortality in the conflict requires a global context. Changing the basis of comparison allows us to recognize the conflict not as the bloodiest civil war, either in terms of absolute numbers of casualties or when weighted by population (these distinctions belong, respectively, to China's Taiping rebellion, which claimed the lives of more than twenty million people between 1850 and 1864, and the Paraguayan War of 1864–1870, which reduced Paraguay's adult male population by more than 75 percent).[1] A global framework provides not only the proper context for understanding the nature of the war but helps explain why the U.S. conflict, while quite destructive, was not worse still. In particular, the practice of retaliation, as defined by international law, limited violence in the conflict.

Union and Confederate leaders used the global law of war to justify their own policies and to condemn those of their opponent. The conspicuous efforts of American leaders to cite European authorities suggest an effort to create a kind of moral genealogy of acceptable and prohibited behavior. More than just intellectual lineage, these efforts—mostly in the U.S. and Confederate States Congresses and in the newspapers of both sections—sought to build international recognition behind claims to legitimacy. An important marker for inclusion in the world of nations was waging warfare like other modern European nations. At its furthest extent, this involved using the principle of retaliation to correct an opponent's breach of the traditional rules of civilized warfare.[2]

Both Federals and Confederates claimed continuity with a long line of thinkers about just war, some going back to Augustine and Aquinas, but most such claims focused on sixteenth-, seventeenth-, and eighteenth-century European writers such as Francisco de Vittoria, Hugo Grotius, and Emerich de Vattel.[3]

Both sides sought historical and contemporary legitimacy as sovereign nations by connecting their methods of waging war to established traditions. Congressman Henry Foote of Mississippi hoped to accomplish this by postponing "the adoption of harsh measures until all other proper resources in vogue among civilized nations were exhausted."[4] He understood the diplomatic importance of positioning the Confederacy as an equal among civilized nations. Just as nations build themselves in a geographic context, they must also do so in a historical context. Eric Hobsbawm and other theorists of nationalism emphasize the historical roots of a given nation—that, to claim nationhood, a people must link themselves to discrete ancestors.[5] In addition to this vertical support, nations require tangential branches on their family tree. These connect the nation to established traditions parallel to its own—distant but related. This practice adds strength to claims for sovereignty because foreign nations see something of themselves in other nations.[6]

Approaching the Civil War from the perspective of international law and conduct also reminds us that claims to statehood exist only in a global context. David Armitage's global history of the Declaration of Independence forcefully and persuasively argues that establishing sovereignty in the U.S. required that other countries accept the declaration, which generally they did.[7] The Civil War revived both the problem of sovereignty and the method that a new generation of American rebels used to establish it. Participants in the Civil War claimed adherence to the rules of war to garner the support of fellow nations. Complying with this entailed sacrifice because it required both sides to limit the force they used in war. The challenge was different for the North and the South; the former had already established itself, but secession presented a serious challenge to American sovereignty and reopened the question of whether a democratic republic the size of the United States could maintain itself over time. In the Civil War, the North and the South sought to use the same set of rules—the loose collection of guidelines known as the law of war—to discredit their opponent and devalue their claims to legitimacy.[8]

Before analyzing the practice of retaliation in the U.S. conflict, it is important to distinguish retaliation from simple revenge. "Retaliation" and "reprisal" (the latter term sometimes substitutes for the former) come from distinct root words, but both emphasize the compensatory nature of the practice. According to the *Oxford English Dictionary,* the Latin root of *retāliāre* means "to make amends for (a wrong done) by an equivalent punishment." Reprisal, from Anglo-Norman and Middle French, indicates the "seizure of property or persons of foreigners as compensation for loss sustained (1353 in Anglo-Norman), retaking, repossessing (early 15th cent.)" Revenge, in contrast, emphasizes the pleasure of payback or, as the *OED* defines it, the "satisfaction obtained by repaying an injury or wrong."[9] Just-war scholars elaborated the concept of retaliation thoroughly before the Civil

War. Grotius insisted that retaliation was lawful only when practiced against the original perpetrators of an unjust act, never as mere punishment.[10] Most military and political leaders on both sides regarded him as the ultimate authority on questions of what was permissible.[11] Building on Grotius, Emerich de Vattel, who was the major eighteenth-century interpreter of the global laws of nations at war, famously discussed the mistreatment of ambassadors. "What right have you to cut off the nose and ears of the embassador [*sic*] of a barbarian who had treated your embassador in that manner?" he asked. Vattel expressed reservations about the role of retaliation but believed that, when practiced, "the punishment ought to bear some proportion to the evil for which we mean to inflict it."[12]

Francis Lieber applied these conceptions to the Union's rules of war (issued as General Order No. 100 in 1863). "The law of war," wrote Lieber, "can no more wholly dispense with retaliation than can the law of nations, of which it is a branch. Yet civilized nations acknowledge retaliation as the sternest feature of war. A reckless enemy often leaves to his opponent no other means of securing himself against the repetition of barbarous outrage." According to the Lieber Code, "retaliation will therefore never be resorted to as a measure of mere revenge, but only as a means of protective retribution, and moreover cautiously and unavoidably."[13] Although Confederates spurned the Lieber Code as an invitation to barbarism, they expressed the same attitude in their discussions of retaliation. In 1864, Confederate congressman Theodore Burnett introduced a resolution demanding that for every Confederate soldier "incarcerated in the dungeons and felon cells of Northern prisons . . . [we] shall . . . administer the same treatment received by our men in the hands of the enemy." But Burnett did not anticipate a limitless cycle of vengeance. Instead, the purpose of his resolution was to "bring the enemy back to a sense of humanity."[14] In practice, both sides used retaliation as a method of ensuring compliance with global standards of conduct.[15]

In many of their public comments, representatives of both sides stressed rules that could curtail violence and ensure a truly civil war. In 1862, Confederate congressman Augustus Wright of Georgia, for instance, proposed a resolution authorizing the appointment of a commissioner to treat with the United States to speak about Northern atrocities, "to prevent, if possible, the inauguration of a war which must shock the humanity and civilization of the nineteenth century." He believed that Northerners and Southerners both wanted a civilized war. We must "treat upon the manner of conducting the war, and, if possible to agree upon the terms whereby its horrors shall be mitigated, and the usages of civilized nations maintained."[16] The Confederacy never codified its principles as the North did, but its use of retaliation reflected the same three core rules: retaliatory violence had to be enacted against the equals of whoever breached the rules of war originally; it had to be proportional in terms of scale; and, most important, it could be intended only to curtail the illegitimate actions of one's enemy.

How did these theoretical pronouncements compare to the actual retaliatory policies adopted by each side? Politicians might well find it useful to condemn violence and explain away their side's atrocities by reference to the initial wrongs of their enemy. Cynics could certainly read the self-aggrandizing speeches of congressmen as mere camouflage for their own brutality, but the record reveals enough consistency in the enactment of retaliation to suggest that most officers pursued it as a last resort and with the intention of ending a cycle of violence rather than initiating one.

Military and political leaders conceptualized and implemented retaliatory policies in a variety of ways. Both sides applied retaliation against soldiers, prisoners, guerrillas, and property.[17] Both sides generally observed the rule of equivalency of target and of degree built into legitimate retaliation. Retaliation could be enacted only against someone of the same category as the original victim: combatant for combatant or noncombatant for noncombatant. Both sides also used the rhetoric of retaliation to appease and inflame public anger against the enemy. It is important to recognize that retaliation held the potential to shade into pure revenge and atrocity. But in the context of the U.S. Civil War, retaliation is most important not because it enabled unrestrained warfare; rather the opposite. In most instances, both sides used retaliation as a way to correct what they saw as the other side's breach of the traditional rules of civilized warfare.[18]

Policymakers conjured and used retaliation in response to actions they deemed beyond the pale. Jefferson Davis articulated his view in a letter to Robert E. Lee. The purpose of retaliation, Davis wrote, was to shock the world "until the outraged voice of a common humanity forces a respect for the recognized rules of war."[19] The best-known use of retaliation was Lincoln's vow to execute captured Confederate prisoners in response to Jefferson Davis's threat to execute or sell into slavery black Union soldiers. Lincoln's decision reflected international law because it sought to correct Confederate policy, noting that "the law of nations, and the usages and customs of war, as carried on by civilized powers, permit no distinction as to color in the treatment of prisoners of war as public enemies."[20] Lincoln's order is rarely discussed within the framework of retaliation and just war, but this was the context from which it sprang. Jefferson Davis's threat to treat black soldiers under Southern state law as enslaved men in the act of rebellion promised to initiate a cataclysmic cycle of violence. Lincoln relied upon the enlistment of black soldiers (almost two hundred thousand served during the war), and he could not afford to deny them the protections of the government. Black Americans and some white abolitionists criticized Lincoln for failing to follow through, but his threat functioned as a preemptive retaliation policy and helped curtail the mass murder of black soldiers.[21] The legislation, orders, questions, and counterorders among Confederate policymakers that followed in the wake of Lincoln's retaliation threat revealed significant confusion among the Southern high command about how to respond in a way that remained consistent with customary norms.[22] Confederate soldiers still murdered black Union troops even after Lincoln's warning, but they did so without official sanction and in smaller numbers. In short, Lincoln's threat of retaliation created a more just and symmetrical conflict.

The practice worked on a smaller scale, as well. The bloodiest episode of this sort came in September 1864 during Philip Sheridan's occupation of Virginia's Shenandoah Valley. Union general George A. Custer authorized the execution of six members of John Singleton Mosby's cavalry regiment. Mosby argued that as members of a regularly commissioned Confederate cavalry unit—Virginia's Forty-Third Cavalry Battalion—his captured men should have received the protection of prisoners of war, and in response he executed six of Custer's men. In an open letter to Sheridan, Mosby defined his action as a policy of retaliation and noted that "hereafter, any prisoners falling into my hands will be treated with the kindness due to their condition, unless some new act of barbarity shall compel me, reluctantly, to adopt a line of policy repugnant to humanity."[23] None did, and no executions followed. In this case, as in others, retaliation worked to end breaches of the customary law of war.

Retaliation worked at the local level to stem bloodshed.[24] Union commanders in the Department of the Gulf, perhaps because of frustration with their inability to eradicate the guerrillas' threat in the region, made frequent use of the threat of retaliation.[25] The unjust behavior of Southern guerrillas demanded retaliation in other regions, as well. In Chattanooga, a Union general reported that he "ha[d] five rebel citizens in custody . . . and intends to execute in retaliation for the Union non-combatants murdered by Gatewood's guerrillas."[26] Confederates did the same. The commanding Confederate general in Atlanta wrote to the Union general in Pensacola, Florida, to inform him that the Confederates were holding two U.S. lieutenants and a captain "in close confinement as *hostages* for Judge Wright, Mr. George Wright, and Mr. Merritt, citizens of Pensacola whom *[sic]* . . . are now inhumanly and contrary to the rules of civilized warfare confined in Fort Pickens for refusing to take the oath of allegiance to the Abolition Government." Five days later, the Union general wrote back to report that the men had been released: "Judge Wright is in Pensacola, George Wright has 'passed out of our lines,' and Merritt left for New Orleans."[27]

Commanders often issued retaliatory threats preemptively. In August 1862 Samuel Cooper, the Confederate inspector general, regretfully announced that a sequence of Union atrocities had "driven [the Confederate government] to the necessity of adopting such measures of retribution and retaliation as shall seem adequate to repress and punish these barbarities."[28] Though the threat was never carried out, it undoubtedly reached Union ears because of its public nature. Similarly, after leaving Savannah and heading into South Carolina, William T.

Sherman left orders to provide for the operation of markets in the city and public assemblies. He also left a warning that if loyal southerners were harassed by pro-Confederates, "the perpetrator if caught will be summarily punished, or his family made to suffer for the outrage; but if the crime cannot be traced to the actual party, then retaliation will be made on the adherents to the cause of the rebellion."[29] In both these cases as in others, a retaliatory policy was announced but not acted on in advance of its being needed in order to deter a specific action.[30]

The most famous episode of property destruction as an act of retaliation came in late 1864, when Jubal Early's Confederate forces burned the town of Chambersburg, Pennsylvania, after holding the town ransom for $100,000 in gold. Early explained his actions as retaliation for the burning of the Virginia Military Institute and of Governor John Letcher's house (both in Lexington, Virginia) by Union general David Hunter earlier in the year. Early defended his actions by noting that "a number of towns in the South, as well as private country houses, had been burned by the Federal troops. I came to the conclusion it was time to open the eyes of the people of the North to this enormity, by an example in the way of retaliation."[31] A true conservative who came to secession quite late, Early saw his actions within the limits of civilized war. In considering the episode from the vantage point of the 1890s, Early baldly stated, "I see no reason to regret my conduct on this occasion."[32]

Participants at all levels of the conflict demonstrated a similar awareness of the function of retaliation. Hannah Johnson, a black resident of Buffalo, New York, whose father had escaped as a slave from Louisiana, implored Lincoln to stand up for black Union soldiers. Johnson's son was serving in the Fifty-Fourth Massachusetts, and she expressed concern over the Confederate policy of selling captured soldiers into slavery. She demanded equal treatment. "Why should not our enemies be compelled to treat him the same, Made to do it." Making them, she knew, would involve having Lincoln "rettallyate" for any discrepancies in treatment suffered by Union men.[33] Johnson did not ask for special treatment—she knew her son risked his life as a soldier—but she expected Lincoln to impose equivalent terms on captured Confederates in order to ensure fair treatment.

Retaliation even influenced the actions of irregular actors. After Robert Cobb Kennedy was sentenced to death for setting a fire in New York City that was part of a Confederate plot to burn the city but that instead killed women and children, he gave a statement in which he admitted setting the fires but explained them as a proportional response. "I wish to say that the killing of women and children was the last thing we thought of. — We wanted to let the people of the North understand and feel that there are two sides to the war, and that they can't be rolling in wealth and comforts while we at the South are bearing all the hardships and privations. In retaliation for Sheridan's atrocities in the Shenandoah we desired to destroy property, not the lives of women and children."[34] Even this decidedly irregular episode bears the hallmarks of classical just war theory—violence committed in the name of retaliation must be proportional within the category of original act; here it was property for property.

The word "retaliation" also functioned rhetorically, but in this medium it blurred easily into simple revenge. Calls for vengeance appeared almost daily in the newspapers around the country, often surrounding events that did not happen as reported and proposing retaliation that never occurred. The repetition of this language and its continuing use in 1865 suggests that it still filled a need for the publics of both sections.

A famous example can be found in the Confederate anthem *"Maryland, My Maryland!"*

> The despot's heel is on thy shore,
> Maryland, My Maryland!
> His torch is at thy temple door,
> Maryland, My Maryland!
> Avenge the patriotic gore
> That flecked the streets of Baltimore.

Grotius had long before identified the source of this desire—the bestial nature of man—and condemned it. "Our Reason tells us, that we ought not to make another Man suffer, unless it be for some Good that may accrue thereby," he wrote. "But in the pain or Sufferings of our Enemy, barely considered in themselves, there can be nothing of Good, but what is false and imaginary."[35] Southerners applied the language of violence and retaliation ("avenge") because they regarded Lincoln's use of the federal army to suppress Baltimore's pro-Confederate community in the war's opening months as a violation of federal law and the rights of protest.[36] Federals engaged in the same arrogant belligerence. Witness Sherman's response to Confederate general Thomas Hindman: "'If, as you threaten [to hang Federal prisoners in retaliation for Union execution of guerrillas], remember we have hundreds of thousands of men bitter and yearning for revenge. Let us but loose these from the restraints of discipline, and no life or property would be safe in the region where we do hold possession and power. . . . You initiate the game, and my word for it your people will regret it long after you pass from earth.'"[37] On the one hand, the rhetoric of retaliation as revenge satisfied a need for people in both sections to fantasize about the damage they could inflict on their opponents.[38] On the other hand, the practice of retaliation revealed the extent to which both sides had access to rules and systems that could curtail and check the war's violence. Retaliation's dual nature fostered fantasies of excess even as it encouraged restraint.

Both sides came close to using retaliation as weapon of vengeance and, in the process, to abandoning global standards of just war. For Confederates, this transpired in response to the Emancipation Proclamation, which an Arkansas editorialist described as a "crime . . . [that] should be ranked, 'amongst those stupendous wrongs against humanity, shocking to the moral sense of the world, like Herod's massacre of the Innocents.'"[39] Confederate senators called openly for a "war of extermination." But moderates in the Confederacy espoused retaliation. One week after Lincoln issued the proclamation, Thomas Semmes, a senator from Louisiana, introduced a resolution calling it "a gross violation of the usages of civilized warfare, an outrage upon private property and an invitation to servile war." But, rather than endorse the attitude of many of his peers—that the black flag should be raised—Semmes proposed that the proclamation be "counteracted by such severe retaliatory measures as . . . may . . . secure its withdrawal or arrest its execution."[40] During the debate over a retaliation measure to the Emancipation Proclamation, Semmes argued that since the war began, "the rights accorded to belligerents by the usages of civilized nations have been studiously denied to the citizens of these States, except in cases where the same have been extorted by the apprehension of retaliation."[41] His final resolution, still not harsh enough for many, proposed to execute all officers in black regiments and to put all captured officers of white regiments to hard labor. Semmes's goal, explained in the resolution, was "to repress the lawless practice and designs of the enemy by inflicting severe retribution."[42]

The closest the United States came to using retaliation as a weapon of vengeance was the early 1865 debate over the treatment of Union prisoners.[43] In mid-1864, the Northern public learned about the conditions in which Union soldiers were confined in Confederate prisons. Woodcuts published in Northern papers appeared to show more skeletons than men, strapping farm boys of the Midwest reduced to ninety pounds of listless bones. Editorials across the country called for vengeance.[44] Congress failed to respond until early 1865, most likely as a Republican strategy to undercut peace negotiations with the Confederacy.[45] Photographs of the men were left on the desks of senators and congressmen.[46] Morton Wilkinson, a Republican senator from Minnesota, responded by proposing that Confederate prisoners held by the United States receive the same "rations, clothing, and supplies" as "those furnished by the rebel authorities to Union troops held by them as prisoners of war." Wilkinson objected to what he regarded as the Confederates' uncivilized method of waging war and also its result—that Union soldiers returned from the South so weak that they could never fight again. His proposal for retaliation thus drew on the argument from military necessity. Although Wilkinson retained doubts about whether this was a truly Christian measure, he concluded that "I think the laws of war would justify a course of retaliation on the part of our Government."[47]

Benjamin Wade, a prominent radical Republican from Ohio, had even fewer qualms. The resolution he introduced a few weeks later would have required that the rations and treatment of captured Confederates correspond to what Union prisoners received.[48] The brutality implicit in Wade's resolution created a divisive debate among Republicans and between Republicans and Democrats in the Senate. It also produced an open debate over the meaning and intent of retaliation. Wade's Republican colleague Edgar Cowan summarized the proposal in plain language: "If the Confederate States of America starve our soldiers, we are therefore justified, or indeed bound, if we undertake to enforce the law of nations, to starve their soldiers." This he refused to do. Although Corwin supported retaliation, by which he meant an action that compensated for the barbarous treatment of Union soldiers, he would not support a perfect equivalency in treatment because this would unjustly kill innocent men. There had been "a time in the history of the world when an eye for an eye and a tooth for a tooth was the *lex talionis* of the universe; but . . . that law, by a higher authority than ours, has been abrogated."[49]

Where Corwin and, especially, Senate Democrats saw simple vengeance, Wade argued that his real purpose was to suppress Confederate atrocities. "Retaliation has in all the ages of the world been a means of bringing inhuman and savage foes to a sense of their duty, and has frequently had the effect to promote the objects of justice," Wade asserted.[50] But other senators believed that Wade's proposal would have entailed deliberately starving Confederate prisoners to death, something that would have cast the United States out of the company of nations. Wade's chief critic, Charles Sumner of Massachusetts, asserted that "Any attempted imitation of rebel barbarism in the treatment of prisoners would be plainly impracticable, on account of its inconsistency with the prevailing sentiments of humanity among us; that it would be injurious at home, for it would barbarize the whole community; that it would be utterly useless, for it could not affect the cruel authors of the revolting conduct which we seek to overcome; that it would be immoral, inasmuch as it proceeded from vengeance alone."[51] The dispute between these two—a surprise to many because they represented the leading edge of radical Republicans in the Northern government—hinged on the importance of proportionality and the limits of retaliation imposed by common consent. Sumner's friend and confidant Francis Lieber expressed the same sentiment in an editorial in Washington's *Daily Globe* during the debate: "These cruelties, therefore, would be simply revenge, not retaliation, for retaliation as an element of war, and of nations in general, implied the idea of stopping a certain evil."[52] Sumner and Lieber won and Wade lost, and Northerners seemed quite glad of it. Although some papers had endorsed the call for vengeance, most celebrated the defeat of the resolution. The Boston *Daily Advertiser* was typical in this respect: "the people were as little willing as the Senate to enter upon retaliation in kind,—and to subject men to the tortures of starvation and cold, because rebels do the same."[53]

Some of the officers and officials who used retaliation seem to have arrived at their position independently after recognizing retaliation as a method of forcing one's opponent to respect the rules of war. But many more came to retaliation because of their awareness of its place in international law. Even ordinary civilians demonstrated an implicit awareness of the parameters of retaliation established by just-war scholars. The examples described demonstrate the influence that global military theory and practice exercised over both northerners and southerners. In the debates on both sides, speakers referenced the laws of nations developed by Emerich de Vattel in the mid-eighteenth century. Charles Sumner raised Vattel in the debate over whether to starve rebel prisoners, citing Vattel's memorable comments on retaliation.[54] Henry Halleck, Lincoln's general in chief and himself the author of a volume on international law in war and peace, used Vattel in an article he wrote on retaliation as well.[55]

Vattel was raised in Neuchâtel (part of today's Switzerland), which was then controlled by the king of Prussia, but he received a polyglot education, studying in Basel, Geneva, and Dresden. His main purpose in the *Laws of Nations* (published in 1758 and translated into English by the end of the eighteenth century) was to apply natural-law theory to the interactions and integrity of nations. Vattel was primarily concerned with political economy and with establishing a system for trade that would enable Europe to advance, but he also explained what was permissible in war and what constituted sovereign authority (especially important for northerners). In short, he embodied established tradition on the question of just war and getting right with Vattel enabled each side to affiliate itself with a respected intellectual and cultural tradition.[56]

It was not just Vattel with whom leaders sought to align themselves. Before Lieber published his rules for Union warfare, he gave a series of lectures in New York that were reprinted in the newspapers. He took particular pains to articulate what combatants could lawfully do to prisoners. Perhaps anticipating the need to retaliate for Confederate treatment of black soldiers, Lieber made clear that previous authorities, such as Grotius, had proved that the enslavement of an enemy's soldiers was unjust.[57] Others used Grotius to condemn the retaliation resolutions considered by the U.S. Senate in early 1865. Lieber himself supported Sumner's argument that they were unjust. Lieber was a useful authority to cite, but opponents of the resolutions grounded their arguments in the writings of Grotius and other European experts on just war.[58]

Throughout the conflict, commanders on both sides larded their comments on which actions were permissible (especially when considering retaliation) with general references to the "laws of war." Henry Halleck, after 1862 the Union's chief military planner, believed that the United States "could not retaliate by adopting the same barbarous mode of warfare, nor can we retaliate by punishing the innocent for the guilty. The laws of war forbid this."[59] Officers and soldiers expressed a similar outlook. After helping burn Chambersburg, Pennsylvania, with Jubal Early's army, a Confederate surgeon expressed his confusion over the legitimacy of their actions: "I am opposed to burning; but I supposed they deserved it & if they desire to retaliate we can play that game with them & play it well but I do hope such warfare may cease." He desired, he wrote, an "honorable" peace.[60] In practice, honor inhered in acting in accordance with Europeans' laws of war. Even the bloodthirsty *Charleston Mercury* sought a more pacific conflict by requiring adherence to international standards: "The sooner and more surely retaliation follows these transgressions of civilized warfare, the more certainly and quickly will our foes cease their barbarities."[61] What this meant in practice was aligning U.S. or C.S. policy and actions with those developed by Europeans over the preceding centuries and decades.

While it is certainly true that the grand pronouncements of senators in Congress did not by themselves determine the actual operations of armies in the field, their discussions broadcast the war's moral frameworks to foreign audiences.[62] Those discussions reveal how both sides engaged global experiences and philosophies to explain and justify the morality of their own policies. Neither side implemented retaliatory policies as often as they discussed them, but the discussions, which situated both nations in a long international tradition of nation building, war, and violence, were central to Confederate and federal national identity and stature. As one U.S. senator explained his position on retaliation: "This law of retaliation is not our law. It is not the law of the Congress of the United States. It is not the law of the President of the United States. It is the law of nations, that is established by their consent, their practice, and their usage . . . it exists as a code independent of all local legislation by any Government upon earth; it exists as the common, general law of the civilized world, that has received the sanction of the nations of the civilized world."[63]

Confederate diplomats aspired to join the nations of the civilized world, and they did so partly by trying to prove that the North had violated the rules of war and that they truly represented the European tradition of civilized military action. Their failure reflects the broader failure of Confederate nationalism abroad, which helped doom the new nation. Even Congressman William Porcher Miles of South Carolina recognized this basic fact when he lamented that "foreign nations had evinced no appreciation of our regard and observance of the laws of humanity."[64] Conversely, Northerners' willingness to comply with accepted international standards of war and the resulting failure of France and Britain to recognize the Confederacy proved an essential element in the North's eventual victory. Beyond this diplomatic component of the war, the rhetoric and practice of retaliation helped diminish the war's severity. In both the worst case —Confederate treatment of black soldiers—and the smaller ones—individual episodes of murder, hostage taking, and torture—the threat and implementation of retaliation brought symmetry and proportionality to this most terrible of wars.

In addition to revealing the dense network of global ideas and principles that shaped the U.S. Civil War, investigating the role of retaliation helps solve another of the conflict's deep riddles. The Civil War produced a huge number of fatalities—it was by any standard a very bloody conflict—but these were mostly the result of clashes between regular army troops. Guerrillas and other irregular combatants contributed to the violence (and received quite a bit back in return), but they played a limited role in terms of total casualty numbers.[65] Further, the fatalities produced by the war (at least 750,000 out of a population of thirty-one million, or almost 2.5 percent of the population) were distributed reasonably symmetrically between the two sides.[66] The Civil War presents the seeming paradox of a bloody conflict that was also restrained and balanced. How do we explain this? Second, civilians and many soldiers on both sides regarded their opponents as having breached the traditional rules for civilized war and called for revenge. Despite the clamor for action, the U.S. Civil War never descended into the spiral of retaliatory violence that defines so many conflicts. Why not?

One answer to both these questions lies in the fact that the practice of retaliation emerged as a method of curtailing violence. Both northerners and southerners deployed retaliation not as an excuse for revenge but as a method of ensuring that their opponent operated in accordance with global standards of war. Retaliation necessarily involves soldiers in a contradiction: they violate the rules of war in order to enforce the rules of war. In this case, however, the threat and occasional use of retaliation deterred unrestrained war. Michael Walzer, the political philosopher and authority on just war, recognizes that the use of retaliation can quickly become a slippery slope. He notes that "it is the express purpose of reprisals . . . . to break off the chain, to stop the wrongdoing *here,* with this final act."[67] From the perspective of just-war theory, the objection to reprisals arises because they punish innocent people for the crimes of others, but even Walzer, whose book is an extended argument for the use of just-war principles in war making, recognizes that the "responsive, restrained, and proportional" nature of reprisals and their goal of ending a breach of the war convention make them valuable. During the Civil War, they played this role. Ironically, retaliation became the last, best hope of man.

NOTES

1. Jonathan D. Spence, *God's Chinese Son: The Taiping Heavenly Kingdom of Hong Xiuquang* (New York: Norton, 1996), and Harris Gaylord Warren, *Paraguay and the Triple Alliance: The Postwar Decade, 1869–1878* (Austin: University of Texas Press, 1978).

2. Though perhaps ironic, retaliation served as one of the hallmarks of "civilized war." The right of retaliation had a long ancestry in European thinking about military conflict, most importantly as a method of restoring order once an enemy has descended into savagery.

3. Many of the most recent treatments of just war in U.S. history have addressed it largely as rhetoric. Jill Lepore's study of King Philip's War in the seventeenth-century Massachusetts colony and Peter Silver's examination of eighteenth-century Indian-European conflict in the Pennsylvania colony both show the power of language to catalyze real violence. They also demonstrate the persistence of a surprisingly robust conversation among European immigrants about who they could attack and in what ways. Jill Lepore, *The Name of War: King Philip's War and the Origins of American Identity* (New York: Vintage, 1999); Peter J. Silver, *Our Savage Neighbors: How Indian War Transformed Early America* (New York: Norton, 2007).

4. Henry Foote, January 19, 1863, in *Proceedings of the First Confederate Congress, Third Session,* reprinted in *Southern Historical Society Papers* (Richmond, Va.: William Byrd Press, 1930), 153.

5. Eric Hobsbawm, *Nations and Nationalism since 1780* (Cambridge: Verso Press, 1990), 73–77; also see the work of Anthony D. Smith, especially *The Ethnic Origins of Nations* (Oxford: Basil Blackwell, 1986) and *The Antiquity of Nations* (Cambridge: Polity, 2004).

6. David Armitage's history of the uses of the Declaration by other nations implicitly shows this process at work when Americans feel sympathy for other people emulating our model of national independence. David Armitage, *The Declaration of Independence: A Global History* (Cambridge, Mass.: Harvard University Press, 2008).

7. Armitage, *Global History of the Declaration of Independence.*

8. "Law of Nations," *Advocate of Peace,* November/December 1863, 357–60, and "International Law: Grotius on War and Peace," *The Knickerbocker Monthly: A National Magazine,* August 1863, 150–57. Several recent books have articulated the ways in which participants in the Civil War relied upon or influenced international laws of war. See Stephen C. Neff, *Justice in Blue and Gray: A Legal History of the Civil War* (Cambridge, Mass.: Harvard University Press, 2010), 56, and Denis K. Boman, *Lincoln and Citizens' Rights in Civil War Missouri* (Baton Rouge: Louisiana State University Press, 2011), 7–8. I am focusing on one aspect of the law of war—retaliation—because it exercised a demonstrable effect in curtailing violence and because its use illustrated the importance to both sides of adhering to global norms. A different essay that highlighted other aspects of the historical law of war in the U.S. conflict could provide numerous ways of showing the conflict's global dimensions.

9. *Oxford English Dictionary,* http://www.oed.com (accessed October 13, 2011).

10. Hugo Grotius, *The Rights of War and Peace,* ed. Knud Haakonssen (Indianapolis: Liberty Fund, 2005), book 2, chap. 21, book 3, 1420–32.

11. "International Law: Grotius on War and Peace."

12. Emerich de Vattel, *The Law of Nations,* ed. Béla Kapossy and Richard Whatmore (1758; repr., Indianapolis: Liberty Fund, 2008), book 2, chap. 28, sec. 339, 459.

13. "Instructions for the Government of Armies of the United States in the Field," General Orders No. 100, Arts. 27–28, U.S. War Department, *The War of Rebellion: A*

Compilation of the Official Records of the Union and Confederate Armies, 127 vols., index, and atlas (Washington, D.C.: U.S. Government Printing Office, 1886–1922), ser. 3, col. 1, 148–64 (hereafter *O.R.*). Available at http://avalon.law.yale.edu/19th_century/lieber.asp (accessed October 16, 2012). See also Union general in chief Henry Halleck's comment: "The law of retaliation in war has its limits . . . the object . . . being, not revenge, but prevention." Henry W. Halleck, "Retaliation in War," *American Journal of International Law* 6 (January 1912): 110. Halleck practiced what he preached, rescinding a retaliatory order issued by General E. A. Paine because "such a policy was contrary to the rules of 'civilized war.' and if its spirit should be adopted the whole country would be covered with blood. Retaliation has its limits, and the innocent should not be made to suffer for the acts of others over whom they have no control." Halleck quoted in Boman, *Lincoln and Citizen's Rights,* 94.

14. Theodore Burnett, January 15, 1864, in *Proceedings of First Confederate Congress —First Session, First Part,* reprinted in *Southern Historical Society Papers* (Richmond, Va.: William Byrd Press, 1923), 244.

15. Though, as I discuss later, both sides did, on occasion, twist the meaning of retaliation to accommodate pure revenge.

16. August Wright, September 10, 1862, in *Proceedings of First Confederate Congress —Second Session,* reprinted in *Southern Historical Society Papers* (Richmond, Va.: William Byrd Press, 1928), 81–82. To be fair, not everyone saw retaliation as a way to balance accounts. Gideon Welles, Lincoln's conservative secretary of the navy, viewed with great apprehension the call for retaliation against the Fort Pillow Massacre. In cabinet discussions about an appropriate response, Welles opposed surrendering to what he called "the barbarity of retaliation." Gideon Welles, May 5–6, 1864, in *Diary of Gideon Welles,* vol. 2: *April 1, 1864–December 31, 1866,* ed. Howard K. Beale (New York: Norton, 1960), 24–25. The plan to use captured Confederate officers as hostages was never implemented, to Welles's relief, though commanders on both sides seized hostages to compel their opponent to surrender men charged with violations of the war convention.

17. Stephen Neff has canvassed the *O.R.* for instances of reprisals against Southern civilians, but the scattered instances he identifies do not constitute a clear Union policy. Also, in a number of the cases he identifies (especially with regard to Pope and Sheridan), the retaliatory orders were announced but never acted upon. Neff, *Justice in Blue and Gray,* 90–94. See also Burrus M. Carnahan, *Lincoln on Trial: Southern Civilians and the Law of War* (Lexington: University Press of Kentucky, 2010), 61–62.

18. My interpretation challenges that of Harry Stout, who has written the fullest just-war analysis of the U.S. Civil War: *Upon the Altar of the Nation: A Moral History of the Civil War* (New York: Viking, 2006). Stout argues that "in too many instances both sides descended into moral misconduct" (xvi). While I do not deny the periodic lapses that marked the extremes of the conflict, what I find more compelling is the attention that both sides paid to the imperatives of just-war doctrine. For other interpretations that emphasize restraint, see Robert Mackey, *The Uncivil War: Irregular Warfare in the Upper South, 1861–1865* (Norman: University of Oklahoma Press, 2004), 14, 21–23; Mark Neely, "Retaliation: The Problem of Atrocity in the American Civil War," Forty-First Annual Fortenbaugh Lecture (Gettysburg, Pa.: Gettysburg College, 2002), 13; Mark E. Neely Jr., *The Civil War and the Limits of Destruction* (Cambridge, Mass.: Harvard

University Press, 2007), 197; Neff, *Justice in Blue and Gray,* 62–65; and Carnahan, *Lincoln on Trial,* chap. 3.

19. Jefferson Davis to Robert E. Lee, July 31, 1862, published in the *Charleston Mercury,* August 5, 1862.

20. General Order No. 252, July 31, 1863, *O.R.*, ser. 2, vol. 6, 163. Roy P. Basler, the editor of Lincoln's papers, notes that the order was drafted by the War Department and signed by Lincoln. *Collected Works of Abraham Lincoln* (New Brunswick, N.J.: Rutgers University Press, 1953), 7: 357n1.

21. James G. Hollandsworth Jr., "The Execution of White Officers from Black Units by Confederate Forces during the Civil War," in Gregory J. W. Urwin, ed., *Black Flag over Dixie: Racial Atrocities and Reprisals in the Civil War* (Carbondale: Southern Illinois University Press, 2004), 60; Theodore Hodgkins to Abraham Lincoln, April 18, 1864, in Ira Berlin, Joseph P. Reidy, and Leslie S. Rowland, eds., *Freedom's Soldiers: The Black Military Experience in the Civil War* (Cambridge: Cambridge University Press, 1998), 118–20; Carnahan, *Lincoln on Trial,* 73.

22. Howard C. Westwood, "Captive Black Soldiers in Charleston: *What to Do*?" in Urwin, *Black Flag over Dixie,* 34–51.

23. Mosby to Sheridan, *O.R.*, ser. 3, vol. 43, 2, 920. Jeffrey Wert, *Mosby's Rangers* (New York: Simon and Schuster, 1991), 246–52. Lee endorsed the action on the same principle—that retaliation might be the only method of preventing "the cruel conduct of the enemy toward our citizens." Lee, quoted in John S. Mosby, "Retaliation," *Southern Historical Society Papers* (Richmond, Va.: Southern Historical Society, 1899), 27: 317.

24. Sherman's use of captured Confederates to clear land mines (as McClellan used them) reflects a retaliatory strategy that also sought to curtail violence (the use of mines in the first place). Mark E. Neely Jr., "Was the Civil War a Total War?," *Civil War History* 37 (March 1991): 13.

25. See, for instance, George L. Andrews to J. A. Logan, August 5, 1863, and Benjamin Butler to Henry W. Halleck, November 14, 1862, both in Department of the Gulf, Entry #1756, Letters Received 1863 (Box #2), Record Group 393, Part 1, National Archives and Records Administration, Washington, D.C. (hereafter referred to as NARA).

26. *Daily National Intelligencer,* February 24, 1865, 2. For more on Gatewood, see Jonathan Dean Sarris, *A Separate Civil War: Communities in Conflict in the Mountain South* (Charlottesville: University of Virginia Press, 2006), 135–38.

27. Simon Bolivar Buckner to Isaac C. Dyer, January 31, 1863, and Dyer to Buckner, February 4, 1863, U.S. Provost Marshal Records, Department of the Gulf, Letters Received 1863 (Box #3), Entry #1756, Record Group 393, Part 1, NARA.

28. S. Cooper, General Orders No. 54, August 1, 1862, in *O.R.*, ser. 2, vol. 4, 836–37.

29. *Baltimore Sun,* January 23, 1865.

30. Henry Halleck observed the utility of retaliatory threats and offered several examples of how they curtailed violence during the war. See Halleck, "Retaliation in War," 117.

31. Jubal Early, *War Memoirs: Autobiographical Sketch and Narrative of the War between the States* (Bloomington: Indiana University Press, 1960), 401.

32. Early, *War Memoirs,* 404.

33. Hannah Johnson to Abraham Lincoln, July 31, 1863, in Ira Berlin and Leslie S. Rowland, eds., *Families and Freedom: A Documentary History of African-American Kinship in the Civil War Era* (New York: New Press, 1997), 81–82.

34. *Baltimore Sun,* March 28, 1865.

35. Grotius, *Rights of War and Peace,* Book 2, 960.

36. Daniel E. Sutherland, *A Savage Conflict: The Decisive Role of Guerrillas in the American Civil War* (Chapel Hill: University of North Carolina Press, 2009), chap. 1; John Lockwood and Charles Lockwood, *The Siege of Washington: The Untold Story of the Twelve Days That Shook the Union* (New York: Oxford University Press, 2011), 113–30.

37. W. T. Sherman to T. C. Hindman, June 25, 1862, quoted in Robert Mackey, *The Uncivil War: Irregular Warfare in the Upper South, 1861–1865* (Norman: University of Oklahoma Press, 2004), 15.

38. Charles Royster has referred to this as "the vicarious war." Charles Royster, *The Destructive War: William Tecumseh Sherman, Stonewall Jackson, and the Americans* (New York: Vintage, 1991). Royster and I differ on whether we think this aspect of the conflict fomented or retarded the practice of actual violence. I believe that the soldiers who had to do the actual killing exhibited more restraint than did civilians engaged only in the vicarious war.

39. John R. Eakin, as quoted in Gregory J. W. Urwin, "'We Cannot Treat Negroes . . . as Prisoners of War': Racial Atrocities and Reprisals in Civil War Arkansas," in Urwin, *Black Flag over Dixie,* 139.

40. Thomas Semmes, September 29, 1862, in *Proceedings of the First Confederate Congress, End of Second Part,* reprinted in *Southern Historical Society Papers* IX (Richmond, Va.: William Byrd Press, 1930), 7.

41. Thomas Semmes, October 1, 1862, in *Proceedings of the First Confederate Congress, End of Second Part,* reprinted in *Southern Historical Society Papers* IX (Richmond, Va.: William Byrd Press, 1930), 25.

42. Thomas Semmes, October 1, 1862, in *Proceedings of the First Confederate Congress, End of Second Part,* reprinted in *Southern Historical Society Papers* IX (Richmond, Va.: William Byrd Press, 1930), 26.

43. Before the debate over prisoner treatment and even before the confirmations of atrocities in rebel prisons, the U.S. Commissary General proposed and the secretary of war approved a 20 percent reduction in the food allotment for Confederate prisoners. W. Hoffman to E. Stanton, May 19, 1864, *O.R.*, ser. 2, vol. 7, 150–51, and "Circular," W. Hoffman, June 1, 1864, *O.R.*, ser. 2, vol. 7, 183–84. Scholars of Civil War prisons argue that this policy shift stemmed from anger among officials (principally the commissary general, W. Hoffman; the quartermaster general, Montgomery Meigs; and Edwin Stanton, the secretary of war). James M. Gillispie, *Andersonvilles of the North: The Myths and Realities of Northern Treatment of Civil War Confederate Prisoners* (Denton: University of North Texas Press, 2008), 58–64. Gillispie's own evidence from the camps at Alton, Rock Island, and elsewhere indicates that the "retaliation" rations did not significantly affect the mortality rates in Union camps. See esp.117, 145, 162, 202, 246.

44. Reporting on Andersonville filled the papers beginning in spring 1864. See, for example, *Columbus Daily Enquirer,* July 27, 1864; *New York Herald,* September 19, 1864; *Philadelphia Inquirer,* November 16, 1864.

45. Neely, *Civil War and the Limits of Destruction,* 187–88.

46. Neely, "Retaliation," 11.

47. *Congressional Globe,* Thirty-Eighth Congress, Second Session, December 20, 1864, 73–74.

48. *Congressional Globe,* Thirty-Eighth Congress, Second Session, January 16, 267.

49. *Congressional Globe,* Thirty-Eighth Congress, Second Session, January 24, 1865, 383.

50. Benjamin Wade, January 23, 1865, *Congressional Globe,* Thirty-Eighth Congress, Second Session, Part 1, 364. Wade's resolution did include a provision for improving conditions in Northern prisoner of war camps once the Confederates demonstrated they had done the same.

51. Charles Sumner, January 24, 1865, *Congressional Globe,* Thirty-Eighth Congress, Second Session, Part 1, 381.

52. Francis Lieber, quoted in Henry W. Halleck, "Retaliation in War," *American Journal of International Law* 6 (January 1912): 113.

53. *Boston Daily Advertiser,* February 4, 1865, 2; *Albany Evening Journal,* April 12, 1865, "Retaliation," 2.

54. Charles Sumner, January 24, 1865, *Congressional Globe,* Thirty-Eighth Congress, Second Session, Part 1, 382. In that same debate, Jacob Howard of Michigan took issue with a third senator's interpretation of Vattel. Jacob Howard, January 26, 1865, *Congressional Globe,* Thirty-Eighth Congress, Second Session, Part 1, 430.

55. Halleck, "Retaliation in War," 112.

56. See, for instance, "The Laws of War," *Richmond Daily Dispatch,* March 15, 1862; *Danville Quarterly Review,* December 1864, 606–9; and *North American Review,* January 1862, 212–14.

57. "Laws and Usages of War," *New York Times,* February 16, 1862.

58. "Retaliation Reply to 'L.,'" *New York Times,* February 3, 1865.

59. "General Halleck and the Poisoners," *New York Times,* March 1, 1862.

60. Isaac White to Jinnie White, August 9, 1864, Isaac White Letters, Special Collections Department, University Libraries, Virginia Tech, Blacksburg, Va.

61. "The President [*sic*] Order for Retaliation in Missouri," *Charleston Mercury,* November 24, 1862.

62. Lacking an extensive foreign press corps that could cover the conflict on the ground, many leading European papers covered the conflict by summarizing reporting from American papers or by quoting public pronouncements from officials on either side. European observers, much more than American ones, relied upon official discourse to understand the conflict. For a discussion of retaliation in this context, see *London Examiner,* December 13, 1862. Wilkinson, December 20, 1864, *Congressional Globe,* Thirty-Eighth Congress, Second Session, Part 1, 73.

63. Davis, January 26, 1865, *Congressional Globe,* Thirty-Eighth Congress, Second Session, Part 1, 427.

64. William Porcher Miles, January 2, 1864, in *Proceedings of the First Confederate Congress, Fourth Session,* reprinted in *Southern Historical Society Papers,* ed. Frank E. Vandiver (Richmond, Va.: Virginia Historical Society, 1953), 172.

65. This is not to deny the important role of guerrillas (primarily pro-Confederate) in shaping Union policy. See Dan Sutherland, *A Savage Conflict and Punitive War: Confederate Guerrillas and Union Reprisals* (Lawrence: University Press of Kansas, 2009) especially.

66. J. David Hacker, "A Census-Based Count of the Civil War Dead," *Civil War History* 57 (December 2011): 307–48.

67. Michael Walzer, *Just and Unjust Wars: A Moral Argument with Historical Illustrations*, 4th ed. (New York: Basic Books, 2006), 207, 208–16.

AARON W. MARRS

Fulfilling "The president's duty to communicate"

The Civil War and the Creation of the Foreign Relations of the United States *Series*

The Civil War was the greatest domestic crisis ever faced by the United States. Yet the character of this crisis—in which one portion of the country bid for independence—required the United States to work abroad to prevent recognition of the southern states as a separate country.[1] This foreign struggle, in turn, had a domestic component: President Abraham Lincoln and his secretary of state, William Seward, had to answer to Congress—and, by extension, to the American people—as to how (and how well) they were defending American interests around the world. In response to a congressional request, the Department of State sent to Congress in December 1861 more than four hundred pages of correspondence between Washington and posts overseas, delivered as an attachment to Lincoln's annual message. One hundred and fifty years later, this compilation of documents has evolved into something wholly different: the *Foreign Relations of the United States* (*FRUS*) series, a comprehensive official history of U.S. foreign policy. The shared sesquicentennial of the Civil War and the *FRUS* series provides an opportunity to investigate the circumstances surrounding the creation of the first volume and to reflect on how the series has evolved over the past century and a half.

Unfortunately, many of the facts about the first volume are shrouded in mystery. There are few Department records from the era that can shed light on the motivations behind its creation. As we shall see, one of the strongest statements of the series' intent is hidden in an 1864 instruction from Seward to Charles Francis Adams, U.S. Minister to Great Britain. To date, I have not encountered an explicit policy statement laying out goals and methods beyond what Seward wrote in 1864. Given the difficulty of finding information, a certain amount of lore has grown up surrounding the publication of the volume, which has suggested that Seward and Lincoln played a more significant role in the publication of the volume than what the extant documentation can prove. Up to the present day, much of what we know about the early history of the series has come from a series of poorly sourced articles (although, in fairness, the dearth of sources makes research difficult).[2] This essay takes a fresh look at the available sources and creates a new narrative that sets out Seward's expectations and illuminates the domestic uses of the first *FRUS* volume. Piecing together the existing documentation and examining the context in which *FRUS* was released can help us fully understand the volume's importance. Several broad conclusions emerge from this investigation: the volume represents an example of the checks and balances between the executive and legislative branches of the federal government, the volume tells modern historians what the Lincoln administration wanted its citizens to know about foreign relations, and the volume had a clear domestic audience.

Early histories of *FRUS* shed precious little light on the origins of the series. Writing in 1938, Clarence Carter stated merely that in 1861 "William H. Seward submitted to Congress for publication the manuscript of a volume containing the general diplomatic correspondence of that year."[3] E. R. Perkins was similarly silent on the subject in 1952, noting only that "This series of publications started when President Lincoln sent to the Congress his first annual message on December 3, 1861."[4] Writing on the one hundredth anniversary of the series, the historian Richard Leopold made no assessment as to who bore responsibility for the first volume but implicitly linked the series with Seward by claiming that "a deterioration set in" the series after Seward left the Department.[5] Department historian William Slany argued in 1989 that Seward "took a personal hand" in the 1861 volume, although the evidence for Seward's role is unclear.[6] Sacha Zala's recent comparative international history of diplomatic documentation suggests only that Lincoln "initiated" the series "without much advance planning or fanfare, and possibly merely as a means of keeping speech short during a time of war."[7]

How involved were Lincoln and Seward in the decision to publish this volume? Unfortunately, we cannot gauge their specific level of involvement; that is to say, we cannot know whether Lincoln or Seward themselves selected the documents included in the volume.[8] But it is difficult to imagine documents of this importance being released without their concurrence. The Department of State was quite small in the nineteenth century, with only forty-two domestic employees in 1860.[9] A project of this type, releasing documents that revealed the workings of American diplomacy, undoubtedly attracted attention at high levels. But the precise nature of Seward's or Lincoln's involvement—did they debate the selection of documents?—remains unclear.

Several years after the publication of the volume, however, Seward explained the necessity of the publication in an exchange with Adams. On February 11, 1864, Adams sent a despatch to Washington noting that "publication of the Diplomatic papers . . . has elicited much comment in Parliament." Adams argued that if diplomatic correspondence were to be published, it should at least be done with adequate context so that his own actions would not come under question in London.[10] Seward responded with a lengthy explanation of the decision to publish the correspondence.[11] For Seward, publishing documentation had a solid constitutional basis: "The Constitution of the United States requires the President from time to time to give Congress information concerning the state of the Union."[12] Above and beyond this constitutional obligation, Seward noted, was the fact that "our foreign affairs have . . . been a subject of anxiety as deep as that which is felt in regard to military and naval events." This widespread interest demanded a government response: "The Government continually depends upon the support of Congress and the People, and that support can be expected only in the condition of keeping them thoroughly and truthfully informed of the manner in which the powers derived from them are executed." Seward linked the publication of documents to democracy. The authority of the government was derived from the people, and so the people deserved to see the correspondence that revealed how policy was being executed.

Thus, Seward told Adams that "Congress and the country . . . had a right" to see the printed instructions that had caused Adams such consternation. Since "history would be incomplete without that account," the president had a "duty to communicate it, unless special reason of a public nature existed for withholding it." Seward did not believe that his instructions to Adams qualified for this exception, and even if they did, "the question which had called out this despatch had been for a time put at rest." Indeed, for Seward the greater error would have been *not* to release the document. Not publishing the documentation "would have seemed to imply a confession that it was improper in itself, while to practice reserve on so great a question would be liable to be deemed an abuse of the confidence which Congress and the people had so freely reposed in the Government." Congress and the American people needed to make an open and honest assessment of the government's foreign policy, and the publication of these documents enabled the constitutional framework of accountability to function.

As we shall see, the theoretical advantages that Seward laid out were not always present in practice. Nevertheless, Seward made explicit in 1864 the reasons for releasing documentation. Evidence from the legislative branch supports the arguments that Seward laid out to Adams. Congress was indeed concerned about foreign relations during the Civil War and did expect to receive documentation reflecting the administration's actions. Seward's defense of publication and the actions of Congress demonstrate that *FRUS* occupies an important place in the federal government's checks and balances: the executive branch carried out foreign policy, but the legislative branch reserved the right to monitor that policy via these requests for documentation.

On July 13, 1861, Samuel Sullivan Cox (Democrat from Ohio) submitted a resolution to the House of Representatives, which was promptly "read, considered, and agreed to." The resolution stated: "*Resolved,* That the President of the United States, at the beginning of the next session of Congress, or at this session, if compatible with the public service, communicate to this House all correspondence with the English, French, Spanish, and other Governments with reference to the right of blockade, privateering, and the recognition of the so-called confederate States."[13] Two days later, a broader version was offered by Erastus Corning (Democrat from New York). The resolution read: "*Resolved,* That the President be requested, if not, in his opinion, incompatible with the public interest, to submit to this House all correspondence between this Government and foreign Powers on the subject of the existing insurrection in the United States." Cox noted that he had already submitted a "similar resolution," and Corning responded that he would "prefer that this should be adopted, if the House will indulge me." With no further debate, the resolution was adopted.[14] Corning's resolution was more expansive than Cox's, casting a wider net for documentation by not limiting it to specific topics within the context of Civil War. On July 25, Senator Timothy Howe (Republican from Wisconsin) made a similar resolution in his chamber, which was adopted by unanimous consent: "*Resolved,* That the President be requested to communicate to the Senate all instructions issued by the executive department to our foreign ministers, since the 4th of March last, in reference to the rebellion now existing in the southern portion of the Union, if, in his judgment, the publication of the same be not incompatible with the public interest."[15] Interestingly, all three resolutions deferred to the president's judgment about whether it would be in the public interest to release the documentation. Thus, while demanding the correspondence, both branches of Congress recognized that the president retained the discretion to determine what was appropriate for the public eye. The House resolutions came from Democrats and the Senate resolution from a Republican, suggesting bipartisan interest in this issue.

The immediate response from Lincoln and Seward was negative. The same day on which Howe put forth his resolution, Seward responded to Lincoln (and Lincoln shared with the House) that it would not be appropriate to share "the correspondence called for" by Corning's resolution.[16] But, by the end of 1861, the decision was made to release the information. Lincoln sent forth a report to Congress and also a note to the House of Representatives (dated December 4), stating that he was fulfilling the request of the July 13 resolution, quoting its text that the documentation covered "rights of blockade, privateering and the recognition of the so called Confederate States."[17] It is unclear whether Lincoln's reference to the narrow resolution of the 13th rather than the broader one from the 15th was an oversight or intentional, but the correspondence forwarded to Congress covered a wide array of issues. If we turn now to the documents, we can learn more about the second conclusion: that these documents have value because they demonstrate what the government wanted its citizens to know about foreign policy.

Lincoln's annual message, dated December 3, covered a range of topics but did touch briefly on foreign affairs. The principal topic of concern was whether the nascent Confederacy had obtained recognition from any other country. On this topic, Lincoln was confident: "The disloyal citizens of the United States who have offered the ruin of our country, in return for the aid and comfort which they have invoked abroad, have received less patronage and encouragement than they probably expected." Lincoln noted that all the Confederacy had to offer to foreign countries was the prospect of commerce. As yet, foreign nations were not ready to "discar[d] all moral, social, and treaty obligations" in order to maintain access to southern commodities and markets.[18] For the time being, the Union's overseas ministers had successfully fended off Confederate advances to other countries' foreign ministries.

The correspondence demonstrated the government's effort to prevent recognition of the Confederacy by foreign countries. The first document published in the volume was from President James Buchanan's administration; it was a circular sent by Secretary of State Jeremiah Black to ministers abroad on February 28, 1861. Black reminded the ministers of the results of the November 1860 election and was blunt about the circumstances of Lincoln's victory: Lincoln was the "candidate of the republican or anti-slavery party," the election "had been confined almost entirely to topics connected, directly or indirectly, with the subject of negro slavery," and Lincoln was as popular in the North as he was despised in the South. Black noted that Buchanan "expected" America's representatives to prevent any Confederate agents from gaining recognition.[19] Secretary of State Seward's first circular, dated March 9, reconfirmed the goals of his predecessor.[20] After the brief section of circulars, the remainder of the volume is a country-by-country publication of correspondence with U.S. representatives abroad in twenty-four countries.[21] Some of the chapters run for only a few pages, while others are much more expansive. Many reprint Seward's initial directions to the ministers.

In these instructions, staving off Confederate agents was key. To the minister to Spain, Carl Schurz, Seward wrote that preventing the Confederacy from gaining recognition was "your chief duty, and no more important one was ever devolved by the United States upon any representative whom they have sent abroad."[22] Even in countries of lesser import, ministers were urged to be on the watch. Although Seward did not believe that the Confederates would attempt to gain recognition immediately from Denmark, he wrote to the representative there that "political action even of the more commanding or more active States is influenced by a general opinion that is formed imperceptibly in all parts of the Eastern continent. Every representative of the United States in Europe has, therefore, a responsibility to see that no effort on his part is wanting to make that opinion just, so far as the true position of affairs in his own country is concerned."[23] Likewise to the minister to Switzerland: "You are in a region where men of inquiring mind and active habit seek a temporary respite from severe studies and exhausting labors. The world's affairs are discussed freely, and the sentiments and opinions which influence the conduct and affect the prospects of nations are very often formed in the mountains and dells of Switzerland."[24] The Union could not afford to let Confederates gain foothold anywhere and wanted their representatives throughout Europe to be alert. This meant that ministers would need to know about events in the United States. Seward urged Norman Judd in Berlin to "fix your attention in the first instance, and to keep it constantly fixed, on the actual condition of affairs at home," rather than being consumed with events in Prussia.[25]

More country-specific directions were required in some cases, and Seward also made note when information was needed from abroad. To Thomas Corwin in Mexico, Seward wrote worriedly that "The actual condition of affairs in Mexico is so imperfectly understood here that the President finds it very difficult to give you particular and practical directions for the regulation of your conduct during your mission." He instructed Corwin to reassure the Mexicans that the United States would not approve of any effort to incite revolution in Mexico.[26] He told Charles Francis Adams not to apologize or make excuses for the present condition of the country: "You will make no admissions of weakness in our Constitution, or of apprehension on the part of the government. You will rather prove, as you easily can, by comparing the history of our country with that of other states, that its Constitution and government are really the strongest and surest which have ever been erected for the safety of any people."[27] Surely Seward was aware that some conservatives in Europe would delight in the collapse of the republican experiment; he wanted Adams to give them no comfort.[28]

The instructions encouraged ministers to not let discouraging news from America cloud foreigners' perceptions of the war effort. "You will hear of a reverse of our arms in Virginia," Seward wrote to Adams after the Battle of Bull Run. He urged the minister to think little of it: "The vigor of the government will be increased, and the ultimate result will be a triumph of the Constitution. Do not be misled by panic reports of danger apprehended for the capital."[29] He likewise wrote to William Lewis Dayton in France: "Treason was emboldened by its partial success at Manassas, but the Union now grows manifestly stronger every day."[30] Foreigners could get their news from any number of sources, and ministers had to stand ready to put a positive spin on events.

The volume also printed despatches from ministers abroad. Some shared good news of the response from foreign governments. From Belgium, Henry Shelton Sanford reported that the Confederate government would "receive no sanction by any act of Belgium" because it would violate the Belgian policy of "strict neutrality."[31] From Great Britain, George Mifflin Dallas relayed that "there was not the slightest disposition in the British government to grasp at any advantage which might be supposed to arise from unpleasant domestic differences in the United States."[32] From Austria, Jehu Glancy Jones noted that the country "hoped to see us re-united" and "was not inclined to recognize *de facto* governments anywhere."[33] In Turkey, the minister of foreign affairs assured the American representative of "the most friendly sentiments towards the government of the United States, and expressions of warm sympathy" for the country.[34] Some of the initial reports, then, were positive.

Other countries had to hedge. Mexico occupied a unique position since the nascent Confederacy was a potential neighbor. Corwin reported that the government was "well affected towards us in our present difficulties" but would be "unwilling to enter into any engagement which might produce war with the south, unless protected by promise of aid from the United States."[35] From France, Dayton reported that, while the "French government was not in the habit of acting hastily upon such questions" as recognizing *de facto* governments such as the Confederacy claimed to be, the French representative was "equally bound to say that the practice and usage of the present century had fully established the right of de facto governments to recognition when a proper case was made out for the decision of foreign powers."[36] In Venezuela, Edward A. Turpin was able to convince the president only that Confederate ships should not be allowed in Venezuela in any case other than distress: "I could not obtain from him their complete denunciation as pirates," he wrote.[37] King Kamehameha IV issued a notice that declared Hawaiian neutrality in the conflict and prohibited subjects "from engaging, either directly or indirectly, in privateering against the shipping or commerce of either of the contending parties, or of rendering any aid to such enterprises whatever" except in cases of distress.[38] This apparent evenhandedness actually legitimized the Confederates and could not have pleased Seward.

Other ministers shared news from the public or other statesmen. In Berlin, Joseph Albert White reported that he was "in the receipt of hundreds of letters and personal calls seeking positions in the American army, and asking for means of conveyance to our shores. So numerous, indeed, are the applications, that I have been compelled to place on the doors of the legation a notice to the purport that 'This is the legation of the United States, and not a recruiting office.'"[39] Dallas forwarded newspaper clippings from the London press featuring debates on the war.[40] From Sweden, Benjamin Franklin Angel informed Seward that "so far as my reading and observations extend, the better informed European statesmen express the opinion that those charged with the administration of public affairs have acted with the greatest moderation" and that the Union "will have the sympathy and best wishes of all conservatives on this side the Atlantic."[41] One month later, James Samils Haldeman relayed that "quite a change is visible in diplomatic circles" and that diplomats in Sweden "speak out openly that the government of the United States should act vigorously and efficiently" and that the "rebellion should be annihilated by force and not by compromise."[42]

Although the volume reproduces only excerpts of some of the instructions and despatches, moments of bluntness still made it through whatever editing was in place. In May 1861, Seward pointedly told Adams that "this government considers that our relations in Europe have reached a crisis."[43] Seward also confided in our representative in Switzerland, George Gilman Fogg, that other European nations would enjoy the downfall of the United States: "I could easily imagine that either Great Britain, France, Russia, Austria, Prussia, Belgium, Spain, or even Denmark, might suppose that it could acquire some advantage, or at least some satisfaction to itself, from a change that should abridge the dominion, the commerce, the prosperity, or influence of the United States. Each of them might be believed to have envious sentiments towards us, which would delight in an opportunity to do us harm."[44] While we cannot know what role Seward had in publication, printing such a statement warned the American people that other countries would cheer their downfall.

The volume also revealed the administration's frustration over Britain's willingness to treat the Confederacy as a belligerent power (and thus with the attendant rights, even if it fell short of full recognition).[45] Such documents exposed British actions to American citizens. Adams reported to the British that the Americans were "irritat[ed]" by the queen's proclamation of neutrality, which was seen as "designed to aid the insurgents by raising them to the rank of a belligerent State." Although Adams demurred that he himself did not feel that this was British intent, he went on to point out that the presence of "pseudo commissioners" from the Confederacy was a continued aggravation. The British responded that "It had been the custom both in France and here to receive such persons unofficially for a long time back. Poles, Hungarians, Italians, &c., &c., had been allowed interviews, to hear what they had to say. But this did not imply recognition in their case any more than in ours."[46] This response did not satisfy Americans, nor were they moved by offers of mediation. Another instruction from Seward refused the idea of European mediation of these disputes: "we cannot solicit or accept mediation from any, even the most friendly quarter."[47]

Although North and South may not have admitted in 1861 that slavery was the "central issue" of the war, slavery does appear throughout the volume.[48] Slavery certainly got credit for causing the war even if the war itself was not yet about emancipation. Seward readily asserted that the slave power and designs of slave owners lay behind the war and emphasized that the rebelling states were operating against the will of the entire people. "The Union was formed upon popular consent and must always practically stand on the same basis," he told Norman Judd in Berlin.[49] But slavery was the root cause of the desire to break with popular consent. "The attempted revolution is simply causeless," Seward wrote to Dayton in France. "It is, indeed, equally without a reason and without an object . . . unless it be one arising out of the subject of slavery."[50] Seward instructed the representative in Russia that although slavery had existed in all the states at the time of the Revolution, "It was expected that under the operation of moral, social, and political influences then existing the practice of slavery would soon cease." The "cause" of the rebellion was the fact that the slave states, having suffered defeat at the polls, "took an appeal from the verdict of the people, rendered through the ballot-box, to the sword, and organized a revolution with civil war."[51] Even if emancipation was not (yet) a defining issue, there could be no denying slavery's role in causing the conflict.

Some of the ministers picked up on this cue and made similar arguments to their foreign interlocutors. In Spain, Horatio J. Perry pointed out to his hosts the parallel between the 1860s "political ambition of our slave owners" and the filibustering of the 1850s in Cuba. "Secession was filibustering struck in," Perry stated, demonstrating the lengths to which the "slave power" would go to maintain its political power.[52] In Russia, Cassius Clay reported that he informed the government that "slaveholders made war upon us because, following in the wake of advancing civilization, we would not allow our government to be longer the propagandist of slavery."[53] James Shepard Pike likewise told the Dutch of "the character of the rebellion, and showed it to be merely a war in behalf of African slavery, and that if we had no slavery we should have no war and no rebellion."[54]

As these quotations demonstrate, there was a great deal in the volume for a domestic audience. The volume shows us what the Lincoln administration wanted the public to know about its foreign relations efforts during the first months of the war. The volume tells some clear stories. Seward immediately wrote to representatives abroad and instructed them in no uncertain terms to resist the efforts of Confederate agents to secure recognition and to demand that countries refuse Confederate ships succor at their ports. Readers of the correspondence were treated to a range of responses from around the globe: some declared their support for the Union, others pledged a neutrality that partially legitimized the Confederates. The documentation from the ministers illustrated the arguments used to sway foreign governments. And the language used makes clear that several ministers and Seward himself placed slavery at the center of war's causation.

Examining the material excluded from publication provides another way to substantiate the conclusion that the 1861 *FRUS* volume was in part designed to fulfill a public affairs function. Printed in an era before federal law dictated how the public should be informed of excisions, this volume printed only rows of asterisks where material was excised. Although we do not know what sort of editorial policy governed these decisions, taking a look at material deleted from the despatches from London can offer some clues. The National Archives and Records Administration holds the copies kept in London of the despatches sent to the United States. London is a good case study, since Great Britain constituted a critical target for the Confederacy, and thus the United States had equal reason to prevent Confederate success. Through a comparison of the originals to the copies printed in *FRUS* we can see some patterns of how the editing was done. Although some deletions were of little consequence, in other cases the excised material reflected efforts to supply the Union with arms, clues about where Adams got his information and his connections with the British government, tidbits on British politics and gossip, and candid assessments of British opinion of the Union.[55]

Clearly, some aspects of the war effort were too sensitive to publish. In the despatch of August 16, Adams wrote that a Mr. Schuyler had arrived and would be overseeing "the whole matter of the selection and supply of arms in Europe as well as of the payment for them." Adams noted that he had promised Schuyler any assistance he could offer. In his September 2 response, Seward noted that he was "pleased" to learn that Schuyler had arrived and noted that he "can scarcely be too active or efficient."[56] Another sensitive category was information that reflected where and how Adams got his information and his connections to the British government; this too was removed by editors. Adams wrote on May 17 that there was to be a debate in the House of Lords on the queen's neutrality proclamation. Adams noted that "the tone" of the newspaper report on the debate was not "generally such as I could wish and that he would be energetic in applying the appropriate pressure. Excised from the passage was Adams's recounting of his meeting with William Forster, "the leading opponent of the measure," who was of "the opinion that it may ultimately subside altogether; if so, it will be a proof of greater discouragement on the part of the Confederate Commissioners than I believe now to exist."[57] That Adams was at work on taking the temperature of the British debate was left in; the precise information about his contacts was cut out.

Another example of the editors removing information on Adams's connections comes from a despatch written in late September. Most of this despatch was excluded from publication, including all of the details about how Adams received an unexpected invitation from Lord John Russell, the British foreign minister, to Abergeldie Castle in Scotland (as Adams caustically noted in a comment not published: "the invitation was very much as if you were to ask [British minister to the United States] Lord Lyons to come and see you and talk of business at

Auburn instead of Washington, with the exception that the expense of traveling here is about six times greater than in America."). The published version notes that the conversation took place at Abergeldie but reproduces only that Adams registered a complaint about the "reception of the insurgent privateer, the Sumter" by "authorities at Trinidad." The majority of the despatch was left out of the publication. In the full version, Adams described his travel, the fact that the journey afforded him "abundant opportunity for full and free conversation" with Lord Russell, a lengthy discussion of European interest in Mexico, and British complaints about "seizure and imprisonment of British subjects." Adams concluded the despatch by noting that "during the whole of my stay at Abergeldie Castle I thought I perceived the symptoms of a more friendly and cordial feeling than had ever been manifested to me before," which "fully compensated me for the length and fatigue of the journey." In this case, the details of Adams's protest about the treatment of Confederate ships was more important (or less sensitive) than his views of how he was treated by the English or discussion of Mexico.[58]

The editors also removed some references to British political or royal gossip. In Adams's first despatch, he noted that "It is generally known that the Queen has been affected by the loss of her mother, to such a degree to render her extremely indisposed to appear or take part in any public proceedings." Despite the queen's condition, Lord Russell arranged for Adams to have an audience with the queen, which to Adams was too "friendly to admit of any possibility of misconstruction." Those quotations were not printed. The printed portion noted that these arrangements put "an end . . . to all the speculations which have been set afloat in some quarters" about the "probable position of the minister of the United States at this court." The editors included the good news about Adams's reception but discreetly left out the information about the queen.[59]

The final principal category of excluded material concerned British opinion of the American war effort. On June 21, Adams sent to Washington a wide-ranging assessment of divisions in British opinion. Adams's basic conclusion, "that the British desire only to be perfectly neutral, giving no aid nor comfort to the insurgents," was published in the volume. But the lengthy reporting that led to this conclusion was excluded. In it, Adams laid out the various political opinions as he saw them. To be sure, he noted, there were many who opposed slavery, yet "those who sympathize the most with the position of the Free States as unfavorable to the extension of domestic slavery are the least inclined to favor their policy of war against the Slave States." Rather, British opponents of slavery seemed to agree with the Confederacy that there should be a "permanent and peaceful separation" of North and South. The reason? British opponents of slavery "fear a reunion of our States because they think it cannot be effected excepting at the expense of principle. They favor a separation because they think it will keep the Free States consistent and determined enemies of Slavery." Such arguments must have struck the editors of the 1861 messages as potentially corrosive to Union morale. Into another category fell the "merchants and the manufacturers," who also "look with great favor on a permanent separation of the States" and assessed the "difficulties" of the United States "in their purely material aspect and in the single interest of their own country." Yet a third category of opinion was "purely political and purely English." Here Adams found conservatives who saw the conflict as "the realization of all their predictions of the failure of republicanism in its most portentous form." This portion of the population "have no preference" for the Union or Confederacy but wanted them to "continue to devour each other." Adams noted that these three sections of opinion were the "very large proportion" of the British population. By contrast, the portion of the population "who really understand the nature of the question at issue and who advocate the cause of the United States as identical with the progress of free institutions all over the world is comparatively insignificant." Only this last group, Adams noted, saw the war as a "necessity"; all others "consider it as more or less the offspring of mere passion."

Was this assessment of British opinion too sensitive to be printed? Did it contain too strong a suggestion that a large portion of the British population would have been satisfied with Confederate independence? Did the Lincoln administration fear that Union morale was too fragile to print these observations? Whatever the reason for its exclusion, Adams's long discussion of British opinion was left out, along with his statement that Seward's strong reaction to any "proclivity to a recognition" had had the desired effect. Only the conclusion that Adams was "earnestly assured" that the "sympathy with the government of the United States is general" made it to the publication, preserving the appearance of support even if it papered over a more complex political situation.[60]

As the volume continued, it excluded other information about the British opinion of America. On August 16, Adams wrote that the effect of the Union defeat at Bull Run was damaging more because of the "ridicule it exposes the country to" than because of the "positive loss" stemming from the battle itself. Reports in the European press did not help the Union cause. Adams noted that the "military spirit of Europe does not reconcile itself to such scenes as have been distinctly painted by the European correspondent of the London Times, and the American press, as well as caricatured in Punch."[61] In the portion of the despatch published in the volume, Adams refers to instructions he received to speak to Lord Russell about the blockade.[62] In the deleted portion, Adams admitted that were he to take a "strong tone" in the midst of such ridicule regarding Bull Run, he would "scarcely likely do more than to provide a smile" on the faces of his interlocutors. Rather, Adams wrote, he should "await an hour doubtless not far distant when the people of the United States will have redeemed their reputation for judgment and skill and courage" and have proved that they can survive war "without the guidance or control of the military or civil officers of the slaveholding States." The demand for a conference and its topic stayed in the volume; the embarrassing reasons for Adams's delay stayed out.

In sum, exclusions from the documents could radically alter the message. When Adams reported that British opinion was neutral, that was acceptable (but not the reasoning or the lengthy longer study that led to his basic assessment). Likewise, it was acceptable to publish material on Adams's willingness to approach the British about vessels on the high seas but not his awkward reason for delaying the meeting, given the Union performance at Bull Run. And, in the case of arms procurement, some matters were better left out of the public—and potentially Confederate—eye altogether.

Once edited and prepared for public consumption, the documents were printed and released. We can infer that the Department intended these documents to have a domestic audience. First, of course, is the fact that they were requested by Congress. But the number of copies printed is also suggestive. The Department ordered two thousand copies for its own use: one thousand copies on November 29 and then an additional one thousand copies on December 12 (just over a week after the initial release—possibly in response to demand?).[63] This was far in excess of the number of foreign posts maintained by the United States in December 1861. Perhaps copies were distributed to congressmen, since they requested the documents. Certainly copies found their way into the hands of journalists. It was through wide distribution to newspapers that most Americans surely were exposed to the documentation in the message of the work the Department was doing to shore up U.S. interests abroad.[64]

Prior to the publication of the annual message, newspapers speculated about the coverage of foreign affairs to be included in the message; the *New York Herald* anticipated that the message would include material on the *Trent* Affair.[65] In this hope they would be disappointed, and the exclusion of *Trent*-related documentation is probably the most glaring example of how the Lincoln administration compiled the documents in the volume with an eye toward shaping public opinion and safeguarding national interests in ongoing negotiations. The affair occurred on November 8, 1861, less than a month before the documents were released to Congress. While few documents beyond October were included in the volume, enough *were* to render it possible that *Trent*-related material could have been included as well. The section on Great Britain includes one document from November 11, and the sections on France and the Netherlands include documents dated November 23.[66] Had the *Trent* Affair happened in June 1861, its exclusion in December would be a clearer case of censorship; the closeness of the event to the publication of the volume makes its purposeful exclusion likely but difficult to establish for certain.

Despite the disappointment of not learning about the *Trent* Affair, newspapers along the Eastern Seaboard published accounts of the correspondence just a few days after the message and documents were released to the public. On December 6, three New York newspapers (the *Times, Commercial Advertiser,* and *Daily Tribune*), three Philadelphia newspapers (the *Public Ledger, North American,* and *Inquirer*), and the Baltimore *Sun* published essentially similar accounts, each reporting the amount of documentation released and highlighting some of the documentation. The next day, the *Albany Evening Journal* and *Boston Daily Advertiser* printed long synopses of the papers. The *Norwich Morning Bulletin* printed a much shorter item and praised the publication: "The diplomatic correspondence submitted to Congress by President Lincoln, reveals as favorable a condition of our relations with foreign Powers as could have been anticipated. This is doubtless owing in a great degree to the firm and decided position maintained by Secretary Seward in his official intercourse with these Governments." In Madison, Wisconsin, the *Weekly Wisconsin Patriot* lauded Lincoln's message, but the correspondence clearly had not made it over the telegraph lines yet: "He refers to the correspondence with foreign powers," the paper noted, "but does not discuss them in detail, or even give us a clue to their contents. So the public must wait for information on that score, till the diplomatic correspondence be published, and they may not be gratified in that respect, as Congress may not consider the public weal sufficiently guarded by their publication."[67]

If the publication of the volume was intended as a public relations measure, it was a success in Northern newspapers. The Baltimore *Sun* reported on December 9 that the correspondence was "receiving that close attention from persons skilled in diplomacy and public law which belongs to its distinguished source and the magnitude of the subject in question." Papers praised the publication of the correspondence and the contents of the documents. The Keene *New Hampshire Sentinel* reported that "in the whole of this correspondence, the Secretary of State exhibits marked ability as a statesman and diplomatist."[68] Others took heart from the correspondence that Seward would continue to act appropriately in the future. "The masterly ability which Gov. SEWARD has shown in his instructions to our Foreign Ministers," opined the *Albany Evening Journal,* "induce strong confidence that he will conduct the correspondence likely to grow out of the MASON and SLIDELL affair, to a successful and satisfactory issue."[69] By January 1862, the correspondence had reached the West Coast; the *San Francisco Daily Evening Bulletin* reported that the diplomatic correspondence was "quite voluminous" and "highly interesting." Seward again came in for praise, his "high-toned" and "courteous" messages were "as nearly perfect models of diplomatic correspondence as are to be found on the pages of modern history." The correspondence with Adams and Dayton "had swept to the winds all the aspersions of those who have accused him of favoring a timid and wavering policy in dealing with the rebels."[70]

Other newspapers hoped that the publication of the correspondence would improve the standing of the United States abroad. The New York *Daily Tribune* predicted that British newspapers that had shown Seward in an unfavorable light "would be surprised if the contents of this volume could be fairly laid before them. In vain would they turn page after page in eager quest of the passages whereon the criminations of their favorite journals were based; they do not appear because they do not exist." The paper praised Seward for his "assured and firm" tone and his faith that the country, "reunited, will be stronger and more prosperous than ever before."[71] Among these newspapers, at least, Seward acquitted himself well.

The publication of the correspondence even attracted notice in the Confederacy. The Columbus [Georgia] *Daily Enquirer* discussed the correspondence with France, under the headline "Whom the Gods Wish to Destroy, They First Make Mad." Naturally, the paper put a different spin on the correspondence; rather than seeing Seward as standing strong in the face of an unfavorable British and French response, the paper focused on the response itself: "It will thus be seen that the relations between the United States and Great Britain and France were far from being securely amicable before the arrest of Mason and Slidell, that there were issues between them of great irritation and danger, and that Great Britain and France are united in the policy to be pursued in reference to political troubles on this continent."[72] Likewise, the New Orleans *Daily Picayune* sneered at the correspondence with France from June 1861, noting that it came from a time when "arrogant confidence" about a speedy end to the war was "universally felt at the North," before "the fervor of the Southern passion for independence" and the subsequent "holy war" had been fully appreciated.[73] In these documents, southerners saw hope that their cause was not lost in Europe and that Union leaders were grasping at straws.

The extent of the newspaper response illustrates the important domestic function that *FRUS* served. Newspapers across the country—including those in the Midwest and on the West Coast—either reprinted or analyzed the correspondence directly. Many papers praised Seward, the decision to publish the correspondence, and the contents of the publication. The volume was a response to a request from Congress, and it retained its domestic character upon release by being widely debated and discussed in the country. While we cannot know exactly how many of the complete volumes were distributed across the country or precisely how it happened, newspaper coverage serves as a good proxy for studying how Americans reacted to the publication of this correspondence.[74]

Much of the early history of *FRUS* remains unknowable. Yet the available evidence reveals much about the beginning of the series and also about the context in which the first volume arose. This preliminary investigation has suggested three broad conclusions: that the volume represents checks and balances between two branches of government, that it contained what the government wanted the public to know about foreign relations, and that there was a domestic audience for its publication.

Perhaps the most significant conclusion is that the idea for *FRUS* represents an example of the checks and balances of the branches of federal government. "Under our form of Government," Senator James Brooks (Democrat from New York) argued in 1864, "we are entitled to all the information from the Executive which is not detrimental to the public interests."[75] Even though Brooks included the familiar caveat of the public interest, it was clear that he expected to receive documentation. And, as Seward argued to Adams that same year, the Constitution obligated the government to provide a framework for accountability. Rather than a project conceived in the executive branch, the process of sharing information represents the checks and balances of the branches of government: the executive executes foreign policy, and the legislative ensures that the policy is being honestly carried out.

This conclusion suggests a second broad conclusion: that even if these volumes may not tell us everything that *we* might wish to know about foreign relations during the Civil War era, they do give us a good picture of what the federal *government* wanted its citizens to know. The early volumes are not "scholarly" in the way that today's *FRUS* volumes are—we do not know anything about the clerks who compiled them, whereas today's volumes are produced by trained historians. Of course, it is anachronistic to castigate the early volumes for not being scholarly when historians in the United States had yet to professionalize.[76] Yet the first volume remains valuable for reflecting the public affairs priorities of the Lincoln administration. Since we have access to the original documentation, we can see how coherent this effort was. Perhaps the most egregious exclusion is the *Trent* Affair, the hottest topic in relations between the Union and Great Britain at the end of 1861. A systematic review of Great Britain–related material excluded from the published volume reveals that some excisions were relatively innocuous, others protected Adams's dealings with the British government, and others reflected Adams's genuine concern with how the United States was perceived in London. Thus, the published volume does not tell us everything that we as historians might like to know about the Union's foreign relations. A modern scholar would have to consult the original documents—not *FRUS* alone—to get the full picture.

The third and final conclusion is that the publication found a domestic audience. Newspapers across the country anticipated and then covered the document release. The volume was surely successful; newspaper editors praised Seward's steadfastness in standing up to European claims of neutrality, and the actions documented in the volume gave people hope that the *Trent* Affair would come to a satisfactory conclusion. The Department ordered an additional one thousand copies of the volume shortly after the original publication date. The number of copies printed and the newspaper response suggest that the volume captured the interest of the domestic audience.

Waging war against the Confederacy required not only fighting Confederates on the battlefields but also combating their envoys in foreign lands. The first volume of *FRUS* was not the country's first publication of diplomatic correspondence, yet it marked an important stage in the evolution of publishing diplomatic documents, and the process has continued to evolve over the past 150 years. The series is now compiled and edited by trained historians, the reasons for exclusion of material are encoded in law, the amount of material excised from a document is always clearly marked in the document, and the office that compiles the series is advised by an independent council of distinguished scholars. If there was a system to the 1861 volume, it requires some intelligent inferences to discern. Today, the process has matured and institutionalized, and the system is subject to public scrutiny. The anonymous clerks who compiled the first volume in the fall of 1861 would surely not recognize what the series has become, but the story of the series' continuing transformation from the Civil War era is an important part of the story of U.S. citizens demanding accountability from their government and the government's response.

NOTES

1. I would like to thank Forrest Barnum, Josh Botts, Peter Cozzens, Edward Keefer, William McAllister, and Melissa Jane Taylor for their comments on earlier drafts of this essay. I also thank the audience at the College of Charleston conference for their comments on the presentation. Finally, I am deeply grateful to Forrest Barnum for his diligent research comparing the printed version of the diplomatic correspondence to the manuscript copies in the National Archives.

2. One exception to this general trend is Rick Moss, "Public Diplomacy and the First *FRUS*: The Origins of the *Foreign Relations of the United States* Series," Fall 2001, unpublished paper in the Office of the Historian, U.S. Department of State. Moss uncovered the resolutions in the House of Representatives that sparked the 1861 volume and also developed the idea that *FRUS* represents checks and balances.

3. Clarence E. Carter, "The United States and Documentary Historical Publication," *Mississippi Valley Historical Review* 25 (June 1938): 13.

4. E. R. Perkins, "'Foreign Relations of the United States': 91 Years of American Foreign Policy," Department of State *Bulletin* (December 22, 1952): 1002. Drawing on Perkins's work, Robert Wilson made a similar assessment in "A Hundred Years of 'Foreign Relations,'" *American Journal of International Law* 55 (October 1961): 947–48.

5. Richard W. Leopold, "The *Foreign Relations* Series: A Centennial Estimate," *Mississippi Valley Historical Review* 49 (March 1963): 597. When Leopold wrote about the series again a decade later ("The *Foreign Relations* Series Revisited: One Hundred Plus Ten," *Journal of American History* 59 [March 1973]: 935–57), he did not comment on the series' history.

6. William Z. Slany, "A Brief History of the *Foreign Relations* Series," July 1989, unpublished paper in the Office of the Historian, U.S. Department of State, 2. Slany cites the work of Gaillard Hunt, although Hunt's article says nothing of Seward's direct interest. Gaillard Hunt, "The History of the Department of State, VIII," *American Journal of International Law* 5 (October 1911): 1018.

7. Sacha Zala, *Geschichte unter der Schere politischer Zensur: Amtliche Aktensammlungen in internationalen Vergleich* (Munich: R. Oldenbourg Verlag, 2001), 93.

8. In addition to the evidence presented in this essay, it is worth noting that *FRUS* volumes during the remainder of the nineteenth century received high-level scrutiny, which also suggests Seward may have been aware of the selection and publication process. During the post–Civil War era, the third-ranking official of the Department (the second assistant secretary of state) was responsible for reviewing content prior to its submission to Congress for publication and for making excisions as he deemed necessary. I am grateful to Peter Cozzens for providing this perspective from his own research.

9. "Frequently Asked Questions: Department Personnel, 1781–1997," http://history.state.gov/about/faq/department-personnel (accessed July 20, 2013).

10. Charles Francis Adams to William Seward, February 11, 1864, vol. 24, U.S. Legation Great Britain, Despatches to the Department of State, Record Group 84, National Archives, College Park, Maryland [hereafter RFSP].

11. William Seward to Charles Francis Adams, March 2, 1864, vol. 98, U.S. Legation Great Britain, Instructions to Diplomatic Officers, Diplomatic Correspondence (1785–1906), Record Group 59, National Archives, College Park, Maryland [hereafter IDO].

12. Seward's reference is to Article II, Section 3, of the Constitution.

13. *Congressional Globe,* Thirty-Seventh Congress, 1st Session, 117. See also Moss, "Public Diplomacy," 4–5.

14. *Congressional Globe,* Thirty-Seventh Congress, 1st Session, 129.

15. *Congressional Globe,* Thirty-Seventh Congress, 1st Session, 253.

16. Roy Basler, ed., *Collected Works of Abraham Lincoln* (New Brunswick, N.J.: Rutgers University Press, 1953), 4: 459. That same day, Lincoln and Seward also declined to provide correspondence with foreign powers relating to maritime rights (ibid., 459–60). Perhaps Howe's resolution (or rumors of it), which occurred early in the day's session, prompted the response from Seward after a nearly two-week delay after Cox's resolution.

17. Basler, *Collected Works of Abraham Lincoln,* 5: 55.

18. *Message of the President of the United States to the Two Houses of Congress at the Commencement of the Second Session of the Thirty-Seventh Congress* (Washington, D.C.: U.S. Government Printing Office, 1861), 3.

19. *Message,* 31.

20. *Message,* 32.

21. These were, in order: Prussia, Belgium, Mexico, Great Britain, Austria, France, Spain, Rome, Russia, Denmark, Italy, Switzerland, the Netherlands, Turkey, Sweden, Portugal, Peru, Guatemala, Nicaragua, Egypt, Venezuela, Chile, the Hawaiian Islands, and Japan.

22. Instruction from Seward to Schurz, April 27, 1861, *Message,* 257.

23. Instruction from Seward to Wood, May 1, 1861, *Message,* 311.

24. Instruction from Seward to Fogg, May 15, 1861, *Message,* 329–30.

25. Instruction from Seward to Judd, March 22, 1861, *Message,* 37. Judd was appointed on March 8 but did not present his credentials until July 1. Joseph Albert White preceded him as minister.

26. Instruction from Seward to Corwin, April 6, 1861, *Message,* 65, 68.

27. Instruction from Seward to Adams, April 10, 1861, *Message,* 76.

28. Howard Jones, *Abraham Lincoln and a New Birth of Freedom: Union and Slavery in the Diplomacy of the Civil War* (Lincoln: University of Nebraska Press, 1999), 50.

29. Instruction from Seward to Adams, July 29, 1861, *Message,* 124.

30. Instruction from Seward to Dayton, August 17, 1861, *Message,* 240.

31. Despatch from Sanford to Seward, May 26, 1861, *Message,* 55–56.

32. Despatch from Dallas to Seward, April 9, 1861, *Message,* 81. Seward found the British response inadequate. See instruction from Seward to Adams, April 27, 1861, *Message,* 83.

33. Despatch from Jones to Seward, April 15, 1861, *Message,* 188.

34. Despatch from Brown to Seward, June 11, 1861, *Message,* 390.

35. Despatch from Corwin to Seward, May 29, 1861, *Message,* 70.

36. Despatch from Faulkner to Seward, April 15, 1861, *Message,* 205.

37. Despatch from Turpin to Seward, July 27, 1861, *Message,* 427.

38. Despatch from Dryer to Seward, September 7, 1861, *Message,* 436.

39. Despatch from Wright to Seward, May 26, 1861, *Message,* 40.

40. Despatch from Dallas to Seward, May 2, 1861, *Message,* 83–85.

41. Despatch from Angel to Seward, June 10, 1861, *Message,* 396.

42. Despatch from Haldeman to Seward, July 28, 1861, *Message,* 399.

43. Instruction from Seward to Adams, May 21, 1861, *Message,* 87.

44. Instruction from Seward to Fogg, May 15, 1861, *Message,* 329.

45. According to Jones, the British "adhered to international law in equating a civil war with a war between nations and then assuming a position of neutrality." Through belligerent status, the Confederates gained "credibility," their raids on Union ships were not considered piracy by the British, and Confederates could do business with British merchants. Howard Jones, *Blue and Gray Diplomacy: A History of Union and Confederate Foreign Relations* (Chapel Hill: University of North Carolina Press, 2010), 51–52.

46. Despatch from Adams to Seward, June 14, 1861, *Message,* 104. For the queen's proclamation, see Jones, *Blue and Gray,* 44.

47. Instruction from Seward to Adams, June 19, 1861, *Message,* 108.

48. Jones, *Blue and Gray,* 3.

49. Instruction from Seward to Judd, March 22, 1861, *Message,* 37.

50. Instruction from Seward to Dayton, April 22, 1861, *Message,* 197.

51. Instruction from Seward to Clay, May 6, 1861, *Message*, 294, 295.

52. Despatch from Perry to Seward, June 13, 1861, *Message*, 261.

53. Despatch from Clay to Seward, June 21, 1861, *Message*, 304.

54. Despatch from Pike to Seward, June 12, 1861, *Message*, 351.

55. For example, the exclusion of information on consular appointments did little to change the tenor of the complete volume. See despatch from Dallas to Seward, March 22, 1861, *Message,* 80, and vol. 22, RSFP, despatch from Adams to Seward, June 21, 1861, *Message,* 109–110, and vol. 22, RFSP, and despatch from Adams to Seward, June 28, 1861, *Message,* 110–11, and vol. 22, RFSP.

56. Despatch from Adams to Seward, August 16, 1861, *Message,* 127–28, and vol. 22, RSFP; instruction from Seward to Adams, September 2, 1861, *Message,* 140–41, and vol. 97, IDO.

57. Despatch from Adams to Seward, May 17, 1861, *Message,* 85–87, and vol. 22, RSFP. For Forster, see Amanda Foreman, *A World on Fire: Britain's Crucial Role in the American Civil War* (New York: Random House, 2011), 95.

58. Despatch from Adams to Seward, September 28, 1861, *Message,* 159, and vol. 22, RFSP. For another example of material on Mexico being excluded, see despatch from Adams to Seward, September 14, 1861, *Message,* 155, and vol. 22, RFSP.

59. Despatch from Adams to Seward, May 17, 1861, *Message*, 85–87, and vol. 22, RFSP.

60. Despatch from Adams to Seward, June 21, 1861, *Message*, 109–10, and vol. 22, RFSP.

61. Despatch from Adams to Seward, August 16, 1861, *Message*, 127–28, and vol. 22, RFSP.

62. Reference is to an instruction from Seward to Adams, July 21, 1861, *Message,* 117–21.

63. Letter from William Seward to John D. Defrees, November 29, 1861, p. 520, vol. 55, reel 52, microfilm publication M40, Domestic Letters, 1784–1906, Record Group 59, National Archives, College Park, Maryland.; letter from Frederick Seward to John D. Defrees, December 12, 1861, p. 22, vol. 56, reel 53, microfilm publication M40, Domestic Letters, 1784–1906, Record Group 59, National Archives, College Park, Maryland.

64. As the war went on, the number of copies desired by the Department grew higher; there was debate in 1864 as to whether or not the Department should be supplied with ten thousand copies of the correspondence (presumably for both domestic and foreign distribution). See *Congressional Globe,* Thirty-Eighth Congress, 1st Session, 495–96.

65. New York *Herald*, December 2, 1861. On November 8, 1861, the USS *San Jacinto* seized Confederate ministers James Mason and John Slidell from the British ship RMS *Trent,* violating British neutrality, Jones, *Blue and Gray,* chap. 3.

66. *Message,* 21–29.

67. Albany *Evening Journal*, Boston *Daily Advertiser*, Norwich *Morning Bulletin*, *Weekly Wisconsin Patriot*, all December 7, 1861. On December 9, the Hartford *Daily Courant* published a synopsis similar to the lengthy ones published on December 6 and 7 by other papers.

68. New Hampshire *Sentinel,* December 12, 1861.

69. Albany *Evening Journal,* December 18, 1861.

70. *San Francisco Daily Evening Bulletin,* January 9, 1862. The paper published additional items on January 10, 13, 14, and 31.

71. *New York Daily Tribune,* December 18, 1861.

72. Columbus *Daily Enquirer,* December 23, 1861.

73. New Orleans *Daily Picayune,* December 25, 1861. For another example of Southern coverage, see *Macon Telegraph,* January 7, 1862.

74. Although this essay focuses on the domestic reaction to the *Message,* there is one aspect of foreign reaction worth noting. Shortly after the volume was released, Lord Lyons sent a copy to Lord Russell. Russell received the correspondence on December 25. Lyons obviously attempted to get his hands on the publication as soon as possible: "As the earliest copies did not come from the press until yesterday afternoon," he apologized, "I have not had time to do more than read somewhat hastily that part of the correspondence which relates to England and France." He then recounted what he considered the highlights of the documents, chiefly the reaction of the United States to the British and French willingness to treat the Confederacy as a de facto government and the U.S. contention that Confederate sailors should be treated as pirates. Lyons also noted that the correspondence left unclear the fate of British consul Richard Bunch: Lyons to Russell, December 6, 1861, British Parliamentary Papers, North America, No. 1, 1862, 115. The correspondence received in London was promptly printed in full by the British: British Parliamentary Papers, North America, No. 2, 1862. No subsequent *FRUS* volume was ever published in the BPP series.

75. *Congressional Globe,* Thirty-Eighth Congress, 1st Session, 1967.

76. For example, the American Historical Association was not founded until 1884, twenty-three years after publication of the first volume. For an opposing view, see Zala, *Geschichte unter der Schere politischer Zensur,* 95.

CHRISTOPHER WILKINS

"They had heard of emancipation and the enfranchisement of their race"

The African American Colonists of Samaná, Reconstruction, and the State of Santo Domingo

In January 1871, in an isolated settlement in northern Santo Domingo, the present-day Dominican Republic, a correspondent of the *New York Standard* witnessed "the extraordinary sight of a real American mass meeting in the midst of a tropical island." The identity of the participants and their reasons for attending added to the meeting's extraordinary character. The speaker, Frederick Douglass, and the audience, two hundred members of a colony of African Americans who had emigrated from Philadelphia to the verdant Samaná peninsula in the mid-1820s, had gathered to discuss the annexation of Santo Domingo to the United States. In his speech, Douglass extolled the benefits annexation would bring to both countries.[1]

The chain of events that led Douglass to Samaná had been set in motion in November 1869, when the Dominican government and President Ulysses S. Grant negotiated a treaty of annexation. The terms provided for Santo Domingo's admission into the Union as a territory placed on a path to statehood and for the incorporation of Dominicans as U.S. citizens.[2] Americans saw Santo Domingo as a "negro republic." In almost any era of the nineteenth century, annexing a black-majority nation on those terms would have been impossible for American politicians to endorse. But during 1870 and 1871, a majority of the U.S. Senate favored annexation. Grant and his allies were, however, unable to achieve the necessary two-thirds majority of the Senate, and the treaty was rejected in June 1870.[3] But Grant refused to concede defeat. Six months later, he proposed that Congress dispatch a diplomatic commission to Santo Domingo to investigate the country's political and economic condition, assess its people's character, determine whether Dominicans desired to "form part of the people of the United

States," and negotiate a new treaty of annexation.[4] In early January, Congress approved the creation of the commission.[5] Although Congress denied the commission the right to reach any new agreement with the Dominican government, Grant nevertheless hoped that its findings would so forcefully vindicate his claims concerning the benefits of annexation that Congress would be compelled to secure annexation by a joint resolution of the Senate and the House of Representatives.[6]

To bolster the commission's credibility among his fellow Republicans, Grant appointed three prominent figures in the Republican party—former senator Benjamin Wade, the social reformer Samuel Gridley Howe, and Cornell University president Andrew D. White—to lead the commission. He also asked former Union army general Franz Sigel and Frederick Douglass to join the commission's staff.[7] Douglass's selection reflected Grant's recognition of African Americans' vital role in the Republican electoral coalition.[8] African American voters in the South had helped to ensure Grant's election in 1868, and the recently ratified Fifteenth Amendment promised to add to their political clout.[9] Grant hoped that if Douglass endorsed annexation, his stance would persuade black voters to follow his lead.[10]

The commission reached Santo Domingo on January 24 and spent its first week in Samaná. Douglass's primary responsibility was to learn more about the colonists and assess their desire for annexation.[11] During the commission's stay, he spoke with the colony's leaders and visited the colonists' homes, school, and church. Their self-reliance and dedicated efforts to build a successful community amid chronic political chaos in Santo Domingo impressed him. After completing his interviews with the colonists, he concluded that they were "anxiously awaiting annexation."[12]

It would be easy to dismiss Douglass's claim. Just prior to his departure for Santo Domingo, he had published an editorial arguing that Reconstruction had transformed the United States into a racially egalitarian democracy and expressing the hope that "San Domingo, Hayti, Cuba, and all the islands of the Caribbean Sea" would join the Union, as long as those islands' inhabitants wished to do so.[13] He believed that incorporation into the American nation would benefit Caribbean peoples. He also welcomed the prospect that Santo Domingo and other Caribbean islands would "have an equal voice with other States in ruling America."[14] When he detected widespread annexationist sentiment among the colonists, Douglass may have simply heard what he wished to hear. His conclusion seems unlikely when one considers the colony's history.

In 1825, the colony's founders resolved to escape the American racial caste system by undertaking a daunting fifteen-hundred-mile journey from Philadelphia to the near-wilderness of the Samaná peninsula, where Jean-Pierre Boyer, the president of Haiti, had offered the colonists citizenship and land in what was then Haitian territory.[15] In the mid-1850s, when they learned that Dominican president Pedro Santana had begun negotiations with the United States to annex Samaná—which came under the Dominican government's control after Santo Domingo's war of independence against Haiti in 1844—the colonists opposed annexation. Those negotiations failed, and they were spared being brought back under the control of the U.S. government.[16]

But in the late 1860s and early 1870s, when the U.S. and Dominican governments discussed Santo Domingo's admission into the Union, the colonists strongly favored annexation. Douglass was correct. The colony's leader, the Reverend Jacob James, judged in early 1871 that among a total population of five hundred to six hundred colonists, "every one of them is for annexation to the United States, praying [to] God earnestly that it may take place."[17] Support for James's claim appears in accounts of the colonists' reactions to pro-annexation church sermons, in transcripts of interviews between the colonists and the commission, and in private letters written by colonists to Grant and Douglass in the summer of 1871.[18] Dominicans who favored Santo Domingo's independence were sufficiently angered by the colonists' pro-annexation stance that an anti-annexationist pamphlet described "most" colonists as "ignorant and wretched."[19]

What accounts for the colonists' annexationism in the late 1860s and early 1870s? Part of that sentiment can be attributed to their enduring cultural ties to the United States. For more than a century after the colony's founding, the colonists maintained their Methodist faith and continued to speak English.[20] The suffering they experienced during the wars that swept over Santo Domingo in the 1850s and 1860s also mattered. But the most significant influence on the colonists' support for annexation was their knowledge of the unprecedented upheaval that the Civil War and Reconstruction brought to U.S. institutions.[21] As the colonists followed news of—and in some cases witnessed—the dramatic changes in the character of the American nation and state that took place during the late 1860s and early 1870s, they reassessed their traditionally bleak view of U.S. institutions. After Douglass returned to the United States, he reported that the colonists had "heard of emancipation and the enfranchisement of their race, and the efforts put forth for their education, and now that the old flag had become the symbol of freedom they were eager to get back under its folds."[22] The colonists embraced annexation because they believed that the U.S. government would extend its reconstructed institutions southward, incorporate Dominicans as equal citizens in the American nation, and inaugurate a new era of stability and prosperity in Santo Domingo.

The colonists' interest in exploring the connections between Reconstruction and U.S. territorial expansion has rarely been shared by historians.[23] In the few histories that address those connections, Reconstruction is usually cast as a deterrent to expansion: white Americans saw the attempt to incorporate African

Americans into the U.S. government as a failed experiment that foreshadowed even more disastrous consequences if the United States attempted to incorporate darker-skinned Caribbean peoples as citizens.[24]

Those histories tell only part of the story. In the late 1850s, Republicans had vigorously opposed proslavery territorial expansion into the tropics. But abolition and the extension of citizenship and suffrage to African Americans created new possibilities. When Grant proposed to extend reconstructed U.S. institutions into the Caribbean by incorporating Dominicans as citizens, many Republicans believed that the moral calculus of expansion had changed dramatically. Some Republican expansionists also cited African Americans' performance under reconstructed institutions in the South as a success that demonstrated that the United States could incorporate black-majority nations in the tropics.[25] During the late 1860s and early 1870s, many Republicans saw Reconstruction as a catalyst for expansion.

Prevailing narratives neglect another significant aspect of Reconstruction's influence on U.S. territorial expansion. They focus on debates within the United States and rarely explore how Reconstruction shaped the way communities in the Caribbean reacted to and sought to influence annexationist initiatives. The colonists were not alone among groups in the Caribbean in considering annexation through the prism of Reconstruction. Some groups feared annexation because they were as alarmed as many Americans were by the likelihood that the U.S. government would extend citizenship and suffrage to the inhabitants of newly acquired territories. In Santo Domingo, the Catholic hierarchy was "deeply disturbed" by annexation because "universal suffrage—which would certainly follow, had been condemned by the Pope."[26] During the Cuban Ten Years' War (1868–1878), an anticolonial struggle against Spain that some observers believed would result in an independent Cuba seeking annexation to the United States, Cuban slaveholders—many of whom had hoped for annexation to the United States during the antebellum era—rejected annexation because they worried that the introduction of reconstructed U.S. institutions would guarantee emancipation and disrupt the conservative Cuban social order.[27]

There were, however, countercurrents. The colonists were far from alone in viewing Reconstruction as a spur to annexation. In 1871, Dominican government officials explained to U.S. diplomats that while American slavery had once "posed a fatal obstacle to cordial relations" between the United States and Santo Domingo, emancipation and the "admission of the former slaves to equality of rights" had encouraged closer ties between the two nations.[28] Between 1868 and 1870, important figures in the Cuban revolutionary movement who desired the emancipation of the island's slaves favored annexation to the United States after it had become an abolitionist power.[29] In 1868, during negotiations for the annexation of the Danish West Indies to the United States, reports from St.

Thomas stated that during a plebiscite on annexation "the colored people [wore] an American cockade in their hats" and spoke of "the liberty and advantages they were to enjoy under the Yankee flag." Sentiment in the islands was "overwhelmingly in favor" of annexation, in part because many Danish West Indians believed that they "would benefit from an extended franchise."[30] Annexationism was never only about Reconstruction, but emancipation and promises of racially egalitarian citizenship helped create configurations of annexationist sentiment very different from those that prevailed before the American Civil War. The articulation by Caribbean communities of alternative readings of the boundaries of the American nation suggests that Reconstruction's influence on U.S. territorial expansion was more contested than traditional narratives acknowledge.

By focusing on the colonists' role in the Santo Domingo annexation controversy, this essay contributes to a better understanding of Reconstruction's international history in three ways. The first stems from the colonists' unique history and highly charged relationship with the United States. No other community in the Caribbean that favored annexation owed its existence to its founders' decision to leave the United States because they believed it was a country where "it is but too certain the coloured man can never enjoy his rights."[31] Eric Foner has described Reconstruction as a "stunning experiment in the nineteenth-century world."[32] The colonists' belief that Reconstruction had transformed U.S. institutions and made annexation to the United States desirable, when viewed in the light of the colonists' profound rejection of life under the power of the U.S. government in an earlier era, is a striking measure of just how stunning some international observers believed Reconstruction to be.

Recovering the colonists' views on U.S. territorial expansion also helps to establish a more accurate understanding of the broader debate over the annexation of Santo Domingo. Conventional narratives have often described annexation as an effort to establish a colonial empire.[33] Those claims do not withstand scrutiny. Grant and his allies presented annexation to Americans as a question of incorporating Santo Domingo into the Union as a territory and future state.[34] Most Americans expected that if annexation occurred, Dominicans would become an integral part of the American nation. The Dominican government also presented annexation to Dominicans as a question of incorporation and eventual statehood, and the colonists hoped that they would gain "admission into the Union."[35]

A close examination of the colonists' interactions with the commission and the dozen newspaper correspondents who accompanied the expedition highlights an episode in the history of American foreign relations when Reconstruction prompted a sweeping change in the political background of U.S. diplomats and the way they thought about and behaved toward Caribbean blacks. In the antebellum era, agents of the U.S. government in Santo Domingo held proslavery opinions, and those views led them to treat black Dominicans with disdain. Douglass's inclusion on the commission was the most obvious sign of change in the identity of American diplomats, but the staunch antislavery background of the commissioners mattered as well. The correspondent of the Democratic-leaning *New York Herald* lamented that "with few exceptions, the party is composed of negro worshipping radicals."[36] Their support for the rights of blacks in the United States predisposed them to treat black Dominicans with respect and to see them as potentially valuable citizens of the United States. Reconstruction influenced not only the broader debate over annexation but also the face-to-face conduct of American diplomacy. The colonists observed firsthand the new identity and behavior of U.S. diplomats, and those changes helped confirm their belief that Reconstruction had genuinely changed the United States.

Historians of Reconstruction have illuminated countless aspects of its impact on American life, but by neglecting the perspective of international observers they have missed an important element of what W. E. B. Du Bois once described as Reconstruction's "world-wide implications." The colonists' story suggests that taking a more accurate measure of Reconstruction's historical significance requires a greater appreciation of the political and ideological upheaval it created far beyond the borders of the United States.[37]

The Colonists and the U.S. Government, 1825–63

When the colony's founders emigrated to Samaná in the mid-1820s, they expected that by moving to a distant Caribbean island they would enjoy the freedom to build new lives unmarred by racist U.S. institutions. But by the 1850s it was clear that the colonists had not gone far enough to avoid the long reach of the U.S. government. Throughout the mid-nineteenth century, Samaná Bay drew the attention of Spanish, French, British, and American military strategists who believed that Samaná might serve as a formidable naval stronghold. Each power intrigued to acquire the peninsula from the Dominican government and to block its rivals from doing the same.[38]

During this era of intense imperial competition, members of the American military repeatedly visited Samaná. Among those visitors was Captain George McClellan, who had been dispatched by Secretary of War Jefferson Davis to survey Samaná Bay in 1854. In his report, McClellan paid the colonists a backhanded compliment. The "mass of [Dominicans]," McClellan wrote, "seem perfectly contented to eke out their existence in cave huts, trusting for support to their bananas and cocoa-nuts. The American negroes of Samaná express more ambition and desire of improving their condition than the others."[39] Raphael Semmes, a young officer in the U.S. Navy and future commander of the CSS *Alabama,* passed through Samaná during the 1840s. In his memoirs, Semmes recalled a conversation with a female colonist and provided a peculiar version of the colonists' history that claimed that soon after the colony's founding, "all the men of the colony had run off, and found their way back, in various capacities, on board of trading vessels, to the land of their birth: leaving their wives and daughters behind to shift for themselves."[40] Agents of the U.S. government who visited Samaná in the antebellum era brought to their encounters with the colonists the same racial attitudes—a mixture of condescension and contempt—that they displayed toward blacks in the United States and undoubtedly gave the colonists no cause to believe that white Americans' racism had diminished since the colony's founders left Philadelphia.

The colonists' correspondence with loved ones and African American churches in the United States provided more information on conditions for blacks in the United States. When individual colonists traveled between Samaná and the United States, they gained more direct evidence of those conditions.[41] That knowledge shaped the colony's reaction to Santana's plans to annex Santo Domingo to the United States during the 1850s. Dominican elites allied with Santana seem to have welcomed annexation, in part because they wished to "enjoy the advantages of the 27 states of the Union."[42] The colonists opposed annexation because they did not share Dominican annexationists' ignorance concerning the advantages non-whites could expect to enjoy in those 27 states.[43]

The colonists' views on the expansion of the U.S. government's influence in Santo Domingo began to shift during the first years of the Civil War. The arrival of foreign newspapers in Samaná allowed the colonists to track the progress of the war and the upheaval it created in U.S. institutions.[44] When Spain annexed Santo Domingo in 1861 and launched a campaign of repression against the colonists because they refused to swear allegiance to the Spanish monarchy, the colonists sought to convince the U.S. government to intercede on their behalf. In April 1863, the colonists sent a petition to "His Excellency, President Abraham Lincoln" requesting his assistance in ending the "arbitrary and intolerable proceedings" of the Spanish government.[45] It is unclear whether the petition reached Lincoln, but the colonists' pleas earned the sympathy of the U.S. consul in Santo Domingo, who routinely submitted reports to the State Department decrying the Spanish authorities' abuse of the colonists.[46] Seeking aid from the Lincoln administration was a much less momentous step than embracing annexation to the United States. But by advocating an expansion of the U.S. government's influence in Santo Domingo in the early 1860s, the colonists built a foundation for a far more sweeping reappraisal of that issue later in the decade.

Annexation

In late 1866, Dominican president José María Cabral offered to lease Samaná to the United States in exchange for the weapons and funding he needed to maintain his hold on power against forces allied with Buenaventura Báez. Secretary of

State William Seward, who hoped to acquire a U.S. naval base in the Caribbean, welcomed that proposal. Seward and Cabral engaged in desultory negotiations over the next year, but those discussions ended when Báez overthrew Cabral's government in January 1868.[47] Báez promptly began his own negotiations with Seward and in late 1868 proposed the admission of Santo Domingo into the Union. Seward agreed to Báez's proposal but left office in March 1869, before he could attempt to build sufficient support for annexation in Congress.[48] Báez—aided by a pair of corrupt American land speculators, Joseph Fabens and William Cazneau—redoubled his efforts in mid-1869 by appealing to recently inaugurated President Ulysses S. Grant.[49] Grant decided to pursue annexation after he concluded that acquiring a Caribbean outpost would provide economic and military benefits to the United States.[50] In November 1869 representatives appointed by Grant and Báez signed a treaty of annexation.[51]

In December 1869, when news of the treaty's signing reached Samaná, the colonists gathered in the colony's chapel to discuss what annexation might mean for their future. When the Reverend Jacob James, the colony's spiritual and political leader, "explained in a clear and forcible manner the character of the great political change about to take place," the colonists "return[ed] thanks to God for the anticipated blessing of a good government, about to be conferred on them." That reaction from the "whole congregation of several hundred" helps explain James's judgment that the colonists unanimously supported annexation.[52]

Although the treaty's defeat in June 1870 seemed to guarantee the disappointment of the colonists' hopes, Grant's suggestion that Congress consider annexing Santo Domingo by a joint resolution reignited the annexation debate and raised the possibility that annexation might still succeed.[53] Understanding that debate is important because the way annexationists framed their project determined what institutions the colonists believed the United States would establish in Santo Domingo. The colonists likely did not know the precise details of the debate, but they knew enough to recognize that annexation meant the incorporation of Santo Domingo into the Union and the extension of citizenship to Dominicans.[54]

A majority of both the Senate and the House of Representatives favored annexation, as did many prominent newspapers.[55] In congressional debates and editorials, annexationists made their case in part by pointing to Santo Domingo's potential agricultural wealth and the military benefits of acquiring a West Indian naval stronghold.[56] Those arguments might just as easily have been made by slaveholders in the antebellum era or imperialists in 1898. But annexationists' partisan identity and political and ideological commitments regarding Reconstruction exercised a crucial influence on their arguments. Annexation was an almost exclusively Republican project on a national level.[57] Republican annexationists therefore often framed their arguments in terms likely to appeal to specifically Republican concerns.

Leading Republican annexationists in Congress went to great lengths to highlight the moral contrast between proslavery expansion and the annexation of Santo Domingo by focusing on the status that Dominicans would hold. Senator William Stewart argued that “the question of annexation now and the question of annexation previous to the abolition of slavery and the adoption of those amendments to our Constitution which secure all men in their equal rights are two very different questions.”[58] William Kelley, one of the most important radical Republicans in the House of Representatives, explained that he had opposed tropical expansion in the antebellum era because its advocates had hoped “to extend the area of slavery and to perpetuate that accursed institution” but that he now supported annexation because it would “extend the area of freedom and give republican institutions, common schools, a free press, our laws, language, and literature, and all the appliances of modern civilization to a tropical people, most of whom are of African descent.”[59] Republican annexationists argued that the moral calculus of expansion had changed because Caribbean peoples would become citizens, not slaves. Stewart dismissed fears that Dominicans would be oppressed if annexation occurred by reminding his audience that the “colored people” of Santo Domingo would possess “all the liberties of American citizens” and “enjoy the same rights and privileges that we do.”[60] In a widely publicized interview, Grant argued that it was precisely the prospect of enjoying those rights that made Dominicans desire to join the United States. They were “drawn to us,” Grant argued, “by our enfranchisement of the colored race and repose implicit faith and confidence in our professions of justice and equal rights.”[61] Representative Job Stevenson affirmed that not only would Dominicans be citizens but also that they would be “better hearted citizens than some of the white race who now struggle against the laws of the land” in the United States.[62] Republican annexationists further reinforced the belief that Dominicans would enjoy equal citizenship by describing annexation as a project of incorporating them into the American nation. Oliver Morton, the leading annexationist in the Senate, predicted that Dominicans would “rapidly incorporate and consolidate with the people [of the United States].”[63]

Republican annexationists also cast annexation as a project of statehood. The *Daily National Republican,* one of the most important Republican journals in Washington, D.C., argued that Americans “contemplate the ultimate annexation of this negro State with complacency.”[64] Some Republican annexationists expected that the creation of new states in the Caribbean would not end with Santo Domingo. The *Christian Recorder,* the journal of the African Methodist Episcopal Church, hoped that the “independent governments of Hayti and

Dominica" would be "dissolved" and that both countries would become "States in the American confederacy."[65] The *New York Tribune* published articles predicting that if Grant should "choose to annex Cuba, Porto Rico, and Hayti, it scarcely admits of doubt that those three states can within three years be legally, peacefully, and honorably incorporated in the Union."[66] The *New York Standard* favored the annexation of Santo Domingo because its editors "hoped to see the admission of the States of Porto Rico, Cuba, and Jamaica into the Union" and believed that if Santo Domingo joined the United States, "in its track will assuredly follow all the sister isles."[67]

The prospect of acquiring black-majority states in the Caribbean profoundly alarmed Democratic leaders. All Democratic senators and representatives opposed annexation, as did virtually every Democratic journal.[68] Their objections centered on Dominicans' race. Senator Thomas Bayard spoke for his party when he described Dominicans as a "semi-barbarous" and "utterly abandoned" population of "black cut-throats" whose society was a "chaotic mass of crime and degradation."[69] And, as Representative Fernando Wood noted, Reconstruction guaranteed that "savage" Dominicans would become "citizens of the United States and exercise, as all do under our present modified system, the privileges of representation and of becoming representatives."[70] Democrats warned that annexation would represent the extension of Reconstruction into the Caribbean. One paper argued that "carpetbaggers from New England . . . will repair to the sunny isle and persuade the niggers to send them as representatives to Congress."[71] The New Orleans *Picayune* predicted that Santo Domingo as well as Haiti would be "speedily brought into the family of states" because radicals "want negro Senators to help pass Constitutional amendments; and negro legislatures to confirm them, in order to secure to the Radical party . . . the control of the Government of the United States."[72] Democrats argued that Cuba and Puerto Rico would follow soon thereafter. They feared that acquiring a band of black-majority, Republican-controlled states stretching across the Caribbean would create a nightmare scenario in which hundreds of thousands of new black voters would provide "a black balance of power," as one newspaper put it, that would allow Republicans to maintain their grip on the federal government and guarantee the permanence of Reconstruction.[73] Those claims seemed plausible in the early 1870s, after Hiram Revels and Joseph Rainey became the first African Americans elected to the U.S. Senate and House of Representatives, state legislatures elected primarily by black voters helped ratify the Fourteenth and Fifteenth Amendments, and more than 500,000 southern African Americans voted in 1868.[74]

A substantial minority of congressional Republicans and many influential Republican newspapers vehemently opposed annexation. They followed Democrats in focusing on Dominicans' alleged racial degradation.[75] Republican anti-annexationists also viewed annexation through the prism of Reconstruction, arguing that Santo Domingo would become essentially another southern state plagued by ignorant and easily manipulated black voters.[76] Because almost all of the most vocal Republican anti-annexationists were also among the greatest critics of Reconstruction, casting annexation as an extension of Reconstruction into the Caribbean came easily.[77] Senator Carl Schurz described the reconstructed South as a "nursery of trouble and embarrassment" and asked Americans if they wished to acquire another such nursery in the Caribbean.[78] "One South is enough," Schurz argued, " . . . we will only have trouble with this second one."[79] Republican anti-annexationists also feared that annexation would not end with Santo Domingo. One New England paper warned that "to annex San Domingo means to annex at no long interval Hayti, and ultimately the whole of the West India islands . . . the scheme must be, and is announced to be, the admission of these islands into the Union as States, not to be governed by us, but actually to participate in controlling us, in proportion to their weight of numbers."[80] Republican anti-annexationists argued that acquiring those states would have catastrophic consequences for American democracy.

A small but vocal cohort of reformers, known for their support for the rights of African Americans, also opposed annexation. Led by Senator Charles Sumner, those reformers rejected annexation for reasons different from those of most anti-annexationists. They argued that Dominicans opposed annexation. They also feared that if annexation occurred, Dominicans would become an exploited, downtrodden people relegated to the margins of political and economic life in their own homeland.[81] Just as important was reformer anti-annexationists' hope that Haiti would establish control over the entire island and serve as the nucleus of a Caribbean-wide black republic. Sumner claimed that Dominicans already desired to rejoin Haiti and that when Cabral regained power he would follow Dominicans' wishes by appealing to the Haitian government to resume its sovereignty over Santo Domingo.[82]

Grant proposed creating a diplomatic commission because he believed anti-annexationists' concerns regarding Dominicans' desire for annexation and capacity for incorporation into the American nation could be allayed by an investigation of conditions in Santo Domingo. On January 12, 1871, Congress authorized the creation of the commission, and one week later the commissioners and their staff departed for Santo Domingo.[83]

Reconstructing U.S. Diplomacy

During the colonists' interviews with the commissioners, they stated that their community overwhelmingly favored annexation.[84] In explaining their support, the colonists discussed how Reconstruction had changed their view of the United States. When Pedro Santana proposed to annex Samaná to the United States in the 1850s, the colonists had objected to annexation because the United States was a slaveholding country. But during the 1860s they had learned of the extension of citizenship, civil rights, and suffrage to African Americans and knew that "everyone was equal before the law" in the United States.[85] The colonists had once feared being enslaved but now believed that the United States was a "country of freedom."[86]

They also pointed to the specific problems they hoped reconstructed U.S. institutions would solve. When they identified their most pressing concern, they spoke the language of free labor. They did not "expect or wish any foreign power to come in with a sack of doubloons to put in every man's pocket." They simply wanted to "work with a prospect of enjoying the fruits of work; that we cannot do now."[87] During chronic political unrest in Santo Domingo, rival armies had repeatedly pillaged Samaná. The colonists believed that the powerful U.S. government would end civil warfare in Santo Domingo and enable the colonists to build more prosperous lives in peace.[88]

The United States' free-labor economy was not the only reconstructed institution the colonists admired. They had heard of "efforts put forth for the education of their race" in the United States.[89] The colonists placed an exceptionally high priority on education. Samaná's schoolteacher explained in one interview that they had "begged" him to open a night school for adults and were "so anxious to educate [their] children" that "they will walk for miles to sell ten cents' worth of provisions" for money to purchase schoolbooks.[90] The colonists had sacrificed what little money they had to sustain two small schools, but their efforts were hampered by the absence of support from the impoverished Dominican government. The colony's leaders promised that if the U.S. government built a public school system it would be "well received and supported."[91]

In many ways, the colonists saw the achievements of Reconstruction as a model for what they hoped the establishment of U.S. institutions in Santo Domingo would achieve. But how had the colonists learned of the changes Reconstruction had brought to the United States? Since the colony's founding, in 1825, the colonists had deliberately embedded themselves in the wider Atlantic World and worked to remain informed about events in the United States.[92] By the late 1860s, the colonists' connections to the United States were more robust than ever. In 1869 trade between Samaná and the United States quickened after an American company established a line of steamships that ran between the city of Santo Domingo, Samaná, and New York. Those ships carried not only goods but also information, including American newspapers.[93] When several families from Maine, Louisiana, and Virginia emigrated to Samaná between 1868 and 1870, they also brought the latest news from the United States.[94] Although Samaná was almost one thousand miles from the nearest American port, Reconstruction was a sufficiently important event that news of the sweeping changes the

United States had experienced reached even seemingly distant corners of the Caribbean.

The commission provided the colonists with additional evidence of Reconstruction's influence on U.S. institutions. In Douglass's speech to the colony, he explained that African Americans had been "exalted from wretched slavery to the right of suffrage and equality with white men."[95] He believed that his place on the commission symbolized the difference between the "OLD TIME and the NEW."[96] The colonists responded enthusiastically to Douglass's inclusion, as did other observers in Santo Domingo. One journalist reported that Báez, after meeting Douglass, had been "charmed with the equality of our mixed commission, furnishing in its white and colored members conclusive evidence that as there are no distinctions of color in Dominica so there are none in the United States."[97]

The commission's treatment of Douglass and the colonists also served as important signs of change in American race relations. One correspondent described the USS *Tennessee,* the warship the commission used to travel to Santo Domingo, as "the most magnificent ship in the navy."[98] During the commission's journey, Douglass ate alongside the commissioners, the ship's senior officers, and the most prominent correspondents in the captain's elegant dining room. In doing so, Douglass did something unprecedented in the history of American race relations. His presence at the captain's table was, he wrote, the first time in the history of the U.S. Navy that a black man had been honored with an invitation to dine with the ranking officers of an American warship.[99] The colonists were aware of the "social equality" that Douglass enjoyed, and at least one colonist had the same respect extended to him. When the *Tennessee* reached Samaná, the first person invited aboard was a colonist, Joseph Hamilton. When Hamilton arrived, both Benjamin Wade and Frederick Douglass "graciously received him."[100] Several days later, Hamilton was again welcomed aboard the *Tennessee* to participate in formal introductions between Dominican officials and the commission and to dine with the combined party. Hamilton, like Douglass, became one of the pioneers of integrating, even for a short time, the elite social spaces of an American warship.[101] The sight of an African American colonist, Frederick Douglass, and mixed-race Dominicans eating alongside and conversing on a level of equality with white American leaders would have shocked most nineteenth-century Americans. Such scenes would have been difficult to imagine in the American racial order the colonists left behind in 1825. The commission also made another major positive gesture toward the colonists. Before leaving Samaná, Douglass took up a collection among the commissioners and correspondents, who provided a large monetary donation to help the colonists purchase lumber and tools to build a new church.[102] The colonists had ample reason for believing that Reconstruction had changed U.S. institutions for the better.

If the colonists doubted that annexation would mean their incorporation into the American nation, the commission provided further confirmation of the terms under which the United States proposed to annex Santo Domingo. The commission discussed annexation with the colonists and other Dominicans as a question of citizenship and eventual statehood. While traveling through several cities in northern Santo Domingo, Andrew White delivered speeches describing Dominicans' relationship to the United States if annexation occurred. "We do not propose to annex you as a colony," White explained, "but as a territory—not as subjects, but citizens. If you are admitted, it will be as equals . . . .we are obliged to be very careful as to who we annex, since all citizens participate in the election of Senators and Representatives, and President of the United States. We should not simply govern you. You would help govern us." White argued that annexation meant Dominicans and Americans would "unite . . . in sustaining the honor and independence of our common country."[103] Benjamin Wade, while speaking to a large crowd in the city of Santo Domingo, discussed Dominicans holding office in the U.S. federal government. "If it should be our fortune to join ourselves together," Wade said, "and you should become citizens of the great republic, there is no man here who may not aspire to be Chief Magistrate of the whole." The correspondent who transcribed Wade's speech reported that his remarks concerning a Dominican potentially becoming a U.S. president caused a "sensation" among the audience.[104]

When the commission departed Santo Domingo in early March, the colonists continued to hope that annexation might be accomplished. The commission's final report, issued in early April, was certainly designed to achieve that aim. The report argued that Dominicans almost unanimously desired to "become part of the people of the United States."[105] It also contained a point-by-point rebuttal of claims that Dominicans were a degraded people. The commission argued that Dominicans' moral decency, general intelligence, and independent character indicated that they had the potential for U.S. citizenship and that Santo Domingo might develop into a "powerful State" of the Union if annexation were to occur.[106] The commission was also impressed that Dominicans "seem to be practically destitute of prejudice of class, race, or color" and cited that racial tolerance as another positive aspect of Dominicans' character. That the commission praised Dominicans for their racially egalitarian society said as much about the commission as it did about Dominicans.[107]

Many of the correspondents took an even more favorable view of Dominicans.[108] The colonists received special praise. The correspondent of the *New York Times,* James Foley, argued that Americans who opposed annexation because they feared "it would be dangerous to further increase the numbers of our ignorant voters" had made a "very grave mistake." "So far as the residents of Samana are concerned," Foley wrote, "[the] men, women, and children who live here are by no means ignorant, and are far more capable of understanding a public question than a great many people in the North, to say nothing of the South, of far greater pretensions. . . . I have no hesitation in saying that they would make excellent citizens."[109]

Promoting Annexation

The colonists were not passive spectators in the annexation controversy; they sought, in multiple ways, to shape its outcome. In 1863 the colonists had attempted to draw U.S. power into Santo Domingo by appealing to the Lincoln administration. In 1870 and 1871 they took more extensive steps to promote the expansion of the U.S. government's influence in Santo Domingo. The most overt method they used to promote annexation was simply speaking with other Dominicans and explaining the nature of U.S. institutions and the benefits of annexation.[110]

The colonists also exercised an important but unacknowledged role in framing the commission's and correspondents' conclusions. Several of the colonists served as translators and guides for the commission's staff and correspondents as they traveled throughout the country.[111] When the colonists told the commission that their own investigations of annexationist sentiment in the country over the past year had led them to believe that most Dominicans favored annexation, that information strengthened the commission's confidence in making the same claim.[112] If the commission had not faced a language barrier in communicating with most Dominicans and not been compelled to rely upon translators brought from the United States and the colonists to serve as conduits of information, the commission might have reached different conclusions about annexationist sentiment among Dominicans and would likely have noticed considerably more opposition to annexation.

The colonists also attempted to influence the annexation controversy in the United States by writing to Douglass and to Grant in the summer of 1871. Douglass had established an emotional bond with the colonists during his time in Santo Domingo. In May, after his return to the United States, he wrote to one of the colonists, Mary Garcia, to inform her of the "gloomy prospects" for annexation. She responded in a somewhat forlorn letter, letting Douglass know that "the children send their love," and expressing her sadness that Americans were unwilling to embrace "our admission into the Union."[113] Douglass wrote in one pro-annexation essay that if Americans had spoken to "the citizens of Santo Domingo . . . and heard their story as I have heard it, your hearts would ache, as mine does," over annexation's failure. That sentiment undoubtedly derived in part from his emotional connection to the colonists.[114]

In a second letter from the colonists to an American leader, General Theophilus James, the brother of Jacob James, wrote to Grant in June 1871, praising him "for the good he is doing for this republic." James affirmed that Dominicans desired annexation. He also struck a more martial tone than had Mary Garcia. He informed Grant that "there are men here as well as myself who are able and willing with sord [*sic*] in hand [to] march from one end [of] this island to the other" if annexation occurred and U.S. forces needed assistance in establishing American authority in Santo Domingo.[115]

The colonists' contributions to the commission's report and attempts to bolster Douglass's and Grant's confidence in seeking annexation reflected the strength of their community's desire for annexation. But their hopes were disappointed. The commission's report did not have the decisive effect on American public opinion that annexationists thought it might. Grant effectively ended his campaign for annexation in early April.[116] Although a majority of congressmen had been willing to annex Dominicans as citizens, the powerful anti-annexationist minority in Congress was too deeply entrenched to overcome. Most anti-annexationists in the United States adopted that stance for the same reason that the colonists desired annexation: because it promised to extend reconstructed U.S. institutions into the Caribbean by making Dominicans citizens of the United States and incorporating Santo Domingo into the Union.

That such a project seemed plausible and desirable to many observers, including a community that had once sacrificed a great deal to escape American racism, is a striking measure of Reconstruction's influence. The colonists concluded that because the racial boundaries of the American nation had expanded as a result of Reconstruction, the geographic boundaries of the United States might prove to be just as malleable. They overestimated the degree and permanence of the change Reconstruction brought to U.S. institutions. The colonists were wrong on that point, but they were not alone.

NOTES

1. Accounts of Douglass's speech appear in the *New York Standard, New York Herald,* and *Cincinnati Commercial* for February 21, 1871. The *Commercial*'s description of his speech and the *Standard*'s summary of the meeting align most closely with Douglass's assessment of his experiences in Samaná. See *New National Era,* May 25, 1871. At the conclusion of Douglass's speech to the colonists, he asked who among them favored annexation. The *Standard* reported that the colonists responded with a "unanimous show of hands."

2. U.S. Department of State, *Report of the Secretary of State in Regard to San Domingo, Transmitted to the Senate, January 16, 1871* (Washington, D.C.: U.S. Government Printing Office, 1871), 98–100. The treaty provided for Santo Domingo's annexation as a territory, but Grant informed the Dominican government that he expected that Santo Domingo would become a state at "no distant day." There is no evidence that he envisioned Santo Domingo holding the legal status to which Puerto Rico was consigned after 1898, remaining a perpetual unincorporated territory. The example of New Mexico, whose statehood was delayed until 1912, when Congress judged that the New Mexican

population had gained a predominant number of white Americans, could serve as a parallel to what might have occurred with Santo Domingo. But that was not Grant's intention. He planned to divide Santo Domingo into multiple "States of the Union . . . under the protection of the General Government," with populations "almost wholly colored."

When Secretary of State Hamilton Fish became alarmed by Grant's "insistence upon a promise of eventual Statehood to the island," he suggested to Grant that annexation might be more likely to succeed if Santo Domingo became a protectorate of the United States. Grant was "totally unwilling" to consider Fish's plan. See John Y. Simon, ed., *Papers of Ulysses S. Grant, November 1, 1876–September 30, 1878* (Carbondale: Southern Illinois University Press, 1995), 430–32; Ulysses S. Grant, *Personal Memoirs of U.S. Grant* (New York: Library of America, 1990), 28: 778; Allan Nevins, *Hamilton Fish: An Inner History of the Grant Administration* (New York: Frederick Ungar, 1937), 327–29; and U.S. Department of State, *Report of the Secretary of State in Regard to San Domingo, January 16, 1871*, 80–82.

3. *New York Times*, July 1, 1870. The treaty failed by a 28–28 vote. However, the *Times* noted that the actual distribution of support was 35–32. The additional senators declined to vote when it became clear the treaty would fail.

4. Ulysses S. Grant, Second Annual Message, December 5, 1870. See *Congressional Globe* (hereafter *CG*), Forty-First Congress, Third Session (Washington, D.C.: Government Printing Office, 1871), 6–7.

5. See *Report of the Commission of Inquiry to Santo Domingo* (Washington, D.C.: Government Printing Office, 1871), 5, for the resolution describing the commission's responsibilities (hereafter *Report of the Commission*).

6. *CG*, Forty-First Congress, Third Session, 6–7.

7. *Report of the Commission*, 36.

8. *New York Herald*, February 21, 1871.

9. Heather Cox Richardson, *West from Appomattox: The Reconstruction of America after the Civil War* (New Haven: Yale University Press, 2007), 92.

10. David Herbert Donald, *Charles Sumner* (New York: Da Capo, 1996), 475.

11. *Report of the Commission*, 38.

12. Ibid., 231–232. *New National Era*, May 25, 1871.

13. *New National Era*, January 12, 1871.

14. "Equal voice" appears in the *New National Era*, April 27, 1871. Douglass published essays on annexation in the *New National Era* on April 6, April 13, April 20, April 27, May 4, May 11, and May 18, 1871. He delivered lectures on Santo Domingo in cities ranging from St. Louis to Bangor, Maine, between April 1871 and January 1873. For more information, see John W. Blassingame and John R. McKivigan, eds., *The Frederick Douglass Papers, vol. 4, ser. 1: Speeches, Debates, and Interviews, 1864–1880* (New Haven: Yale University Press, 1991), 342. Also see "Santo Domingo," Folders 1–5, Speech, Article, and Book File, Papers of Frederick Douglass, Library of Congress, Washington, D.C.

15. Julie Winch, *A Gentleman of Color: The Life of James Forten* (Oxford: Oxford University Press, 2003), 216–20. H. Hoetink, "'Americans' in Samaná," *Caribbean Studies* 2 (April 1962): 3–22.

16. Luis Martinez-Fernández, "Caudillos, Annexationism, and the Rivalry between Empires in the Dominican Republic, 1844–1874," *Diplomatic History* 17 (October 1993):

585–89, describes Santana's negotiations with the United States during the 1850s. See *Report of the Commission,* 227, 230, for the colonists' rejection of annexation to the United States "because it was a slaveholding country" and concerns that white Americans might "pour in and make them slaves."

17. *Report of the Commission,* 230.

18. Theophilus James to President Ulysses S. Grant, June 1, 1871, in John Y. Simon, ed., *Papers of Ulysses S. Grant, June 1, 1871–January 31, 1872* (Carbondale: Southern Illinois University Press, 1995), 22: 28. Letter from Mary Garcia to Frederick Douglass, July 1871, in General Correspondence File, Papers of Frederick Douglass. Joseph Fabens to Hamilton Fish, December 30, 1869, Notes from the Legation of the Dominican Republic in the United States, 1844–1906, T801, Department of State, National Archives and Records Administration (hereafter NARA).

19. Varios Dominicanos, *Breve Refutación del Informe de los Comisionados de Santo Domingo Dedicado al Pueblo de Los Estados Unidos* (Curacao / New York, 1871), 15, 19.

20. Hoetink, "'Americans' in Samaná," 18–19.

21. I use Reconstruction at times to refer to the attempt to redefine the position of African Americans in the United States as a whole via the Thirteenth, Fourteenth, and Fifteenth Amendments. At other points I refer specifically to the struggle to implement those amendments in the American South by creating a free-labor economy and racially egalitarian democracy under the auspices of Republican state governments backed by the power of the federal government.

22. *New National Era,* May 25, 1871.

23. See Mark M. Smith, "The Past as a Foreign Country: Reconstruction, Inside and Out," in Thomas J. Brown, ed., *Reconstructions: New Perspectives on the Postbellum United States* (New York: Oxford University Press, 2006), 117–40. Smith's essay contains a useful summary of current work on the international history of Reconstruction. Jay Sexton, in "Toward a Synthesis of Foreign Relations in the Civil War Era," *American Nineteenth Century History* 5 (2004): 50–73, discusses diplomatic historians' relative lack of interest in the broader Civil War era.

24. Walter LaFeber, in *The Cambridge History of American Foreign Relations, vol. 2: The Search for Opportunity, 1865–1913* (Cambridge: Cambridge University Press, 1993), 67, argues that anti-annexationists feared that annexing Santo Domingo would "compound racial problems already plaguing the United States." Robert Beisner, in *From the Old Diplomacy to the New, 1865–1900* (Arlington Heights, Ill.: Harlan Davidson, 1975), 50, 82, also focuses on antiexpansionists' use of Reconstruction as evidence that proved tropical annexation would harm the United States. Eric T. L. Love, in *Race over Empire: Racism and U.S. Imperialism, 1865–1900* (Chapel Hill: University of North Carolina Press, 2004), 27–72, argues that white Americans' fear of extending U.S. citizenship to nonwhite Dominicans was one of the central causes of annexation's failure.

25. *CG,* Forty-First Congress, Third Session, 408–10. *New York Standard,* May 19, 1870.

26. Nevins, *Hamilton Fish,* 267.

27. Luis Martinez-Fernández, *Torn between Empires: Economic, Society, and Patterns of Political Thought in the Hispanic Caribbean, 1840–1878* (Athens: University of Georgia Press, 1994), 207. Many groups in the Caribbean feared U.S. territorial

expansion and saw Reconstruction as irrelevant. A pamphlet published by Dominican anti-annexationists offered a different analogy from U.S. history to predict Dominicans' fate if annexation occurred: "what reason have we to expect to be more fortunate than the Creeks, the Winnebagoes, the Cherokees. We shall also be dispossessed by the Yankees of our lands, our rights, and our liberties." See "To Arms, Dominicans, to Arms!," signed "A Thousand Patriots," reprinted in the *Chicago Tribune,* January 30, 1871.

28. *Report of the Commission,* 174–76, 265.

29. Martinez-Fernández, *Torn between Empires,* 206–7.

30. Isaac Dookhan, "Changing Patterns of Local Reaction to the United States' Acquisition of the Virgin Islands, 1865–1917," *Caribbean Studies* 15 (April 1975): 54–59. *New York World,* January 21, 1868.

31. Winch, *Gentleman,* 217.

32. Eric Foner, *Nothing but Freedom: Emancipation and Its Legacy* (Baton Rouge: Louisiana State University Press, 1983), 40.

33. Ernest May, in *American Imperialism: A Speculative Essay,* 2nd ed. (Chicago: Imprint Publications, 1991), 98, argues that the annexation controversy was an effort by Grant to "put before the American public the issue of whether or not to acquire a colonial empire." Charles C. Tansill, in *The United States and Santo Domingo, 1798–1873: A Chapter in Caribbean Diplomacy* (Baltimore: The Johns Hopkins University Press, 1938), 338, refers to the annexation controversy as a question of "colonial expansion." Also see William J. Nelson, *Almost a Territory: America's Attempt to Annex the Dominican Republic* (Newark: University of Delaware Press, 1990), 67. See Nicholas Guyatt, "America's Conservatory: Race, Reconstruction, and the Santo Domingo Debate," *Journal of American History* 97 (March 2011): 974–1000, for an important analysis of the annexation debate as a question of statehood.

34. Allison L. Sneider, *Suffragists in an Imperial Age: U.S. Expansion and the Woman Question, 1870–1929* (Oxford: Oxford University Press, 2008), 47, argues that during the Santo Domingo affair, "the United States did not have in place a legal apparatus for governing colonies, and the ruling presumption was that any new territory under U.S. control would eventually enter the Union as a new state."

35. *Boletín Oficial,* 19 de Febrero de 1870. Letter of Mary Garcia to Frederick Douglass, July 1871, Papers of Frederick Douglass, Library of Congress. On February 7, 1871, the *Baltimore American* published an excerpt from the *Boletín Oficial,* written in early January 1871, which described annexation as a question of "union" with the United States.

36. *New York Herald,* February 24, March 17, 1871. See Hans L. Trefousse, *Benjamin F. Wade: Radical Republican from Ohio* (New York: Twayne, 1963); Harold Schwartz, *Samuel Gridley Howe, Social Reformer, 1801–1876* (Cambridge, Mass.: Harvard University Press, 1956); and Glenn C. Altschuler, *Andrew D. White—Educator, Historian, Diplomat* (Ithaca, N.Y.: Cornell University Press, 1979).

37. W. E. B. Du Bois and David Levering Lewis (introduction), *Black Reconstruction in America, 1860–1880* (New York: Free Press, 1998), 708.

38. Martinez-Fernández, "Caudillos, Annexationism, and the Rivalry between Empires," 572–592. Emilio Rodríguez Demorizi, *Samaná, Pasado y Porvenir* (Santo

Domingo: Impreso en la Editora del Caribe, 1973), 15–50. A. de St-Merant, *Samaná et Projets de Cession, 1844–1891* (Paris: Marchal et Billard, 1896).

39. *Report of the Secretary of State, 77.*

40. Raphael Semmes, *Memoirs of Service Afloat: During the War between the States* (Baltimore: Kelly, Piet, 1869), 189.

41. Daniel Alexander Payne, *History of the African Methodist Episcopal Church* (Nashville: Publishing House of the A.M.E. Sunday School Union, 1891), 64–68. U.S. diplomatic records mention a colonist who immigrated to Santo Domingo in the mid-1820s, lived in Baltimore in 1840, and died in the city of Santo Domingo on Christmas Eve, 1864, with "letters found in her possession" from her siblings in the United States. William Read to William Seward, January 2, 1865, Reel 5, Despatches from U.S. Consuls in Santo Domingo, Record Group 59, Department of State, NARA. Another colonist recounted in 1871 how he had "several times visited the United States . . . [in] New England, [and] several of the Middle and Southern States." *Report of the Commission,* 229. For references to correspondence between Samaná and the United States in the colony's early years, see *Niles' National Register,* April 2, 1825, and *Zion's Herald,* February 23, 1825, which describe "hundreds" of letters being sent from Samaná to the United States.

42. Martinez-Fernández, "Caudillos, Annexationism, and the Rivalry Between Empires," 577.

43. *Report of the Commission,* 227.

44. Ibid., 230. In 1871, Jacob James recalled that "we had newspapers here during the war, telling us all the news when the rebellion was going on." The newspapers he referred to may have been editions of the Dominican government newspaper, *Gaceta de Santo Domingo,* which republished excerpts from papers from Havana that carried news regarding the secession crisis and the American Civil War. See *Diario de la Marina de la Habana* in *Gaceta de Santo Domingo,* 21 de Marzo, 1861.

45. William Jaeger to William Seward, April 6, 1863, Reel 4, Despatches from U.S. Consuls in Santo Domingo, NARA.

46. William Jaeger to William Seward, February 5, 1862, April 6, 1863, July 7, 1863, July 1, 1864, Reel 4, Despatches from U.S. Consuls in Santo Domingo, NARA.

47. Tansill, *The United States and Santo Domingo, 1798–1873,* 232–59.

48. Ibid., 258–86.

49. Ibid., 343–48. See Nevins, *Hamilton Fish,* 252–56, and Robert E. May, "Lobbyists for Commercial Empire: Jane Cazneau, William Cazneau, and U.S. Caribbean Policy, 1846–1878," *Pacific Historical Review* 48 (August 1979), 383-412.

50. Ulysses S. Grant, "Reasons Why San Domingo Should be Annexed to the United States," in John Y. Simon, ed., *Papers of Ulysses S. Grant, November 1, 1869–October 31, 1870* (Carbondale: Southern Illinois University Press, 1995), 20: 74–76.

51. A second treaty would have annexed only Samaná, but after the failure of the primary treaty, the second was never brought before the Senate. *Report of the Secretary of State,* 98–102.

52. *Report of the Commission,* 230; *New York World,* February 21, 1871. A description of the colonists' church service appears in Joseph Fabens to Hamilton Fish, December

30, 1869, Notes from the Legation of the Dominican Republic in the United States to the Department of State, 1844–1906, T801, NARA.

53. On March 3, 1871, the Washington, D.C., correspondent of the *Springfield Republican* reported that "probabilities favor [annexation]'s success." On March 17, 1871, the *New York Tribune* reported that the commission's work had "undoubtedly had a powerful effect in reconciling public opinion to the probable acquisition of the island." But, on the same day, the *Tribune* reported that a "a prominent opponent of [annexation] in the Senate now claims to be certain that not only will it be impossible to obtain a two-thirds vote for annexation, but there will be found to be a clear majority against the treaty." Annexation was still a contested issue in the spring of 1871, and the outcome of the annexation controversy was by no means self-evident to observers in Washington.

54. For evidence that the colony's leaders were aware of the content of debates in the U.S. Congress concerning annexation, see Theophilus James's dismissal of claims that "had been said in Congress" concerning Dominicans' opposition to annexation. Theophilus James to President Ulysses S. Grant, June 1, 1871, in John Y. Simon, ed., *Papers of Ulysses S. Grant June 1, 1871–January 31, 1872* (Carbondale: Southern Illinois University Press, 1995), 22: 28.

55. On March 10, 1871, Senator Timothy Howe stated that a majority of the Senate favored annexation. *CG*, Forty-Second Congress, First Session, 48. On January 11, 1871, Representative John Ela of New Hampshire estimated that a majority of Republicans in the House supported annexation. *CG*, Forty-First Congress, Third Session 411. Among the major national newspapers that favored annexation between early 1870 and mid-1871 were the *New York Times, New York Herald,* and *New York Tribune.* The *New York Standard, Baltimore American, Philadelphia North American and U.S. Gazette, Daily National Republican, Christian Recorder,* and *Zion's Herald* also enthusiastically backed annexation.

56. *CG*, Forty-First Congress, Second Session, Appendix, 408–9. *CG*, Forty-First Congress, Third Session, Appendix, 17–18. *New York Times,* March 9, 1870.

57. The *New York Herald* was the only major Democratic paper in the United States that endorsed annexation. The twenty-eight affirmative votes for the annexation treaty on June 30, 1870, were all Republicans. Annexation remained an exclusively Republican project in Congress throughout the annexation controversy. *New York Times,* July 1, 1870.

58. *CG*, Forty-First Congress, Third Session, 428.

59. Ibid., 794.

60. Ibid., 428.

61. *New York Times,* April 6, 1870.

62. *CG*, Forty-First Congress, Third Session, 409–10.

63. Ibid., 238. Morton also predicted that Cubans and Puerto Ricans would also become rapidly incorporated into the American nation, if they wished to join the United States. *New York Tribune,* February 25, 1871.

64. *Daily National Republican,* February 19, 1870.

65. *Christian Recorder,* February 13, February 20, 1869.

66. *New York Tribune,* March 5, 1869.

67. *New York Standard,* February 22, 1871.

68. In early 1869, a Democratic congressman summarized his party's position by promising that Democrats would unanimously oppose annexation because "there was too much nigger involved in it." *New York Times,* February 2, 1869.

69. *CG,* Forty-First Congress, Third Session, 225.

70. Ibid., 385–87.

71. *Pomeroy's Democrat,* February 24, 1869.

72. New Orleans *Times-Picayune,* April 15, 1869.

73. *Atlanta Constitution,* April 14, 1869.

74. Both Rainey and Revels endorsed annexation. See *Charleston Daily News,* December 13, 1870, Guyatt, "America's Conservatory," 982., and Xi Wang, *The Trial of Democracy: Black Suffrage and Northern Republicans, 1860-1910* (Athens: University of Georgia Press, 1997), 41.

75. *Nation,* April 15, 1869, March 7, 1871. *Cincinnati Commercial,* May 9, 1870. *Chicago Tribune,* March 21, 1870. *Springfield Republican,* March 24, 1871.

76. *Chicago Tribune,* March 26, 1870, December 7, 1870. *Nation,* February 3, 1870, March 7, 1871.

77. See Andrew Slap, *The Doom of Reconstruction: The Liberal Republicans in the Civil War Era* (New York: Fordham University Press, 2007), 117–22, for evidence of the overlap between Republicans opposed to annexation and Republicans opposed to Reconstruction.

78. *CG,* Forty-First Congress, Third Session, Appendix, 30.

79. Sabine Freitag, *Friedrich Hecker: Two Lives for Liberty* (St. Louis: St. Louis Mercantile Library, 2006), 267.

80. *Bangor Daily Whig and Courier,* December 31, 1870.

81. Prominent reformers such as William Lloyd Garrison, Wendell Phillips, Lydia Maria Child, Gerrit Smith, and Henry Highland Garnet also opposed annexation. Sneider, *Suffragists in an Imperial Age,* 36–40. Donald, *Sumner,* 442–44. *CG,* Forty-First Congress, Third Session, 227–31. *Independent,* April 13, April 27, 1871.

82. *CG,* Forty-First Congress, Third Session, 228. *CG,* Forty-Second Congress, First Session, 295. William Lloyd Garrison referred to Haiti and Santo Domingo as "absurdly divided" republics in the *Independent,* December 22, 1870.

83. For anti-annexationists' claims that the commission report would be meaningless, see *CG,* Forty-First Congress, Third Session, 195–96, 267, 407. Grant also sought vindication from charges that he and his advisers had acted corruptly and pursued annexation because they hoped to benefit financially.

84. *Report of the Commission,* 228–31. *New York World, New York Times, Cincinnati Commercial,* February 21, 1871.

85. *Report of the Commission,* 212. A government official stated that "all" the people of Samaná understood that equal rights had been established in the United States. Also see *New National Era,* May 25, 1871.

86. *Report of the Commission,* 229–31.

87. Ibid., 228–29.

88. *New York Times,* February 21, 1871.

89. *New National Era,* May 25, 1871.

90. *Report of the Commission,* 227.

91. Ibid., 229.

92. See note 41. Martha Willmore, an historian and descendant of the colonists, emphasized the Atlantic worldview of her ancestors in a recent interview. See Martha Ellen Davis, "Asentamiento y vida económica de los inmigrantes afroamericanos de Samaná: Testimonio de la profesora Martha Willmore (Leticia)," *Boletín del Archivo General de la Nación,* Año 69, 119, Septiembre–Diciembre (2007): 728.

93. In his letter to Grant from July 1871, Theophilus James described newspapers reaching Samaná. Douglass also described copies of the *New York Tribune* arriving on the ship that passed through Samaná on its way to the city of Santo Domingo. See Diary of Frederick Douglass (Santo Domingo 1871), FRDO 2090, at http://www.nps.gov/frdo/historyculture/upload/Douglass-Diary-1871.pdf (accesssed November 10, 2012).

94. *New York Tribune,* July 3, 1869. U.S. Senate Executive Documents, Forty-First Congress, Second Session, *Report of the Select Committee Appointed to Investigate the Memorial of Davis Hatch* (Washington, D.C.: Government Printing Office, 1870), 168–69. *Report of the Commission,* 213–18. *New York Standard,* February 21, 1871, mentions six American families that had recently settled in Samaná.

95. *New York Standard,* February 21, 1871.

96. Frederick Douglass, *Life and Times of Frederick Douglass* (Hartford, Conn.: Park, 1882), 500–501.

97. *New York Herald,* February 21, 1871.

98. *New York World, Cincinnati Daily Gazette,* February 21, 1871. *New National Era,* April 13, 1871.

99. Douglass, *Life and Times,* 500–1.

100. *Cincinnati Commercial,* February 21, 1871.

101. *New York Herald,* February 21, 1871.

102. *New York World, Cincinnati Daily Gazette,* February 21, 1871. *New York Herald,* February 22, 1871. Douglass gathered $64, a sum equivalent to $1,000 in 2012.

103. *Cincinnati Commercial,* March 31, 1871.

104. *New York Tribune,* February 24, 1871.

105. *Report of the Commission,* 11.

106. Ibid., 13–20, 33, 97, 112, 126.

107. Ibid., 13.

108. *Baltimore American,* April 3, April 22, 1871. *Philadelphia North American and U.S. Gazette,* February 21, February 24, 1871. *Report of the Commission,* 115.

109. *New York Times,* February 21, 1871.

110. *Report of the Commission,* 11.

111. Ibid., 95, 112.

112. Ibid., 228–32, 251–56.

113. Mary Garcia to Frederick Douglass, July 1871, Papers of Frederick Douglass, Library of Congress.

114. *New National Era,* April 27, 1871.

115. Theophilus James to President Ulysses S. Grant, June 1, 1871, in John Y. Simon, ed., *Papers of Ulysses S. Grant June 1, 1871 - January 31, 1872* (Carbondale: Southern Illinois University Press, 1995), 22: 28.

116. *Report of the Commission,* 3.

JANE E. SCHULTZ

Nurse as Icon

Florence Nightingale's Impact on Women in the American Civil War

I study Florence as if she were a language and as she is a deep one I have not mastered it by any means.

Mary Mohl to Parthenope Nightingale, February 16, 1853

In the five short years between her departure from Balaclava on the Crimean Peninsula and the start of the American Civil War, Florence Nightingale became the most talked-about civilian in the British Empire despite her legendary seclusion.[1] Though medical historians now believe that Nightingale suffered from a bacterial infection called brucellosis[2] and not the nervous exhaustion that Lytton Strachey attributed to her,[3] this season away from the world—an eleven-year stretch during which she wrote thousands of letters, gave few audiences, and orchestrated new paradigms for hospital management—fed a transnational imaginary that captains of print and media culture gladly attempted to gratify. Afflicted perhaps just as much with what Jane Addams would later call "the snare of preparation,"[4] Nightingale directed, from bed, the construction of the first professional school of nursing in London in 1860, St. Thomas's, a project whose reverberations would not only mobilize thousands of American women to seek relief assignments during the Civil War but would also influence the development of nurse-training schools in the United States after it.

American readings of Nightingale as a multifaceted text were well established even before the story of Crimean relief work had been publicly disseminated or fully evaluated—readings, according to one critic, that eclipsed the nursing work of Catholic sisterhoods from the Middle Ages to 1830s London.[5] That story—the one that eluded most Americans and Britons until the twentieth century—revealed Nightingale's noble but failed attempt to keep soldiers alive at Scutari across the Bosphorus Strait from Constantinople during the winter of 1854–55, when more than ten thousand of them died in a five-month period, sometimes more than seventy per day, due to inadequate sanitation and a lack of supplies.[6] Nightingale's star ascended despite this frightful mortality, for which she might as easily have been vilified as lauded on the eve of the Civil War. But the laudatory tone associated with Nightingale's name as early as 1855 was like a snowball rolling downhill, incorporating everything in its path. Once the magnitude of the American conflict became clear, whole armies of women wanted to be "Nightingales." Wartime narratives illuminated these motives in the context of a broader international discourse: eager to demonstrate that both sections could produce their own Florence Nightingales, writers expressed a competitive zeal that reflected the States' fervent wish to gain the global respect enjoyed by Britain and, in so doing, glimpsed the imperial ambitions of the young, fractured nation.[7]

Nightingale's 1860 opus on hospital design and patient care, *Notes on Nursing,* traveled across the Atlantic as the States' sectional rupture became a fait accompli and as the U.S. Army Medical Department recognized that its hundred hospital beds and thirty surgeons would not adequately serve the needs of warring troops.[8] The timeliness of Nightingale's book and its wide distribution encouraged women to volunteer in military hospitals long before there was any agreement among American medical administrators that their presence was practicable or desirable.[9] Nightingale's much-touted declaration that "every woman is a nurse" sanctioned a link between gender and nursing in an era when military nursing had been the province of men. Her contention that women's domestic knowledge made them ideal nurses—even better than men—gained traction among women when the American war began, despite her conviction that women ought to steer clear of regimental hospitals.[10] Whether Nightingale's horrendous months in the Barracks Hospital at Scutari created her reluctance or pride and egotism, the international broadcast of her labors in everything from tabloids to works of art gave American women the precedent to argue that there was no better outlet for their patriotic energies than war nursing.[11]

The history underpinning Nightingale's coronation as the World's Nurse is complex, but it is not my chief aim here. Instead, I want to look at Nightingale as a *linguistic* export and mid-nineteenth-century icon that drew American civilians enthusiastically into relief work. As others have observed, Nightingale's name became synonymous with female heroism,[12] obviating the need, for those with something to gain from the comparison, to explain their motives. Ultimately, Unionists' and Confederates' interpretations of Nightingale and her story—the iconic materials of her image and the triumphal narrative created around her—urged thousands to seek war work. Much like the "cult" of Giuseppe Garibaldi that Lucy Riall revealed in her 2007 study,[13] the adulation and excitement that attached to the figure of Nightingale satisfied a popular wish to find heroes in a time of political instability and national doubt. Apart from the nurse herself, Nightingale's name took on a life of its own when both northerners and southerners used it as a reference point, as a part of speech, and as a trope by which their enthusiasm for the prosecution of the war could be mapped. Indeed, as Barbara Cutter has suggested, reference to Nightingale appealed to people on both sides of the Mason-Dixon Line because she was not associated with either section.[14] Exploring the utility of the name reveals the multiple layers of meaning that constituted the icon and that owed its accretion to the expanding role of media in nineteenth-century lives. The migration of the name westward from Europe not only attracted Americans' attention but also became a source of British pride. London newspapers covering the American war referred to Nightingale's impact on medical relief systems, and the British press expressed satisfaction that its own Sanitary Commission, established in the Crimea to augment Nightingale's work, became a model for the U.S. version launched by elite New Yorkers in 1861.[15]

In his 2008 biography, Mark Bostridge reads the Nightingale legacy as a dynamic construct, one in which the legend of Nightingale imbricated her life even as it was lived. As in the media-fed "cult" mentioned earlier, the mythology that grew up around Nightingale had a life of its own, and that mythos affected the outlines of Nightingale's life in peculiar ways, causing her both to "manipulate her fame to masterly effect" and also to shun the limelight.[16] Nightingale's letters to the London *Times* in 1855, as well as dispatches from journalists to the London *Daily News,* revealed the medical mayhem at Scutari and implored Britons to take action. Such appeals resulted in widely read encomiums to her in the press and more than $200,000 in donations for her hospital work.[17] Parthenope Nightingale's publication of British soldiers' testimonials to her sister only heightened public enthusiasm about Nightingale's "pattern" virtues. And yet Nightingale would not sit for photographs, nor would she agree to write an account of her Crimean sojourn when the U.S. publishing house Childs and Petersen, smelling a profit to be made, came calling in 1855.[18] The woman who opined that even a handful of women in a military hospital might be too many and who skewered her nursing colleague Mary Stanley was also the woman being enshrined as "the most distinguished military figure of her time."[19] The saintly warrior image—a curious emulsion of masculinized feminine traits—had already captured the public imagination, rendering moot any assessment of Nightingale's character or actions. At a time when the carefully articulated domesticity of American women was straining toward revision, the image of Florence Nightingale offered relief: women believed that they could bring their domestic tools to the war front without unsexing themselves; they could fall into line with soldiers without fear of gendered reprisals. The active, progressive qualities that might have made them vulnerable to censure in peacetime were now approved and even applauded as demonstrations of patriotism.[20]

The transatlantic movement of Nightingale's name and its use as a shorthand for war nursing in the United States were evident by 1861. Just after the fall of Fort Sumter, one of the Woolsey sisters of New York contemplated becoming "a member of the Nightingale Regiment." Others "had read of Florence Nightingale and the noble work she did in the Crimean War," planning "a course of action, and a career of usefulness, that would in effect be reproducing the Crimean heroine under our flag." By June, Mary Boykin Chesnut, diarist extraordinaire of the Confederacy, observed with irony, "Every woman in the house is ready to rush into the Florence Nightingale business."[21] Though others had served alongside Nightingale, only a handful of Americans knew their names and learned them only when circumstances obliged them to do so through common purpose. Working on the Virginia Peninsula in the spring campaign of 1862, Sanitary Commission nurse Katharine Wormeley praised her coworker "Mrs. Reading, an excellent surgical nurse trained in the Crimea under Miss Nightingale," but never mentioned her subsequently. Alabama's Kate Cumming was warned by two sisters-in-law who had worked with Nightingale in the Crimea to avoid service altogether. But she ignored their advice and went on to become a three-year nursing veteran of the Confederate Army of Tennessee.[22] In a striking and unique example, direct knowledge of Nightingale's Crimean debacle did little to deter the Confederate nurse, already obedient to the icon.

The iconic figure was under construction right after the Crimean War, aided by versifiers in Britain and the United States. Longfellow's "Santa Filomena," a thinly veiled tribute to "a lady with a lamp" published in 1857, caught fire with Americans and Britons alike, and the appearance of the poem in the *Atlantic Monthly* made palpable the connection between the heroine of the Crimea and the virgin martyr of fourth-century Greece, also known as the patron saint of the sick. Though Longfellow twice invokes the phrase "a lady with a lamp," Nightingale quickly became "the" lady with "the" lamp, the indefinite article being supplanted by a definite one in the service of bringing together the nurse with the martyr. The liquid, alliterative sobriquet contributed a brand-like identity that could be grafted onto the image of Nightingale by 1858, when the *Illustrated London News* featured a sketch of her on February 24. Personal and commemorative accounts, in addition to the journalistic record, indicate the extent to which the icon was taking hold as the Civil War began. Even before 1861, Nightingale had become a household name in the United States because of substantial press coverage on both sides of the Atlantic.[23] In her study of wartime suffering, Frances Clarke has demonstrated the power and immediacy of telegraphic and photographic reportage to forever alter public reaction to war news. The evolution of mid-nineteenth-century information technologies captured an audience willing to insist that soldiers' comfort be made a high priority.[24] As that audience grew to understand the exigencies of military medicine, it also grew to love the figure associated with improving the quality of care.

Media sources in both countries helped seal Nightingale's unassailable reputation. References to her were common after 1855 in American and British newspapers and magazines. Between 1856 and 1861 alone, some 571 American and 253 British articles about her appeared in diverse venues such as *Godey's Lady's Book, Scientific American, Punch,* and *John Bull.* The *New York Times* alone mentioned her fifty-eight times between 1855 and 1861 and forty more times during the war years. American papers that followed Nightingale ran the gamut from Charleston, South Carolina, to Montpelier, Vermont, and from Cleveland to San Francisco, ensuring broad regional coverage.[25] Many of these articles were biographical in nature, establishing Nightingale as a woman of sterling antecedents and character—and appealing to the upwardly mobile. Patrons could obtain Nightingale's views about infection in the *Milwaukee Daily Sentinel* or consult *Frank Leslie's Illustrated Newspaper* to learn about the lamp-bearing lady's own health. The female operatives of the Lowell, Massachusetts, cotton mills could access Nightingale's opinions about women's dress or portraits of her home; papers catering to African Americans also featured Nightingaleana.[26] Even publications about publications used Nightingale's celebrity to garner advance subscribers. The *American Publishers' Circular and Literary Gazette* of December 26, 1857, included an advertisement for D. Appleton's 1858 gift book, which featured Nightingale as a "world-noted" woman.[27]

Much of the press on Nightingale between the Crimean and Civil wars appeared in 1860, after the publication of *Notes on Nursing.* In addition to two editions of the work published in the United States, one of which became a best-seller, the Danish, French, Swedish, Italians, and Germans could read translations in their native tongues. U.S. reviews appeared in the weekly *Literary Gazette,* the *Saturday Evening Post,* the *Literary Intelligencer, Godey's,* and the *Southern Literary Messenger,* the same organ that had vilified Stowe and *Uncle Tom's Cabin* eight years earlier. *Godey's* influential editor, Sarah Josepha Hale, referred to Nightingale as "a woman of genius" and advised her 150,000 subscribers to "study the work and practice its precepts" because "the benevolence, philanthropy, and excellent sense which have distinguished the career of Miss Nightingale are apparent on every page."[28] Such praise suggests that before the war, Americans identified Nightingale as a model and paragon. Among those who later wrote about their wartime nursing experiences were several who mention having read *Notes on Nursing* in 1860. Women like Hannah Chandler Ropes of Massachusetts, an abolitionist who had moved to Kansas Territory in the 1850s to prevent slaveholders from moving in, received *Notes on Nursing* from a nephew who promoted it as an example of what could be accomplished by women who modeled Nightingale's Christian virtues.[29]

It is no coincidence that American coverage of Nightingale emphasized her religious merits. Her reputation for heroism stoked the evangelical ambitions of the nation throughout the sectional fracas, a symbol of what conservative Protestant womanhood could achieve. In 1857 Byron Sunderland, the minister of Washington's First Presbyterian Church, underscored this point by encouraging his female parishioners to use their moral instincts for the good of the Union. Distinguishing between "true women" and "strong-minded women," he noted that the former, including women like Nightingale, "feareth the Lord," whereas the latter were "infidels" whose radicalism would bar them from participation.[30] Other, less conservative, voices concurred that Nightingale offered a set piece on advancing women's rights through her model of steady pressure and moral suasion. Like Longfellow, Julia Ward Howe made her the object of poetry in the 1850s, five years before "The Battle-Hymn of the Republic" became a Unionist anthem. But instead of heaping praise on the icon, Howe stressed the ordinary, achievable nature of what Nightingale had done and the dangers of icon making: if praise and hyperbole were the only registers reserved for Nightingale, then American women might shrink before the impossibility of attaining her level. Though Howe urged American women to pursue the work of reform, her husband, Samuel Gridley Howe, thought her too bold. Even if he had been engaged to Florence Nightingale, he told his wife, he would have "given her up" as soon as she commenced her career as a "public woman."[31] Reluctant to see women exhibiting themselves in public, Samuel Howe got to the heart of the matter: only those who did not make spectacles of themselves would garner his admiration. In spite of his petulance, the Nightingale icon was so successful precisely because most Americans did not perceive an assault on middle-class virtue. In fact, when compared with Elizabeth Blackwell, a British transplant to America, Nightingale appeared positively tame. Arguing that women should study medicine instead of nursing, Blackwell (who became America's first woman physician) took a more radical line and fumed that "there was a perfect mania amongst [American women] to act Florence Nightingale."[32] Although both resisted evidence of the germ theory and believed that morality was the key to preserving good health, only Nightingale achieved heroine status, applauded for work in keeping with feminine prescriptions for modesty.

American papers continued to lionize her after the war began, but instead of biographical and medical pieces featuring her innovations in ventilation, diet, sanitation, and hygiene, papers waxed editorially about her exemplary conduct. By 1861 Americans already knew a great deal about Nightingale-the-person, having read her words, digested paeans to her virtuous conduct and executive acumen, and glimpsed the lady with the lamp in an array of pictorial images, including those literally depicting her with a lamp.[33] Once women had cause to point to Nightingale-the-example to legitimate the propriety of war nursing, the iconography evolved in more metaphorical directions. It no longer served solely as a repository for tributes and became more of an expository site enunciating women's suitability for military partnership. In the first winter of the war, for example, when thousands of Union and Confederate soldiers were suffering from dysentery, measles, and diphtheria, readers were reminded of Nightingale's 1854 winter of misery by journalists like William Howard Russell, who had reported it for the London *Times* and who covered the Army of the Potomac as a foreign correspondent for the *New York Tribune*.[34] Russell had even noted in a diary entry as early as the first battle of Bull Run that "there were lady nurses in attendance on the patients who followed—let us believe, as I do, out of some higher motive than the mere desire of human praise—the example of Miss Nightingale."[35] Concerned that too many thrill seekers might invade the ranks of female relief workers, Russell offered an injunction that they look instead to his countrywoman. Though his diary was not published until 1863, it is clear that he saw her as an archetype from the start, poised paradoxically like a virgin matriarch before American womanhood, the exponent of some immaculate conception.

American publications used the Crimean War as a comparative reference point to enhance national aspirations. Illuminating the motives and aspirations of citizens who were eager to demonstrate that the young nation could produce its own Florence Nightingale, such accounts were tinged with a competitive zeal that reflected the States' fervent wish to gain the global respect enjoyed by Britain.[36] An 1862 number of *Peterson's Magazine* lauded "the ladies and the hospitals" as competitors to Nightingale's achievement: "When the Crimean war broke out, and Florence Nightingale went to Scutari to nurse the wounded and sick in the hospitals, all England exulted at her name. Nor England alone. In this great republic the pride and glory in her as a woman was not less than in her native land. We knew then, from this outburst of generous admiration, that, if the occasion ever should arise, America would show her Florence Nightingales also."[37] Emphasizing Nightingale *as a woman* to admire, the *Peterson's* editorial implied that it was uncommon for an entire republic to bestow an honor of this magnitude on a member of the weaker sex. In hindsight, it appeared as if Nightingale had always already lit the way forward for women in the American war and that they would show themselves similarly worthy of her patriotic conduct. Nightingale was mentioned so often in stories linking the Crimean conflict with the American one that her name served as a standard by which volunteers could make claims about American ingenuity. Illinois nurse Jane Hoge compared the formation of the U.S. Sanitary Commission in 1861 to Nightingale's work as a justification for women's activism: "The experiment of rendering . . . such assistance had been successfully made in the Crimean War, and had saved thousands of lives, elevated the morale of the army, and made the name of Florence Nightingale not only immortal, but a household word wherever Christianity prevails, as the pioneer of female effort and relief in camps and battlefields."[38] Hoge's reference to Nightingale as a pioneer Americanized this formula, as did delimiting the icon's influence to Christendom.

In some cases, women's relief credentials were cited retrospectively, as if both to demonstrate and to justify to future generations the extent of Nightingale's reach. Mary Livermore's 1889 *My Story of the War* cited the problem of distribution in the Crimea as a cautionary example: "All [supplies] were tied up with the red tape of official formalism until Florence Nightingale, with her corps of trained nurses, & full power to do and command, as well as advise, landed at Scutari, and ordered the storehouses opened. Then want gave place to abundance and through her executive skill and knowledge of nursing and hospital management, the frightful mortality was arrested."[39] Livermore's Nightingale is a fully realized hospital executive instead of the neophyte that her Crimean letters adumbrate. All Nightingale had to do, she believed, was to say the word, and loaves and fishes would appear. Such a perspective had little to do with what actually happened in the Crimean winter of 1855, when British provisioners were thwarted by an autumn hurricane in the Black Sea. In fact, Nightingale's biographers have argued that mortality at the Barracks Hospital in Scutari was far worse than that on the peninsula, near Balaclava and Sebastopol, and that Nightingale, Parliament, and even Queen Victoria did their best to cover these things up.[40] While Livermore's use of this example reprised the heroic iconography of Nightingale, it also justified the bureaucratic measures taken by the U.S. Sanitary Commission to circumvent a reprise of the debacle at Scutari. With exceptionalist fervor, Livermore one-upped the British by remarking at the ingenuity of American benevolence, insinuating the superiority of American know-how. Thus, in one stroke, she marked the continuing vitality of the icon and the legitimacy of the United States as an international player.

The magazine culture of the war era, as Kathleen Diffley has reminded us, both shaped and reflected public attitudes about the war's conduct.[41] Early in the war, both *Frank Leslie's* and *Harper's Weekly* featured images that showed women in active war pursuits both as evidence of their war front commitment and as visual rhetoric to persuade naysayers that they belonged there. A two-page illustrated spread in *Harper's Weekly* of September 6, 1862, depicted "the influence of woman" at soldiers' bedsides, at the washtub, and in sewing circles—Catholic Sisters of Charity and Protestant women alike—in poses that emphasized industry and a common purpose. The accompanying text intoned, "This war of ours has developed scores of Florence Nightingales, whose names no one knows, but whose reward [is] the soldier's gratitude and Heaven's approval." Evident here and elsewhere, American editors used Nightingale's name metaphorically, implying that American women would not be outdone by the Crimean exemplar. Reaching thousands of readers at a time, such content both sanctified women's voluntarism and calmed the fears of those who wanted assurances that their personal privacy would be respected. While foregrounding the personal in its use of the plural possessive ("this war of ours"), *Harper's* also alluded to American anxieties about national survival. The identification of the war as a strictly American phenomenon demonstrated Northerners' political competence on the world stage and urged Parliament to hold off on intervention, despite its inclination to recognize the Confederacy as a sovereign state.[42]

The partisanship implicit in such maneuvering is also visible in the sectional politics relating to the Nightingale icon. While pundits of both sections worked to secure the good opinion of Britain, northern and southern women found themselves in an analogous competition to emulate the World's Nurse, believing that the more successful group could lay greater claim to a feminine ideal that mirrored masculine honor and courage. Enthusiastic in the righteousness of secession, Confederate women were out of the gates first. A teen-age Mississippian, Cordelia Scales, crowed to a friend in the first month of the war that she "[was] going [to nurse soldiers] in the capacity of a Florence Nightingale, [t]hough I would prefer doing a little fighting to dressing wounds."[43] Scales's youthful bravado suggests the richness of her imaginative world, where she could do one better than Nightingale by taking up arms instead of offering them to fallen warriors. In crafting language for a correspondent's benefit, Scales could compress her patriotic ardor into one metonymic sentiment via Nightingale. Ada Bacot of Darlington County, South Carolina, was less certain. The widow and daughter of planters, she had lost her husband and both of her children in the five months before the war and wanted nothing more than to consecrate her grief in the service of Confederate troops. A living embodiment of Augusta Evans Wilson's heroine Macaria, Bacot appealed to officers to help her: "I saw & spoak [*sic*] to Generals McQueen & Harllee. They said, 'I hear you are going to be a Florence Nightingale,' I said yes but was afraid nobody would send for me. Oh! How I wished I could go down with them."[44] More confident than Bacot, Kate Cumming was surprised when obstacles appeared. Within a few days of arriving at Tishomingo Hospital to nurse rebels at Shiloh, she chafed at being held back by surgeons with an overly precious view of feminine delicacy: "I only wish that the doctors would let us try and see what we can do! . . . Is the noble example of Miss Nightingale to pass for nothing?" It was not until a few months later, in October 1862, that she began to comprehend how the image of Nightingale differed from the lived experience of the individual: "Have had one of the most trying days of my life," she wrote. "I wonder if Miss Nightingale had any of the hardships to endure that we have?"[45] Only when Cumming experienced setbacks could she begin to understand challenges that must have beset the flesh-and-blood Nightingale.

Elite southern nurses found in Nightingale an especially apt metaphor for the romance of war, fascinated by rumors of Nightingale's lovelorn status and steeped as they were in the chivalric traditions of the cavaliers. Several of them referred to Tennessean Ella Newsom, who gave up her entire fortune to fund hospitals and was left penniless after the war, as "the Florence Nightingale of the Confederacy"[46]—playing on Nightingale's personal sacrifices, which did not, incidentally, require her to jettison her own fortune. Not only did Kate Cumming's Louisville publisher, John Morton, advertise the sale of her diary in 1866 with the same verbal garland, but the phrase caught on with authors of commemorative volumes after the war, who used it to correct the misperception that "noble women of the North" were the only ones worthy of such comparisons.[47] In 1888, J. B. Lippincott touted Fannie Beers, a nurse-memoirist from Virginia, as yet another "Florence Nightingale of the Confederacy," imitating the postwar advertising strategy that Cumming's publisher had employed.[48] As a Jew, Phoebe Pember, a well-connected widow from Charleston, South Carolina, was reluctant to compare herself to Nightingale, but she recognized the metonymic power of the icon in the domestic chores she assumed as head matron of Chimborazo Hospital Number Two in Richmond: "Nature may not have intended me for a Florence Nightingale, but a kitchen proved my worth. Frying-pans, griddles, stew pans and coffee-pots soon became my household gods."[49] In a moment of studied modesty, Pember readily admitted that nursing was not her forte. Still she equated Nightingale's name with culinary attainments, elevating the homely language of domesticity to more poetic heights—subject matter she would otherwise have resisted as déclassé.

Northern women were no less likely than their Confederate counterparts to force comparisons with Nightingale, especially when the honor was posthumously bestowed. Aunt Lizzie Aiken's funeral oration in 1906 noted that when Illinois soldiers heard the name of this "angel of the hospitals of Memphis and Paducah," they would "raise their hands to the salute, out of respect and love to America's Florence Nightingale."[50] A similar tribute to Margaret Elizabeth Breckinridge, a British immigrant to the United States, seemed an even more fitting testimonial to the icon. Commemorative editors Linus Brockett and Mary Vaughan took linguistic possession of Breckinridge by naturalizing her: "We feel that we may call her, without offense to the other, our Florence Nightingale," once again signifying on the international stage America's arriviste desires as a world power.[51] If iconic associations with Nightingale's name were evident at the start of the war as citizens leveraged support for relief ventures, they were no less evident as Americans began to perceive the war as a prima facie site of commemoration, long before Robert E. Lee handed over his sword at Appomattox.

In the American publishing bonanza that began as early as 1863 with books like Louisa May Alcott's *Hospital Sketches*, memoirists suggest how Nightingale's name became a touchstone for postwar memory—in effect imbricating Civil War narrative history as it was being written. At the start of the war, for example, there was little agreement about the Union army's nursing superintendent Dorothea Dix. Some employees covertly labeled her a "dragon," while others publicly censured her, such as one volunteer who reported to the *New York Times* on December 4, 1861, that Dix did "not live in the hospitals, but in her comfortable house in Washington, and has never nursed a sick soldier, nor folded a shroud over a dead one since the war began."[52] By midwar, however, writers had already begun to assess Dix's legacy more generously through analogy to Nightingale. Alcott noted in 1863, "Daily our Florence Nightingale climbed the steep stairs, stealing a moment from her busy life to watch over the stranger, of whom she was as thoughtfully tender as any mother."[53] Dix's biographer Thomas Brown notes that "at the peak of her career, she had pursued the heroic role of an American Florence Nightingale as carefully as a hunter might stalk a beast in the jungle," suggesting that Dix never garnered the reverence that Nightingale did for her administrative work.[54] The inapplicability of the comparison was reinforced by factors that made Dix unpopular with military superiors and a target of surgical wrath: she was homely, painfully thin, and sixty years old at the time of her service, not in her thirties like the prepossessing Nightingale. If Brown is correct in ascribing to Dix solicitousness where Nightingale's image was concerned, Surgeon General William Hammond put an end to the fond notion by circumventing her authority in 1863.[55] This action rendered Dix useless as the chief of Civil War nursing, and her purview and control as a military regulator waned from this point forward. Her war history, in contrast to Nightingale's, was one of shrinking power.

If memoirists' attempts to resurrect Dix in the image of Nightingale were not successful, they found other, more utilitarian applications. Chicago's Mary Newcomb invoked the icon in *Four Years of Personal Reminiscences of the War* (1893) as she remembered what prompted her to serve. Initially attaching herself to her husband's Illinois regiment, she stayed on to nurse when injuries necessitated his discharge. Although Newcomb had one of the boldest voices among nurse-authors—a confidence born of thirty years of narrative retrospection—she struck a self-effacing pose when mentioning Nightingale: "I was vain enough to suppose that I was the only woman that was willing to be a Florence Nightingale; for women were scarce in the army at that time."[56] Early in the war in the sparsely populated western theater, as Newcomb recalled, Nightingale's name had given her entrée. The increasingly common syntax among relief workers—using an indefinite article before "Nightingale"—indicated both the metonymic force and the extent to which the passage of time had not diminished the iconic impress of the name.

In effect, Nightingale iconography retained its power in postwar memory, regardless of who was invoking it. Commemorative editor Frank Moore praised "women of the war" for "surpass[ing] the charity of Florence Nightingale and repeat[ing] the humility and gentle sacrifices recorded of Mary in the Sacred Scriptures."[57] Volumes such as Moore's and Brockett and Vaughan's subliminally urged women back into domesticity via hagiography: *Woman's Work in the Civil War* (1867) noted of Emily Parsons of Cambridge, Massachusetts, that "her gentle ministrations so faithful and cheering, might well have received the reverent worship bestowed on the shadow of Florence Nightingale so admirably described by Longfellow."[58] The memorable image of the 1850s heroine was still at work in postwar America, despite the reference to Nightingale's shadow—an interpretation of "Santa Filomena" that emphasized, in the conventional gendered idiom, her airy, angelic movements ahead of her grit and substance.

As shapers of middle-class culture, postwar commentators were more inclined to enshrine elite women in the Nightingale regiment than nonelites, but there is evidence that working-class women also earned the distinction in a way that neutralized their social inferiority. Bridget Divers, an Irish immigrant who received lots of attention in the press for "sleeping on the ground like a soldier and enduring hardships like the rest," achieved near-legendary status in the Union during the war. In the customary coding of women used to manual labor, Frank Moore described Divers's face as "browned by exposure and her figure grown athletic by constant exercise and life in the open air. But," he went on, "the heart that beats under her plain cassock is as full of womanly tenderness as that of any princess . . . ; and though her hand is strong and brown, it is as ready to do an act of generous kindness as that of Florence Nightingale herself."[59] Moore's word choice resuscitated Divers's social pedigree by emphasizing her truehearted loyalty and by recognizing her as part of Nightingale's court. Not only was Divers's class inferiority mitigated in such language, but the masculine idiom often invoked to describe women who could not be classified as "ladies" was mollified. This graphic example of female embodiment, where tanned skin, athleticism, and a beating heart were referenced, had the potential to offend polite citizens—or at the very least to mark Divers as irreparably different—but Moore's reference to Nightingale's reputation rescued Divers's femininity and diminished the tarnish on her class identity. Similar language characterized another working-class nurse, Annie Etheridge, of Michigan, whom Maine infantryman Charles Mattocks observed dressing wounds on the field, a place that "few surgeons dared show themselves." Mattocks wrote, "That girl is Anna Etheridge, a second—a more than—Florence Nightingale," demonstrating once again how Americans laid claim through hyperbole to international distinction.[60]

Aside from journalists, soldiers, and editors, relatively few of Nightingale's male contemporaries traded on the utility of her name. The evidence we do have suggests that men regarded Nightingale's apotheosis much as women did: as historically secure and powerful enough to recruit a nation of relief volunteers. But women obviously saw the imagery as more immediate to their own experience; something that allowed them to assert political claims before suffragists won for them a more direct link. We might expect to find something about Nightingale in Walt Whitman's nursing accounts, *Specimen Days* and *Memoranda during the War,* but these works are strangely silent on the subject. Given Whitman's predilection for universalizing the transformations of war through the common, the uncelebrated, and the homosocial, Nightingale's absence from his pages may not be so surprising. Still, soldiers were more likely to mention Nightingale than surgeons. In more than thirty surgical narratives of the war, I found no reference to Nightingale at all. If this absence looks puzzling, given that both the Union and the Confederate surgeons general had utilized Nightingale's plan for pavilion-style hospitals, one need only consider that surgeons were engaged in raising their own professional sights and that their service was constantly under the scrutiny of military superiors and the public. They were not in search of a figure that connoted domesticity, sacrifice, or religiosity. More to the point, Nightingale's example had greatest utility for women themselves, who wanted to tap into the rich trove of qualities associated with the icon without seeming to claim too much. If the icon conferred authority and female independence, it also presented these qualities in an evangelically inflected haze of feminine approbation.

The enormous influence of Nightingale's reputation in America was made possible by timely transatlantic media coverage and the advent of a civil war following so closely on the heels of the Crimean War. Nightingale's belief that women ought to be strong moral centers in hospital work was something American women embraced wholeheartedly as this supported their sense of themselves as religiously ordained to perform relief work. Moral guardianship of hospitals was also consistent with the maternal role that women were expected to play in their homes. This idea became a flashpoint in the professionalization of nursing in both Britain and the United States, as nursing leaders insisted that students gain competency in scientific practice and that they move away from domestic work to gain the respect of medical professionals.[61] The development of nurse training schools in the United States after 1870 is characterized by a struggle between "sympathy and science"—what Gina Morantz-Sanchez has defined as the terms that confounded women pursuing medical careers in the nineteenth century but that apply just as persuasively to the dilemmas inherent in the professionalization of nursing. As nursing leaders tried to reverse an unearned public perception of nurses as slatternly by holding their students to the highest ethical and moral standards, they sometimes gave short shrift to the scientific knowledge that could garner for student nurses the esteemed title of "the physician's hand."[62] The wedge between character and competency has defined the history of American nursing and is especially visible in the nursing narratives of the late nineteenth and early twentieth centuries. More recently, books like Margarete Sandelowski's *Devices and Desires* (2000), which charts the increasing interface between nurses and machines to deliver care, have reflected the broader medical impetus to master scientific practice ahead of bedside manner.

The assertion of Mary Mohl, in 1850, with which this essay begins, that Florence herself was like an inscrutable language foreshadows the process by which Nightingale's interpreters would continue to dig for clues to her motives, to peel away the layers of sediment that constructed the icon. The linguistic application of Nightingale's name in war narratives shows how the icon assisted in underwriting a new institutional concept at a time of national crisis but before nursing was universally acknowledged as appropriate work for the middle class. Women used the Nightingale name not only to gain entry to a relief world but to make claims about individual expertise in the immediate postwar years, claims that implicitly argued for women's greater participation in the polity. Americans exploited Nightingale's image, contributing to her apotheosis, because it helped them gain civilian support for a war that had terrible costs and might have been averted. It was good propaganda. Also, it gave the neophyte nursing community a foundation on which to begin constructing a professional identity. Civil War nurses and relief workers did not consciously see themselves as inaugurating a new profession because the work they did in this military context was familiar to them. However, the medical culture they created, which certainly evolved *because* of Nightingale's professional mandate, is still visible in nursing today.

Nightingale's name became a rallying cry for women, whose entrance into American military circles was initially questioned, but it also became the expressive shorthand by which military doubters could ultimately enact détente with those whose work was central, in its restoration of sick and wounded bodies, to the political objectives of the Union and the Confederacy. An iconic presence in the media culture of the mid-nineteenth century, the name also had staying power, giving memoirists the opportunity to reproduce its meanings for readers well into the twentieth century. Anyone who doubts the memorial longevity of Nightingale's image need only consider the Nightingale memorabilia available on eBay today: Turkish and Guinean stamps embossed with her profile, children's books and nurse costumes, figurines from Royal Doulton, and an 1887 Bible with Nightingale's signature on sale for $7,777.[63] Britons and international visitors to London can visit the Florence Nightingale Museum, which has made it a point to archive Nightingale's life and artifacts but which has also sought to make sense of the Nightingale legacy in terms both mythic and poetic. Such institutionalized memory suggests that the World's Nurse will not be soon forgotten.

NOTES

1. For their helpful suggestions on this essay, I wish to thank Kathleen Diffley, Annemarie Rafferty, Ruth Richardson, Elizabeth Duquette, Natasha McEnroe, and Lyn McDonald. The epigraph is quoted in Mark Bostridge, *Florence Nightingale: The Woman and Her Legend* (London: Viking, 2008), iii.

2. See, for example, Hugh Small, *Florence Nightingale, Avenging Angel* (New York: St. Martin's, 1998), 1; and Bostridge, *Florence Nightingale*, 20.

3. Lytton Strachey depicted the cause of Nightingale's post-Crimean collapse as neurosis. See *Eminent Victorians: Eminent Victorians: Cardinal Manning, Dr. Arnold, Florence Nightingale, General Gordon* (New York: Modern Library, 1999 [1918]).

4. Jane Addams, *Twenty Years at Hull-House. With Biographical Notes* (New York: Macmillan, 1912), 65. "The Snare of Preparation," the title of "Chapter 4," befell well-educated women whose societies had no channel for their talents.

5. Siobhan Nelson, *Say Little, Do Much: Nurses, Nuns, and Hospitals in the Nineteenth Century* (Philadelphia: University of Pennsylvania Press, 2001), 56, 60–63.

6. Small, *Avenging Angel*, 54.

7. Frances Clarke, "'Let All Nations See': Civil War Nationalism and the Memorialization of Wartime Voluntarism," *Civil War History* 52, no.1 (2006): 66–93.

8. See *Medical and Surgical History of the Civil War*, vol. 1 (Philadelphia: Broadfoot, 1990–92); and George W. Adams, *Doctors in Blue: The Medical History of the Union Army in the Civil War* (New York: Henry Schuman, 1952), 4, 26.

9. For a discussion of national resistance to women's pursuit of relief work, see my *Women at the Front: Hospital Workers in Civil War America* (Chapel Hill: University of North Carolina Press, 2004), chap. 2. Alice Fahs observes a similar resistance in the popular literature of the day in *The Imagined Civil War: Popular Literature of the North and South, 1861–1865* (Chapel Hill: University of North Carolina Press, 2001), 140.

10. See Florence Nightingale, *Notes on Nursing: What It Is and What It Is Not* (Mineola, N.Y.: Dover, 1969), 41.

11. British and American periodicals published images of hospital settings in the Crimea, as well as of Nightingale. An elegant engraving by Jerry Barrett, completed in 1856 and titled "The Mission of Mercy: Florence Nightingale Receiving the Sick and Wounded of Scutari," was widely reproduced on both sides of the Atlantic. Bostridge notes that by May 1855, numerous engravings of Nightingale's image were circulating. See *Florence Nightingale*, 265.

12. See, for example, Barbara Cutter, *Domestic Devils, Battlefield Angels: The Radicalism of American Womanhood, 1830–1865* (DeKalb, Ill.: Northern Illinois University Press, 2003), 160.

13. Lucy Riall, *Garibaldi: Invention of a Hero* (New Haven: Yale University Press, 2007).

14. Cutter, *Domestic Devils, Battlefield Angels*, 160.

15. See, for example, "The U.S. Sanitary Commission," *All the Year Round* 1, no. 295 (December 17, 1864): 439–43; and "War Charities, National and International," *Good Words* 6 (January 1865): 213–20.

16. Bostridge, *Florence Nightingale,* xxii. Mary Poovey has made a similar point, observing that once Nightingale's celebrity was established, there was little she could do to control public perception. See Poovey, *Uneven Developments: The Ideological Work of Gender in Mid-Victorian England* (Chicago: University of Chicago Press, 1988), chap. 6.

17. Edgerton notes the reportage of Russell, as well as that of E. L. Godkin and Thomas Chenery, from Constantinople. See Robert B. Edgerton, *Death or Glory: The Legacy of the Crimean War* (Boulder, Colo.: Westview Press, 1999), 148; and Marjorie Barstow Greenbie, *Lincoln's Daughters of Mercy* (New York: G. P. Putman's Sons, 1944), 46–47.

18. Bostridge, *Florence Nightingale,* 260, 266, 268.

19. Greenbie, *Lincoln's Daughters of Mercy,* 47.

20. Nina Silber regards the war as prompting an increase in Northern women's civic participation and awareness through more active forms of conduct. See Silber, *Daughters of the Union: Northern Women Fight the Civil War* (Cambridge, Mass.: Harvard University Press, 2005), 9–13, 39–40.

21. Sarah Chauncey Woolsey to Georgeanna Woolsey Bacon, *Letters of a Family during the War for the Union,* ed. Georgeanna Woolsey Bacon and Eliza Woolsey Howland (New Haven, Conn.: Tuttle, Morehouse & Taylor, 1899), 1: 53. The second quotation refers to Maria Hall, a four-year nursing veteran. See Frank Moore, *Women of the War: Their Heroism and Self-Sacrifice* (Hartford: S. S. Scranton, 1866), 398; and Mary Boykin Chesnut, *A Diary from Dixie,* ed. Myrta Lockett Avery (New York: D. Appleton, 1905), 22.

22. See Wormeley letter of May 28, 1862, in *The Other Side of War with the Army of the Potomac* (Boston: Ticknor, 1889), 85; and Kate Cumming Collection, Alabama Department of Archives and History (hereafter ADAH), Montgomery, Ala.

23. See, for example, Eliza P. Gurney's mention of a woman who "is a perfect Florence Nightingale" in a letter of July 1855 in *Memoir and Correspondence of Eliza P. Gurney,* ed. Richard F. Mott (Philadelphia: J. B. Lippincott, 1884), 247. A British publication even began with a story that claimed Nightingale "is now a household name." See "Something of What Florence Nightingale Has Done and Is Doing," *St. James's Magazine* (UK), April 1861, 1.

24. Frances Clarke, *War Stories: Suffering and Sacrifice in the Civil War North* (Chicago: University of Chicago Press, 2011), 54–55.

25. These figures were tabulated by using "Florence Nightingale" as a search term in the following databases: Proquest Historical Newspapers, 19th-Century US Newspapers (Gale), Historical New York Times (Proquest), 19th-Century UK Periodicals (Gale), and 19th-Century British Library Newspapers (Gale).

26. See, for example, *Littell's Living Age,* February 17, 1866, 8, 560; *Milwaukee Daily Sentinel,* March 26, 1860, column B; *Frank Leslie's Illustrated Newspaper,* August 27, 1859, 159, column C; and the *Lowell Daily Citizen and News* (Massachusetts), February 14, 1860, column B, and May 15, 1860, column F. See Cutter, *Domestic Devils, Battlefield Angels,* 72, for information about black press coverage of Nightingale.

27. *American Publishers' Circular and Literary Gazette,* December 26, 1857, 3, 52.

28. For translations of *Notes,* see Bostridge, *Florence Nightingale,* 361. See also *Godey's,* "Florence Nightingale's Book," September 1860, 61; and Kathleen Diffley, ed.,

To Live and Die: Collected Stories of the Civil War, 1861–1876 (Durham: Duke University Press, 2002), 10.

29. Hannah L. Ropes, *Civil War Nurse: The Diary and Letters of Hannah L. Ropes*, ed. John R. Brumgardt (Knoxville: University of Tennessee Press, 1980), 29.

30. Quoted in Cutter, *Domestic Devils, Battlefield Angels*, 126–27.

31. Cutter, *Domestic Devils, Battlefield Angels*, 160–61. Samuel Howe material quoted in Marilyn Mayer Culpepper, *Trials and Triumphs: The Women of the American Civil War* (East Lansing: Michigan State University Press, 1991), 316.

32. Julia Boyd offers this elegant comparison in "The Art of Medicine: Florence Nightingale and Elizabeth Blackwell" in *Lancet* 373 (May 2, 2009): 4–5. She goes on to point out the remarkable similarities between the two women.

33. See the February 24, 1855, rendering of Nightingale in the *Illustrated London News*.

34. See Amanda Foreman, *A World on Fire: An Epic History of Two Nations Divided* (London: Penguin, 2010). 72. Coincidentally, Russell (1820–1907) was a close contemporary of Nightingale (1820–1910).

35. William Howard Russell, *My Diary North and South* (London: Burnham, 1863), 408.

36. Clarke, "'Let All Nations See.'"

37. *Peterson's Magazine*, September 1862.

38. Jane Hoge, *The Boys in Blue: Or, Heroes of the Rank and File* (New York: E. B. Treat, 1867). 60.

39. Mary A. Livermore, *My Story of the War: A Woman's Narrative of Four Years Personal Experience* (Hartford, Conn.: Worthington, 1889), 127–28.

40. See, for example, Small, *Avenging Angel*, 2–3.

41. Diffley, *To Live and Die*, 1–24.

42. See Howard Jones, *The Union in Peril: The Crisis over British Intervention in the Civil War* (Lincoln: University of Nebraska Press, 1992), 1–9; and Brent E. Kinser, *The American Civil War in the Shaping of British Democracy* (London: Ashgate, 2011), 1–12.

43. Cordelia Scales to Loulie, May 1861, Mississippi Department of Archives and History, Jackson.

44. Ada Bacot, *A Confederate Nurse: The Diary of Ada W. Bacot*, ed. Jean V. Berlin (Columbia: University of South Carolina Press, 1994), 25 (entry for January 8, 1861).

45. Cumming, *A Journal of Hospital Life*, April 9, 1862, October 12, 1862. Apparently, she had not read Harriet Martineau's 1859 book on the subject.

46. See, for example, Jane Stuart Woolsey, *Hospital Days* (New York: Van Nostrand, 1868).

47. See John L. Underwood, *The Women of the Confederacy* (New York: Neale, 1906). The phrase plays on the title of Sylvia Dannett's book about Northern military nurses, *Noble Women of the North* (New York: Thomas Yoseloff, 1959).

48. See Cumming Collection, ADAH; and Fannie A. Beers, *Memories: A Record of Personal Experience and Adventure during Four Years of War* (Philadelphia: J. B. Lippincott, 1888), 336.

49. Phoebe Yates Pember, *A Southern Woman's Story: Life in Confederate Richmond*, ed. Bell I. Wiley (Jackson, Tenn.: McCowatMercer, 1959), 6.

50. Frank Atherton, "Memorial, Aunt Lizzie Aiken, with Sketch of Her Life, Funeral Service, Tributes, and Resolutions," n.p., 1906.

51. Linus P. Brockett and Mary C. Vaughan, *Woman's Work in the Civil War: A Record of Heroism, Patriotism, and Patience* (Philadelphia: Zeigler, McCurdy, 1867), 188–89. Even the book's table of contents refers to Breckinridge as "The American Florence Nightingale."

52. Quoted in Thomas Brown, *Dorothea Dix, New England Reformer* (Cambridge, Mass.: Harvard University Press, 1998), 303. Nurse Cornelia Hancock was similarly critical, noting in August 1863 that Dix "does not work at all, and her nurses are being superseded very fast." See Cornelia Hancock, *South after Gettysburg: Letters of Cornelia Hancock from the Army of the Potomac, 1863–1865*, ed. Henrietta Stratton Jaquette (Philadelphia: University of Pennsylvania Press, 1937), 17.

53. Alcott, *Hospital Sketches and Fireside Stories* (Boston: Roberts Brothers, 1871), 71.

54. Brown, *Dorothea Dix*, 322.

55. Order 351, issued by the Surgeon General's Office in October 1863, gave staff surgeons the power to appoint their own nurses, rendering Dix's authority ineffectual.

56. Mary Newcomb, *Four Years of Personal Reminiscences of the War* (Chicago: H. S. Mills, 1893), 19.

57. Moore, *Women of the War*, 17–18.

58. Brockett and Vaughan, *Woman's Work in the Civil War*, 278.

59. Moore, *Women of the War*, 112.

60. Philip N. Racine, ed., *Unspoiled Heart: The Journal of Charles Mattocks of the 17th Maine* (Knoxville: University of Tennessee Press, 1994), 30.

61. See Patricia D'Antonio, *American Nursing: A History of Knowledge, Authority, and the Meaning of Work* (Baltimore: The Johns Hopkins University Press, 2010).

62. Barbara Melosh, *The Physician's Hand: Work, Culture, and Conflict in American Nursing* (Philadelphia: Temple University Press, 1982).

63. http://www.ebay.com (accessed May 31, 2011).

LESLEY MARX

Race, Romance, and "The spectacle of unknowing" in *Gone with the Wind*

A South African Response

A young girl who will one day become my mother plays on the pavement in front of her local cinema in the erstwhile mining town of Springs several miles east of Johannesburg, looks up and sees a poster of a "handsome man" holding a "beautiful woman" in "the most romantic pose."[1] The little girl cannot stop looking at it, but, alas, there is an age restriction—no one under the age of twelve may see the film—and so she has to wait for its re-release. She will see it in 1948 at the Metro Cinema in Johannesburg, "sitting upstairs in the front row, so that we could have a perfect view." She continues: "It was the most amazing experience of my young life. Just sitting there, drinking in every minute of this magnificent spectacle." Twenty years after my mother's epiphany, I had my turn. Having grown up with movie-struck parents, who loved acting out their favorite scenes, I felt I already had an intimate knowledge of *Gone with the Wind*. I knew all about Big Sam asserting his authority over his fellow slave ("I'se the foreman, I'se the one who says when it's quittin' time at Tara. Quittin' tiiiime!") or over the horse that must carry Scarlett away from her would-be rapist: "Hoss, make tracks!" I knew of Mammy disapprovingly telling Rhett that Scarlett was indeed going to come downstairs to see him after Frank Kennedy's death: "I don't know why she's a-comin', but she's a-comin'." And of course I knew that Scarlett would never go hungry again, that tomorrow is another day, and that Rhett doesn't give a damn.[2]

The 1967 re-release was a gala event (it reached South Africa in 1968). My mother still has the glossy, generously illustrated program announcing the technical enhancements to this version of the film: "'Gone with the Wind' is being shown for the first time in wide-screen projection. The original 35mm negative has been converted to 70mm through the wizardry of technicians at the MGM studio in Culver City. . . . New color processes were applied to 'enliven' the hues of the original film and technicians isolated portions of the soundtrack to provide a six-track stereophonic rendition. The result is the best presentation of 'Gone with the Wind' in its illustrious history."[3]

In 2004 a four-disc collector's edition was released with several extra features tailored to nostalgia, so duplicating the appeal of the narrative itself. Five years later, to commemorate its seventieth anniversary, the film was once again released in high definition Blu-ray format with yet more extras, many focusing on technical accomplishments. The hoopla around the film is of a piece with the epic genre to which it subscribes. Vivian Sobchack has written of the way in which the "surge and splendor" of the Hollywood historical epic engages in a series of repetitions: the much-vaunted labor behind the making of the film mimics the vast scope of the narrative being represented; the weighty tones of the voiceover or, in the case of *Gone with the Wind,* the written prologue and intertitles, call attention to the film's significance as much as to that of its content; the "extended duration" and "expanded space" of the genre mimic the sense of extension and expansion of the "historical field" that it dramatizes.[4] All these aspects of excess are also to be felt on the body of the spectator. Amusingly, she describes how "writing on the body of the model American spectator/consumer, the Hollywood historical epic is *transcoding* the culture's emphasis on literalism and materialism into specific carnal terms, reprinting its version of History not only for posterity but also on our posteriors. This is, philosophically and carnally, a profound form of repetition."[5]

What, though, of the non-American spectator? Sobchack argues that the Hollywood epic was concerned with offering a different inscription of its (American) spectators into history from that to which academic history aspires: where the latter is the "objectification and projection of *ourselves-now* as *others-then,* the expansive and transparent work of Hollywood's epic histories seems to be the subjectification and projection of *ourselves-now* as *we-then.*"[6] But for the starstruck teenager watching the film thousands of miles away in another country and another culture, the attraction lies in the adventure of living through "others-then." A nostalgia for (American) otherness marked my youth; a nostalgia for the films of yesteryear marked my upbringing ("they don't make them the way they used to"). A powerful seduction by classical Hollywood thus informed both my and my parents' initial response to *Gone with the Wind.* We were entranced by the spectacle of otherness.

As seen above, I am framing my exploration of *Gone with the Wind* by means of a personal narrative that takes its cue especially from Helen Taylor and Molly Haskell's work on the novel and the film. The narrative here is a specifically South African one that emerges out of one particular set of circumstances that are nevertheless not unique and that enable me to reach into a wider range of narratives that dramatize correspondences between the history and the fictions of the American South and those of South Africa: crucially, racism and the "spectacle of unknowing" that have mediated white consciousness in both cultures; the consequences, for the black community, of the American Civil War and the Anglo-Boer War; the mythologizing of both wars in the twentieth century; the double-edged effect of Mammy in the film version of *Gone with the Wind* and her resonance with South Africa's myths of the Mammy figure; the regressive agrarian dream common to both southern and Afrikaner cultures; and, finally, the shifting relationship among knowledge, agency, desire, and affect.

What is apparent from this account is how divorced our appreciation of the film was from the social and political tumult going on around us. While the lines of the film's slaves were frequently quoted as among the best in the film, the realities of slavery were elided by our unquestioning acceptance of the film's version of the antebellum South and the power of the love story, an acceptance at one with our immersion in a certain, limited view of life in South Africa. What irony that my mother saw the film in the same year that the National Party came to power and that I saw it at the end of a decade of violent escalation of apartheid, starting with the withdrawal of the country from the Commonwealth as the nationalist government under Hendrik Verwoerd, the so-called architect of apartheid, declared the country a Republic. That decade saw the Sharpeville Massacre, the imprisonment of Nelson Mandela, the assassination of Verwoerd—as well as the rise of the counterculture, the flower children, the Beatles, the hippies who hung out at the Dunka Donout on Pretorius Street in Hillbrow. My younger brother saw the film only a year after military conscription was introduced, resulting in his generation being embroiled in a decades-long, misbegotten "Border War," an expression of mounting paranoia on the part of the government, that, while expressed in terms of anticommunism, was profoundly racially inflected.

But we lived in middle-class white suburbs and went to middle-class white schools where the most pressing antagonisms and sense of difference were generated not by white and black but by English and Afrikaans, where South African history lessons repetitively started with the Great Trek and ended with the Anglo-Boer War. Classes in twentieth-century history were superficial surveys of the two World Wars, Europe and the United States, with some nineteenth-century European history thrown in. Only in my final year of high school (and my sixth school) did I encounter a superb history teacher who flouted the rules of the syllabus and encouraged us to explore farther afield and to see history as an arena for debate and interpretation rather than as a list of dates. This was also the year I "discovered" America and became enthralled by a history that seemed so much more varied than the story of "The Great Trek to the Boer War" with which I'd been inundated. That there were intriguing connections between the South African history I knew and the American history I was reading about would become more obvious over time, notably the westward expansion of the American settlers at the expense of the indigenous inhabitants, the racism of the South, and the imbrication of South Africa's "Border War" with the war in Vietnam (all sources for many white South Africans of indignation at American critiques of apartheid: "look at what they did to the Indians and the slaves; see how they abandoned us in Angola during the anticommunist struggle").

I had spent only my final high-school year in Cape Town and had not been part of the growing politicization of the students at that particular school. At the end of the year, I won a prize for Afrikaans and disappointed my Afrikaans teacher by choosing a hardback copy of *Gone with the Wind* instead of the book everyone else seemed to be choosing: André Brink's second novel *Kennis van die Aand* (translated as *Looking on Darkness,* although the title means literally "knowledge of the evening").[7] The urgency of getting hold of Brink's novel before it was banned was palpable among my schoolmates. Even though I was under the joint spell of nineteenth-century literature and classical Hollywood, I became aware, rather like Dylan's Mr. Jones, that there was something happening, even if I didn't quite know what it was.

Arriving to study English and Afrikaans literature and drama at a white university that prided itself on being in the vanguard of liberal revolt against apartheid, I was soon provided with evidence of the ways in which lives other than those of the white middle class were lived in South Africa. The Afrikaans curriculum introduced me to sophisticated and subversive work that I never knew existed. In Drama, I learnt about Athol Fugard and Adam Small. In English, there was a palace revolution against the emphasis in the syllabus on the British canon. Moreover, I shared classes and bus rides home with Coloured students. Ironically, the only buses that rode past the suburb we lived in were the Coloured buses, so apartheid had to be compromised. Through the eighties, as a young teacher, I had to make decisions about how to respond to politically motivated class boycotts: would I cancel the class? Would I teach it in spite of the boycott (the rationalization was that one had to give the students something to boycott), or would I teach the class but use the opportunity to open up discussion about the issues at stake?[8]

During these years, my affection for the film *Gone with the Wind* did not abate, although my growing interest in southern literature, especially Faulkner, alerted me to its historical inaccuracies. But still the film enraptured because of its visual magnificence and because of Scarlett and Rhett. Like my mother, I was captivated by the love story and the spectacle. I felt, with my mother, that the book did not live up to the film, largely at that time because of its prolixity. It was decades after leaving high school before I read it again in preparation for a series of public lectures on film adaptation. This time it was hard labor to wade through its 1,042 pages, mostly because I was acutely aware of how awful the racism of the book is. In Patricia Yaeger's felicitous description, this is "a story that drives through slavery and Reconstruction like the Energizer bunny—its racism just keeps going and going."[9] Focusing critical attention on Mitchell's novel rather than the film, Yaeger writes of the "unthought unknown . . . a residue of childhood imprinting us with expectations about the way the world will shape itself (or fail to shape itself) about us. These early experiences are lodged in the sensorium but not available to consciousness—hence known but unthought or unacknowledged."[10] She develops this concept in an analysis of the novel, which she sees playing out a double misrecognition: "the romantic structure that allows Scarlett to make her way to one recognition (the discovery of her own 'erotic truth') is also a structure primed to ward off another set of political recognitions about race as the very ground that makes Scarlett's infatuation with whiteness possible. In other words, misrecognition is not just the heroine's fatal flaw but the author's problem as well."[11]

Yaeger concludes that "*Gone with the Wind* offers an unwitting anatomy of *the spectacle of unknowing* built into the very structures of white southern life."[12] She sees this enthrallment to the spectacle of unknowing playing itself out in real-life experiences as well. She gives the example of southern white citizens of the 1920s being shocked at discovering that "municipal services and paved roads did not extend to the black sections of town."[13] Yaeger's unequivocal judgment of these citizens is evident as she writes of a "deliberate *sequestration* of knowledge" by those who "drive maids home, ride through this section of town to get to church or go to the country," yet "*act as if* they are blind to the conditions they see all the time" (my emphasis).[14]

What if one is dealing with apartheid geography where white citizens never need to drive anywhere outside their white domain? Their pervasive unknowing may still be a cause for astonishment. Whether the bearers of such unknowing are to be seen as agents in their ignorance is a trickier matter. There are, indeed, critics even of Mitchell who have used kinder language in acknowledging her misrecognitions. Helen Taylor quotes Mitchell on her use of the Klan: "As I had not written anything about the Klan which is not common knowledge to every Southerner, I had done no research on it." Taylor argues that this "confidence in her knowledge" may be "startling," but it reveals the extent to which she "had accepted as gospel the Wilson-Rhodes-Dunning version of Reconstruction and the Klan's development, and drew deeply on that accepted, 'common-sense' version of racial history."[15] Writing from an intimate knowledge of what it meant to grow up in the South, Molly Haskell notes how in thrall Mitchell was to her parents "and lined up behind them were a phalanx of 'givens' one didn't challenge or question, such as the existence of God or the lawfulness of racial discrimination, the superiority of man over woman, white over black."[16] Even Bruce Chadwick, in his strong critique of the film, comments: "It wasn't that Margaret

Mitchell wanted to nostalgically glorify the Old South . . . it was that she could not help doing so."[17] Summarizing her conflicting attitudes, Thomas Cripps notes how she wanted at once to please southern traditionalists but to avoid replicating Uncle Remus; she admired the critical exploration of W. J. Cash while gushing over Thomas Dixon's work; she cared deeply about her black servants but accepted the Ku Klux Klan as a "historic necessity."[18] She remained, writes Cripps, "ever Southern and, despite her literary celebrity, yearned to be accepted by Southern readers. As one of her characters says: 'Miss Scarlett, tain' gwine to do you no good to stan' high wid de Yankees ef yo' own folks doan' 'prove of you.'"[19] Finally, Ralph McGill speculates that, "[h]ad she lived, she might . . . have developed new attitudes. But she was always the unreconstructed Southerner, with a fierce pride in, and loyalty to, the old code that a Southern white person scrupulously 'looked after' servants and decent colored persons in distress."[20] While white South Africa was always a fractured entity, the section of it from which I came espoused this notion of "benign paternalism," a phrase Haskell applies to "the enlightened scions of the Old South," from which Mitchell and her novel's lead characters took their cue. One instance of this benign paternalism relates to how we name race. Where Mitchell's preferred term for blacks was "darkies,"[21] we were encouraged as children to be respectful of blacks and always call them "natives," which indeed they were, native to the country, in ways that our mixed Scottish-English-French-Dutch-German-Jewish roots could not claim. (The abusive alternatives were "nigger" in the South or "kaffir" in South Africa, a term we invariably associated with the radical racists, the unreconstructed Boers).

The difficult interweaving of love, condescension, and fear that often marked attitudes of white South Africans towards their black countrymen and -women is only one echo of the southern complex identified by critics of Margaret Mitchell's brand of southern-ness. Beyond that link lie the commonalities of a history of repression culminating in war, the Civil War in the United States and the Anglo-Boer War in South Africa. While the differences of context between these two wars must be acknowledged, parallels in their outcomes have been explored by George Fredrickson in his pioneering study of white supremacy (1981)[22] and, later, by Anthony Marx in his 1998 study, *Making Race and Nation: A Comparison of the United States, South Africa and Brazil.* In brief, the key consideration for both victors—the North in the case of the Civil War and Britain in the case of the Anglo-Boer War—was to strengthen white unity, between the North and the South in the case of the former and between "Boer and Brit" in the case of the latter. So the eighth clause in the Peace of Vereeniging reads: "The question of granting the Franchise to the Natives will not be decided until after the introduction of Self-Government."[23] White unity was proposed at the expense of political recognition for the black population. In Marx's words: "Appeasing the South to reaffirm stability was of greater importance than black rights. The North had tried to achieve both its aims; when it tired of the effort, it turned its attention to more pressing matters than that of the black minority. Like the British victors in the Boer War two generations later, the North faced the strategic imperative to abandon its commitment to blacks in favor of encouraging white reconciliation and peace. And, as in South Africa, pervasive racial prejudice reinforced this impetus."[24]

In his recent update on the Anglo-Boer War, Bill Nasson remarks on the very precise analogies drawn by the British with the American Civil War: "Winston Churchill welcomed the day 'when we can take the Boers by the hand and say as Grant did to the Confederates at Appomattox 'Go back and plough your fields.'"[25] Marx outlines the differences between the two cases: where the rule in South Africa was by a white minority feeling threatened by the black majority as well as urged on by white racism, apartheid policies grew apace and in a linear determination to strangle black social and political aspirations. In the United States, "only after Radical Reconstruction further inflamed regional tensions, thereby undermining the prospect of unified white loyalty to the nation-state, would the salve of racial domination be applied—not by central authority weakened by the failed reform experiment, but by resurgent local authorities. Race-making and nation-state consolidation remained linked, but the United States embraced this linkage more fitfully."[26] Even with a more centralized government during the Depression and the receding of states' rights, Marx argues, the disproportionate suffering of blacks failed to receive the attention it needed because of the influence of party politics: Roosevelt needed the support of southern Democrats to pass the New Deal.[27]

At the same time that racial discrimination continued to blight the lives of southern blacks, white southerners were reinventing their past in ways that entrenched the myth of the Lost Cause, what Catherine Clinton calls "a remembrance of things imagined,"[28] a lost agrarian dream, an Eden, as Louis Rubin Jr. puts it, where "[t]here is no evil . . . it comes from outside with Sherman's army."[29] He continues: "Miss Mitchell liked to think of herself as a historical realist, but when it came to antebellum life she was as whole-souled a perpetuator of the plantation myth as Thomas Nelson Page or Stark Young at their most eulogistic."[30] Comparing Mitchell with Page and Young may be accurate, if a cruel cut, given her express desire not to reproduce the genre of southern writing epitomized by these writers. Darden Asbury Pyron quotes her expression of embarrassment at finding herself "included among those writers who picture the South as a land of white columned mansions whose wealthy owners had thousands of slaves and drank thousands of juleps,"[31] and yet she gives us Ashley Wilkes taking his courage from the memory of Twelve Oaks, replete with images of moonlight, magnolias, climbing roses, and "the darkies coming home across the fields at dusk, tired and singing and ready for supper."[32] Patricia Yaeger remarks of this passage how the "African Americans become atmosphere,"[33] but this was in keeping with the national trend toward rehabilitating the antebellum and wartime South in the twenties and thirties, absolving it of slavery. Bruce Chadwick enumerates the several commemorative events that helped to restore white southern pride: a tribute to Robert E. Lee by the American Bar and a vote of funds by Congress to print a commemorative coin with Lee's and Stonewall Jackson's images in 1924. The following year, Congress voted to restore Lee's mansion, and in 1928 "President Calvin Coolidge sent the U.S. Marine Corps band to entertain crowds gathered at several national reunions of Confederate veterans groups," while two years later headstones were allowed to be placed on the graves of Confederate veterans. At the same time, there was a rush of publications on key Confederate heroes.[34] And underpinning these gestures of reconciliation was the work of the women in the years after the surrender of the South. Catherine Clinton writes, in *Tara Revisited: Women, War and the Plantation Legend,* of the significance of the formation of the United Daughters of the Confederacy, which raised funds for commemorative causes, influenced how southern history was taught by funding libraries, essay contests, and college scholarships and by establishing the Children of the Confederacy, whose members were taught what Richard Harwell wittily describes as "an unbiased history of the war from the Southern point of view."[35] The UDC also campaigned for the renaming of the conflict: not the "Civil War" but "The War between the States."[36]

One might argue that a similar process of wresting myths of heroism from defeat was being played out in South Africa, notably through the embryonic film culture. Deployed in the figuring of select moments of Afrikaner history as nationalistic myth, the film *De Voortrekkers* (1916) is a landmark in South African film history.[37] The film's manifest content may have been the Great Trek, but its latent content was surely the epic memorializing of the Afrikaans heroes of the Anglo-Boer War. Made with British backing, the film had to shape this history in ways that would not destabilize the uneasy rapprochement between English and Afrikaans. Thus, the forging of the new nation is projected back in time where the conflict is between black and white.[38] The crisis moment is the betrayal and murder of the Boer hero Piet Retief by the savage Zulu chief Dingaan, a martyrdom avenged by the outnumbered but well-armed Boers at the Battle of Blood River. Edwin Hees has offered an intriguing comparison of the film with Griffith's *Birth of a Nation,* noting, however, that where the latter became increasingly marginalized, "*De Voortrekkers* and its ideology were gradually incorporated into the ideals of the group that was to dominate South African political history for much of the twentieth century."[39] The more brazenly nationalistic *Bou van 'n Nasie,* released in 1938 as part of the centenary celebrations of the Great Trek, abandoned all pretense at an improved relationship between English and

Afrikaans.[40] This was, quite unambiguously, a film about the building of an Afrikaans nation (made after *The Birth of a Nation* had reached South Africa, apparently, in 1931).[41] The film ends with an abbreviated montage of the Anglo-Boer War, followed by the heavy-handed symbolism of a woman sowing seeds, suggesting an agrarian dream of nation similar to the dream propagated by southern revivalists.

The elision of racial realities in favor of a sanctification of (white) loss in both Afrikaans films (and in the renovation narratives of the South) bears a fugitive relationship to the way in which the pariah status and the loss of power of the Afrikaner-led apartheid government are potentially being rehabilitated even now through a recovery of the heroism of the Anglo-Boer War. Bill Nasson's new history of the Anglo-Boer War is especially valuable for the analysis of how the war has been remembered during the twentieth century and the careful *toenadering* [rapprochement] between the ANC and the Afrikaners, culminating in the 1999 centenary commemorative events that saw the war as both part of a common history of resistance to European imperialism and an occasion to restore the memory of the blacks who had suffered and died during that war.[42] As the new century dawned, young Afrikaners also looked back to a time before apartheid for an identity that would not carry shame. One instance of this may be seen in a documentary, made by a group of my students in 2004, called *Algemeen Befokte Afrikaans,* whose title plays on the phrase "Algemeen Beskaafde Afrikaans" (translated literally as General Civilised Afrikaans). Focusing especially on the resurgence of Afrikaner youth culture and a renewed relationship to their language, the students shot location footage at the Klein Karoo Nasionale Kunstefees [Little Karoo National Arts Festival], a very successful forum started in 1994 to bring multiracial Afrikaans performers together. An interesting moment was the appearance of images of Paul Kruger on posters and T-shirts. One of the academic commentators suggested that, for young Afrikaners, going back to the heroic preapartheid days of the Boer War when a small band of intrepid soldiers took on the might of the British Empire was a way of reclaiming pride in their past. That Paul Kruger himself "fled" to Europe on the eve of the outbreak of the second Anglo-Boer War was something handed down to me by my father, who took a rather dim view of him, especially given that my paternal grandmother had been incarcerated in a British concentration camp. Nevertheless, Kruger attained iconic status at the festival. More recently, Bok van Blerk's rousing anthem to the great Boer general De La Rey took the country by storm, even reaching into the heart of the so-called Black Boer, the subject of another student documentary.[43] Piet Dlamini, the "black Boer" of the title, reveres Eugene Terre' Blanche, murdered leader of the defanged Afrikaner Weerstandsbeweging [Afrikaner Resistance Movement], and the documentary opens with Dlamini solemnly singing "De La Rey":

> Op ‘n berg in die nag / lê ons in donker en wag/in die modder en bloed lê ek koud, / streepsak en reën kleef teen my / en my huis en my plaas tot kole verbrand sodat hulle ons kan vang, / maar daai vlamme en vuur brand nou diep, diep binne my.
>
> Chorus: De La Rey, De La Rey sal jy die Boere kom lei? / De La Rey, De La Rey / Generaal, generaal soos een man, sal ons om jou val. / Generaal De La Rey.
>
> Oor die Kakies wat lag, / ’n handjie van ons teen ‘n hele groot mag / en die kranse lê hier teen ons rug, / hulle dink dis verby. / Maar die hart van ‘n Boer lê dieper en wyer, hulle gaan dit nog sien. / Op ‘n perd kom hy aan, die Leeu van die Wes Transvaal. (Chorus)
>
> Want my vrou en my kind lê in ‘n kamp en vergaan, / en die Kakies se murg loop oor ‘n nasie wat weer op sal staan. (Chorus)[44]

The tropes of closeness to the land, the courage of the underdog, and the violence perpetrated on the sanctity of the family are all brought together with the heroic image of the “lion of the West Transvaal,” itself a metaphor that merges De La Rey with the untamed strength of Africa (and, of course, using the pre-1994 name for the region bears its own nostalgic resonance in the “heart of the Boer”). But there are “southern accents” here as well in the image of the burnt farmhouse and lands: Kitchener’s scorched-earth policy mirrored Sherman’s. The last line of the chorus also echoes the post–Civil War sentiment that “the South shall rise again.”[45]

If these postapartheid instances of rehabilitation of the Afrikaner past echo, in however partial a manner, the revisions of history seen in the moonlight-and-magnolia school of southern mythmakers, they emerge after the spectacle of unknowing has been resolutely shattered, especially by the broadcast of the Truth and Reconciliation Commission hearings, images and stories of other South African lives erupting into living rooms across the country. This counterspectacle effectively put paid to any lingering unknowing, certainly any view that we could not have known. Now we could know, even if only through the mediations of spectacle, but then the power of spectacle to change consciousness can never be underestimated. Yes, one could switch off the TV, but not without registering what was about to appear, and even those glimpses would ensure that the present would be fissured and haunted by those many different pasts with their many forms of pain and suffering.

What, then, of the endurance of a film like *Gone with the Wind* for South Africans, or for this South African? Molly Haskell describes the “seven stages” of one’s possible relationship to *Gone with the Wind* (the film): “Love, Identification, Dependency, Resentment, Embarrassment, Indifference, and then something like Half-Love again.”[46] The continuing ambivalence even in that “Half-Love” is seen in other writers on the subject: the redoubtable Leslie Fiedler, for example, describes how he chose to talk about the novel at a symposium on James T. Farrell and Nelson Algren, admitting in parentheses that he "had secretly enjoyed both book and film for a long while," although this was the first time he had "come out of the closet."[47] Helen Taylor pays homage to the ways in which age, experience, and wider knowledge have changed her attitude toward the novel and the film but concludes: "in case all that sounds too pious for words, I freely admit to an enduring pleasure in all those gorgeous costumes, lavish Southern social gatherings, and spectacular events and effects. And like many other women, I still sigh weakly at Clark Gable's first appearance at the staircase, and sob bitterly as he slams the door for the last time."[48]

Catherine Clinton, whose study is concerned with unraveling the "distorted if splendid myths"[49] perpetuated by the novel and the film, cannot resist concluding her discussion by quoting from the text that generated her critique. Like Taylor, she acknowledges that "certain legends endure. Tara remains contested yet transcendent—bewildering, unbending and beguiling. And its distinctive, compelling image prods us to re-examine a fascinating crossroads of history and memory, beckoning us to revisit, yet again, another day."[50] In his much more acerbic dismantling of Tara, even Bruce Chadwick feels compelled to end his chapter with Rhett's famous last words as his own parting shot at American audiences' failure to care about the film's "muddled history and racism."[51]

If one does, indeed, feel that "half-love" for the film, it can only be through the difficult accommodation of the spectacle of *knowing* and acknowledging its "muddled history and racism," perhaps acknowledging too that the film's treatment of race tries to eschew the extreme offensiveness of the novel. The complication in analyzing the film from this point of view is that one may merely be sustaining that "spectacle of unknowing," allowing spectacle to appease one by not acknowledging that the less obvious racism may be more insidious. This is suggested by Carlton Moss's trenchant critique of the film: "Whereas 'The Birth of a Nation' was a frontal attack on American history and the Negro people, 'Gone with the Wind,' arriving twenty years later, is a rear attack on the same. Sugar-smeared and blurred by a boresome Hollywood love story and under the guise of presenting the South as it is in the 'eyes of the Southerners,' the message of GWTW emerges in its final entity as a nostalgic plea for sympathy for a still living cause of Southern reaction."[52]

Moss's alert to the "sugar smearing" of the film affects a reading of Mitchell's views on how the slave characters should be performed and poses problems of how to interpret her own "unknowing." She is on record, for example, as saying that the part she would most like to have played was that of Prissy. The performance by Butterfly McQueen was a great disappointment to Mitchell, who observed that she had meant Prissy to be "shiftless," not "stupid."[53] Indeed,

Mitchell's description of Prissy scarcely squares with the character as the film presents her, a character that has drawn much angry criticism, especially from African American spectators, Malcolm X and Alice Walker being among the most distinguished.[54] In the novel we read: "[Dilcey] reached behind her and jerked the little girl forward. She was a brown little creature, with skinny legs like a bird and a myriad of pigtails carefully wrapped with twine sticking stiffly out from her head. She had sharp, knowing eyes that missed nothing and a studiedly stupid look on her face."[55] While there are clear echoes of Topsy here, there is also an interesting disturbance in Prissy's portrayal, her "studied stupidity" suggestive of the skilled performance, masquerade, and mimicry that subvert white authority. Mitchell was especially concerned that the film version not succumb to stereotypical cinematic depictions of the southern black community and writes feelingly and amusingly to Katharine Brown:

> Even more wearying than the choral effects are the inevitable wavings in the air of several hundred pairs of hands with Rouben Mamoulian shadows leaping on the walls. This was fine and fitting in "Porgy" but pretty awful in other shows where it had no place. I feared greatly that three hundred massed Negro singers might be standing on Miss Pittypat's lawn waving their arms and singing "Swing low, sweet chariot, Comin' for to carry me home" while Rhett drives up with the wagon.[56]

Selznick avoided such excesses, also toning down the more violent instances of racism: Scarlett's would-be rapist in the Shantytown is a white man, not a black as in the novel; overt reference to the Klan is deleted, as well as any mention of Rhett's killing a black man for being "uppity" to a "lady."[57] Notably the racist language used relentlessly through the novel to describe the slaves is missing, including the use of the word "nigger." Through these changes and excisions Selznick sought to avoid the outcry that had greeted the overt racism of D. W. Griffith's *The Birth of a Nation.*

Arguably, however, the key transformation with regard to the representation of black characters in the film is in the role of Mammy and the performance of Hattie McDaniel.[58] Scarlett's relationship with Mammy is, in Camille Paglia's view, the most powerful in the film.[59] Working subterraneanly, it emerges more and more fully after each viewing. Scarlett's fiercest and most loving critic, Mammy is also the source of moral vision, a position strengthened in the film by giving her Will Benteen's lines when Ashley is seen stumbling back to Tara and Scarlett wants to rush after Melanie: "He's her husband, ain't he?" Our alliance with Mammy is most powerfully present in Hattie McDaniel's final scene, that with Melanie after the death of Bonnie, a radical revision of the way in which the novel develops the action. In the novel, Mammy goes to Melanie's home and tells her, at very great length, of the terrible alienation between Rhett and Scarlett.

Melanie returns to the Butler house with her and leaves Mammy huddled outside Rhett's room while she works her magic on Rhett. She then asks Mammy to bring coffee and sandwiches, after which she proposes to spend the night watching over Scarlett. Mammy is thus merely the grieving tale bearer, Melanie the strong ministering angel, of a piece with Scarlett's epiphany about her dying sister-in-law: "She was seeing through Rhett's eyes the passing, not of a woman but a legend—the gentle, self-effacing but steel-spined women on whom the South had builded its house in war and to whose proud and loving arms it had returned in defeat."[60]

Instead, the succoring arms become Mammy's in the film. Here, Melanie visits the bereft couple. Mammy opens the door to her, commanding a sense of authority and sanity. Her account of the grief in the house is severely abbreviated and thus much more dramatically effective, strengthening the sense of her authority to describe this dysfunctional household. The two women process in a slow dignified manner up the stairs, the rapport between them palpable. Implicitly in this scene, one might argue, they are both great ladies, and the staircase, a place of transformations, transitions, revelations, collapse, disaster, and recovery, is here an image of a journey that these two women take together. Mammy prays outside Rhett's room and then, in a key deviation from the novel, welcomes Melanie's news as Melanie, long gone in her dangerous pregnancy, collapses. Mammy catches and holds her in a pièta scene that may indeed tap into the stereotype of the plantation mammy but that, given Hattie McDaniel's bravura performance, also suggests a strength and stability indispensable to any hope that tomorrow might be another day. Even the steel magnolia that is Melanie must collapse into Mammy's arms, arms that become a sustained metaphor of maternal strength. In the documentary included in the recent Blu-ray release, Paglia's observation on the crucial significance of the Scarlett/Mammy relationship is framed by the scene in which a worn and weary Scarlett finally makes it through enemy lines and reaches Tara. The look of relief and happiness on Scarlett's face as she falls into Mammy's waiting arms bears out Paglia's insight.

How to transcend the stereotype that still lurks in this image is a major challenge for the film, as it was in the mixed reception accorded McDaniel's performance: an Academy Award on the one hand and disapproval from members of the NAACP on the other for playing yet another mammy. Molly Haskell has documented the racism practiced against her even while her accomplishment was being celebrated, notably her being seated separately from the white cast members at the Academy Award banquet.[61] McDaniel's off-screen experiences extend the ambiguities of her onscreen role, focalizing the matrix of love, dependency, and patronage accorded the black woman who mothers her white charges, indeed performs the true mothering in texts such as *Gone with the Wind* as well as in the society the novel seeks to reflect. This matrix has been and still is a well-recognized feature of innumerable white South African families. Under apartheid the black female servant's indispensable presence was, like McDaniel's on- and off-screen for *Gone with the Wind,* constantly in tension with the humiliating limitations imposed on that presence—arriving early in the morning and leaving late for wherever it was she lived, or, if she was a "live-in maid," returning to her (invariably) small room in the backyard every night. Darrell Roodt's *Sarafina* demonstrated memorably the way in which the black "maid" was torn between her servitude to a white family's needs, in this case a child's birthday party, and the crisis suffered by her own child, an increasingly politicized daughter who tries to come to terms with the abject status of the mother she adores.[62] The mother was played, significantly, by Miriam Makeba, Mama Africa, a choice of casting that brought multiple layers and painful ironies to the idea of "mother" in the film. The black woman whose mothering is forcibly displaced from her own biological children onto white surrogate children is also recalled in Koos Kombuis's autobiography. Describing his dysfunctional family, he tells us: "Of all these people Kytie was closest to me. She was even closer to me than my mother, because Kytie dressed me in the morning, Kytie fed me, Kytie was there when I took my first steps, and Kytie sat talking to me in the afternoons on the staircase behind our house."[63] He writes a song for his "nanny" that, loosely translated, means "Kytie, you did not stay with us for nothing for twenty years. Kytie, you were not just a maid, but a mother for me." "Sadly," he adds, "Kytie died during childbirth on the eve of her forthcoming wedding to her umpteenth unsober boyfriend. She who was so good at babysitting, she who excelled at domestic duties, was never to have a house and children of her own. She who was the best mother I ever had, she who had made my childhood bearable."[64]

In a connected, if differently inflected dynamic, the role of the black surrogate mother cannot be divorced from the relationship between the white mistress and her black female servant. While Mitchell's novel kills off Ellen O' Hara rather than explore this dynamic, Willa Cather's *Sapphira and the Slave Girl* engaged with it in tortured ways analyzed most potently by Toni Morrison.[65] Recently, one of the most celebrated Afrikaans novels, Marlene van Niekerk's densely woven narrative, *Agaat,* took the relationship between white mistress and black servant as the focus for a wide-ranging scrutiny of Afrikaner history and identity under apartheid. Liesl Schillinger lyrically articulates Van Niekerk's achievement: "It is apartheid itself that Agaat and Milla embody, two women, black and white, ink and paper, who together, over 50 years, inscribed upon each other a scroll of wrongs, betrayals and sacrifices that cannot be redressed, only reread."[66]

The task of re-reading proposed here is also the task of re-vision, of seeing again and seeing anew. In the case of reading the Mammy of the film version, this may enable a favorable interpretation of her role in Selznick's film, but it would also necessitate the awareness that the film fails her in one crucial moment, and that is the final scene of the film, where her voice is silenced. At the end of the novel, Scarlett's decision to return to Tara echoes her earlier flight out of Atlanta. Where, then, she wanted her biological mother but found the comfort of her real mother, now she knows whom she seeks: "And Mammy would be there. Suddenly she wanted Mammy desperately, as she had wanted her when she was a little girl, wanted the broad bosom on which to lay her head, the gnarled black hand on her hair. Mammy, the last link with the old days."[67] This image of Mammy is supplanted in the film by the voiceovers of the three most significant men in Scarlett's life: her father, Ashley, and Rhett, telling her that Tara is where she belongs. The final image before the credits roll is of Scarlett alone under the same tree where she once stood with her father. In spite of that image of Scarlett alone, the elision of Mammy in favor of the male voices diminishes the powerful narrative of female survival that Selznick has developed up to that point, taking his cue from Mitchell's express focus on survival: "I wrote," she said, "about the people who had gumption and the people who didn't."[68] Two of the most stirring scenes are the ones that mark the halfway and the final moments of the film: Scarlett clutching her radish against a burning sunset and swearing never to go hungry again, Scarlett in close-up revisiting her old stand-by, "Tomorrow is another day," but investing it with new meaning. No longer part of the throwaway expression of denial and procrastination—"I won't think about that now. I'll think about that tomorrow"—her climactic insight is that she cannot think about it tomorrow but that she can think about tomorrow as another day, with a revived sense of hope and possibility. Yet, in both novel and film, the postbellum Scarlett and the New South are finally judged as wanting. The novel ends with a return to the past, "the old forms . . . the leisured manners, the courtesy, the pleasant casualness in human contacts, and, most of all, the protecting attitude of the men toward their women."[69] James Boatwright suggests that this conservative turn is one of the great disappointments of the novel: "It turns out that [Rhett and Scarlett] weren't bad, irresponsible, free—some grand Promethean figures—they were going through a *phase* . . . what we witness is not transformation through suffering (although both characters have certainly suffered plenty) but a simple victory for the home folks."[70] In this reading the power of Mammy in the novel is repressed, for she becomes merely "the last link with the old days." That repression is even more acute in the film, where her presence is simply obliterated.[71]

In *Gone with the Wind*—novel and film—this desire to return to the past has both political and personal resonance. The containment of Mammy in a narrative of nostalgia in the novel and her excision from the return to Tara in the film are both functions of prioritizing the narrative of romance. After all, Scarlett wants to return in order to "regroup" and figure out how to win Rhett back.

Yet the suspended ending, with Scarlett alone under the spreading tree on her beloved farm, also foregrounds the agrarian dream of the Depression South that contested the burgeoning materialism and industrialism assailing Americans not only after the Civil War but, even more acutely, after the First World War. Chadwick explores the appeal of the myths propagated by the Civil War films, released "when Americans felt smothered by materialism, the growth of cities, consumerism, the growth of industrialization, assembly-line work lives, unfair labor practice and the new corporate world that sprawled about them. They longed for the simple, rural life of the mid-nineteenth century, a time, they believed, when the stress and anxiety that were crippling them did not exist."[72]

As he points out, *Gone with the Wind*'s huge success was of a piece with the success of other films that longed for home, such as *The Wizard of Oz* and the Depression-era work of John Ford and Frank Capra.[73] So, too, the agrarian dream was there in the iconography of the last images of 1938's *Die Bou van 'n Nasie:* the farmer (or "boer" in Afrikaans) plowing the fields with his black servant, the young woman sowing her seeds, all intimately linked to the land.[74] More than sixty years later, Van Niekerk's magisterial exploration of this Afrikaner myth takes as one of its epigraphs an excerpt from the *Manual for Farmers in South Africa,* published in 1929, that, in its invocation of the Bible, explicitly sanctifies the role of the farmer: "Net soos die Bybel die pad wys tot geestelike volmaaktheid so sal hierdie Hulpboek ook op middels en maniere wys tot meer winsgewende boerdery en tot groter welvaart vir elke boer in elke deel van die land."[75]

Answering the call of the men's voices to return to the land that is "the only thing that matters, the only thing that lasts," the land that, Ashley tells her, she loves more than him though she may not know it, the land from which, Rhett tells her, she gets her strength, Scarlett is at last silhouetted against the backdrop of Tara as we return to her origins and the beginning of her story. And it is, at the end of the day, *her* story, as Chadwick reminds us, "her saga, her soap opera, her love story, her vanquished people, her rebirth, her individualism and her struggle."[76] In this account, romance (both the love story and the agrarian fantasy) trumps race.

The spectacle of unknowing with which I may have read the book and watched the film in my salad days encouraged me to elide the problematic representation of race and its echoes in my South African world, to be easily captivated by the romance, both that of Scarlett and Rhett and of the "world that only wanted to be graceful" that they inhabited. This easy response has given way, over time, to a more entangled experience of the film. I find myself in agreement with Molly Haskell, perhaps because her southern sensibility speaks to my own complicated feelings about being a white South African. The final stage for Haskell in one's response to the film of *Gone with the Wind,* as noted earlier, is a return to "half-love," in the knowledge that there are distortions and betrayals of history. Much of this half-love is dependent on the appeal of Vivien Leigh and her powerful entrenchment of the myth of Scarlett.[77] Haskell offers a very fine description of the power of the film star that "bears away our faith" (to misappropriate a phrase from André Bazin).[78] Hollywood's female stars, she writes, are "space-devouring presences who, having learned how to be singularly, erotically, religiously alive in close-ups, the visual lexicon of stardom, would stop time and break down the two-dimensional barrier of the frame."[79] Watching the film (yet again!) in order to respond to my questions, the scene that stirred my mother most was the moment when Rhett throws a glass against the portrait of Scarlett hanging on the wall. The camera cuts back, not to Scarlett but to Vivien Leigh, hair flowing over her shoulders, fragile, exquisite, breaking out of the frame of narrative. It is that doubleness—of character and performer—that complicates one's response to any film, including this one. We may know that Scarlett is a spoilt brat and a devious hussy, but how ravishing is Vivien Leigh! We may register that Mammy is a stereotype, but how splendid is Hattie McDaniel! What the "surge and splendor" of *Gone with the Wind* push to breaking point is the question of how we choose to be seduced.

NOTES

1. The quotations are from my mother's written memoir.

2. David O. Selznick, *Gone with the Wind,* Selznick Pictures International, Culver City, Hollywood, Calif., 1939. All quotations from the film are my own transcription. Even as the film was part of my growing up, both the book and the film have had a great impact on generations of readers and viewers, especially women. Helen Taylor did a survey of British women fans' experiences and finds time and again how mothers have passed the book down to their daughters, how women have found the comfort of escape or counsel in its pages, how "Tomorrow is another day" became a coping mechanism for women, particularly during World War II. See Helen Taylor, *Scarlett's Women*: Gone with the Wind *and Its Female Fans* (London: Virago Press, 1989).

3. Bob Thomas, *The Story of* Gone with the Wind (Culver City: Metro-Goldwyn-Mayer, 1967), n.p.

4. Vivian Sobchack, "'Surge and Splendor': A Phenomenology of the Hollywood Historical Epic," in Barry Keith Grant, ed., *Film Genre Reader II* (Austin: University of Texas Press, 1995), 295.

5. Ibid., 296.

6. Ibid., 283–84.

7. André Brink, *Kennis van die Aand* (Cape Town: Buren, 1973).

8. Teaching Whitman on democracy was one strategy that produced some interesting debate.

9. Patricia Yaeger, *Dirt and Desire: Reconstructing Southern Women's Writing, 1930–1990* (Chicago: University of Chicago Press, 2000), 99.

10. Ibid., 101.

11. Ibid., 102.

12. Ibid.

13. Ibid., 103.

14. Ibid., 103–4.

15. Taylor, *Scarlett's Women,* 55–56.

16. Molly Haskell, *Frankly, My Dear:* Gone with the Wind *Revisited* (New Haven: Yale University Press, 2009), 108–9.

17. Bruce Chadwick, *The Reel Civil War: Mythmaking in American Film* (New York: Knopf, 2001), 205.

18. Thomas Cripps, "Winds of Change: *Gone with the Wind* and Racism as a National Issue," in Darden Asbury Pyron, ed., *Recasting:* Gone with the Wind *in American Culture* (Miami: University Press of Florida, 1983), 140.

19. Ibid.

20. Ralph McGill, "Little Woman, Big Book: The Mysterious Margaret Mitchell," in Richard Harwell, ed., Gone with the Wind *as Book and Film* (Columbia: University of South Carolina Press, 1983), 75.

21. Leslie Fiedler, "*Gone with the Wind*: The Feminization of the Anti-Tom Novel," in Fiedler, *What Was Literature: Class Culture and Mass Society* (New York: Simon and Schuster, 1982), 200.

22. George Fredrickson, *White Supremacy: A Comparative Study in American and South African History* (New York: Oxford University Press, 1981).

23. Hermann Giliomee, *The Afrikaners: Biography of a People* (Cape Town: Tafelberg, 2003), 261.

24. Anthony W. Marx, *Making Race and Nation: A Comparison of the United States, South Africa, and Brazil* (Cambridge: Cambridge University Press, 1998), 133.

25. Bill Nasson, *The War for South Africa: The Anglo-Boer War 1899–1902* (Cape Town: Tafelberg, 2010), 257.

26. Marx, *Making Race and Nation,* 131.

27. Ibid., 145–46.

28. Catherine Clinton, *Tara Revisited: Women, War, and the Plantation Legend* (New York: Abbeville Press, 1995), 174.

29. Louis Rubin Jr., "Scarlett O' Hara and the Two Quentin Compsons," in Darden Asbury Pyron, ed., *Recasting:* Gone with the Wind *in American Culture* (Miami: University Press of Florida, 1983), 81–103.

30. Ibid.

31. Pyron, *Recasting:* Gone with the Wind *in American Culture,* 185–201.

32. Margaret Mitchell, *Gone with the Wind* (1939; repr., London: Macmillan, 1972), 214.

33. Yaeger, *Dirt and Desire,* 101.

34. Chadwick, *The Reel Civil War,* 207.

35. Richard Harwell, "Introduction" to Harwell, Gone with the Wind *as Book and Film* (Columbia: University of South Carolina Press, 1983), xvii.

36. Clinton, *Tara Revisited,* 183.

37. Harold Shaw, *De Voortrekkers,* African Film Productions, Johannesburg, 1916. For detailed accounts of the film, see Edwin Hees, "The Birth of a Nation: Contextualising

De Voortrekkers (1916)," in Isabel Balseiro and Ntongela Masilela, eds., *To Change Reels: Film and Culture in South Africa* (Detroit: Wayne State University Press, 2003), 46–69; Jacqueline Maingard, *South African National Cinema* (London: Routledge, 2007); and Lucia Saks, *Cinema in a Democratic South Africa: The Race for Representation* (Bloomington: Indiana University Press, 2010).

38. It may be worth noting that when my mother saw *Gone with the Wind*, she was working at the SA Club, the South African Party Club that served members of the Party led by Louis Botha and Jan Smuts, known for its espousal of continued ties with Britain and, relative to the rising National Party, its more ameliorative stance on race relations. When Jan Smuts lost the elections in 1948, writes Koos Kombuis in his phlegmatic autobiography, it was because he was either "too slow or too quick (no-one is quite sure which) in giving political power to the natives" (21). Kombuis was one of the group of young rebel Afrikaners whose music flew in the face of the repressive South African regime. Their "voëlvry" (literally "free-as-a-bird," but connoting "fugitive" status) concert tour in the 1980s was a memorable moment in the rise of Afrikaner anti-apartheid expression.

39. Hees, "Contextualising *De Voortrekkers,*" 61.

40. Joseph Albrecht, *Die Bou van 'n Nasie,* African Film Productions, Johannesburg, 1938.

41. Hees, "Contextualising *De Voortrekkers,*" 67.

42. Nasson, *The War for South Africa,* 300. "Toenadering" means literally "an approach," a word that carries different connotations, from the obsequious notion of making overtures to the gentler sense of drawing together.

43. Xolani Gumbi, *The Black Boer* (Cape Town: University of Cape Town, 2010).

44. On a mountain in the night / we lie in darkness and wait / In the mud and blood I lie cold, / grain bag and rain cling to me. / And my house and my farm, burned to ashes / so that they can catch us / But those flames and fire burn now deep, deep within me.

Chorus: De la Rey, De la Rey, / will you come to lead the Boers? / De la Rey, De la Rey / General, General, as one man / we'll fall in around you / General De la Rey

And the Khakis [Brits] that laugh / a handful of us / against whole great might / And the cliffs to our backs, / they think it's all over / But the heart of the Boer lies deeper and wider, / They'll still see this. / On horseback he comes, / the Lion of the West Transvaal

Chorus

Because my wife and my child, / lie in a camp and perish / And the Khakis' marrow runs over a nation that will rise up again

Chorus

45. My thanks to Simon Lewis for pointing out this analogy. The potential for the song to bring black and white together is also ambiguously explored in Jann Turner's comic road movie, *White Wedding*, when the bridegroom, Elvis (Kenneth Nkosi), sings the song with the stereotyped white Boer racists in a country bar. The whites are duly pleased. Jann Turner, *White Wedding,* Stepping Stone Pictures, Johannesburg, 2009. The connections between this kind of Afrikaner revivalism and the latter-day resurrection

of southern pride may perhaps be seen through the success of the two concept albums, *White Mansions* and *The Legend of Jesse James* (released in 1978 and 1980) with songs sung by such hugely successful, even iconic, performers as Johnny Cash and Emmylou Harris (see Johnny Cash et al., *White Mansions / The Legend of Jesse James* [Santa Monica: A and M, 1999]). Notable is the plaintive waltz "The Last Dance and the Kentucky Racehorse," a duet sung by Jessi Colter (as "Polly") and John Dillon (as "Matthew"), redolent not only of the scene in the film of *Gone with the Wind* in which Ashley and Melanie stand on a balcony at Twelve Oaks and speak of a world that "only wants to be graceful" but also of the love story that underpins Charles Frazier's *Cold Mountain* (New York: Atlantic Monthly Press, 1997) and its 2003 film adaptation, directed by Anthony Minghella.

46. Haskell, "Frankly, My Dear," xiii.

47. Fiedler, "*Gone with the Wind,*" 202.

48. Taylor, *Scarlett's Women,* 234.

49. Clinton, *Tara Revisited,* 213.

50. Ibid.

51. Chadwick, *The Reel Civil War,* 231. On the other hand, in *Algemeen Befokte Afrikaans,* it is notable how often young Afrikaners declare themselves uninterested in the past (see Nicky Comninos, Kristen Broberg, and Carole Bezuidenhout, *Algemeen Befokte Afrikaans* [Cape Town: University of Cape Town, 2004]). This desire to "move on" is there among certain of my black students as well, while courses in South African film after 1994 invariably involve giving history lessons on even the recent past, with most contemporary undergraduates born in 1990 or later. Kombuis's revised autobiography and the significant trilogy of works by Antje Krog testify to an older generation's more complex struggle to embrace a past that takes account of what we, unavoidably, know now. See Koos Kombuis, *Short Drive to Freedom: A Personal Perspective on the Afrikaans Rock Rebellion* (Cape Town: Human and Rousseau, 2009); Antje Krog, *Country of My Skull* (Johannesburg: Random House, 1998); Krog, *A Change of Tongue* (Johannesburg: Random House, 2003); and Krog, *Begging to be Black* (Cape Town: Random House/Struik, 2009).

52. Carlton Moss, "An Open Letter to Mr. Selznick," in Richard Harwell, ed., Gone with the Wind *as Book and Film*, 157.

53. Harwell, *Gone with the Wind,* 170.

54. Taylor, *Scarlett's Women,* 178

55. Mitchell, *Gone with the Wind,* 66.

56. Cripps, "Winds of Change," 142.

57. Mitchell, *Gone with the Wind,* 625.

58. At the most obvious level, the regressive racist language used to describe Mammy is missing from the film. When she grieves, for example, she is described as having "the uncomprehending sadness of a monkey's face" (417) and, later, "the sad bewilderment of an old ape" (997).

59. Camille Paglia et al. "*Gone with the Wind*: The Legend Lives On," DVD Special Feature, Seventieth Anniversary Blu-ray re-release, 2009.

60. Mitchell, *Gone with the Wind,* 1030.

61. Haskell, *Frankly, My Dear,* 213–14.

62. Darrell Roodt, *Sarafina*, Distant Horizons et al., BBC, Johannesburg, 1992.

63. Kombuis, *Short Drive*, 26.

64. Ibid., 27.

65. Toni Morrison, *Playing in the Dark: Whiteness and the Literary Imagination* (New York: Vintage, 1993).

66. Marlene Van Niekerk, *Agaat* (Cape Town: Tafelberg, 2004); English version, Van Niekerk, *Agaat*, trans. Michiel Heyns (Jeppestown: Jonathan Ball, and Cape Town: Tafelberg, 2006). Liesl Schillinger, "Truth and Reconciliation," *New York Times* Sunday Book Review, May 21, 2010, n.p., www.nytimes.com/2010/05/23/books/review/Schillinger-t.html (accessed October 16, 2012).

67. Mitchell, *Gone with the Wind*, 1042.

68. Mitchell, "Margaret Mitchell," in Richard Harwell, ed., Gone with the Wind *as Book and Film*, 37–38.

69. Mitchell, *Gone with the Wind*, 609.

70. James Boatwright, "Reconsideration: Totin' de Weery Load," in Richard Harwell, ed., Gone with the Wind *as Book and Film*, 216–17.

71. Helen Taylor also notes Mammy's silencing at the end of the film (*Scarlett's Women*, 173). The uncritical expression of nostalgia for the Old South is, of course, a white dream and resonates with a similar desire for apartheid in South Africa, where the gruesome effects of apartheid are overwhelmed by a sense that things now are not what they should be or, simply, much worse. The litany of woes experienced by the country—AIDS, crime, domestic violence and abuse of women, government corruption, unceasing poverty especially among the black population, ineffectual service delivery, increasing disillusionment expressed by those who fought on the side of the ANC—lead to a different kind of spectacle, the spectacle of forgetting and, with it, the risk of repetition. So, for example, the documentary about the "black Boer" mentioned earlier includes an unnerving scene where Piet Dlamini's fellow black townsmen complain volubly about the lack of jobs and food that they would never have suffered under the old regime, or so they say. The relationship between Boer and farming is explicitly evoked when one of the interviewees urges that "The Boers must come back to teach us how to plant."

72. Chadwick, *The Reel Civil War*, 34.

73. Ibid., 222.

74. At one level the image realizes Churchill's hope that the Boers would go back to plowing their fields, but, in the context of the nationalist propagandizing of the film, it speaks more to Bill Nasson's observation that, in "hounding" the Boers, the British "produced Afrikaner nationalism and, in turn, the excesses of apartheid." Nasson, *The War for South Africa*, 299.

75. The English translation by Michiel Heyns reads: "Just as the Bible points the way to spiritual perfection so will this Handbook also point to ways and means to more profitable farming and to greater prosperity for every farmer in every part of the country." Of additional interest here are the farm novels of the Afrikaans writer C. M. van den Heever, whose Depression-era work offers a romantic and often anguished, account of the relationship between protagonists and their natural environment: *Droogte* [Drought] (Pretoria: Van Schaik, 1930); *Groei* [Growth] (Pretoria: Van Schaik, 1933);

Somer [Summer] (Pretoria: Van Schaik, 1935); and *Laat Vrugte* [Late Harvest] (Bloemfontein: Nasionale Pers, 1939).

76. Chadwick, *The Reel Civil War,* 222.

77. When I discussed the film with one of my third-year students (of German-Hungarian background) who completed her schooling in South Africa, she identifies the beauty of Vivien Leigh as the key factor in her love for the film.

78. André Bazin, *What Is Cinema?,* trans. Hugh Gray (Berkeley: University of California Press, 1967), 1: 14.

79. Haskell, *Frankly, My Dear,* 73.

Coda

Roundtable on Memory

Wars linger far longer than the treaties, victories, or defeats that "end" them. Vanquished enemies have generally been dealt with on a continuum from prosecution to absorption. In the Roman civil wars that led to the establishment of Octavius's rule as emperor, losers could expect to find themselves on proscription lists, slated for summary execution; the less prominent might find themselves exiled or facing lustration, the banning from holding public office (a practice followed by the United States in contemporary Iraq). The twentieth and twenty-first centuries have seen legal prosecutions for war crimes brought against defeated political leaders and generals (as in the Nuremburg Trials or the recent trials of Liberian, Sierra Leonean, and Bosnian war criminals at the Hague or of Hosni Mubarak in Egypt).[1] Other civil conflicts or periods of severe internal repression have ended with negotiated settlements aiming at reconciliation. The turnover of power from dictatorship and military rule in Spain and Chile or the negotiated settlements that brought about the end of apartheid or the Good Friday Agreement in Northern Ireland are among the most notable examples of such arrangements. In postconflict Rwanda, the sheer number of perpetrators of the 1994 genocide necessitated a strikingly innovative response to civil conflict: the simultaneous use of traditional gacaca courts (allowing for the possibility of reparation, reconciliation, and reabsorption) and of international tribunals for those deemed most responsible for the killings. No matter what the approach, though, memory is rarely, probably never totally expunged, the tinder of long-nursed grievance rarely if ever totally damped down.[2]

In the case of the defeated Confederacy, the experience of Reconstruction, the federal retreat from Reconstruction, and the subsequent Jim Crow era, memory itself has remained a field of conflict.[3] The lines from William Faulkner's *Requiem for a Nun* "The Past is never dead. It's not even past" have been quoted and paraphrased so frequently that they've become clichéd, but in relation to the American Civil War their continuing validity seems assured. In December 2010 and again in April 2011, when journalists and scholars covered the various public ceremonies and events commemorating South Carolina's secession from the Union and the firing on Fort Sumter, respectively, they almost routinely reached for some version of Faulkner's phrasing. Headline after headline repeated the notion that the Civil War was and is still being fought—"civilly," perhaps, as the National Public Radio report of December 19, 2010, had it, but doggedly nonetheless.[4] The battlefield now is a virtual one rather than a real one, and the struggle may be for control over narrative rather than nationalism, but the battle over whom, what, and how to remember rages unabated.

At 150, the ongoing Civil War can even look back at previous high points in the process of memorialization, notably the "troubled commemoration" of 1961–65 whose initial assumption that a reconciliatory national narrative was possible almost immediately encountered the evidence of its impossibility when a black New Jersey member of the Civil War Centennial Commission (CWCC) was refused accommodation at the Francis Marion Hotel in Charleston, South Carolina.[5] Although 2010 and 2011 saw large numbers of commemorative events around the country, there was no national attempt quite on par with the CWCC to commemorate the sesquicentennial. In fact, as Ari Kelman put it in a review of four important new books by prominent historians, "reaction has remained oddly muted, suggesting that people in the United States, though apparently still obsessed with the Civil War, remain uncertain about how to remember this troubling event collectively: as triumph or tragedy, as rebirth or mass murder, or as something else again."[6]

Even during the war, memory mattered. Drew Gilpin Faust argues that the overwhelming death toll of the Civil War changed the way Americans remember. Alongside new modes of mourning, new types of cemeteries, new holidays dedicated to commemorating the war's victims, the "presence of death" remains with us, leading to a "fundamentally elegiac understanding of the Civil War."[7] As far as historiography is concerned (as O. Vernon Burton's piece in this section especially illustrates), the war thus continued throughout and beyond Reconstruction, with white southerners' need to forget the violence in order to reestablish their power over blacks going hand in hand with their memorial reconstruction of the Lost Cause of southern honor and victimhood in the "War of Northern Aggression." Although this continued historiographical struggle looks local, even parochial, perhaps, it, like the war itself, has a global dimension. Because of America's ascendance to world power status, the narrative of Lincoln the Liberator created a usable past for groups as diverse as Republican forces in the Spanish Civil War and anti-apartheid writers in South Africa.[8] At the same time, because of Hollywood's global ascendancy, the single most dominant cultural narrative has been provided by the glamour and schmaltz of the movie version of *Gone with the Wind.* Lesley Marx's essay in this volume on the impact of the movie in South Africa gives just one indication of that iconic film's cultural power and global reach.

But if this long Civil War's end is not neatly marked by the date of Lee's surrender at Appomattox in 1865, its beginning cannot neatly be marked by South Carolina's secession in December 1860 or by Beauregard's shelling of Fort Sumter in April 1861. Rather, we have to consider whether it was not in fact the culmination of what Kevin Phillips called the "cousins' wars," inevitably and inextricably connected to earlier postconflict agreements—the stipulations and silences first in the Treaty of Paris and then in the Constitutional Convention's compromises over slavery and slave trading embodying the memory and forgetting that allowed a nation founded on the principle of individual liberty to fail to act against the institution of unfree labor.[9]

It was the French historian and philosopher Ernest Renan who first formulated the notion that the ability to forget ("*savoir oublier*") was frequently important in creating a sense of national identity—especially after military conflict.[10] If the losing side clings to its memory of its own self-righteousness, it is less likely to be absorbed into the new national narrative. The winning side needs to allow a level of amnesty based on a shared amnesia of the grudges that both sides might otherwise have carried with them and that might have led to a perpetual cycle of retaliation. Aaron Sheehan-Dean's essay, which outlined the bounds within which retaliation was actually kept during the war itself, might be balanced against the continuing sense of grievance nursed by some in the former Confederacy, notably towards Sherman's attritional tactics. As Lesley Marx's essay indicates, a similar sense of grievance drove white Afrikaner historiography of the South African War of 1899–1902; in both wars the competing historiographies to a large degree overlooked black agency and created the conditions of possibility for the reestablishment of white supremacy in the birth/building of the "new" postconflict nation. In South Africa, the struggle to dismantle the structures of that white supremacy led to violent resistance and a decade-long situation of low-level civil war, followed in 1990–94 by a negotiated transfer of power to the country's black majority that was frequently touted as a miraculous turnaround. The new nation's dependence on remembering *and* forgetting was exemplified by the Truth and Reconciliation Commission's guarantee of amnesty to perpetrators of gross violations of human rights who told the full truth about their actions and could demonstrate a political (rather than criminal) motive for them. The commission thus created a record of public memory so that individuals and their crimes could be "forgotten" in a state sense and, perhaps, forgiven, if not by the victims at least by the new state itself.[11]

Like the compromises of the Treaty of Paris, negotiated by, among others, Henry Laurens, the American slave trader, and Richard Oswald, his British supplier, the end of apartheid allowed the apparent losers of the conflict, those whom we might rather simplistically present as leading the resistance to the forces of liberty, to continue business pretty much as usual: F. W. de Klerk shared the Nobel Prize for Peace with Nelson Mandela and has maintained a highly distinguished career as an international statesman. The postconflict settlement, to the dismay of many, appeared to make moral equivalence between the enforcers of apartheid and its opponents.[12] Amanda Foreman's piece in this section highlights a similar compromise of memory and forgetting in the comparative context of the American Civil War and the conflict in Ulster. Comparing the postwar careers of Confederate agents Luke Blackburn and Jacob Thompson with the careers of IRA leaders Gerry Adams and Martin McGuinness after the U.S.-brokered Good Friday Agreement of 1998, Foreman asks "what kind of reconciliation is possible without punishment or atonement for wrong doing" and bemoans the "corrosion of moral clarity surrounding the Civil War and its meaning in American history."[13]

In light of these kinds of seemingly intractable questions, we asked a number of historians with special interest in the South and the Civil War to give us short "think pieces" on the issue of memory. We asked each writer to consider what we remember about the war and what we *should* remember, as well as why and how we remember what we do and why and how we *should* remember it. Each writer wrote from his or her distinctive position as someone whose memory of *this* war as a still living phenomenon both locally and globally is colored by his or her experience of other global conflict, from the Vietnam War to the Holocaust. We print their various responses here, starting with the longest, by O. Vernon Burton, which provides a broad historiographical introduction to the section as a whole.

O. Vernon Burton, Remembering the Civil War

Among all there is to cover on remembering the Civil War, I will concentrate on three major ideas, and I will use Abraham Lincoln as the fulcrum around which these ideas swirled. First, the Civil War was about slavery. Second, the war changed the meaning of liberty and therefore changed the power structure in the political system. Third, the war was not over in 1865 but continued through Reconstruction.

The Civil War was fought to preserve slavery. Although both North and South profited from slavery, although it was the engine of economic prosperity for the whole country as cotton from the South filled textile mills in the North, nevertheless, as the North moved away from enslaved labor, the South clung to it more tenaciously. In his second inaugural address, Lincoln assumes that slavery was an offense against God and that is why God "gives to both North and South, this terrible war." Because slavery is such a shameful part of our history, some to this day are in a state of denial that the underlying cause of the Civil War was slavery. We need to overcome this distortion.

This is *not* to say that Southern soldiers went to war to preserve slavery or that Northern soldiers went to war to end it. Often in war the reason for conflict is political, and often the reason soldiers enlist is cultural. Both Northern and Southern soldiers enlisted on behalf of their community, neighborhood, state, and with their family, and friends.

This is *not* to say that the war was not to preserve the Union. The Union was threatened because of the slave system.

Some who deny that the war was about slavery declare that it was about states' rights. Not so! Prior to Lincoln's election, southerners controlled the majority in Congress and on the Supreme Court and either occupied the White House or had a southern sympathizer in the presidency. They looked to the Union to defend them against states' rights. Their objection was to "Liberty Laws," wherein the states of Massachusetts, Rhode Island, Connecticut, Vermont, Michigan, Maine, Wisconsin, Ohio, Kansas, and Pennsylvania refused to send back fugitive slaves without a trial.

As to the cause of this terrible war, historians have the smoking gun of historical evidence. The seceding states left documents that challenge those who deny that slavery was the heart of the rebellion. Again and again, the men who made the southern revolution laid out their purposes. Alabama reacted to "a sectional party, avowedly hostile to the domestic institutions and to the peace and security of the people of the State of Alabama," its domestic institution being slavery. Texas reacted to a federal government that wanted "to strike down the interests and property of the people of Texas, and her sister slave-holding States," that property being human beings.

The Georgia state assembly passed a resolution in January 1861 condemning the Republican Party, instituted as it was "for the avowed purpose of destroying the institution of slavery." When Georgia sent a representative to Virginia to try to persuade that state to secede, their advocate was Henry L. Benning, a lawyer, a Democrat, and a man who held ninety slaves. As to why Georgia seceded, he pronounced: "This reason may be summed up in a single proposition. It was a conviction, a deep conviction on the part of Georgia, that a separation from the North was the only thing that could prevent the abolition of her slavery."

Mississippi's official statement on secession, issued in January 1861, also explained its position as "thoroughly identified with the institution of slavery." If the state did not secede, militants calculated, the resultant abolition of slavery would mean "the loss of property worth four billions of money." The new vice president of the Confederacy, Alexander Stephens, was explicit that slavery "was the immediate cause of the late rupture and present revolution."

The bill of grievances Robert Barnwell Rhett drew up for South Carolina was especially frank—if melodramatic. The North, he charged, had "encouraged and assisted thousands of our slaves to leave their homes; and those who remain, have been incited by emissaries, books and pictures to servile insurrection."

Lincoln knew the war was about slavery. In his first inaugural, he stated that "One section of our country believes slavery is *right* and ought to be extended, while the other believes it is *wrong* and ought not to be extended. This is the only substantial dispute." Although the South instigated war to protect slavery, the northern call for defense against rebellion was not a call against slavery. Lincoln defined the war in 1861 as a need to put down an uprising that threatened the United States and its democratic, constitutional system of government. Lincoln was actually willing to sign a constitutional amendment that would have guaranteed noninterference with slavery in the states where it existed. Fortunately for America, this amendment was not successful because it did not go far enough for the slaveholders who believed in a constitutional right to expand slavery into the territories.

A southern man, born in Kentucky after all, Lincoln was honor bound to defend the United States. As he told a committee of the Young Men's Christian Association (YMCA, April, 22, 1861) from Baltimore that was trying to persuade him to let the South go, "You would have me break my oath and surrender the Government without a blow. There is no Washington in that—no Jackson in that—no manhood nor honor in that." More important, however, was Lincoln's understanding that the Constitution dictated that it was his job as president to keep the Union intact.

When Lincoln was looking for army commanders, the Italian hero Giuseppe Garibaldi considered taking the post. He was interested in a war to end slavery. When Lincoln clarified that this was a war to preserve the Union, Garibaldi declined the appointment. Because Lincoln defined the war as one to preserve the union and constitutional government, we do not know what nonslave-holders in the South would have done if Lincoln had announced he was fighting the war to end slavery. We do know, however, that if he had defined the war initially as one to end slavery, Lincoln could not have got a corporal's guard of Northerners to have fought. Lincoln could not call up volunteers to end slavery, but he could ask American citizens to preserve the Union.

In *The Age of Lincoln* I have argued that Lincoln was a southerner. This contrasts with many historians, including William Cooper, who argued the point in his 2010 Southern Historical Presidential Address, who claimed that Lincoln did not understand the South. And, Lincoln did believe that there were many unionists in the South. Lincoln himself declared, "You know I am by birth a southerner." His best friend was a slaveholding southerner. His wife was southern, and, while she opposed slavery, the Todd family were southern slaveholders.

Some historians fervently claim that Lincoln did not understand Southerners, but I think his southern roots were important to his interpretation of events. Many historians have argued that Lincoln did not know the South because he believed that nonslave-owners would not fight a war to preserve slavery. Lincoln was correct about the many southerners who supported the Union. The public has given too much credence to much of the *Gone with the Wind* and *Birth of a Nation* mythology that all white southerners supported the Confederacy. They did not. Every Confederate state but South Carolina had a regiment fighting for the Union. And some white South Carolinians went over to Georgia, North Carolina, and Tennessee to join the Union army. Many of the white southerners who were in the army in 1861 stayed after the outbreak of the Civil War. James Henry Hammond, the South Carolina senator and proslavery writer remembered for his phrase "Cotton is king," had a brother who as a surgeon remained with the Union army. One of the more radical of the Republicans, a general whose order to free Missouri slaves was countermanded by Lincoln, was John C. Fremont, the Pathfinder. He was born in Savannah, Georgia, and reared in Charleston, South Carolina, and he attended the College of Charleston—clearly a southerner. Fighting for the Union were also cultural southerners from Kentucky, Missouri, southern Ohio, Indiana, and Illinois. Moreover, approximately 180,000 African Americans fought for the Union, most of whom were southerners. Probably close to 40 percent of Southerners fought for and supported the Union. An interesting caveat when considering pro-Union and pro-Confederacy southerners is the realization that South Carolina and Mississippi had a black majority, that is, that most people in South Carolina and Mississippi were enslaved African Americans and wanted the Confederacy to lose and the Union to win. One can say that the Confederate states of Mississippi and South Carolina lost in the Civil War, but one cannot accurately say that South Carolina and Mississippi lost in the Civil War; they won.

Although begun to preserve slavery, although defended to preserve the Union, the war changed in its definition, its scope, its ramifications. War changes culture. As the conflict progressed, reaction against the Civil War's underlying root of slavery became its cause célèbre. The second point to remember is that the war to preserve the Union against the perpetrators who wanted to preserve and expand slavery evolved into a war that ended slavery and, in doing so, redefined freedom and liberty in the world.

Lincoln often spoke about the differences between two antagonistic groups who "declare for liberty." Some, he said, used the word "liberty" to mean that each man could "do as he pleases with himself, and the product of his labor." Others held the word "liberty" to mean "for some men to do as they please with other men, and the product of other men's labor." He proffered a parable to nail the point. "The shepherd drives the wolf from the sheep's throat," he said, "for which the sheep thanks the shepherd as a liberator, while the wolf denounces him for the same act as a destroyer of liberty, especially as the sheep is a black one."

David Hackett Fischer found five hundred ideas (not definitions) of liberty and freedom about the time of the Civil War. What freedom meant to an enslaved person on a plantation in North Carolina was, of course, quite different from what freedom meant for the slaveholder or for an overseer but was also different for a young woman or twelve-year-old boy working in a shoe factory sewing soles on shoes in the Northeast. Freedom meant different things for struggling yeomen, like Tom Lincoln, or a more prosperous Sam Davis in the slave state Kentucky and influenced whether they moved to the border Midwest or to Mississippi. Thus, both Union and Confederate soldiers understood the war as a war about freedom and liberty, but they defined those terms differently.

Lincoln saw the Union and liberty in a global context. He knew what was happening to democracy around the world at the time. The American Revolution had unleashed the forces of democracy and constitutional government, or at least the practice of adult white men governing themselves, and begun to change the world. But following the French Revolution, Napoleon returned the French Republic to a monarchy. The European Revolutions of 1848 failed. The republics in South America were failing; Napoleon III put Maximilian on the throne in Mexico. And even though Garibaldi reunited Italy, it became a monarchy, not a republic. Thus, the forces of history were with the Confederacy and the move away from democracy and self-government. And European powers wanted the Confederacy to win to lessen the power and influence of the United States. Lincoln was aware that the preservation of the Union was "the last best hope of earth" (annual message to Congress, December 1, 1862). For Lincoln, a government of laws, a republic, and a democratic government were about opportunity and the ability to work hard and rise in society—what we now call the American Dream.

Lincoln believed that the Emancipation Proclamation was "the central act of my administration and the great event of the nineteenth century." It was actually Lincoln's understanding of liberty that became the greatest legacy of the age and of the Civil War. Told as a story of freedoms and liberty rather than of the enslaved's emancipation, the Civil War and the nineteenth century make greater sense. Emancipation is one point on a long continuum of freedom and unfreedom.

In his Gettysburg Address, delivered in November 1863, even as rivers of American blood continued to flow, President Abraham Lincoln articulated the meaning of the war. He called for a "new birth of freedom." Lincoln implied that the dedication of the new cemetery, only half finished, was a waste of time and effort if creating a place of burial was all it accomplished. "The brave men, living and dead, who struggled here," he noted, "have consecrated it, far above our poor power to add or detract." But they had left their work "unfinished." A "great task" lay ahead. The task was not simply restoration or reconstruction; it was a rebirth. Human liberty and democracy themselves were at stake. Lincoln's vision was at once conservative and revolutionary. There would be overflowing cemeteries, vacant chairs at family tables, men broken bodily and spiritually, but "government of the people, by the people, for the people shall not perish from the earth." More than simply preserving the liberty of the fathers, the nation, Lincoln's new nation, "under God," would have "a new birth of freedom."

Lincoln revolutionized personal freedom in the United States by ensuring that it was protected by law. Basically Lincoln inserted the Declaration of Independence (our mission statement) into the Constitution (our rule book) of the United States. Part of the legacy of Lincoln, especially his "new birth of freedom," involves a redefinition of the role of government in securing liberty. Prior to the Civil War Amendments, the Thirteenth, Fourteenth, and Fifteenth, the latter two passed after Lincoln's death, we the people wanted freedom from government. The Bill of Rights institutionalized protection from federal abridgement. Amendment One reads: "Congress *shall make no law* respecting an establishment of religion, or prohibiting the free exercise thereof; or abridging the freedom of speech, or of the press; or the right of the people peaceably to assemble, and to petition the Government for a redress of grievances." The Thirteenth, Fourteenth, and Fifteenth Amendments state that "Congress *shall have power to enforce* . . ." (italics mine). Lincoln and, after his assassination, his legacy institutionalized positive liberty.

New amendments notwithstanding, citizenship for African American men (and later for black and white women) did not come easy. Ultimately, a meaningful vote was necessary for citizenship, and Lincoln was killed for such an idea. On April 1, 1865, from the White House balcony, Lincoln made some remarks to the gathering crowd about postwar efforts: "We must simply begin with, and mould from, disorganized and discordant elements." He spoke about the need for citizenship for the valiant African Americans who had fought for the Union. One listener at this speech, John Wilkes Booth, read his darkest fears into Abraham Lincoln's vision and told his companion, "That is the last speech he will ever make." Lincoln was killed for advocating voting rights for African American soldiers.

And the third point to remember is that the Civil War continued in the South as people fought for and against the idea of an interracial democracy. I would like people to realize that the Civil War did not end in 1865 with the surrender of Lee and Johnston. Reconstruction is part and parcel of the long civil war.

The bloodiest war in our history, the Civil War posed in a crucial way what clearly became persistent themes in American history, the character of the nation and the fate of African Americans (read large, the place of minorities). Consequently, scholars have been vitally interested in the Civil War, searching out clues therein for the identity of America. But if the identity of America is in the Civil War, the meaning of America and what we become is found in Reconstruction. We have bookended American history in the classroom so that the Civil War closes out one era of our history and Reconstruction begins the next period or second half of American history. Actual history defies such simple categorization.

Although Robert E. Lee countermanded Jefferson Davis's orders to keep on fighting, some Confederate leaders refused to surrender. For more than a decade after the war officially ended, these commanders continued to lead their troops in terrorist, guerrilla warfare. Civil war continued in the South where neighbor fought neighbor and whites fought blacks and some white Republicans. Some of the men who fought in these terrorist paramilitary groups in 1876 and 1878, those who were too young to fight in the Civil War, actually applied for their state's Confederate War pensions! They believed Reconstruction was part of the Civil War. I would also like people to remember that most whites in the South were not part of counterrevolutionary terrorist organizations like the Ku Klux Klan. The tragedy is that most good people just did nothing and did not stand up for the rule of law.

Although we are finally moving away from the *Gone with the Wind* and *Birth of a Nation* mythology about the antebellum period and slavery, the view of an overreaching and doomed Reconstruction still predominates in the popular culture. Even our language as historians is wrong. Adelbert Ames wrote that the people who served during Reconstruction were "all young, each and every one believed he was doing God's service and that the final result of his labors would be the elevation of an unhappy class of the human race." People coming south after the Civil War included African Americans who were returning home without fear of being re-enslaved. Harriet Beecher Stowe moved to Florida in 1867, taken with the natural beauty of the land and the "tumble-down, wild, panicky kind of life—this general happy-go-luckiness which Florida inculcates." Laura Towne came to the South Carolina Sea Islands to begin a Penn School for African Americans; she remained there for forty years, teaching. These men and women, teachers, nurses, ministers, missionaries, philanthropists, and honest businessmen barely made a living, and their lives were in daily jeopardy, but all are painted with the same smear of "carpetbaggers" applied to unscrupulous speculators who came south with all they owned packed in cheap suitcases made of carpet material. Some southern whites also stood up for reconciliation and racial justice at a time when the majority of whites refused to do so. An Alabama newspaper described any white who joined the Republican Party as "a mangy dog, slinking through the alleys, haunting the governor's office, defiling with tobacco juice the steps of the capital." Men who advocated reconciliation and African American citizenship, including the Confederate cavalry hero John Mosby (the "Gray Ghost") and General James Longstreet, Lee's "Old Warhorse," were labeled, as they still are today, with the epithet "scalawag." But nothing so insults the legacy and sacrifice of these and others as the term still used in historical writings for the time when fraud and violence prevailed: the use of the term "Redemption" to signify the restoration of an elite white rule takes a beautiful religious term and applies it to the coup d'état against a legitimate interracial government.

Today's history books remember the attack on the United States on December 7, 1941, as a "Day of Infamy." We are aghast over the attack upon the United States on September 11, 2001. Thus, it is Jefferson Davis's not knowing the North, not knowing that firing on the American flag would unify a North to preserve the Union, more than Lincoln's not knowing the South, that brought on the Civil War. I hope that as we remember the Civil War, we do not "celebrate" a time when the Confederacy fired on the flag of the United States.

Edmund L. Drago, How Do We Bring Forth Real Reconciliation?

What should we remember 150 years later? When South Carolina's leaders urged its people to war in 1860, they gambled with the future of the children in our state and lost. Our children, of all races, are still suffering from its impact. During the war the number of orphans rose dramatically, and the failure of the state to accept a multiracial democracy undermined the education of our children, white and black. Our public schools still suffer from inadequate support. During Congressional Reconstruction, the Ku Klux Klan in the Upcountry made war on Republicans who supported it. Home invasions in the black community were brutal; children themselves were attacked in their homes as their parents looked helplessly on.

Our people are still of two minds when it comes to remembering the past. Some glorify the Lost Cause and lionize their ancestors, while others lament the failure of the state to become a truly multiracial democracy. As a result, our state is still not fully healed from the wounds of the war. How do we bring forth real reconciliation?

First, we can do so only with good will and genuine humility. I say this as someone from California who has spent most of his life as an educator in South Carolina. But I also say this as a former captain in the U.S. Army. I served in Casualty Reporting in the United States and in Long Binh, Vietnam. In 1964, when my classmates and I graduated from ROTC at Santa Clara University, as unbelievable as this may sound, we had no idea what was in store for us. One of my dearest friends, a second lieutenant, a tank commander, died shortly after arriving in Vietnam. I still remember his sunshine personality. I admire his sacrifice and courage. Regardless of any ideology, the young man gave up his life for what he thought was a noble cause. I had no such illusions when I arrived in 1970.

How is that experience relevant to a reconciliation process? We can agree that it is proper and fitting for people to honor the sacrifice of loved ones who have fallen in war. But reconciliation in the case of Civil War memory demands an acceptance that slavery was an important cause of the war. When I wrote *Broke by the War: Letters of a Slave Trader,* in 1991, I recognized how dehumanizing slavery was both for the slaves and for some of the free people involved in it. Like many South Carolinians before the war, the slave trader Andrew Jackson McElveen, from Sumter District, barely eked out an existence in the 1850s. His experience as a Confederate soldier left him both physically and mentally broken.

Last year, a young woman in my class took a copy of *Broke by the War* to one of her friends, who happened to be a descendant of Andrew Jackson McEleveen. The family history acknowledged that several family members had been involved in the trade. This could not have been an easy thing for them to come to grips with, but they used the original *Broke by the War* to augment their own research. This suggests that reconciliation is possible. Despite the shouting matches that dominate twenty-four-hour television, the seeds of real renewal and reconciliation process may take root. The greening of our state may slowly be under way.

September 27, 2011

W. Eric Emerson, A Time to Learn, Teach, and Grow:
Why We Should Commemorate the Civil War 150th

In 2008 the South Carolina legislature passed a law creating the South Carolina Civil War Sesquicentennial (150th) Advisory Board. The legislation tasked the board with promoting "a suitable statewide observance of the sesquicentennial of the Civil War," and the board held a series of statewide meetings to collect citizen input regarding the forthcoming commemoration. The one unifying thought expressed by hundreds of participants at those meetings was that the Civil War 150th would afford an excellent opportunity for all South Carolinians to learn about this pivotal event that shaped the world in which we live.

Two years later, the state and nation marked the anniversary of South Carolina's secession and the bombardment of Fort Sumter. The economic downturn that struck South Carolina and the nation during the planning process significantly limited commemorative efforts for both anniversaries. Government funding for commemorative events was not forthcoming, so organizations were forced to compete for dwindling private donations. Commemorative groups in South Carolina faced the added challenge of overcoming public malaise resulting from the ongoing debates over the public display of the Confederate flag. Despite these obstacles, commemorative organizations pressed forward with their efforts.

Their determination to mark this anniversary is vital for a variety of reasons. The Civil War defines who we are today. It was our nation's bloodiest conflict, resulting in the deaths of well over six hundred thousand men, as well as countless thousands of women and children. It led to the emancipation of nearly four million enslaved African Americans and the creation of the Thirteenth, Fourteenth, and Fifteenth Amendments, which fundamentally altered our nation's definition of citizenship. It also resulted in the economic and physical destruction of our state and much of the South. To ignore these events is to deprive South Carolinians of the knowledge that their forebears sacrificed, struggled, and experienced both grief and pain to secure their most basic freedoms.

Fifty years ago, South Carolina commemorated the Civil War Centennial but missed an opportunity to broadly engage its citizens. Led by the Confederate War Centennial Commission, South Carolinians celebrated South Carolina's significant role in the Civil War but overlooked the role that African Americans and women played in the conflict. In addition, the commission supported a series of celebratory events that presented only one view of the war's causes and outcomes.

Much has changed for the better in South Carolina since the Civil War Centennial in 1961. Our state continues to evolve and to strive toward ensuring an improved life for all of its citizens. By acknowledging and embracing our past, we can educate ourselves about the most formative event in the past two centuries and belatedly acknowledge the vital roles played by African Americans as well as women and children in a war where events on the home front significantly impacted events on the battlefield.

In some ways, South Carolina's task is made easier because the Civil War is the most popular topic in American history. The conflict and its origins have been the source of much debate, which intensified with the approach of the 150th anniversary of South Carolina's secession. At the center of this dispute were the two claims competing for recognition as the primary cause of the war: slavery and states' rights. Public discourse was so lively that some advocated that South Carolinians disregard differences of opinion regarding the war and instead focus on finding consensus. Though such sentiments are understandable, they ultimately ignore the key role that debate plays in developing critical thinking.

Genuine discussion over the war's causes is healthy, necessary, and educational. It can lead people to do more than simply accept what they read on the Internet. It can motivate budding historians to visit archives and museums to view firsthand the documents and artifacts that tell the history of the war. If conducted in a spirit of enlightenment, debate regarding the war's origins can be a first step to a deeper understanding and appreciation of our state and nation's rich past.

The 150th anniversary, however, should not be merely a referendum on the war's causes. If South Carolinians come to the end of the sesquicentennial with only an understanding of why the war began, the commemoration has been a failure. If we spend the next four years battering each other with "the true history of the war" or provoking each other with arguments about the legality of secession, South Carolinians will grow tired of the sesquicentennial long before we reach 2015.

We should instead concentrate on those tangible links to the past that not only capture our attention but also fire our imaginations. If we view for the first time the original Ordinance of Secession or a photograph of our Civil War ancestor or if we step inside a slave cabin or look at a battle flag that has been dyed with the blood of its color bearer, then we invite the past into our life. It is the story of artifacts such as these and the people who produced them that generate interest, curiosity, and education.

The 150th anniversary of the Civil War provides South Carolinians with an excellent opportunity to learn, teach, and grow. The past provides lessons for the future, and it is our responsibility to seek out those lessons. The American Civil War was the most cataclysmic event in our nation's 235 years of existence. It is our *Iliad:* a story, both tragic and triumphant, that encompasses and magnifies all of the virtues and foibles that characterize our humanity. Millions of Americans experienced the conflict, and they left letters, diaries, memoirs, and service records for future generations. Their accounts are fascinating, and, for the sesquicentennial to be successful, we must embrace their stories.

Joseph McGill, Telling the Rest of the Story

The sesquicentennial of the American Civil War presents to us a chance to tell the rest of the story. The rest of the story is that story that for so long has been neglected, relegated to the back pages, or that has been just a footnote in our history books. A vital part of that neglected story is African Americans'participation in the Civil War and the idea that slaves were happy with their status in life.

Fifty years ago, when the centennial of the Civil War was being commemorated, African Americans did not participate in great numbers if they did at all. The main reason was that African Americans were deeply involved in their struggle for their civil rights—civil rights that, as a result of the Civil War, should have been granted by the Thirteenth, Fourteenth, and Fifteenth Amendments to the Constitution. The fact of the matter is that African Americans did not stand idly by during the Civil War waiting to be freed. They took an active role in obtaining that freedom.

Since the centennial of the Civil War, research has made the knowledge of African Americans' participation more prominent. Additionally, the movie *Glory,* in 1989, made the knowledge of African Americans' participation more mainstream. That movie sparked a desire among the general public to be more cognizant of that participation.

For the past twenty years, I have been a Civil War reenactor. This role has allowed me to tell the stories of the two hundred thousand or so African American men who fought for the Union during the American Civil War. It has also allowed me to tell the stories of the women who supported them. The sesquicentennial presents the opportunity for me to increase the audience(s) for the stories that I have been telling for the past twenty years.

Because of the sesquicentennial, I have aligned myself with several entities that will use various means to commemorate the Civil War. The entities include the Fort Sumter/Fort Moultrie Trust, the South Carolina African American Heritage Commission, the South Carolina African American Historical Alliance, and Penn Center, Inc.

More recently, I have taken on another quest, called the Slave Dwelling Project. This project allows me to spend nights in slave dwellings throughout the nation. It is my attempt to bring attention to and to save as many of these dwellings as possible. This also affords me the opportunity to conduct lectures on the subject of slave dwellings, bringing to light a major cause of the war.

All that I do—Civil War reenacting, sleeping in slave dwellings—are my methods of telling the rest of the stories that were not regularly told in the past. Taking on these tasks sometimes puts me before audience members that are hostile to my intent and message. This hostility has not yet deterred me from my goal of telling stories that have not often been told. In fact, I welcome that hostility. It is that hostility that lets me know that there is still a lot of work to be done. Location dictates that the Confederacy will be commemorated in various ways during the sesquicentennial of the Civil War. As in the past, I will continue to participate in some of those commemorations. More important, as a presenter or an audience member, I will use the sesquicentennial of the American Civil War to tell the rest of the story.

Theodore Rosengarten, Why Study the Civil War?

The Civil War tore our nation apart. We were a new country, and, just as we were getting going, things went to pieces. For the past hundred and fifty years we have been asking ourselves how it was possible for this to happen and how a war that was so appallingly costly could have gone on for so long with nobody stopping it. Just the expense of fielding the two armies, never mind the losses of property, could have bought freedom for the slaves five times over at market value. As a portion of the population, the 620,000 soldiers killed on both sides would be the equivalent of more than six million today. Horrendous, unacceptable. Yet the people accepted it: those who believed they were repelling an invasion, and those who were fighting for re-union and the liberation of the enslaved. If you live in the South, you know it took many decades for your region to recover. If you live in the North, well, your forebears probably came to the United States in one of the great waves of immigration after the War. For them, and that includes me and my family, the Civil War turned this country into an object of desire where a person could dream big dreams, make a good living, and aspire to become anything imaginable without being held back by social class or place of origin or because he or she spoke accented English. With the war over, slavery ended, federal law strengthened from sea to sea, and the northern states embarked on a path of rapid industrialization that would require importing a working class, the country swiftly completed its geographic task—at a huge human cost paid by indigenous people, who stood in the way of white expansion.

Meanwhile, America projected itself into the world by welcoming not only the tired, poor, huddled masses "yearning to breathe free" but ambitious, creative, untiring individuals aching to build new lives of meaning. Thus, the Civil War brought out the full import of the Bill of Rights and the Constitution. The country had become more civilized, outlawing slavery and granting citizenship to the former bondsmen and women. True, by the middle of the twentieth century, black people were asking what kind of freedom they had. It was unkind to make people wait any longer for equality before the law as guaranteed by the Fourteenth and Fifteenth Amendments, crafted in the heady days of 1868 and 1870. As Thurgood Marshall said in defense of black families who petitioned for better schools in segregated South Carolina in 1950, "ninety years is gradual enough."

Now the sorry, wasteful era of Jim Crow is past, and the American legacy of nation building ushered in by the outcome of the Civil War embraces people of all colors from all parts of the globe. The historian Ira Berlin was inspired to write his latest book on the making of African America by the discovery that more people of African ancestry have migrated to America since 1965 than came, whether under duress or as free men and women, in the three previous centuries. Had he lived, President Lincoln would not have been surprised. Lincoln once fantasized sending the freed slaves to West Africa, but by enrolling black men in the Union army and navy he removed the stigma and threat of statelessness—from them and from the rest of us.

I feel a debt of gratitude to Lincoln. He was ridiculed during the war for freeing the slaves in the rebellious states where he had no authority and leaving them enslaved in the states and territories where he ruled. But his Emancipation Proclamation was not only the central policy directive of the era and the lightning rod to battle that made Union victory inevitable; it turned the conflict into a territorial war, so that emancipation would be ongoing, enacted place after place as the Northern armies advanced. Similarly, the passage from old world despotism to new world democracy, from statelessness to citizenship, would be experienced by millions of immigrants over the next century and a half, mimicking the slave's passage to freedom and keeping the country safe and strong.[14]

Amanda Foreman, Memory and Responsibility:
The Civil War and Its Moral Legacy across the Atlantic

On the 150th anniversary of the Civil War, the debate over whether the North and the South fully discharged their separate moral obligations remains unresolved and a source of ongoing tension. The discussions in this section on the war and how it should be remembered demonstrate just how deeply these questions still trouble us today. Nor are these discussions solely an American phenomenon. In Great Britain and Northern Ireland the peace accord between the mainland government and the Provisional IRA has led to a renewed interest in the moral dimension of the Civil War and its diverse interpretations over time.

Given Ireland's massive contribution of manpower during the Civil War, it is perhaps not surprising that the war still carries a special resonance for communities on both sides of the Irish border. The peace achieved in America after 1865 remains a contradictory source of anxiety and inspiration today for those asking what kind of reconciliation is possible without punishment or atonement for wrongdoing. How postwar America dealt with the leaders of the Confederate guerrilla movement is particularly instructive. The fate of two Confederate operatives, Colonel Jacob Thompson and Dr. Luke P. Blackburn, remains an example of the moral contradictions inherent in peace building.

First, a reminder of Thompson's and Blackburn's roles in the Civil War. On April 7, 1864, Confederate president Jefferson Davis sent a wire to Colonel Jacob Thompson, a former cabinet secretary under President Buchanan and a veteran of Vicksburg, who had returned to his plantation in Oxford, Mississippi, after its surrender: "If your engagements will permit you to accept service abroad for six months, please come here immediately." Thompson arrived a few days later and accepted the appointment of "Commissioner for special service in Canada." Thompson's mission was to foment anti-Northern feeling in Canada until it created a crisis in Anglo-American relations. Davis also wanted him to supervise propaganda operations in the Northwest. The existence of the Knights of the Golden Circle and its sister organization, the Sons of Liberty, had convinced Confederate secretary of state Judah P. Benjamin and Davis that there were tens of thousands, if not hundreds of thousands, of disaffected midwesterners who, with the right encouragement and sufficient funds, would take up armed resistance against the Republican administration.

Thompson supervised a number of plots during his campaign in Canada. One involved leading a revolt and prison break in Chicago; another involved setting fire to New York and freeing the prisoners at Fort Lafayette. A third involved the liberation of the Confederate prisoners of Johnsons Island in Lake Erie, and another plan included equipping a steamer named the CSS *Georgian* to fire on towns along the U.S. side of Lake Erie. Southern support for these plots was strong. The idea that the Confederacy should burn New York in retaliation for the damage to the Shenandoah Valley was a popular one in the Southern press. On October 15, 1864, the *Richmond Whig* urged Jefferson Davis

> to burn one of the chief cities of the enemy, say Boston, Philadelphia, or Cincinnati. . . . If we are asked how such a thing can be done, we answer, nothing would be easier. A million of dollars would lay the proudest city of the enemy in ashes. The men to execute the work are already there. There would be no difficulty in finding there, here, or in Canada, suitable persons to take charge of the enterprise and arrange its details. . . . New York is worth twenty Richmonds. They have a dozen towns to our one; and in their towns is centered nearly all their wealth. It would not be immoral and barbarous. It is not immoral nor barbarous to defend yourself by any means or with any weapon the enemy may employ for your destruction. They choose to substitute the torch for the sword. We may so use their own weapon as to make them repent, literally in sackcloth and ashes, that they ever adopted it. If the Executive is not ready for this, we commend the matter to the secret deliberation of the Congress about to meet.

Luke P. Blackburn, a Kentucky doctor, undertook a completely separate operation, this one inspired by the yellow fever epidemics in Bermuda. Dr. Blackburn was an expert on the disease and twice in 1864 offered his services to the Bermudan authorities, once in the spring and once in the autumn. Mistakenly believing that yellow fever could be transmitted via the clothes of deceased victims, Blackburn nursed the dying patients and then stored their belongings in large trunks. He had them transported to Halifax, Nova Scotia, where a Confederate agent shipped them to Washington to be auctioned off to unsuspecting civilians. Blackburn's ignorance of the fact that yellow fever is spread via mosquito bites rather than by human contact prevented the plan from working. None of Thompson's plots were successful, either. The Chicago conspirators were arrested before they could carry out their insurrection. The New York conspirators inadvertently sabotaged their fire bombs, and the *Georgian* was impounded before it could receive its shipment of arms. These were intercepted by British agents, who discovered the Confederates' rifles and ammunition in three large boxes marked "potatoes."

After the war Thompson and Blackburn both became public servants with unblemished records. Thompson endowed the University of the South at Sewanee and served on the board of trustees. Blackburn was arrested in Canada for violating its neutrality during the war but was acquitted and returned to the United States in 1867. Once home, he aided efforts to combat an outbreak of yellow fever in Louisiana. Although the full details of his Civil War activities became known, Blackburn was elected governor of Kentucky in 1879.

To recap for those unfamiliar with the history of the so-called Troubles in Northern Ireland: in 1998 the Provisional IRA and the British government signed the Good Friday Agreement, which resulted in a ceasefire in the IRA's twenty-eight-year campaign for a united Ireland. The violence continued for another seven years until, in 2005, the IRA Army Council announced an end to its armed struggle. Since then, Sinn Fein, the political wing of the IRA, has remained a dominant player in Northern Ireland and Irish politics, and its leaders have held office in Dublin and Belfast. For the victims of violence and their respective communities, the progress of political integration and the acceptance of normalization without, in most cases, the prospect of any legal restitution or representation in court has been a painful and difficult process. The modern equivalent of Thompson and Blackburn are Martin McGuiness and Gerry Adams, two former leaders of the IRA who have gone on to forge successful political careers in peacetime.

Arguments for not pursuing legal redress against McGuiness and Adams have included a lack of concrete evidence of wrongdoing and the potential harm that stoking community tensions could pose to the post-Troubles peace. Similar arguments were used in the cases of Thompson and Blackburn. In both eras, apathy combined with an overriding desire for peace proved stronger than the cries for due process. In the short term, the decision to put the "needs" of peace above justice can be said to have proved successful. However, in the long-term the accumulated effect of placing expediency ahead of all other concerns has been a corrosion of moral clarity surrounding the Civil War and its meaning in American history. Divisions have yet to be healed; the truth about the war and its roots in slavery is still competing with myriad myths and wishful thinking about moral and social responsibility. This is the real lesson to be taken and the reality that should be remembered, both in America and across the Atlantic.

NOTES

1. They may be having a profound effect on world politics . See Kathryn Sikkink, *The Justice Cascade: How Human Rights Prosecutions Are Changing World Politics* (New York: Norton, 2011).

2. For this international context see, for example, Priscilla B. Hayner, *Unspeakable Truths: Transitional Justice and the Challenge of Truth Commissions*, 2nd ed. (New York: Routledge, 2010); Robert I. Rotberg and Dennis Thompson, eds., *Truth v. Justice: The Morality of Truth Commissions* (Princeton: Princeton University Press, 2000) ; Graham Dawson, *Making Peace with the Past? Memory, Trauma and the Irish Troubles* (Manchester, UK: Manchester University Press, 2011); Paloma Aguilar, *Memory and Amnesia: The Role of the Spanish Civil War in the Transition to Democracy* (New York: Berghahn Books, 2002); Dacio Viejo-Rose, *Reconstructing Spain: Cultural Heritage and Memory after Civil War* (Brighton: Sussex Academic Press, 2011).

3. W. Fitzhugh Brundage, *The Southern Past: A Clash of Race and Memory* (Cambridge, Mass.: Harvard University Press, 2008).

4. For a sampling of such articles, see Eric Foner's " The American Civil War Still Being Fought," http://www.guardian.co.uk/commentisfree/cifamerica/2010/dec/20/american-civil-war-usa (accessed June 19, 2012); Michael Wolf, "Is the Civil War Still Being Fought?," http://voices.yahoo.com/is-civil-war-still-being-fought-8263921.html (accessed June 20, 2012); National Public Radio, "The Civil War Is Still Being Fought, Civilly," http://www.npr.org/2010/12/19/132180688/The-Civil-War-Is-Still-Being-Fought-Civilly (accessed June 20, 2012); Harold Meyerson, "150 Years later, We're Still Fighting the Civil War," http://www.washingtonpost.com/opinions/150-years-later-were-still-fighting-the-civil-war/2011/04/12/AFFLFeSD_story.html (accessed June 20, 2012); CNN,"Civil War Still Divides Americans," http://politicalticker.blogs.cnn.com/2011/04/12/civil-war-still-divides-americans/) (accessed June 20, 2012); Konrad Yakabuski, "Remembering a War That Is Still Being Fought," http://www.theglobeandmail.com/news/world/remembering-a-war-that-is-still-being-fought/article551561/ (accessed June 20th, 2012).

5. David Cook, *Troubled Commemoration* (Baton Rouge: Louisiana State University Press, 2008).

6. Ari Kelman, "An Impertinent Discourse," *Times Literary Supplement,* February 24, 2012, 7–8.

7. Drew Gilpin Faust, *This Republic of Suffering: Death and the American Civil War* (New York: Knopf, 2008), xiii.

8. For the Lincoln Brigade, see the Abraham Lincoln Brigade Archives at http://www.alba-valb.org/ (accessed June 20, 2012). Examples of South African works in which Lincoln appears as an icon of liberation include Athol Fugard, "*Master Harold" and the Boys* (Fort Worth: Harcourt Brace, 1997), 32, and Alan Paton, *Cry, the Beloved Country* (New York: Scribner's, 1950), 143–47.

9. Kevin Phillips, *The Cousins' Wars: Religion, Politics, Civil Warfare, and the Triumph of Anglo-America* (New York: Basic Books, 1999).

10. Ernest Renan, "*Qu'est-ce qu'une nation*?" (Paris: Calmann Levy, 1882), 19.

11. Hayner, *Unspeakable Truths*, 27–32. For the weaknesses of truth commissions see Paul Gready, *The Era of Transitional Justice: The Aftermath of the Truth and Reconciliation in South Africa and Beyond* (New York: Routledge, 2011).

12. Among the many critics of the TRC, Mahmood Mamdani accused the commission of producing a "diminished truth" by considering "as a gross violation only that which was a gross violation under the laws of apartheid!" Wilmot James and Linda van

de Vijver, eds., *After the TRC: Reflections on Truth and Reconciliation in South Africa* (Cape Town: David Philiip, 2000), 60. For a strong case against the criminality of apartheid itself, see Kader Asmal, Louise Asmal, and Ronald Suresh Roberts, *Reconciliation through Truth: A Reckoning of Apartheid's Criminal Governance* (New York: St. Martin's, 1998). Given his position as chair of the commission, Desmond Tutu remains one of the TRC's strongest defenders, but in his memoir, *No Future without Forgiveness* (New York: Doubleday, 1999), 51, he admits that he would have "vehemently opposed" the Nobel Committee's decision to award its Peace Prize to F. W. de Klerk "had I known then what I know now." On the Treaty of Paris, see Ronald Hoffman and Peter J. Albert's edited collection, *Peace and the Peacemakers: The Treaty of 1783* (Charlottesville: University of Virginia Press, 1986). On the counterrevolutionary consequences of the Treaty of Paris, see Eliga H. Gould, "American Independence and Britain's Counter-Revolution," *Past and Present* 154 (February 1997): 107–41. Oswald's and Laurens's partnership in the slave trade is evident from Laurens's letter-books; see, for example, Kenneth Morgan's "Slave Sales in Colonial Charleston," *English Historical Review* 113 (September 1998): 905–27.

13. This reconciliation without atonement seems to have been consummated by Queen Elizabeth II with her handshake with Martin McGuinness in June 2012. See "SF's Martin McGuinness shakes hands with queen in Belfast," *Irish Times*, June 27, 2012, http://www.irishtimes.com/newspaper/breaking/2012/0627/breaking2.html (accessed June 29, 2012).

14. Editor's note: Professor Rosengarten's point is all the more telling if we accept that the consensus figure of 620,000 Civil War dead is in fact an underestimate. See David Hacker, "Recounting the Civil War Dead," *New York Times*, September 20, 2011, http://opinionator.blogs.nytimes.com/2011/09/20/recounting-the-dead/ (accessed June 12, 2012).

CONTRIBUTORS

O. VERNON BURTON is the executive director of the Carolina Lowcountry and Atlantic World (CLAW) program at the College of Charleston. He is emeritus university distinguished teacher/scholar, professor of history, African American studies, and sociology at the University of Illinois and is currently the director of the Clemson University Cyber Institute, distinguished professor of humanities, and professor of history and computer science. Among his sixteen books are *The Age of Lincoln* and *In My Father's House Are Many Mansions: Family and Community in Edgefield, SC.*

EDMUND L. DRAGO is a professor of history at the College of Charleston. His latest book is *Confederate Phoenix: Rebel Children and Their Families in South Carolina.*

HUGH DUBRULLE is an associate professor at Saint Anselm College in Manchester, New Hampshire, where he teaches modern European history. A book review editor for H-CivWar, he focuses his research on the Anglo-American relationship during the American Civil War. He is currently working on a book-length study of the way Britain constructed lessons from the American conflict.

NIELS EICHHORN is an assistant professor at Middle Georgia State College in Macon, Georgia, specializing in mid-nineteenth-century transatlantic interactions, with a particular interest in Civil War diplomacy. He has recently completed his dissertation, "'Up Ewig Ungedeelt' or 'A House Divided': Nationalism and Separatism in the Mid-Nineteenth Century Atlantic World," exploring the role and experiences of post-1848 immigrants from Schleswig-Holstein in the United States. Dr. Eichhorn has presented at a number of scholarly conferences, including SHAFR and BrANCH, and has book reviews on H-CivWar and H-Diplo and in *The Southern Historian.*

W. ERIC EMERSON is director of the South Carolina Department of Archives and History and chair of the South Carolina Civil War Sesquicentennial Advisory Board.

AMANDA FOREMAN is a senior visiting scholar at Queen Mary, University of London. Her book on Anglo-American relations during the Civil War: *A World on Fire: Britain's Crucial Role in the Civil War*, won the Fletcher Pratt Award for Civil War writing.

DAVID T. GLEESON is a reader in American history at Northumbria University in Newcastle upon Tyne, England. His most recent book is *The Green and the Gray: The Irish in the Confederate States of America* published in the Civil War America Series by the University of North Carolina Press in 2013. His essay here is part of the Locating the Hidden Diaspora Project on the English in North America, which is being supported by the Arts and Humanities Research Council of the UK.

MATTHEW KARP is an assistant professor of history at Princeton University. He is working on a book that explores the relationship between slavery and U.S. foreign policy.

SIMON LEWIS is associate director of the Carolina Lowcountry and Atlantic World program at the College of Charleston. He teaches African literature and is the author, most recently, of *British and African Literature in Transnational Context*.

AARON W. MARRS is a historian in the Office of the Historian at the U.S. Department of State. He is the author of *Railroads in the Old South: Pursuing Progress in a Slave Society*.

LESLEY MARX teaches at the University of Cape Town in the Centre for Film and Media Studies, of which she was the founding director. She taught American literature in the English department at UCT for many years and published a monograph on John Hawkes in 1997. Her current teaching and research interests focus on Hollywood and the Great Depression, the interface between American and South African history and culture, and South African film. Among her publications are articles on country music and Afrikaner culture, Vietnam and the South African Border Wars of the apartheid era, gangster films, and films of the TRC.

JOSEPH MCGILL is a field officer for the National Trust for Historic Preservation in the Charleston, S.C., Field Office. Founder of Company I, Fifty-Fourth Massachusetts Reenactment Regiment, he is the creator of the Slave Dwelling

Project. Blogs documenting his more than fifty overnight stays in extant former slave dwellings throughout the United States can be found at http://blog.preservationnation.org/tag/slave-cabin-project/; http://blog.lowcountryafricana.net/following-in-her-fathers-footsteps-daughter-accompanies-dad-on-slave-cabin-preservation-mission/; and http://www.aboutourfreedom.com/2011/05/teen-has-great-educational-adventure-in.html.

JAMES M. MCPHERSON is the George Henry Davis '86 Professor of American History Emeritus at Princeton University, where he taught for forty-two years. He is the author of numerous books on the era of the American Civil War, including *Battle Cry of Freedom: The Civil War Era,* which won the Pulitzer Prize in 1989, and *Tried by War: Abraham Lincoln as Commander in Chief,* which won the Lincoln Prize in 2009.

ALEXANDER NOONAN is an advanced graduate student in the history department at Boston College. His primary research focuses on the relationship between political violence, American foreign relations, and national security in the late nineteenth and early twentieth centuries.

THEODORE ROSENGARTEN is the Zucker-Goldberg Chair in Holocaust Studies, at the Yaschik/Arnold Jewish Studies Program, at the College of Charleston. His classic oral history work *All God's Dangers: The Life of Nate Shaw* won the National Book Award in 1974.

EDWARD B. RUGEMER is an associate professor in the departments of history and African American Studies at Yale University. He is the author of *The Problem of Emancipation: The Caribbean Roots of the American Civil War*, which won the Avery Craven award of the Organization of American Historians and was a co-winner of the Francis B. Simkins Award of the Southern Historical Association.

JANE E. SCHULTZ is a professor of English and the medical humanities and director of literature at Indiana University-Purdue University-Indianapolis. Her recent book, *This Birth Place of Souls*, is the annotated diary of Harriet Eaton, a Civil War nurse from Portland, Maine. *Women at the Front* was a finalist for the Lincoln Prize. Schultz's article in this volume began as a presentation to the Florence Nightingale School of Nursing at King's College, London, on the occasion of its sesquicentennial anniversary in 2010–11.

AARON SHEEHAN-DEAN is the Fred C. Frey Professor of Southern Studies at Louisiana State University. He is the author of *Why Confederates Fought: Family and Nation in Civil War Virginia,* the *Concise Historical Atlas of the U.S. Civil War*, and the editor of several books. He teaches courses on nineteenth-century U.S. history, the Civil War and Reconstruction, and southern history.

CHRISTOPHER WILKINS is an assistant professor in the department of history at William Jewell College. His research interests include the international history of the American Civil War and Reconstruction, the history of the U.S. South and the Caribbean as a single region, and the United States' emergence as a great power in the late nineteenth century.

INDEX

abolition of slavery, 15, 18–19, 23, 41, 217, 277; in Brazil, 14–15, 22–24; in British West Indies, 7; in Cuba, 22–24, 27, 28; in Massachusetts, 20; in Vermont, 18
abolitionism, 15, 18, 20, 23–24, 26, 29–30, 33n32, 37, 39, 40–41, 45, 48, 54n40, 59–60, 65
Adams, Charles F., 152, 188, 192, 195, 197, 199–203, 205
Adams, Ephraim Douglass, 59
Aiken, Aunt Lizzie, 244
Alcott, Louisa May, 245
Alabama, 122, 216
Alexander II, 117, 120, 124, 126, 127–128, 129, 133–35, 144n109, 144n116
Alexander Nevskii, 116,
Algemeen Befokte Afrikaans, 259, 270n51
Alvensleben, Gustav von, 158–9
American Civil War, 7–11, 12n5, 12n6, 15, 18, 26–27, 30, 36, 43, 52n26, 58–59, 63–64, 66, 67, 75, 83n104, 89, 94, 102, 107–8, 111, 116–17, 118, 120, 122–23, 125, 127, 130, 132, 133, 135, 146–47, 149–51, 153, 158, 159–61, 164, 170–73, 181, 183n18, 188, 190–91, 196, 203–4, 211, 213, 233, 253, 256–58, 274–77, 279–80, 281–89, 291
The American Union; Its Effect on National Character and Policy with an Inquiry into Secession as a Constitutional Right, and the Causes of the Disruption, 67
Angel, Benjamin Franklin, 196
Anglo-Boer War, 10, 255, 258–59, 260–61,
Anglo-Saxon race, 7, 64–65, 67, 75–76, 89, 93, 107
Appeal to the Colored Citizens of the World, 19
Aquinas, 172
Archibald, Edward, 102, 103
Arkansas, 17, 179
Arrango, Francisco, 21
Augustine, 172
Austria, 38, 118, 121, 146, 147, 148, 150, 151, 155, 157, 158–159, 161–162, 163, 194, 195

Bacot, Ada, 243,
Baez, Buenaventura, 215–16, 221
Baker, E. D, 104–5
Battle of Bull Run, 193, 199–200, 239
Bayard, Thomas, 220
Bazin, Andre, 269
Beers, Fannie, 244
Belgium, 38, 85, 152, 163, 194, 195
Benjamin, Judah P, 92, 291
Bernstorff, Albrecht Graf von, 154, 158, 160, 161–162, 163, 164, 170 n83
Berthoff, Rowland, 100
Birth of a Nation, The, 258–59, 261, 262, 279, 282
Bismarck, Otto von, 86, 157, 158, 159, 160, 161, 162, 163, 164
black soldiers, 30, 173, 179, 180
Black, Jeremiah, 194
Blackett, R. J. M., 59, 63, 76
Blackwell, Elizabeth, 240

Blake, Peter, 74
Bleak House, 68
Boatwright, James, 267
Boernstein, Henry, 157
Bonaparte, Napoleon, 148
Bonner, Robert E, 54, 76, 84
Boston, Massachusetts, 16, 292
Boston Daily Advertiser, 178, 203
Bou van 'n Nasie, Die, 258, 266
Bower, Robert, 109
Brazil, 7, 14–18, 20–27, 28, 29–30, 31n5, 33n32
Breckinridge, Margaret, 242, 250n51
Brink, Andre, 256, 269
British attitude toward Civil War, 40, 58–59, 74–75, 100, 103, 149, 197–200
British press, 5, 40–41, 63, 66, 74, 202, 235, 237
Brooks, James, 205
Brown, John, 30, 63–64
Buchanan, James, 132, 192, 289
Buffalo, New York, 101, 175
Burnett, Theodore, 172
Butler, Fran, 56, 57–58, 77–78
Butler, Pierce, 18, 56–58, 84n115

Calhoun, John C, 25, 37–38, 39, 40–41, 49n8
Campbell, Duncan Andrew, 59
Capra, Frank, 268
Carlyle, Thomas, 60, 68
casualties, 172, 293n14
Cather, Willa, 266
cavaliers, 7, 90–94, 96n24, 242
Cavour, Camillo Benso, Conte di, 146
Chambersburg, Pennsylvania, 175, 180
Charleston Mercury, 44, 180
Chartism, 101
Chattanooga, Tennessee, 174
Chesnut, Mary Boykin, 236, 248n21
civic nationalism, 8, 86–88, 89, 90, 92, 93, 94, 107, 111
civilizational perspective, 60
Clay, Cassius, 121, 125–126, 128–129, 132, 196
Clinton, Catherine, 2, 257–58, 261
Cobden, Richard, 68
common law (English), 105
Confederacy, 14–15, 26–27, 36, 48, 59, 66, 68, 75–76, 83n92, 88–89, 91–94, 102–3, 108, 109, 114n122, 123–24, 129–30, 147, 154, 163, 171–172, 177, 180, 192, 194–95, 197, 198–99, 202, 204, 208n74, 218, 236, 241, 242, 246, 258, 273, 279–80, 283, 287, 290
Confederate Congress, 174
Confederate diplomats, 129, 180
Confederate press, 75, 89, 91, 93, 172, 176, 290
Cooley, C. C., 106
Cooper, Samuel, 174
Copperheads, 74, 109
Corn Laws, 37
Corning, Erastus, 193
Cortes of Cadiz, 20–22, 28
Corwin, Thomas, 178, 193–194
Cossham, Handel, 75
cotton, 7, 15, 17, 36–38, 41–44, 46, 48, 49n3, 50n13, 51n16, 52n26, 53n30, 64–65, 67, 108, 132, 152, 237, 276
Cowan, Edgar, 178
Cowley, Henry Richard Charles Wellesley, Lord, 148, 152, 157, 158, 160, 166
Cox, Samuel Sullivan, 191, 205n16,
Crimean War, 9, 117, 120, 124, 126, 132–134, 140n55, 157, 161, 165; and professionalization of nursing, 233, 235–237, 239–41, 245
Cripps, Thomas, 258
Cuba, 2, 7, 14, 15–18, 20–29, 30, 38, 39, 44, 45, 46, 55n43, 105, 196, 210, 212, 218
Cumming, Kate, 236, 241–42
Custer, George A., 174

Dallas, George Mifflin, 196
Damascus, 149
Davis, Jefferson, 41, 139, 173, 214, 282–283, 289–90
Dayton, William Lewis, 126, 193–194, 196, 201
DeBow, James B. D., 14–15, 39–40, 42–43, 45–46, 53n31, 90

DeBow's Review, 37, 44, 49n3, 51n19, 53n31, 90, 91
De la Rey, General Koos, 259–260, 269n44
Democrat Party, 20, 178, 218
Denmark, 20, 39, 151, 157, 158, 161–63, 168n37, 192, 195
de Vattel, Emerich, 174, 179
de Vittoria, Francisco, 174
Dicey, Edward, 64, 66, 78, 81n68
Dickens, Charles, 68, 100
Dilke, Charles, 76
diplomacy, 2, 19, 21, 52n26, 118–19, 122, 135, 146–47, 148, 153, 157–59, 161–162, 164, 189, 201, 214, 219
Divers, Bridget, 244
Dix, Dorothea, 243, 250n55
Dlamini, Piet, 259, 271n71
Dominican Republic (*see also* Santo Domingo), 9, 209–213, 215–224, 224n2, 225n14, 226n24, 228n41, 231n93
Douglass, Frederick, 26, 62–63, 106, 209–211, 214, 221, 223–24, 224n1, 225n14, 231n93
Dred Scott, 87
Drescher, Seymour, 31n4, 64

Early, Jubal, 175, 180
Eastern Question, 148–49, 157
Emancipation Proclamation, 26, 28, 68, 107, 109–10, 144n116, 157, 177, 280, 288
Eminent Victorians, 247n3
Erickson, Charlotte, 100
Essay on the Inequality of the Human Races, 75
Etheridge, Annie, 244
ethnic nationalism, 7–8, 85–90, 91–92, 94
ethnology, 60
European attitudes toward Civil War, 6, 58–59, 75, 118
European views of slavery, 7, 21, 41, 56, 58–62, 63, 75, 127
evangelicals, evangelicalism, 60, 81n68, 238, 245

Fabens, Joseph, 216
Ferdinand VIII of Spain, 20, 21–22
Fiedler, Leslie, 261
Fifteenth Amendment, 11, 30, 210, 218, 226n21, 281, 285, 286, 288
Fitzhugh, George, 25, 45–46, 54n38, 55n43, 90
Fish, Hamilton, 225n2
Foote, Henry, 171
Ford, John, 266
Fogg, George Gilman, 195
foreign assistance to the United States, 66, 69, 98–99, 103–104, 106–108, 125–26, 197
foreign recognition of Confederacy, 26, 75, 108, 122–124, 163, 180, 188, 191–92, 194–96, 199, 241
Foreign Relations of the United States, 9, 188–204
Forster, William, 76, 197
Fourteenth Amendment, 11, 30, 94, 218, 226 n21, 281, 285, 286, 288
France, 3, 4, 8, 17, 37, 38, 39, 42, 46–47, 93, 117, 118, 121, 124, 126, 129, 131–33, 135, 146, 148–51, 152, 154–64, 165n13, 170n83, 180, 193–96, 200, 202, 208n74, 236
France and slave emancipation in West Indies, 14, 37, 39
Fredrickson, George, 60, 256
free blacks, 19, 25, 29 74, 87
free trade, 37–40, 46, 48, 49n8, 50n9, 50n13, 51n16, 149
Fremont, John C., 107, 279
Fugitive Slave Act, 25, 26, 63

Garcia, Mary, 223–224
Garibaldi, Giuseppe, 150, 234, 278, 280
Garrison, William Lloyd, 19, 63
General Admiral, 126–27, 129–30, 141n66
Gerber, David, 101
Gladstone, William Ewart, 157
Gobineau, Arthur de, 75
Gorchakov, Alexander Mikhailovich, 118, 121, 122–124, 127–28, 129, 133, 139n36, 144n109, 160
Grant, Ulysses S., 209–12, 213, 216–18, 219, 223–24, 225n2, 227n33, 230n83, 257

Grattan, Thomas Colley, 63
Great Britain, 2, 4, 8, 14, 17, 18–19, 20–23, 26–27, 29, 37–39, 40–42, 47, 58–59, 62–63, 76–77, 99, 102–103, 105, 118, 146–149, 151–57, 159–64, 194, 195, 197, 200, 202–3,
Greater Britain: A Record of Travel in the English-Speaking Countries, during 1866–1867, 76
Gregory, William, 74
Grotius, Hugo, 172, 174, 176, 179
Guerrillas, 121, 150, 173, 174, 176, 181, 187n65, 282, 289

Haiti, 3, 9, 14–15, 16–17, 20, 21, 26, 30, 63, 68, 209–213, 215–24, 224n2, 225n14, 226n24, 227n34, 228n41, 228n44, 230n82, 231n93
Haldeman, James Samils, 195
Hall, Catherine, 61
Halleck, Henry, 179, 183n13, 184n30
Hammond, James Henry, 20, 37, 41–42, 279
Hawaii, 194
Heaney, Seamus, 5–6
Hindman, Thomas, 176
Hobsbawm, Eric, 166n10, 171
Hoge, Jane, 239–240
Hospital Sketches, 243
Hospitals: Barracks, Scutari, 234, 235, 239–40; Chimborazo, 242; design and management, 233–34, 240, 245; moral guardianship in, 245; pavilion-style, 245; St. Thomas's, London, 233; Tishomingo, Shiloh, 241
Hotze, Henry, 75–76, 83n104, 84n108
Howe, Julia Ward, 238
Howe, Samuel Gridley, 210, 238
Howe, Timothy, 191, 205n16, 229
Hunt, James, 60, 75, 79n28
Hunter, David, 107, 175

international law, 9, 121, 154, 170–171, 173, 179, 182n8, 206n45
Italy, 2, 127, 146, 149–50, 152, 157–58, 160, 164, 280
Ivanhoe, 89
Iverson, Alfred, 88

Jackson, Andrew, 20, 99
Jackson, William, 20
Jamaica, 47, 218
Jamaican Rebellion, 59
James, Jacob, 211, 216, 223, 228n44
James, Theophilus , 223, 229n54, 231n93
Jefferson, Thomas, 12n6, 18–19
Johnson, Hannah, 175
Jones, Charles C. Jr., 88, 89
Jones, Jehu Glancy, 194
Journal of a Residence on a Georgian Plantation in 1838–1839, 56–58
Journeys and Explorations in the Cotton Kingdom, 67
Judd, Norman, 193, 196, 206n25
Junta de Informacíon sobre Ultramar, 27
just war, 170, 171, 173, 176, 179, 181

Kemble, Fanny, 7, 56–58, 63, 74, 77–78
Kendall, Amos, 20
Kennedy, Robert Cobb, 175
King, Rufus, 18
King Cotton, 15, 36–37, 42–44, 48, 51n16, 52n26, 53n30
King Kamehameha IV, 194

La Tour d'Auvergne, Henri de, 154, 157
Laird Rams, 130, 134, 142n83, 161, 164
Laurens, Henry, 18, 275–76, 293n12
Laurens, John, 18
Lawrence, George Alfred, 69
Lawley, Frank, 74
Laws of Nations, 179
laws of war, 177, 179–80, 182n8
Lee, Robert E., 93, 102, 173, 242, 258, 282
Leigh, James, 57
Leigh, Vivien, 267
Lewis, Sir George Cornewall, 65–66
Lhamon, W. T., 64
Lieber, Francis, 93–94, 172, 178–79
The Liberator, 19
Lincoln, Abraham, 1, 4, 12n6, 14, 15, 26, 28, 87, 88, 91, 92, 94, 98–99, 106–7, 109,

120, 124, 127–28, 131–32, 134, 144n116, 149, 154, 173–74, 176–76, 177, 179, 188–89, 191–92, 201, 205n16, 215, 274, 276–83, 288
Lindsay, William S., 161
Lisovskii, Stepan, 116, 119–21, 123–24, 131, 132, 133–34, 135n3, 138n33
Livermore, Mary, 240
London, 41, 51n20, 75, 147–48, 151, 197, 233, 246
London Anthropological Society
London, Protocol of, 151, 161–63
Longfellow, Henry Wadsworth, 236, 238, 244
Lorimer, Douglas, 59, 61, 64, 67, 73, 75, 80n42
Lott, Eric, 62
Louisiana, 17, 135
Lyons, Richard Bickerton Pemell, Lord, 153, 197–98, 208n74

Magna Carta, 106, 111
Mandela, Nelson, 12n6, 253, 276
Mandler, Peter, 60
Martin, Luther, 18
Martineau, Harriet, 67, 68
Marx, Antony W., 256–57
Maryland, 17, 24, 176
Mason, George, 18
Mason, James, 105, 123, 153–54, 201, 202, 207n65
Massachusetts, 16, 103, 109, 182n3
Mattocks, Charles, 244
McClellan, George, 110, 115n43, 214
McCord, Louisa S., 46
McDaniel, Hattie, 262–64, 267
McGill, Ralph, 256
McGuinness, Martin, 267, 293n13
McQueen, Butterfly, 261
Meagher, Thomas Francis, 103
Meer, Sarah, 62
Mexico, 2, 21, 25, 36, 38, 54n38, 118, 132, 157, 159, 193, 194, 198, 280
Miles, William Porcher, 180
minstrelsy, 61–62, 64, 69, 71–73, 80n42, 80n43, 83n92
Mohl, Mary, 233, 246
Moore, Frank, 244
Moret Law, 28–29
Morrison, Toni , 264
Morton, Oliver P., 217, 229n63
Mosby, John Singleton, 174, 283
Moseley, Thomas, 101
Moss, Carlton, 261

Napoleon III, 124, 129, 131, 146, 147, 149, 151, 152, 155–59, 161, 162–3, 280
Napoleon Bonaparte, 17, 19, 20, 135, 148, 280
nationalism, 2, 4, 6, 7, 8, 85–95, 107, 111,159, 171, 180, 271n74, 274
nativism, 87–88
Netherlands, the, 38, 148, 200
Neuchâtel, Switzerland, 149, 179
New York, New York, 3, 8, 16, 98, 102, 103, 111, 116–17, 119–21, 123, 126, 127, 129, 131–34, 138n33, 175, 290
New York City Draft Riots, 111
Newcomb, Mary, 243
Newsom, Ella, 242
Nice, 146, 149, 157
Nightingale, Florence, 9, 233–46
Nightingale, Parthenope, 233, 235
noncombatants, 173–74
Normans, 7–8, 90–91, 94
Notes on Nursing, 234, 237
nurses, 7, 9, 233–46; and relief work, 233–35, 239, 240, 242, 243, 245, 246; Confederates as, 234, 236, 239, 241–42; nuns as, 233

"Occasional Discourse on the Negro Question," 60
Ohio, 26, 109, 277
Olmsted, Frederick Law, 67
Osliaba, 116
Owen, Wilfred, 10

Paglia, Camille, 262–63
Palmerston, John Henry Temple, Lord, 146, 152–53, 157, 160–61, 162–63
Paraguayan War, 3, 12, 27, 30, 170

Paris, 133, 149, 151, 158, 275
Parsons, Emily, 244
particularism-generalism, 60
Party of Order, 23
Patrick, Francis, 110
Peace of Zanjon, 28
Pedro I of Brazil, 22–23
Pedro II of Brazil, 23, 27, 28, 30
Pember, Phoebe, 242
Pensacola, Florida, 174
Periodicals: *Atlantic Monthly,* 236; *Frank Leslie's Illustrated Newspaper,* 237, 240; *Godey's Lady's Book,* 237; *Harper's Weekly,* 120, 121–22, 126, 130–31, 240; *Illustrated London News,* 69, 236; *John Bull,* 237; *New York Times,* 116, 130, 134, 234, 246; *New York Tribune,* 201, 218, 239; *Peterson's Magazine,* 239; *Punch,* 199, 237; *Saturday Evening Post,* 237; *Southern Literary Messenger,* 47, 90, 91, 237; *Times* (London), 40, 41, 47, 64, 73, 74, 77, 126, 128, 199, 235, 239
Perry, Horatio J., 196
personal liberty laws, 26
Pickering, Michael, 62, 80n43
Pike, James Shepard, 196
Pinckney, Charles, 18
Poland, 86, 89, 117, 120–21, 123, 126, 128–29, 132, 134–35, 150–52, 158–61, 164
Polish Uprising, 118, 120, 122, 123, 128–29
Pollard, Edward, 94
Popov, Andrei, 117, 120, 122, 137n21
Portugal, 4, 16, 20–23, 38
postcolonialism, 59
Prichard, James Cowles, 60
prisons, 172, 173–74, 176, 177–79, 185n43, 290
prisoners of War, 172, 173–74, 176, 177–79, 186n50
Prussia, 93, 147–164
Puritans, 90–92
Pyron, Darden Asbury, 257

Queen Elizabeth II, 293n13
Queen Victoria, 98, 102–3, 105–6, 108, 110, 111, 150, 163, 195, 197, 198, 240

racism, 4, 58–64. 69, 73–76, 80n42, 215, 224, 253–57, 261–63
Rainey, Joseph, 218, 230n74
Ramsay, James, 18
Republican Party, 25, 87, 99, 107, 109, 149, 177–78, 191–92, 210, 212, 216–219, 226n21, 229n55, 229n57; 230n77, 277, 279, 282–283. *See also* Lincoln, Abraham
Republicans (Jeffersonian), 19
Republicans (Spanish), 274
retaliation, 171–86, 275
Revels, Hiram, 281, 230n74
Revenge, 82n81; 171–73, 176, 181, 183n13, 183n15
Richmond Dispatch, 91
Richmond Enquirer, 89
Richmond Examiner, 94
Ricker, Samuel, 150
Rio de Janeiro, 20, 24
Rio Branco Law, 28–29
Roebuck, John A. 161
Roebuck, John, 76
Roodt, Darrell, 264
Ropes, Hannah Chandler, 237–38
Rubin, Louis, Jr., 257
Ruffin, Edmund, 94
runaway slaves, 25–26, 107
Russell, Lord John, 38, 82n8, 151, 153, 157, 159, 160, 197–99, 208n74
Russell, William Howard, 73–74, 239
Russia, 3, 8, 38, 44, 47, 85–86, 88–89, 116–119, 122–27, 129, 131, 133–35, 149–5 ,155 157–161, 195–96

St. George, Societies of, 98–99, 102–105, 108–111
Sala, George Augustus , 74, 93n97
Sanford, Henry Shelton, 94
Sanitary Commission: British, 235; U. S., 236, 239–40
"Santa Filomena," 236, 244. *See also* Longfellow, Henry Wadsworth
Sapphira and the Slave Girl, 264
Sarafina, 264
Savoy, 146, 149, 156

Scales, Cordelia, 241
Schillinger, Liesl, 264
Schleiden, Rudolph M., 154–55
Schleswig-Holstein, 150–51, 157, 162–64
Schofield, Charles, 102
Schurz, Carl, 192, 219
Scott, Sir Walter, 7, 89
second party system, 20, 23, 26
Sedgwick, Elizabeth, 56
Selznick, David O., 9, 262, 264–65
Semmes, Raphael, 214–15
Semmes, Thomas, 277
Seward, William H., 9, 88, 99, 120–21, 125, 128, 131–32, 135, 153–56, 188–97, 199, 201–204, 205n6, 205n8, 205n16; 216
Sharp, Granville,18
Sheridan, Philip, 174–75, 183n17
Sherman, William T., 93, 175–76, 184n24, 257, 260, 275
Simms, William Gilmore, 43–44, 88
slave insurrections, 14–15, 20, 63, 68, 82n82, 278
slavery,1, 3–7, 14–31, 31, 32n10, 33n32, 36–48, 53n35; 56–77, 81n68; 87–91, 94–95; 106–108, 110–11, 120, 127–30, 173, 175, 192, 195–99, 212, 217, 221, 253, 255, 258, 275–79, 285, 291
Slidell, John, 105, 123, 153–54, 201–202.
Smith, Sidney, 61
Sobchack, Vivian, 252
soldiers, 1, 18, 27, 30, 93, 102–105, 122, 173–75, 177–81, 185n38, 234–35, 237, 239–45, 259, 277, 280–81, 288
Somersett Case, 107–108
South Carolina, 4–5, 16–18, 72–73, 93, 174, 274–75, 278–79, 284–85, 289
Southern Literary Messenger, 47, 90, 91, 237
Southern Quarterly Review, 39, 42–43, 45, 88
sovereignty, 171, 219
Spain, 4, 14, 17, 21–23, 27–30, 33 n.32, 38, 44, 86, 118, 192, 195–96, 212, 215, 273
Spence, James, 67–68, 76–77,
Starkey, T. A., 105–106
Stephens, Alexander H., 42, 89, 277
Stoeckl, Edouard, 116, 12223, 127, 133, 135, 139n36
Stowe, Harriet Beecher, 27, 41, 62, 237, 282
Sumner, Charles, 47, 121, 126, 129, 132, 134–35, 178–79, 219
Sumter (CSS), 122, 198
sugar, 14–17, 22, 24, 29, 37–40, 44, 46, 49, 50, 55n43;
Sweden, 38, 86, 194–95,
Switzerland, 132, 155–56, 179, 193, 195
Syria, 149–50, 167n20

Taiping Rebellion, 11–12 n14; 170
Tallmadge, James, 19
telescopic philanthropy, 68, 74
Ten Years on a Georgia Plantation since the War, 57
Ten Years War, 26, 28, 30, 212
Thackeray, William, 60
Thouvenel, Antoine Edouard, 154, 157
Timrod, Henry, 91
Tocqueville, Alexis de, 68–69,
transatlantic slave trade, 17–22, 27, 33 n.32
Trent Affair, 8, 105–106, 108, 123, 153–56, 200, 203
Truth and Reconciliation Commission [TRC], 260, 275
Turkey, 85–86, 89, 130, 194
Turpin, Edward A., 194
Tutu, Desmond, 293n12

Ulster, 5, 276
Uncle Tom's Cabin, 27, 31, 62
U.S. Army Medical Department, 234
U.S. Colored Troops, 30, 173, 179–181
U.S. Congress, 9, 20, 25, 94, 104, 107, 120, 170, 180, 188–92, 200–202, 209–10, 216–19, 224, 258, 277, 281, 290
U.S. Constitution, 7, 18–19, 26, 30, 64, 67, 86, 88, 91, 94, 98, 107, 190, 193,203, 217–18, 275, 278, 281, 286, 288
U.S. Department of State, 9, 215
U.S. diplomats, 119, 125, 212–13,
U.S. foreign relations, 9, 118–119, 130–32, 189–90, 196, 203, 213

U.S. foreign relations, popular opinion of, 135, 200, 224
U.S. Surgeon General's Office, 243

Vallandigham, Clement, 109
Van Vugt, William, 100
Venetia, 146, 150, 152, 157, 159
Venezuela, 194
Vesey, Denmark, 20
Victor Emmanuel, 150
Victoria, Queen, 98, 102, 111, 150, 163, 240
Vinton, Alexander Hamilton, 98–99, 103, 107
Virginia Military Institute, 175
von Brunnow, Philipp, 123

Wade, Benjamin, 177–78, 211, 221–22
Walcott, Derek, 10
Walker, Alice, 262
Walker, David, 19
Walzer, Michael, 181
Washington, George, 12n6; 92, 98, 111, 120
Webb, William H., 126–27
Welles, Gideon, 93, 116, 120, 132–33, 183n16
Whig Party, 20, 38, 99
White, Andrew D., 222
White, Joseph Albert, 194
Whitman, Walt, 10, 245
Wilberforce, William, 18, 41, 47
Wilhelm I, 149, 157, 159–60
Wilkes, Charles, 153, 155
Wilkinson, Morton, 177
William the Conqueror, 90–91
Wittke, Carl, 100
Woman's Work in the Civil War, 244
Women of the War, 244
Wormeley, Katharine P., 236
Wright, Augustus, 172

X, Malcolm, 262

Yaeger, Patricia, 10, 255, 258